# Architectural Detailing in Residential Interiors

# Architectural Detailing in Residential Interiors

Wendy W. Staebler



Whitney Library of Design
an imprint of Watson-Guptill Publications/New York

*At Whitney, special thanks for their perseverance and patience to:*
Cornelia Guest
Mindy Nass
Areta Buk
Hector Campbell
Marilyn Litvin

Illustration opposite Table of Contents: Axonometric view of kitchen hood *in situ,* Lawrence Residence, Hermosa Beach, California. Architecture: Morphosis. From detail on pages 128 and 129.



First published 1990 by Whitney Library of Design
an imprint of Watson-Guptill Publications
a division of BPI Communications, Inc.,
1515 Broadway, New York, N.Y. 10036

**Library of Congress Cataloging-in-Publication Data**

Staebler, Wendy W.
Architectural detailing in residential interiors / Wendy W. Staebler.
p. cm.
ISBN 0-8230-0253-5
1. Architectural drawing—Detailing. 2. Architecture. Domestic—United States—Designs and plans. I. Title.
NA2718.S7 1990
729—dc20 89-48856
CIP

Distributed in the United Kingdom by Phaidon Press Ltd.,
Musterlin House, Jordan Hill Road, Oxford OX2 8DP



Manufactured in Japan

First printing, 1990

1 2 3 4 5 6 7 8 9/95 94 93 92 91 90

*To Andrew, Jonathan, and "Team Adiri":*
*Florence Agnew, Ken Hutchinson, David Murray,*
*Kelly Petoskey, and Chesapeake.*

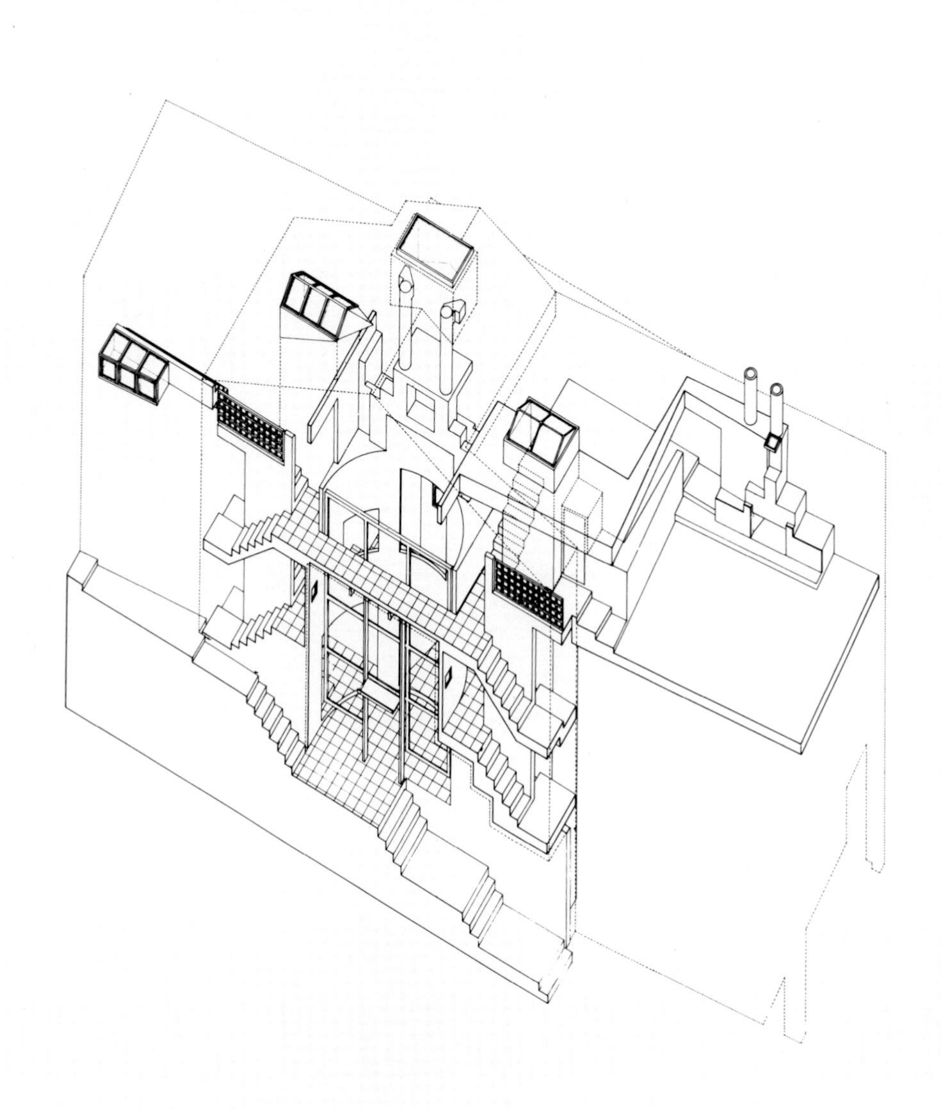

# CONTENTS

# Preface

**Dorothy, (of *Wizard of Oz* fame)** is not alone in expressing the belief that "There's no place like home." Statistics culled from recent nationwide polls reveal that most adult Americans now choose to spend their leisure time at home—preferring, for example, home videos to movie theaters; an informal gathering of family and friends to a night on the town; or a private recreation room, swimming pool, or tennis court to membership in an athletic or country club.

The impetus for this homing instinct may signify a long-term sociological shift or, instead, may be just a measure of the "circle the wagons" pragmatism that evolves during uncertain financial times. In either case, an identifiable, responsive trend has emerged in today's architecture and interior design—a trend toward quality in personal space, expressed not in numbers of square feet but, rather, by attention to finish detail. In consequence, as offices and public buildings are being developed with a renewed appreciation of form as well as function (see *Architectural Detailing in Contract Interiors*, Whitney, 1988), housing manifests an even greater enrichment of detail designed and crafted to ever more exacting standards.

Architects and interior designers now offer "dream houses" that, regardless of budget, enhance their residents' lives with details of real meaning: details that—no matter how few or how many—resolve practical problems as they subtly and sometimes flamboyantly evoke icons of either historical connection or current culture. As family life once centered around the hearth or fireplace, modern family life may revolve around the kitchen island, the media center, or the Jacuzzi.

*Architectural Detailing in Residential Interiors* is a compilation of the best residential detailing work produced by both mainstream and "New Wave" American architects and interior designers during the last five to seven years. Some architects represented in this volume are well known; others are new faces. All are demonstrably committed to thoughtfully planned, beautifully rendered detailing that is appropriate to its function and distinguished in its form.

The details selected for inclusion in this volume are intentionally divergent in stylistic expression, as they represent every region of the United States. By comparing the design solutions of often ideologically polarized architects—architects whose work may also be, to a greater or lesser extent, discernibly influenced by their own regional climate and cultural values—it is possible to see the almost infinite range of creative solutions that may be utilized to resolve universal detailing problems.

The work in *Architectural Detailing in Residential Interiors* epitomizes, in both substance and method of presentation, the American devotion to individual expression. Therefore, with appropriate apologies to all the architects and interior designers who graciously redrafted and rephotostatted their work to meet our editorial format, we celebrate, rather than censure, the divergent, freewheeling, and idiosyncratic expression of creativity that is, in fact, the strong suit of current American architectural and interior design practice.

Wendy W. Staebler

© H. Durston Saylor

*Shope Reno Wharton's contrasting rendition of window detailing is proof positive that the visual impact of detailing may be derived by isolation as well as by repetition.*

© 1989 H. Durston Saylor

*A "piano" bar in Steven Spielberg's Manhattan apartment, designed by Gwathmey Siegel Associates, exemplifies an urbane wit that is characteristic of current residential detailing. Smooth, minimalist paneling designed by the firm for another city apartment evokes, nonetheless, a comforting sense of connection to the past.*

*In Spalding Taylor's apartment, San Francisco architect Ira Kurlander emphasized the continuing, if updated, importance of fireplace detailing as he gave taut, elegant expression to a new domestic icon: the sybaritic bath/shower environment.*

© Peter Aaron/ESTO

© Peter Aaron/ESTO

© Paul Warchol

*The New York firm SITE brought its considerable expertise in creative visualization to bear in developing an appropriate new persona for a circa 1826 Greenwich Village house—a persona that evolved from its existing identity. SITE's solution was to evoke the building's history by embedding unobtrusive personal objects, or artifacts, into the walls. The concept seemed uncannily prescient when, during the initial phases of the renovation, an antiquated perfume bottle and a portrait of the original owner were recovered. From both planned and found artifacts, therefore, a series of "narrative architecture" details were conceived and woven throughout the house. According to SITE principle Alison Sky: "By embedding fragments of historical artifacts into the walls, the walls function as planes between the past and present; in other words, as planes of memories." More pragmatically, the details also conceal newly installed plumbing stacks and electrical lines.*

*SITE's unique "built-in historical layering" wall treatment was accomplished, technically, in three straightforward steps: artifacts appropriate to a particular wall section were wired into the lath through often disintegrating original plaster, after which each wall was carefully replastered. Walls and embedded objects were then finished with a monochromatic "skin" of white paint, which "separates past and present." The result is evocative, mysterious, and haunting.*

© Paul Warchol

# Archway

## Adams Residence
*Connecticut coast*

**Architect**
Centerbrook Architects

**Design Team**
Mark Simon, AIA, Partner-in-Charge; Nick Deaver, AIA, Project Manager/Design; Walker Burns, AIA, Project Manager/Construction

**Structural Engineer**
Besier Gibble Norden

**General Contractor**
John Landon, Landon and Hall

**Photography**
© Norman McGrath

Commanding a steep escarpment of stone outcroppings overlooking Long Island Sound, the Adams residence—designed by Centerbrook Architects of Essex, Connecticut—epitomizes the thoughtful integration of structure to site. As initially glimpsed from the curved drive (which rises 30 feet in 100 yards), the Stick-style, stone house emerges "organically" in elevation—rooted in a foundation excavated from rocky ledges and topped by soaring stone chimneys.

The walls of the entry hall—clad in roughly square cut stone—were designed as a transitional device to reiterate, in more refined form, the complementary work outside of nature and architect. The transitional quality of the entry hall is specifically reinforced by its most prominent detail, a massive archway, which draws visitors into the cave-like space and beyond, to expansive rooms with spectacular views.

The jogged wall of the archway and its impressive stone lintel were not designed as merely aesthetic embellishments, however. Both serve practical, structural purposes. The wall encases the back of a first-floor fireplace; the lintel, in conjunction with the wall, serves as a secondary support for an asymmetrically positioned fireplace above, which was laid on an 8-inch reinforced concrete slab on the second, bedroom floor (*axonometric*).

Supporting tons of weight "on air" was not the only sleight-of-hand technique Centerbrook used in the construction of the Adams house. The stone itself is a teaser. Twelve-inch-deep "stone" walls actually consist of 4-inch cut stone veneer, which has been reinforced with corrugated masonry ties and mortared to 8-inch cinderblocks. The cinderblocks form the true structural spine of the house, above grade. Below grade, 12-inch concrete masonry units rising from a poured slab over footings provide a solid shelf to support both 8-inch concrete block and the stone veneer upward from the first-floor level (*stone veneer @ 1st floor construction*).

At Centerbrook's behest, builder John Landon incorporated another subtle masonry construction technique into the essentially trompe l'oeil stone composition. After the stone veneer was laid in horizontal courses, the mortar between both vertical and horizontal joints was raked to a depth of ½ inch. Because the mortar is recessed from view, the new finished walls appear to be old, dry-laid constructions. The "aged" quality of the walls was given additional credibility by the juxtaposition of a genuinely old floor—20-inch-wide pine planks unearthed at a salvage company by the Adamses themselves. To cap the composition, Centerbrook added its signature crown molding, rendered in cherry, which was stained to match the floor.

Despite the impressiveness of both its exterior and interior detailing, the 4,000-square-foot house was built, according to Nick Deaver, project manager of design for Centerbrook, on "a surprisingly modest budget," made possible by using stone quarried from both the actual site and local resources.

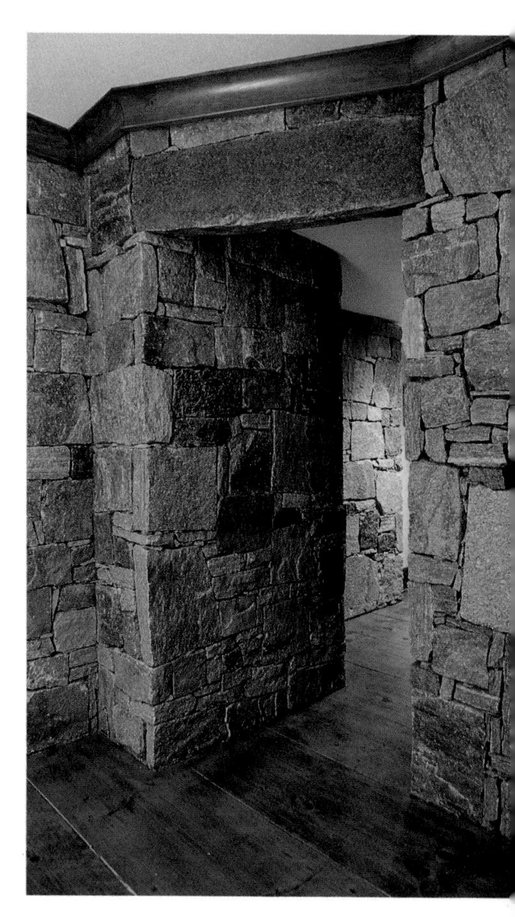

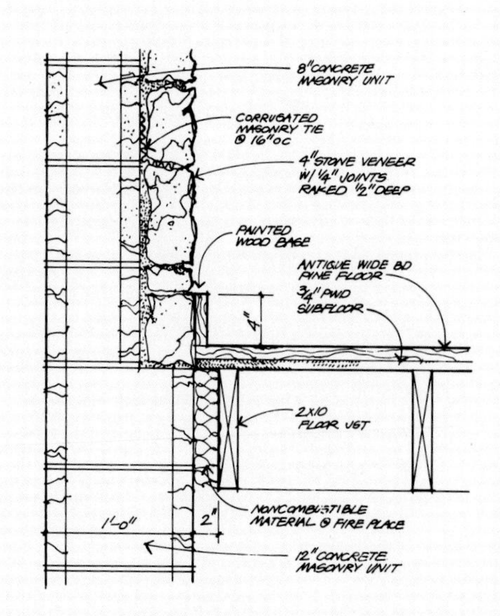


2 STONE VENEER @ 1ST FLOOR CONSTRUCTION
1½" = 1'-0"

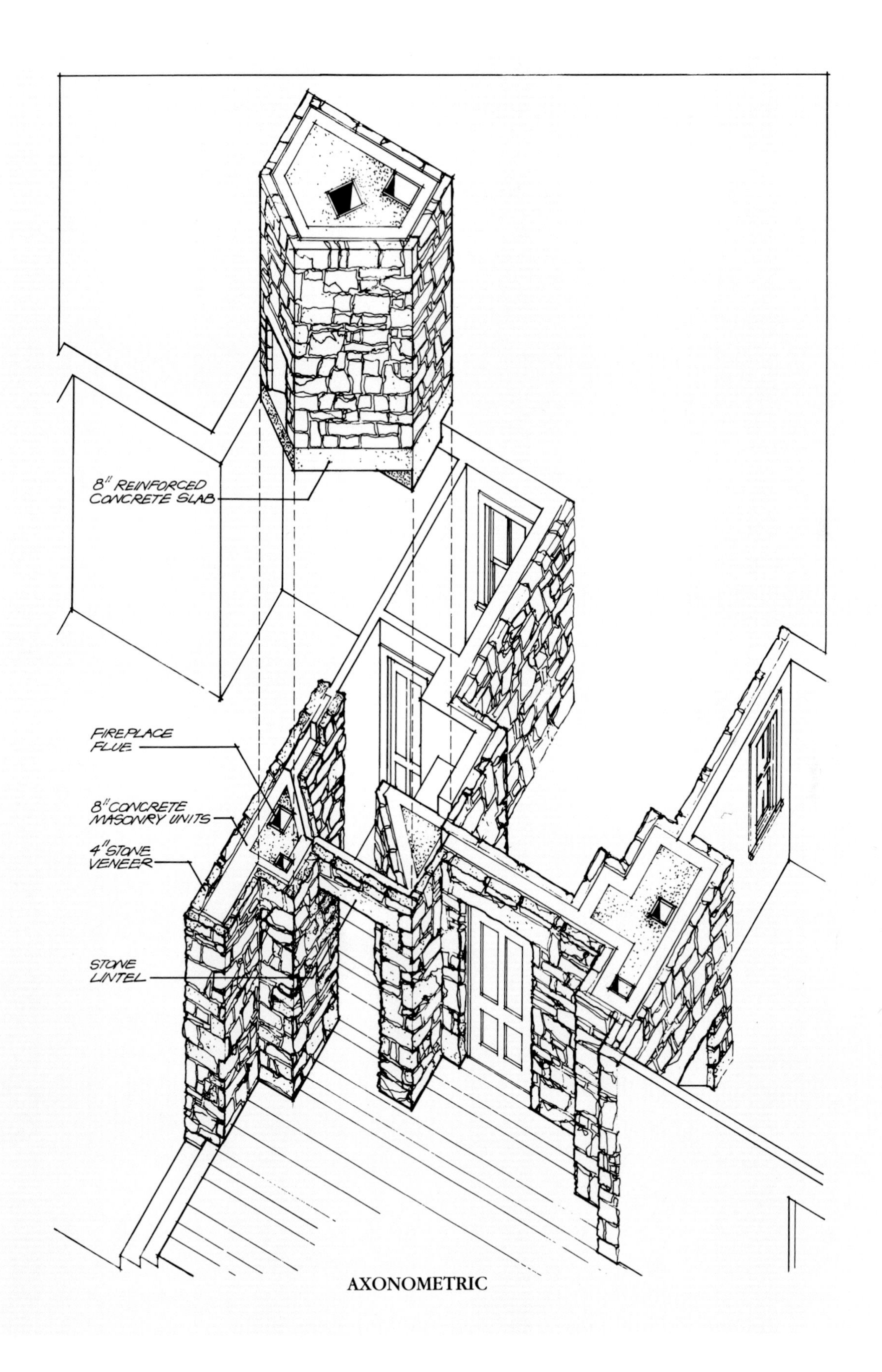


AXONOMETRIC

## LOS FELIZ HILLS RESIDENCE
*Los Angeles, California*

**Architect**
J. Frank Fitzgibbons, AIA, Architect

**Joint-Venture Partners**
Duncan and Wendy Craven

**Design Team**
J. Frank Fitzgibbons, AIA, Principal;
Jeremy Baldwin, M. J. Neal, Assistants

**Fabricators**
John Slaughter (sheet metal);
Marisa Geisy (custom finishes)

**Photography**
© Toshi Yoshimi

IN 1988, architect J. Frank Fitzgibbons collaborated with joint-venture partners Duncan and Wendy Craven to design and build an atypical speculative house of 3,900 square feet on a generous budget.

The house that Fitzgibbons built is situated at the end of a cul-de-sac on a precipitous site overlooking panoramic views of "L.A. to the ocean." Because the project program called for "three bedrooms, a two-car garage, and a pool," the steep slope became the primary consideration in the development of the final design solution.

Fitzgibbons designed a tri-level house that integrates building forms with terrain in terraces that follow and intersect the topography. According to the architect, planes were established that "intersect or overlap, nonaggressively. Sculptural solids and voids are balanced by their opposites within the overall composition."

Within the house, a similar sense of intersecting and overlapping planes, positive and negative, balanced solids and voids, is evident. To create an interior environment that "promotes mental stimulation as it establishes physical ease," the architect adapted classical proportions to contemporary ergonomic data in the details he designed.

The most prominent—and eye-catching—detail in the house is a monumental wedge-shaped archway that serves several, separate purposes. The archway "grounds" the house to the hillside; reflects the two axes that move through the house by connecting the three floors; separates the living and dining rooms as it maintains their visual connection; and accommodates a concealed wet bar within invisible, bifold doors. And the archway does more: because it is finished in wire-brushed copper sheathing, and its portal planes are lacquered in fiery orange/red, it becomes a sculptural art object that "alludes to Christo and Diebenkorn."

The 4′–4″-deep end of the archway narrows at an 18½ degree angle along its 13′–0″ width to a knife edge termination that is emphasized, at its base, by its projection beyond the lowest stair riser and tread (*axonometric*).

For all its graphic impact, the archway was simply constructed. A plywood and stud frame was covered in a skin of drywall, onto which individual copper sheet panels were riveted. A concealed metal strip secures the meeting edges of copper sheets, which were butt-fitted without gaps by expert craftsmen.

Fitzgibbons characterizes the archway as "a Ying-Yang detail"—a machine product that is hand-rubbed and textured. One might also refer to it as "the thin edge of the wedge"—the wedge that should stimulate speculative housing developers to incorporate design work of like quality into their projects.

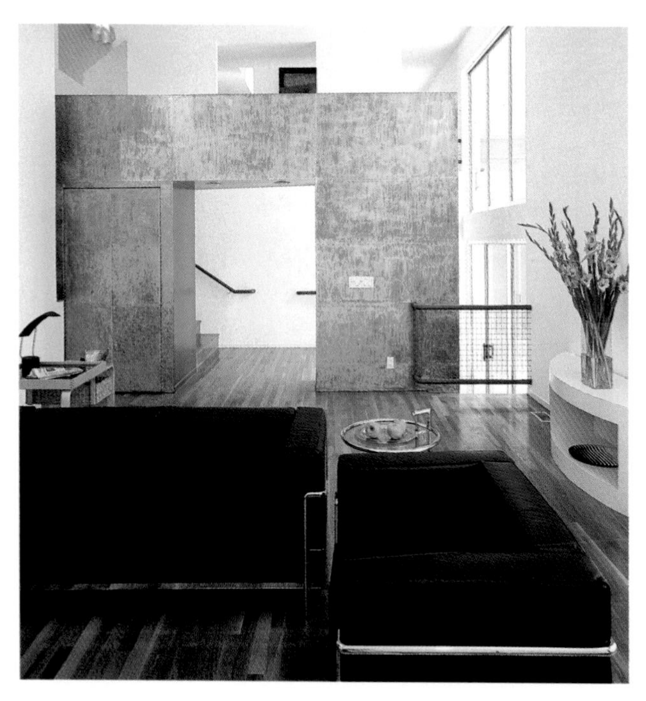

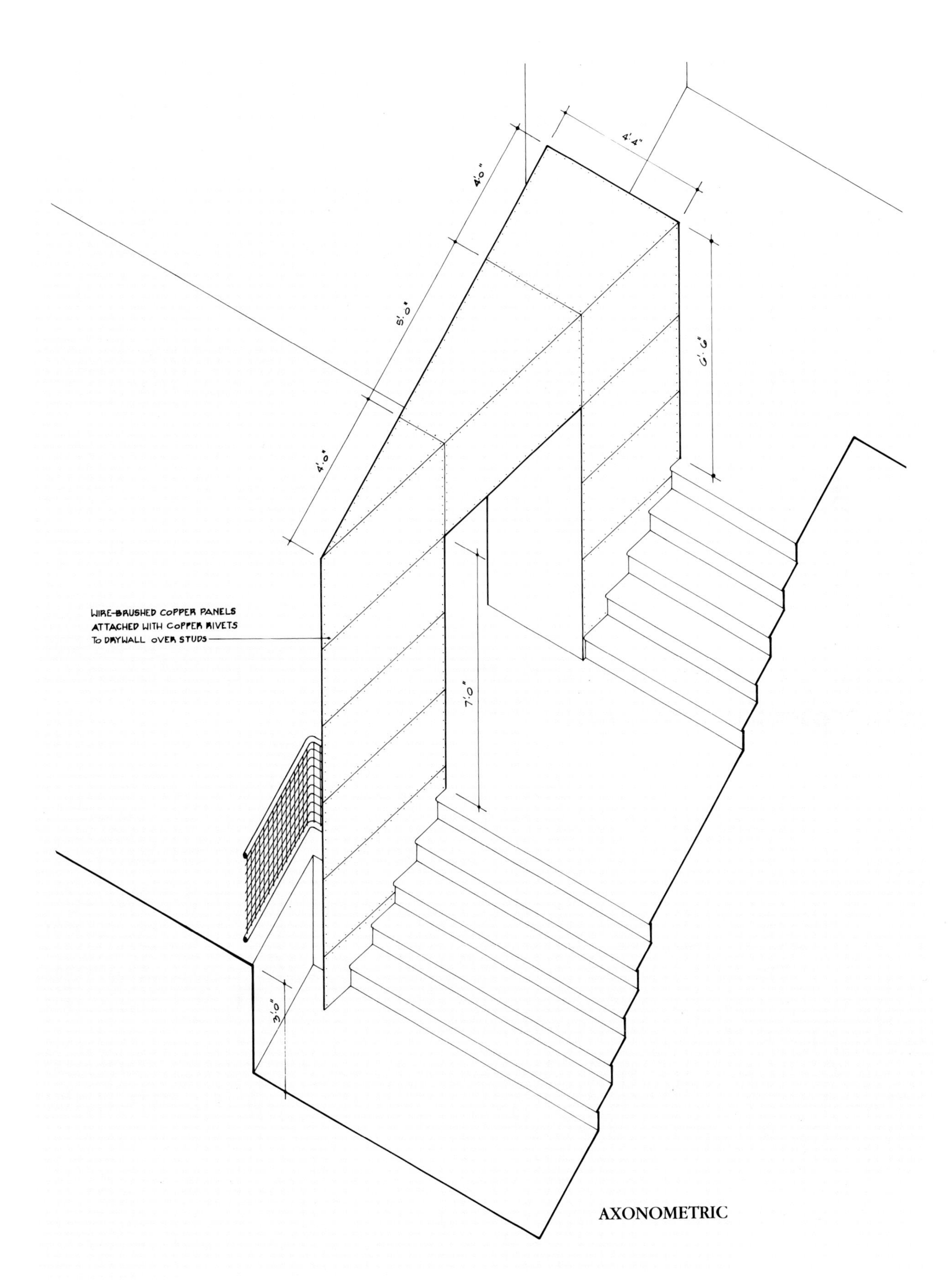


AXONOMETRIC

## Bennett–Novak Residence

*Cincinnati, Ohio*

**Architect**
Michael Schuster Associates:
Michael Schuster, Principal/Designer

**General Contractor**
Jeff Stevens, J & B Construction

**Feasibility Consultant**
Chip Hunter, Hunter/Haas Real Estate

**Photography**
© Ron Forth

Jim Bennett and Mary Novak—two young commercial real estate developers—formed a partnership in 1986 to renovate a nineteenth-century Mt. Adams rowhouse in Cincinnati. Happily, both the project and the partnership flourished; halfway through the renovation Bennett and Novak were married.

Architect Michael Schuster and craftsman Jeff Stevens rounded out this particularly copacetic project team, which was united by a focused common vision: the house was to be restored from multi-family to single-family use; the building's nineteenth-century charm was to be reclaimed as both its systems and ambience were to be updated to a "contemporary classic" standard; and the south-facing wall of the house was to be opened up so that transmission of light and spectacular views of the Ohio River could be maximized.

During the initial feasibility and cost-analysis phase of the project, the architect surveyed an existing structure replete with renovation impedimenta. According to Schuster: "The house was really dark; its floors were covered in linoleum; and rough joists and brick walls had been exposed during a crude early seventies 'update.' "

In discussing revisions to the floor plan, the clients and the architect agreed that a defined, formal pattern of circulation should be maintained on the ground floor. Therefore, to simultaneously increase light penetration through the connecting rooms, the design team decided to take a direct and simple approach to problem solving: a number of doors and archways were enlarged from 5′–0″ widths to 7′–0″ spans. Because the first-floor ceilings were high, the archways were also expanded vertically, increased from 6′–8″ to 9′–10″.

To restore a harmonious sense of scale to the enlarged openings without obstructing the new flow of light, Schuster designed base, column, and frieze details that, installed in combination, allude to the original archway proportions. Schuster explains: "We've balanced large openings between small-scale rooms by utilizing, within the openings, small-scale components."

The wood base of the archway detail is subtly raised 2 inches above the height of the tangential baseboard to give it added "emphasis and prominence." The column itself, a stock porch element, was reduced in height by cutting a 1′–0″ section off the top, a decision the architect and Jeff Stevens made together so that the column's 6-inch base circumference would taper to an appropriately scaled 4½-inch capital. The frieze consists of a cruciform, cross-sectional, articulated grid (*elevation*). Traditional in its first-floor application, the chameleonlike grid reappears throughout the house in incrementally more modern form (*see* Partition, page 150).

The details of the archway were constructed of moderately priced, finely grained poplar indigenous to Ohio. The project was completed in August 1987.

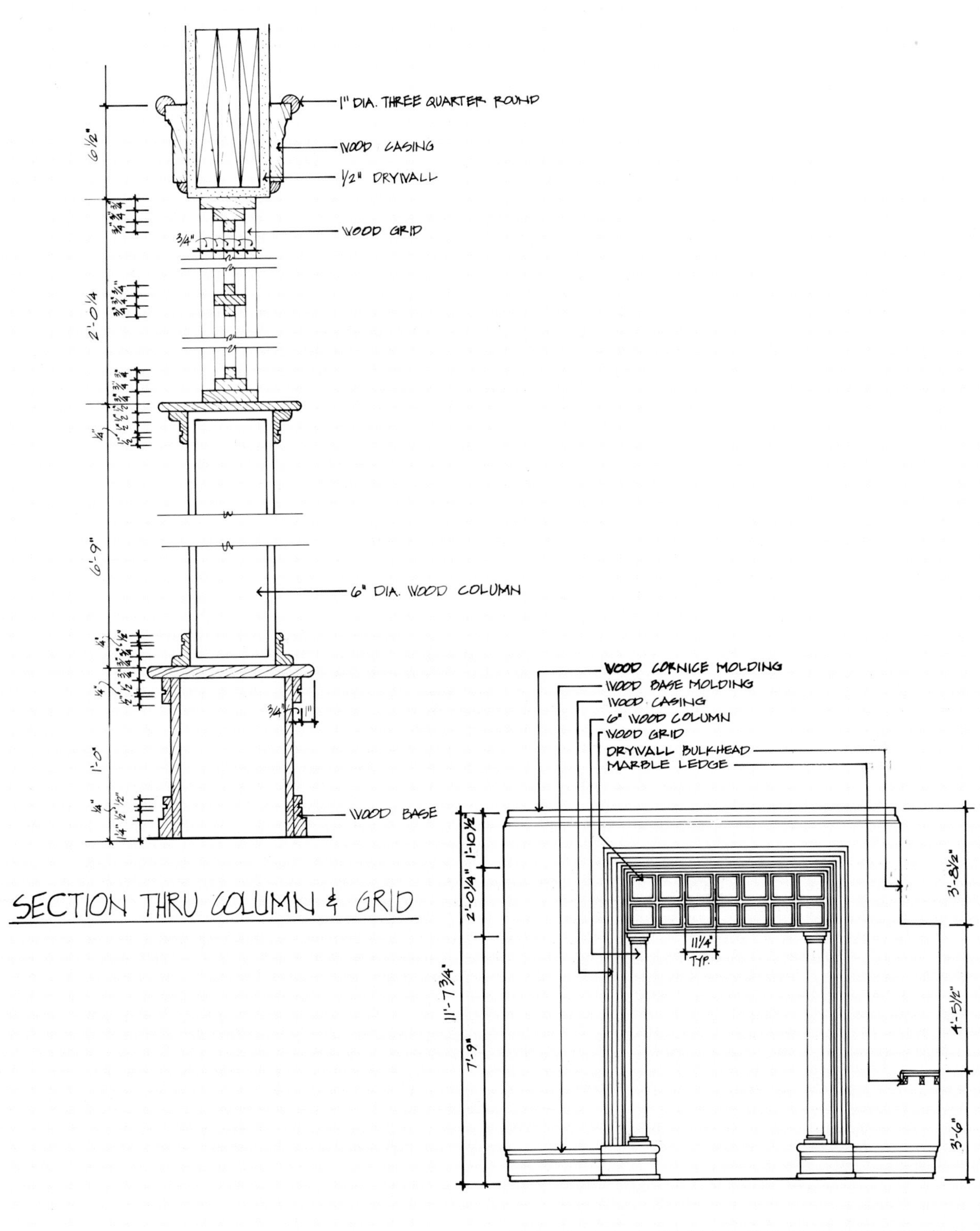
1" DIA. THREE QUARTER ROUND
WOOD CASING
1/2" DRYWALL
WOOD GRID
6" DIA. WOOD COLUMN
WOOD BASE
6 1/2"
2'-0 1/4
6'-9"
1'-0"
SECTION THRU COLUMN & GRID
WOOD CORNICE MOLDING
WOOD BASE MOLDING
WOOD CASING
6" WOOD COLUMN
WOOD GRID
DRYWALL BULKHEAD
MARBLE LEDGE
1'-10 1/2
2'-0 1/4"
11'-7 3/4
7'-9"
11 1/4"
TYP.
3'-8 1/2"
4'-5 1/2"
3'-6"
ELEVATION · DINING ROOM DOORWAY

# Archway/Alcove

## Private Residence
*Paoli, Pennsylvania*

**Architect**
David C. S. Polk &
Linda O'Gwynn, Architects

**Design Team**
David C. S. Polk, Principal-in-Charge;
Linda O'Gwynn, Project Architect;
Alina Brajtburg, Assistant Architect;
Ellen Concannon, Assistant Architect

**General Contractor**
Hallowell Construction Company

**Mechanical Engineer**
Basil Greene, Inc.

**Structural Engineer**
Nicholas L. Gianopulos and Charles Bloszies, Keast and Hood Company

**Photography**
© Matt Wargo

The building site selected by a horticulturalist is bound to be one of natural beauty; this house, built for an amateur horticulturalist and her banker husband, is built on a site bounded by two streams. Philadelphia architects David C. S. Polk and Linda O'Gwynn were asked by their clients to design a house that would seem to extend into its landscape to terraces, gardens, and water (*see* Railing, page 164).

The clients had an unusually specific program, the prime requisite of which was flexibility. Both of their children were away at school; consequently, the couple preferred their son's room to be self-contained and, to allow for the possibility of rental, to have its own entrance. Their daughter's room, conversely, was to be connected to the master bedroom by a guest room that might serve as a sitting room when the house was without children or guests.

The architects interpreted this program by creating rooms and pavilions that integrate exterior space into the overall plan.

Since the rooms vary in size and definition—some exterior, some interior, some combined—the line between room and detail becomes blurred. One such "room" is an alcove off the living room. Defined by four concrete columns, this room is exactly large enough to hold one built-in sofa. The identity and purpose of this room are simple and singular: it is a place just for sitting, a place identifiable and sheltering. As Polk puts it, "The seat feels as if it were given to you by the building."

The alcove lies at a critical juncture at the edge of the house, helping to define the boundary between interior and exterior. Sitting on the sofa grants one views to both: on the outside, a garden and pool, and in the distance, a valley and stream; on the inside, the living room with its large fireplace. Another significance of the alcove is that its back wall serves to define the exterior entry court.

The alcove is formed by four 1′–5″ concrete block piers covered in stucco. The columns rise from the plinth of the house, becoming a vertical extension of it. The tops of the four piers are tied together with eight 4-inch-wide concrete lintels that bear on the concrete block, a symbiotic union that creates a rigid structure.

The tops of the lintels, which are flush with the ceiling, and the faces of the lintels, which overhang ⅝ of an inch from the face of the concrete block, allow them to be flush with the final finish of tinted stucco.

Between each pair of lintels, an infill panel of red oak is set off by a narrow reveal, reiterating the oak of the ceiling and wall trim, as well as that of the floor and sofa base.

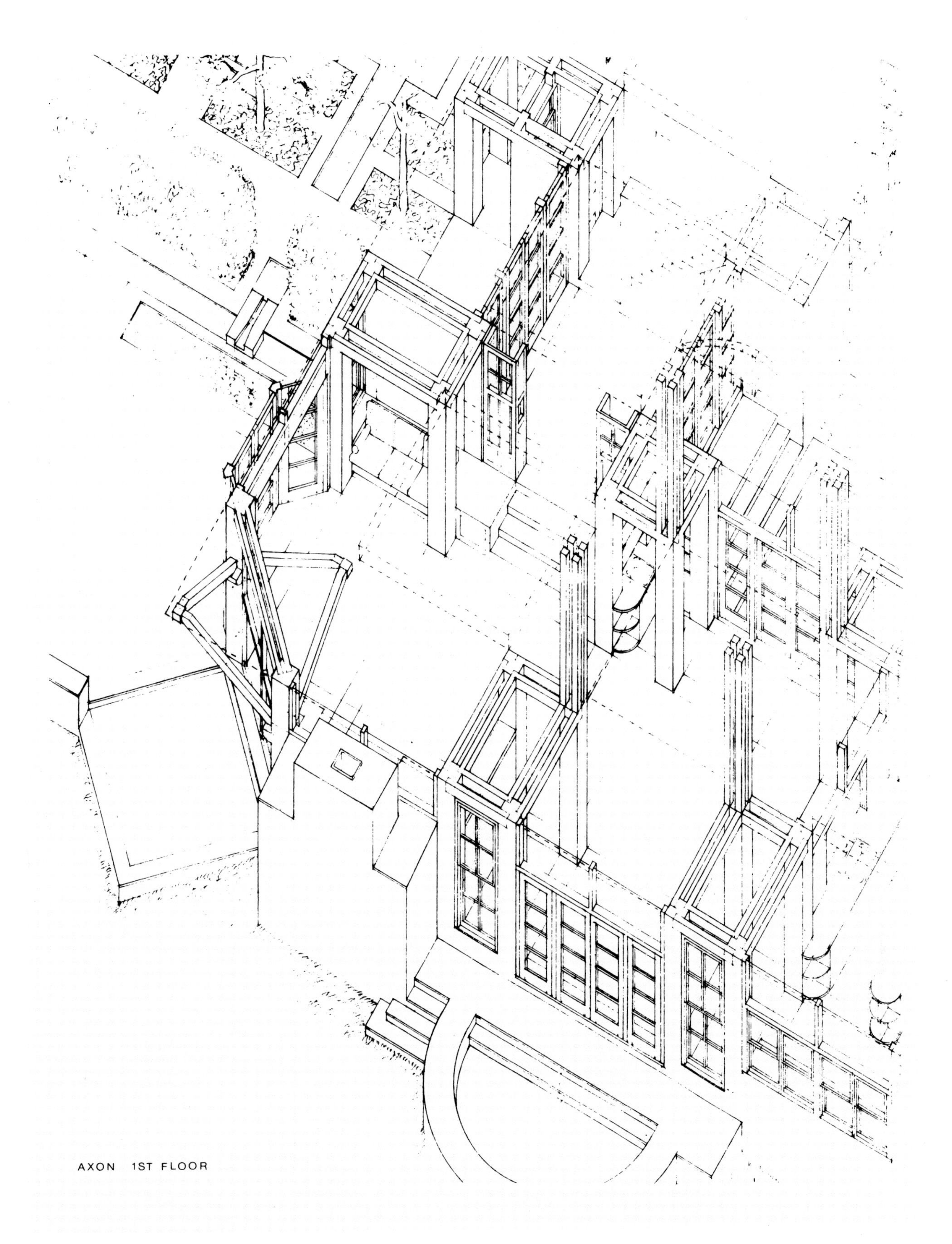

AXON 1ST FLOOR

# Audiovisual Cabinet

**Lewis Residence**
*Beverly Hills, California*

**Interior Design**
Sally Sirkin Interior Designs

**Design Team**
Sally Sirkin Lewis, Senior Designer;
David Wheat, Project Designer/Coordinator;
Dante Amato, Project Architect;
James Picotte, Assistant

**Fabricators**
Audio Command Systems (audiovisual equipment); J. Robert Scott (cabinets); Jim Bohn, Inc. (paint/wall coverings)

**Photography**
© Jaime Ardiles-Arce

The fireplace, formerly the focus of nocturnal family gatherings, has largely been eclipsed—for those honest enough to admit it—by television. In 1985, designer Sally Sirkin Lewis faced this fact and closed off one-half of a double-sided fireplace in the house she shares with her husband, Bernard Lewis, to "architecturally accommodate" a media center and sculpture niche.

The original, double-sided firebox was replaced with a model that faces only the living room. The remaining, mirror-image cavity was then enlarged by framing, which added 1′–0″ to its depth and extended its width to 6′–3″ (*plan*).

A welded steel frame, recessed and bolted with angle irons into the back-wall masonry, serves a dual purpose: it maintains the structural integrity of the active chimney and, thanks to the frontal inclusion of two ½-inch-diameter steel rods hung from a horizontal steel plate, also supports the "very heavy" Roman bust that resides in the new niche (*section*). The display niche was enhanced by mirroring its anterior wall and by lacquering its side elevations.

The cubic space of the firebox itself was requisitioned for the installation of audiovisual componentry. The cabinetry is constructed of both ½-inch and ⅜-inch black-lacquered plywood, segments of which were dovetailed and glued into the shelves that hold the center's electronic equipment (*elevation*).

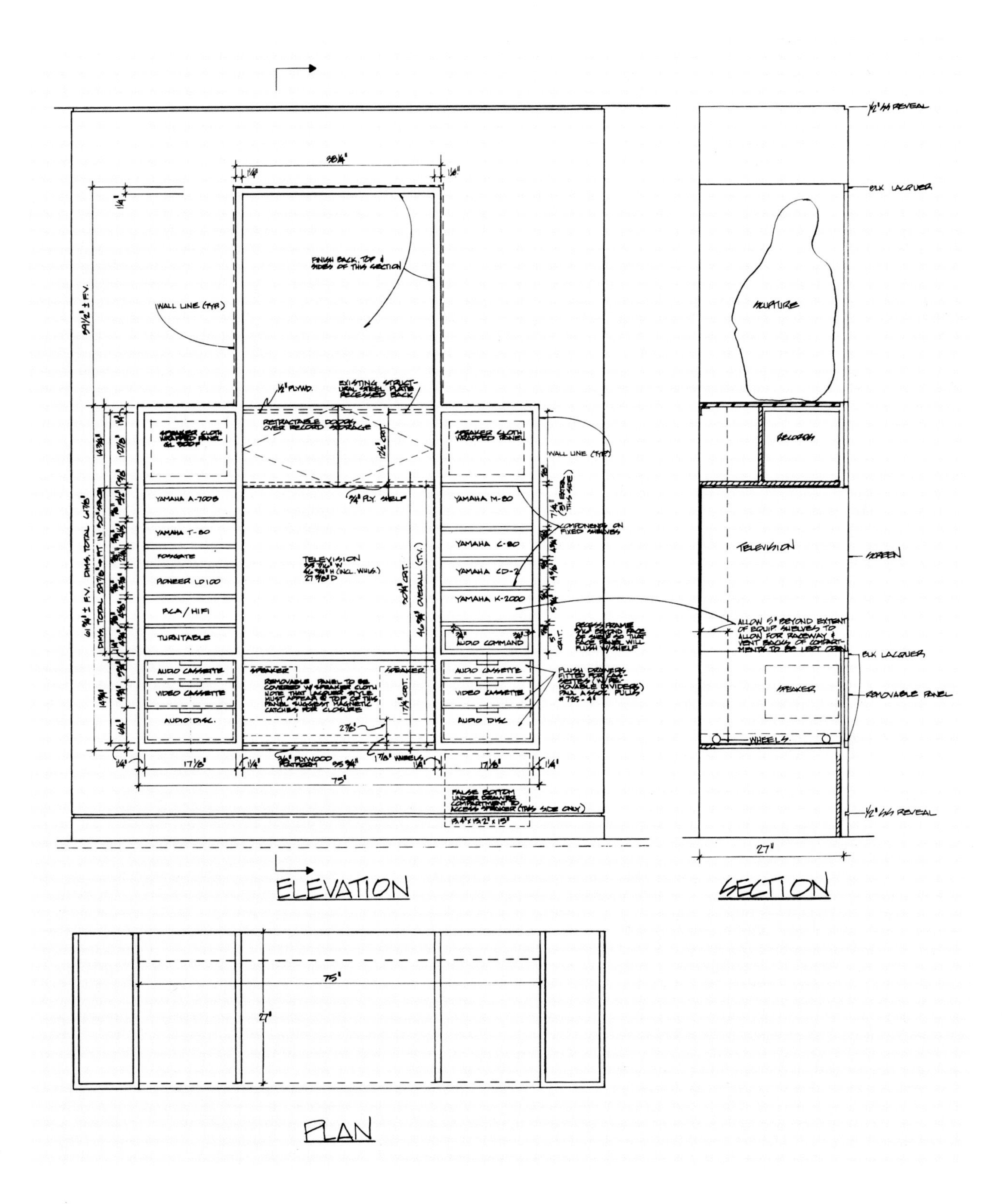

ELEVATION
SECTION
PLAN
WALL LINE (TYP)
FINISH BACK, TOP & SIDES OF THIS SECTION
1/2" PLYWD.
EXISTING STRUCTURAL STEEL PLATE RECESSED BACK
RETRACTABLE DOORS OVER RECORD STORAGE
SPEAKER CLOTH WRAPPED PANEL
3/4" PLY. SHELF
YAMAHA A-700B
YAMAHA T-80
FOSGATE
PIONEER LD100
RCA / HIFI
TURNTABLE
YAMAHA M-80
YAMAHA C-80
YAMAHA CD-2
YAMAHA K-2000
AUDIO COMMAND
COMPONENTS ON FIXED SHELVES
TELEVISION
AUDIO CASSETTE
VIDEO CASSETTE
AUDIO DISC
AUDIO DISC.
SPEAKER
3/4" PLYWOOD PLATFORM
WHEELS
75"
27"
SCULPTURE
RECORDS
SCREEN
BLK LACQUER
REMOVABLE PANEL
1/2" REVEAL

# Audiovisual Enclosure

**Private Residence**
*Edgartown, Massachusetts*

**Architect**
MacNelly • Cohen Architects

**Design Team**
Bruce MacNelly, AIA, Principal-in-Charge; Linda Joy Cohen, AIA, Principal; Margaret Smart, Construction Drawings; Jill Neubauer, Renderer

**General Contractor**
Richard Knight

**Fabricator**
Alexander & Wright Millworks, Inc.

**Photography**
© Bruce MacNelly

For many, hunting equipment, fishing equipment, and antique American furniture are laden with as much sentimental as factual meaning. Considered together, they evoke images of a cosy country cottage equipped with a rocking chair, a roaring fire, and a stalwart dog asleep on the hearth. Hoping to transcend that stereotype, a sophisticated New England couple commissioned architects MacNelly • Cohen to design an addition to their home.

The clients allowed a generous budget for the 600-square-foot addition, which was to contain a primary space, or library, replete with storage space for books, hunting and fishing equipment, and a television, as well as display space for artwork. Elsewhere within the addition, a small study, a hot tub room, and a potting shed were to be included.

The most prominent characteristic of the library consists of two pairs of opposing elements: along the main axis of the room a gable end wall with windows opening to the garden and harbor view opposes an inglenook that is sheltered below a curved, projecting balcony. The two elements are also functionally opposite: the open glass wall projects outward into the landscape, while the intimate inglenook, with its built-in seating and imposing fireplace, clearly focuses on home.

It was in detailing the two side walls with cabinets that the architects most clearly transcended stylistic expectations. The cabinets, far from exhibiting Colonial-style sensibilities, instead manifest contemporary qualities—including handsomely integrated clerestory windows.

Lower cabinets hold books, sporting equipment, and a television in wood-paneled cases with glass doors and adjustable interior shelves. Above, the clerestory windows are set in beveled window wells; the central, double-beveled bay that accommodates the television is wider than the two single-beveled bays that flank it.

The curly maple paneling that was used to finish the display cases and window frames is supported on a ¾-inch plywood armature (built over a wood frame) that projects 2′–0″ into the room from the exterior wall. The armature also serves to stabilize the roof structure and allows shimming space for attaching paneling and cabinets. The interior "carcasses" of the cabinets were shop-constructed and screwed into the plywood armature. At the top of the armature, a 1′–5″ piece of trim molding hides a duct chase, with an HVAC return set into the wood soffit of the window well.

Because the curly maple paneling was narrower than the surfaces it had to cover, it was "bookmatched." The cabinet doors and trim were rendered in solid maple, the window wells in curly maple veneer plywood. Both were screwed into the plywood armature at the sides and concealed by the trim; corner joints were mitered and glued.

Typically, each element or panel is surrounded by a ⅛-inch reveal. The reveals allowed the wall to be constructed in sections, leaving space for squaring and shimming. They also absorb differential movement, shrinkage, and cracking, and become, according to MacNelly, "expressive of the joint."

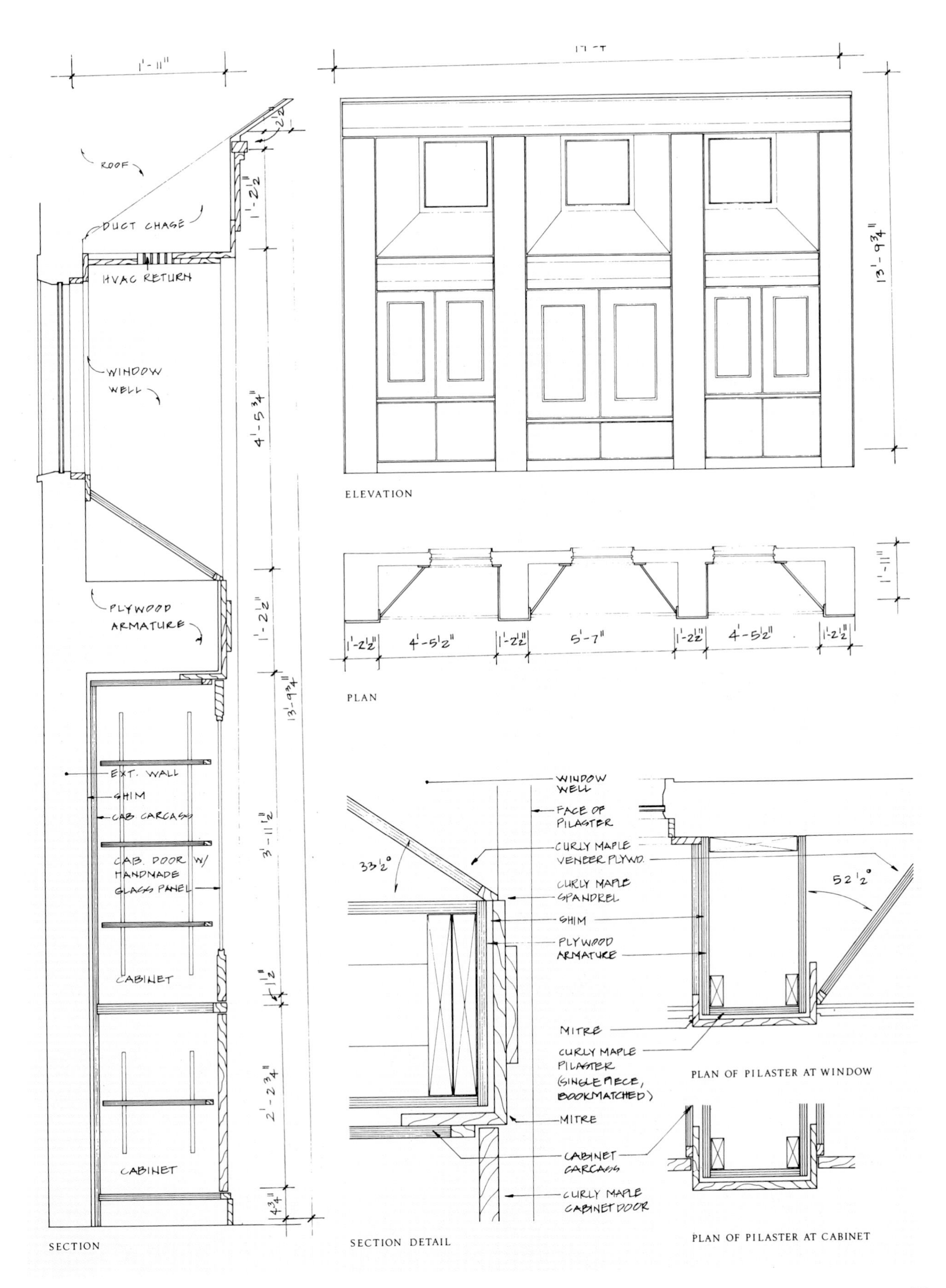


SECTION

ELEVATION

PLAN

SECTION DETAIL

PLAN OF PILASTER AT WINDOW

PLAN OF PILASTER AT CABINET

# Bathroom Cabinet

**Townhouse Residence**
*Chicago, Illinois*

**Architect**
Rudolph & Associates, P.C.

**Design Team**
Christopher H. Rudolph, AIA, Principal;
Lawrence M. Petitti, Architect;
Janet L. Steidl, ASID, Designer

**General Contractor**
S. N. Peck, Builder, Inc.

**Photography**
© Bruce Van Inwegen

For clients who requested a "re-discovery of paradise lost" in their 1860s Chicago townhouse, architects Rudolph & Associates designed what might be described as a very private paradise—a sumptuous 1,000-square-foot master suite that incorporates a luxurious 250-square-foot bathroom.

The development of the master suite/bathroom design was just one part of the 4,500-square-foot renovation the firm undertook within the house, originally owned by an organ company magnate. According to the architects, the house had suffered severe despoilation in the intervening century—its once-grand interior had been repeatedly subdivided into smaller, awkward spaces. In developing the renovation plan for the house, the design team created new spatial equations and detailing forms consistent with both the monumental scale of the house and the specific use of marble the clients had requested.

Both prerequisites were accomplished in the master bathroom by the development of a subtly curved bathroom sink cabinet that is appropriately massive and powerful from a frontal perspective, but which is relatively slim and light from the side. A marble countertop rests on a subframe, which is divided into four storage spaces. Rectilinear end cabinets are hidden behind recessed and trimmed lacquered panel doors. In striking—and graceful—contrast, two pivoting bins with quarter-circular fascias are mounted between the end piers, their curved form complementing the curved countertop. Hinged, the bins' downward swing is braked by pneumatic flapstays.

The scale of the bathroom sink cabinet is accentuated by two vertically mounted fluorescent light fixtures, rendered as simplified columns that rise 3′–4″ behind the counter surface to continue the line of the pierlike end cabinets. The fixtures' exterior surface of sand-blasted glass over a clear Plexiglas frame is bolted to strips of laminate, which in turn are bolted to the wall. An incandescent bulb concealed within the cornice molding (*section-light column*) further illuminates the upper walls and ceiling.

Six mirrored surfaces, each in a different plane, open up the rather narrow concavity in which the sink cabinet is recessed with a "hall-of-mirrors" effect. Each mirror adjacent to the cabinet opens to reveal a recessed, glass-shelved medicine cabinet (*section-storage unit; lower level plan*). All mirrors are double-beveled.

Rudolph took advantage of the niches on either side of the cabinet to build in marble seating benches. The architects tempered the cold feel of the marble bench tops by installing them next to radiator vents. Storage is provided in lacquered drawers under each bench.

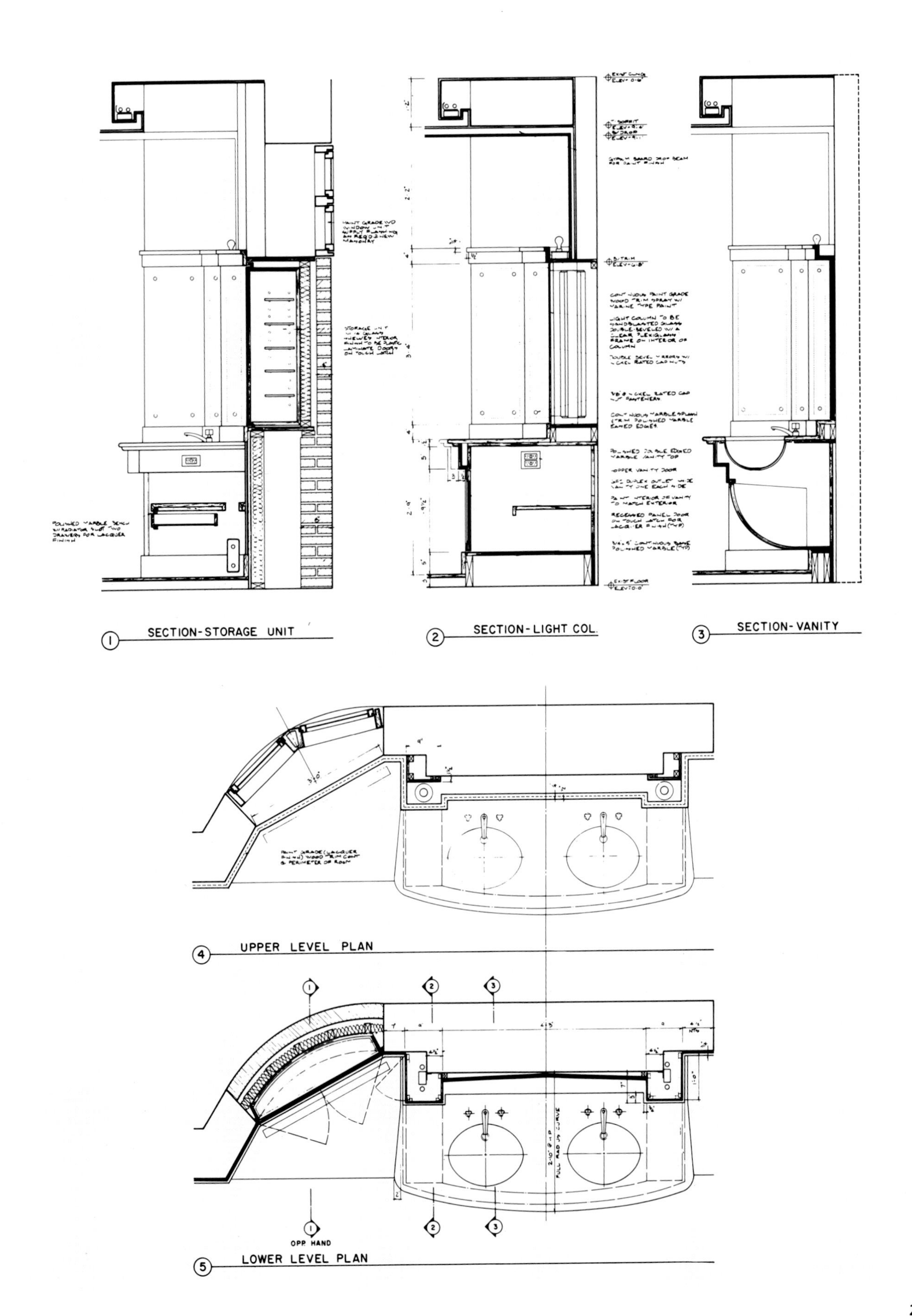

SECTION-STORAGE UNIT
SECTION-LIGHT COL.
SECTION-VANITY
UPPER LEVEL PLAN
OPP HAND
LOWER LEVEL PLAN

# Bathroom Cabinets

**Harborside Residence**
*Baltimore, Maryland*

**Interior Designer**
Rita St. Clair Associates, Inc.

**Design Team**
Rita St. Clair, FASID, Principal;
Ted Pearson, ASID, Project Designer

**Fabricators**
The Valley Craftsmen, Ltd. (finishes and murals); Hough Woodworks (millwork and cabinetry); Crystal Interiors (beveled mirrors)

**Photography**
© Tim Fields

Although the owners of this residence considered themselves fortunate to have acquired one of the last new waterfront townhouses in Baltimore Harbor's historic district, they still wanted their new home to have a rich, traditional feel. They therefore commissioned Rita St. Clair Associates to design and oversee construction within the 4,500-square-foot shell, entrusting the firm with a generous budget (*see also* Door, page 86; Railing, page 168; Storage Cabinets, page 208). The owners also made clear their wish to stay heavily involved in the project, hiring their own cabinetmaker, with whom they worked closely throughout the renovation.

St. Clair utilized rich wood surfaces, natural light, and leaded glass to provide her clients with a neo-Edwardian environment, which assimilated their various treasured objects as it showcases their interests in sailing, Eastern religions, and art.

One of the owners' major priorities was the development of a large multipurpose master bath with generous storage space. As part of this room, St. Clair designed a formal, symmetrical, 8′–3″-long master bath vanity cabinet with beveled mirrors, verde issorie marble sinktop and backsplash, and a mahogany base with numerous drawers.

The vanity cabinet's design is strongly neoclassical; the entire piece is framed by two 1′–0″-wide by 7½″-deep mahogany "pilasters," the mirrored surfaces of which open to reveal medicine cabinets. These end pieces are continued below by ¾-round, 6-inch-diameter, mahogany "corner columns" that project out from the ends of the vanity. The marble sinktop's ogee edge, set 3′–0″ from the floor, wraps the tops of these columns, giving them "capitals" and defining the cabinet plan.

Inset between the two mirrored pilasters, a pair of brass sconces emerge from the large central mirror, further emphasizing its symmetry. Below, two sets of double-door cabinets conceal a clothes hamper and more storage space, flanked by sets of four stacked clothing drawers. Sink basins are pewter; the hardware is polished brass.

The antique zinc-lined bathtub is decorated with a wave design of gold leaf and glaze. The floor of the bath is random length walnut edged by a cherry and ebony border; the window shutters are cherry with translucent silk panels.

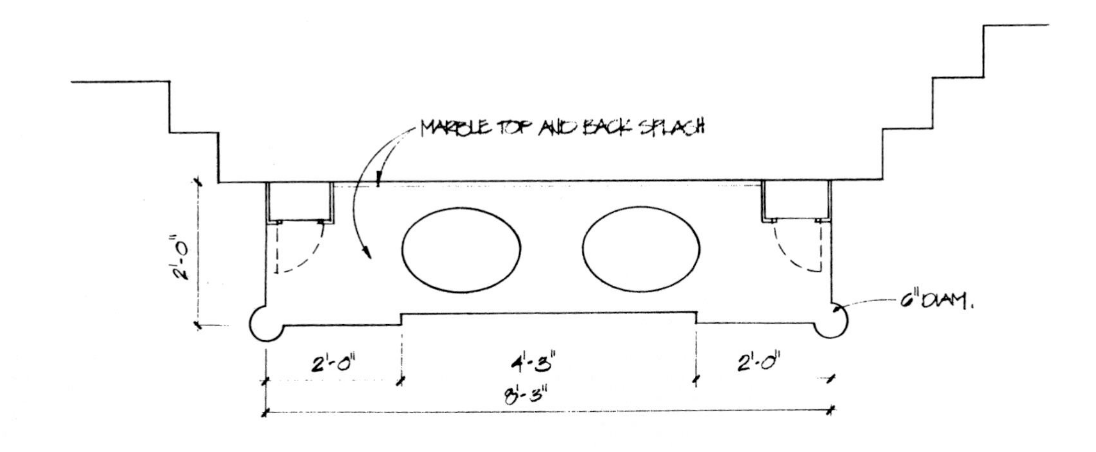
MARBLE TOP AND BACK SPLASH
2'-0"
6" DIAM.
2'-0"
4'-3"
2'-0"
8'-3"

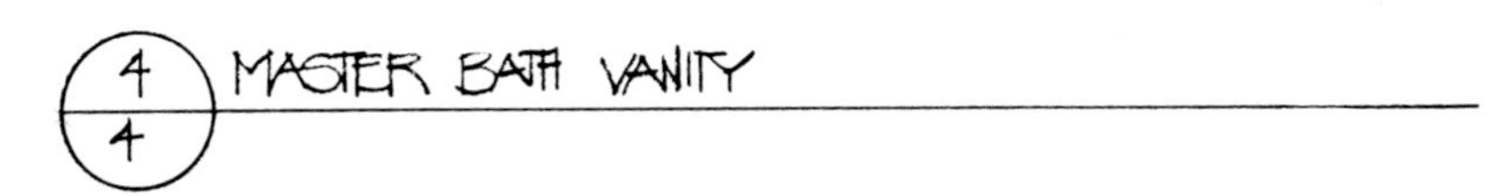
4
4
MASTER BATH VANITY

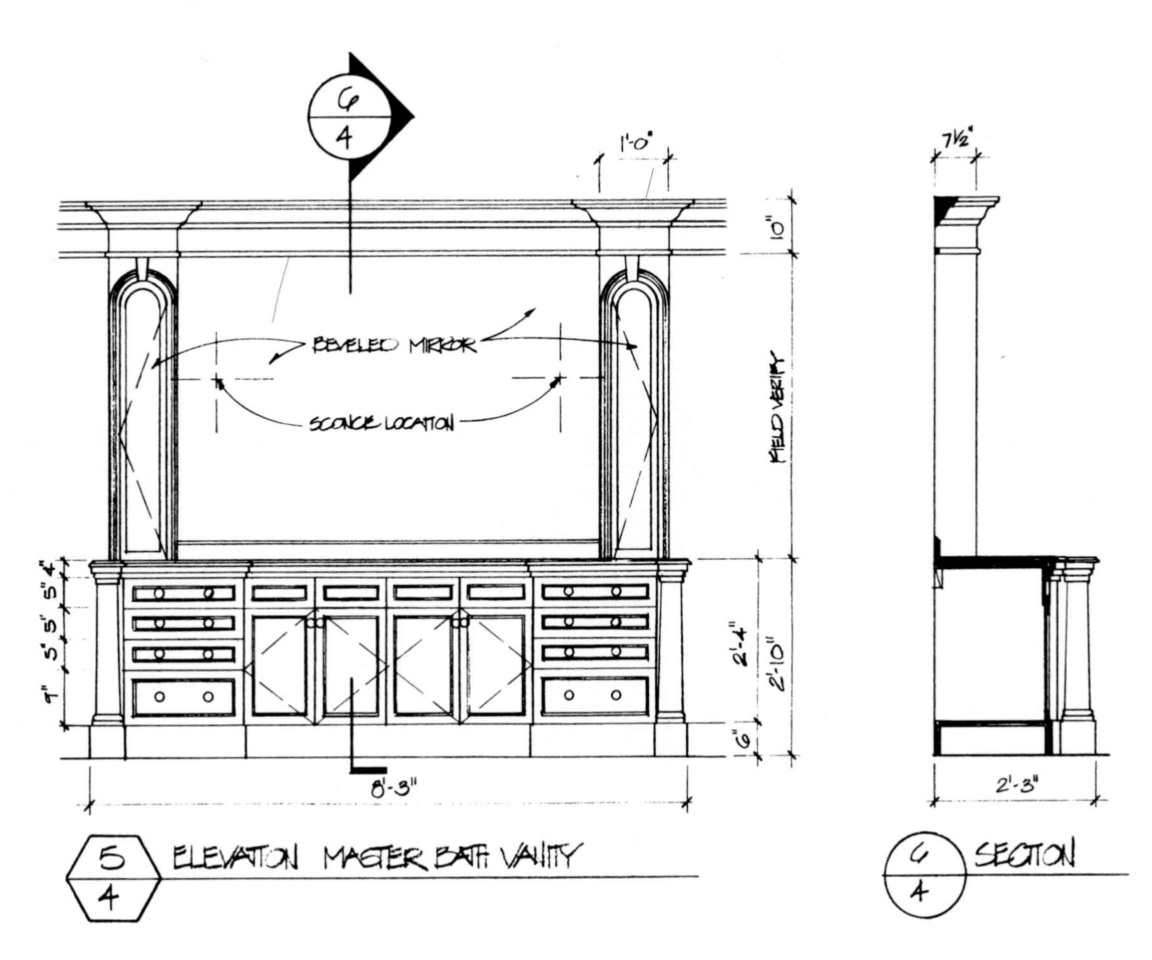
6
4
1'-0"
10"
BEVELED MIRROR
SCONCE LOCATION
FIELD VERIFY
2'-4"
2'-10"
6"
8'-3"
5
4
ELEVATION MASTER BATH VANITY
7½"
2'-3"
6
4
SECTION

# Bathroom Cabinets

## Lewis Residence
*Beverly Hills, California*

**Interior Design**
Sally Sirkin Interior Designs

**Design Team**
Sally Sirkin Lewis, Senior Designer;
David Wheat, Senior Project Designer;
Dante Amato, Project Architect;
Mitchell N. Quigley, Staff Decorator

**Fabricators**
Best Way Marble Company (marble);
J. Robert Scott (cabinets);
Paul Associates (fixtures)

**Photography**
© Jaime Ardiles-Arce

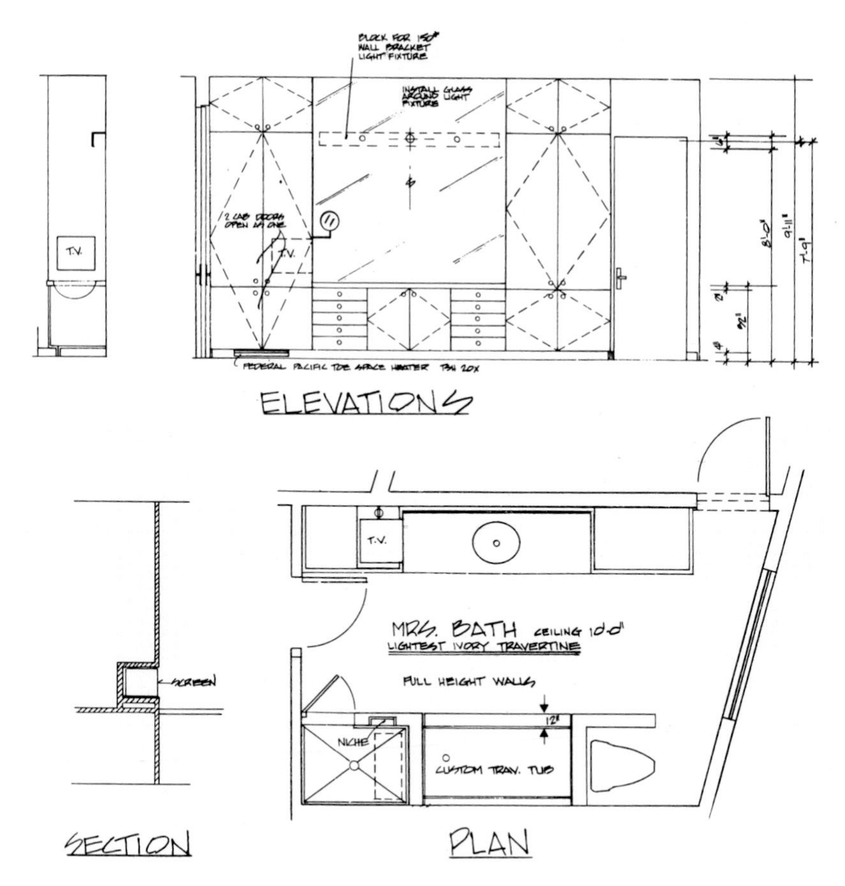


Sally Sirkin Lewis is an early riser who insists on getting "a daily update on news of world affairs" while, simultaneously, minimizing the time required to ready herself for the office. To maximize efficiency, Lewis designed a self-sustaining "hers" bathroom that also contains both kitchen and media center elements.

The bathroom allows immediate access to linens and Lewis's business wardrobe closet/dressing room, as well as to an automatic coffeemaker and a television (*plan*). The television is recessed neatly into a wall niche and, thanks to the number of mirrors in the room, is visible from almost any angle.

Because the bathroom floor area—5′–0″ × 17′–0″—is long but not wide, artful use of facing mirrors, as well as floor-to-10′–0″-ceiling cabinetry averts claustrophobia (*elevations; plan*).

Standard particleboard and plywood construction underlie the elegant craftsmanship of the cabinet exteriors, finished in many coats of polished polyester lacquer toned to match the travertine that faces the counter and walls.

The same attention to simple elegance and quality craftsmanship is evident in visible fixtures: a silvered sink and appendant hardware, a stainless steel makeup mirror supported by a pivot arm, and a stainless steel bracket light fixture (which was first custom-built in Sirkin's own shop and then bolted through the wall mirror to heavy-duty blocking). The light fixture diffuses potential glare from the many small low-voltage incandescent bulbs that wash the mirror. The bathroom floor is heated; in addition, toe-space heaters were installed.

# Bathtub Enclosure

**Riverside Drive Penthouse**
*New York, New York*

**Interior Design**
Claudia Librett Design Studio

**Design Team**
Claudia Librett, Design Principal;
Gayle Kenigsberg, Design Associate

**Filing Architect**
Michael Sapinsky, AIA

**Construction Consultant**
John Deak, Jr., Deak Construction, Inc.

**Photography**
© H. Durston Saylor

Straightforward simplicity in detailing should never be confused with lack of quality, as demonstrated by the powerful, yet tautly disciplined, bathroom finish detailing created by Manhattan-based interior designer Claudia Librett. The key to success in this carefully planned detailing package lay in the designer's sure knowledge of what to eliminate rather than what to impose. (*See also* Display Niche, page 72).

The result is a sleek composition in which nothing is extraneous. No-nonsense fixtures from American Olean are sensibly placed; luxurious brass accessories—heated towel rail, shower curtain rod, faucets, antique pendant light fixture, and custom-designed brass-bracketed glass shelf—are dramatically offset by a soothing backdrop of gray-toned terrazzo tile (*bathroom elevation*).

Construction methodology was similarly straightforward. The tub was set into a vermiculite and concrete bed to minimize the load on the floor (*bathroom tub detail*); wall and tub surround tiles were glued to waterproof Wonder-Board with silicone adhesive.

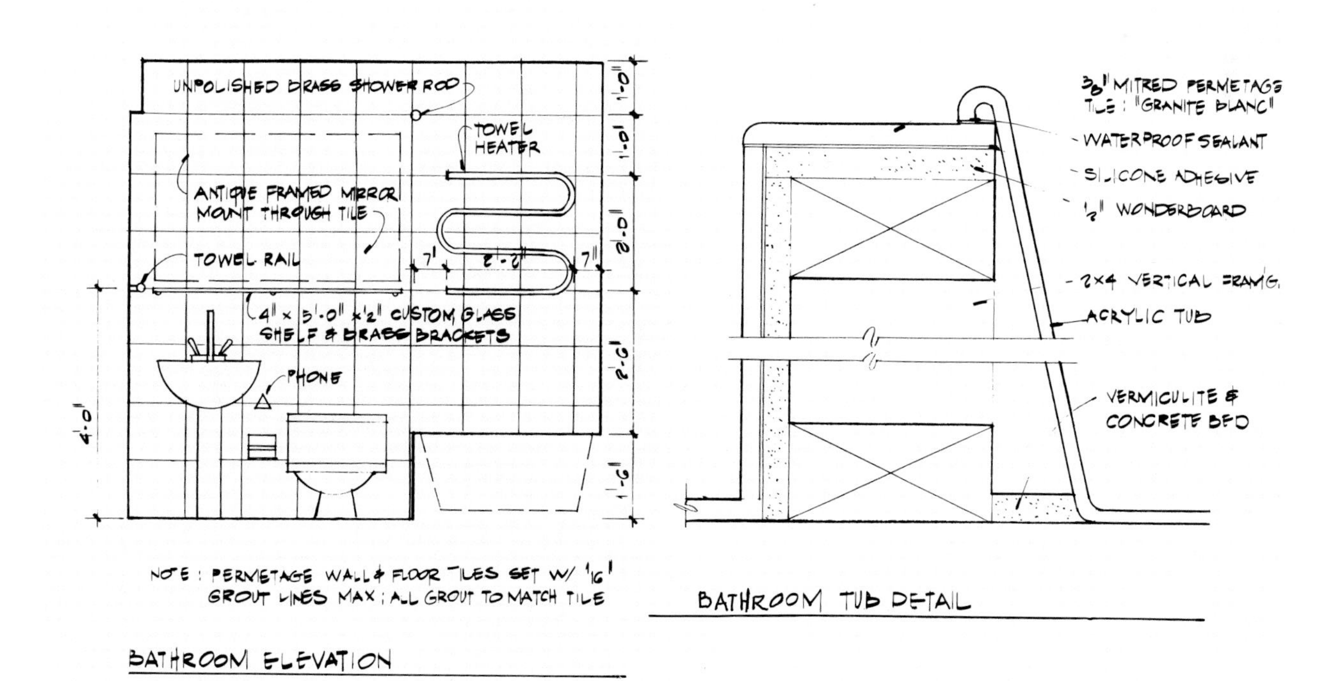

# Bathtub Enclosure

**Private Residence**
*Austin, Texas*

**Architect**
Dick Clark Architecture:
Dick Clark, Architect

**General Contractor**
Robert Coe Builders, Inc.

**Fabricators**
Tim Donovan Tile (tile);
Dutchman Plumbing (plumbing);
Max Rockoff Cabinets (cabinets)

**Photography**
© Greg Hursley

THE OWNER of this 1,800-square-foot home in Austin, Texas, is a single businesswoman who works in advertising. Because her schedule is hectic and her work is stressful, she asked architect Dick Clark to place special emphasis on the bathroom when she commissioned him to renovate her house. She specifically asked for "a relaxing atmosphere," defining her goals as "comfort and luxury." The architect was given a $20,000 budget with which to create "a functional and sparkling solution."

It was important to the client that natural light and a lovely garden view be maximized within the bathroom, while at the same time it was essential that privacy from nearby neighbors be ensured. In response, Clark developed a solution that utilized three varieties of window glazing—clear glass, glass block, and a skylight—to provide daylight views of the garden and nighttime views of the stars.

Clark combined tile with the several types of glass to add elegance and plasticity to his curvilinear forms. Basic tile work was fabricated in versatile 2″ × 2″ × ½″ white and aquamarine blue ceramic tile. Contrast was provided by 2″ × ½″ tiles which replace the 2″ × 2″ on the shower wall and in the trim. All tile is mud set, in grout over wire mesh.

For convenience, Clark built the shower and the tub next to each other (*axonometric*). The shower is separated from the access ramp that leads up from the sink/toilet area to the tub (which is a custom Jacuzzi) by an arc of glass blocks, which act as a permanent shower curtain bordered on three sides by the smaller tile (*axonometric*).

To build the shower wall, Clark used 4″ × 8″ glass blocks. Thus, the inner sink/toilet area receives light from the windows that overlook the tub, without sacrificing privacy.

The tub itself had to be raised for mechanical reasons. Clark turned an apparent awkwardness into a virtue by rendering the wide steps up to the tub as a ceremonial passage past the curved shower wall. The extra height of the tub also allows a much closer proximity to the windows.

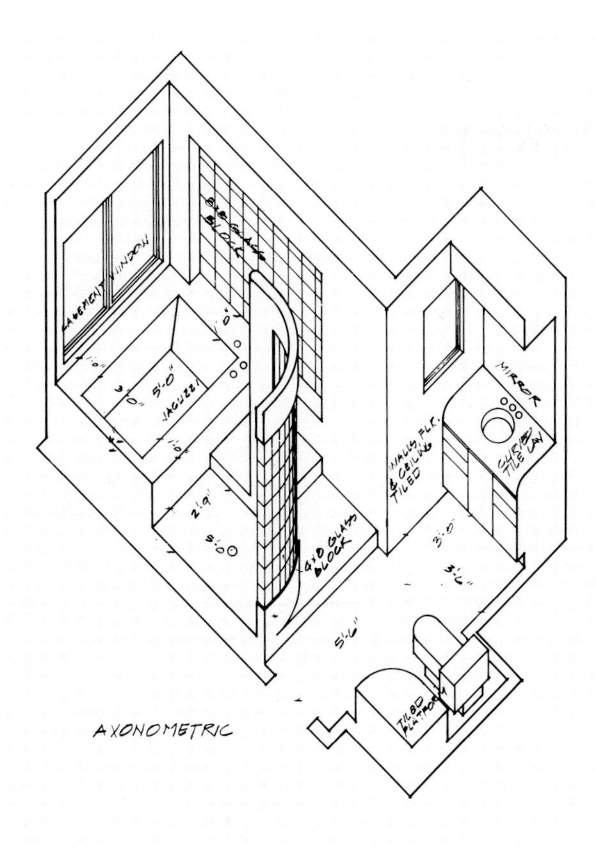

# Bathtub Enclosure

**Printers Row Loft**
*Chicago, Illinois*

**Architect**
Pappageorge Haymes Ltd.

**Photography**
© John Alderson

In 1983, a young, then-single doctor commissioned architects Pappageorge Haymes to space plan and detail his Printers Row loft condominium in Chicago. The owner gave the design team a concise, definitive tri-part list of priorities: "maximize the two-story, open quality of the space; enclose some areas of privacy; and, last—but certainly not least—incorporate a large whirlpool into the plan."

With a modest $50-per-square-foot budget, Pappageorge Haymes pragmatically left certain existing structural elements alone: the design team worked around the building's plumbing stack; and to save finishing costs, the heavy timber beams and outer masonry walls were left exposed.

As carefully balanced by the design team, these rough, textural materials enhance—rather than detract from, by comparison—the focal point of the finished plan: a sleek and shining wall fabricated of 8-inch glass block. The juxtaposition of rough and smooth materials within the open plan works because, in George Pappageorge's words, "like brick, glass block is another, more refined, industrial material."

The undulating partition exemplifies design, as well as economic, efficiency—satisfying all the client's program priorities in just one detail. But the wall accomplishes much more than merely separating the new whirlpool bathroom from primary living space. As a design device, it exuberantly breaks through the marginal rigidity of otherwise right-angle vertical and horizontal planes.

Pappageorge Haymes delivered extra, long-term value to the owner by utilizing two simple but effective passive energy conservation techniques in the construction of the 115-square-foot bathroom, the "open" appearance of which is illusory. In fact, a flat, waterproofed "roof" prevents both heated air and humidity from escaping into the larger space. And because the "flush" whirlpool tub deck is raised 2′–8″ from the floor, dense layers of insulation packed into the plywood subframe help to maintain a consistent temperature (*section*).

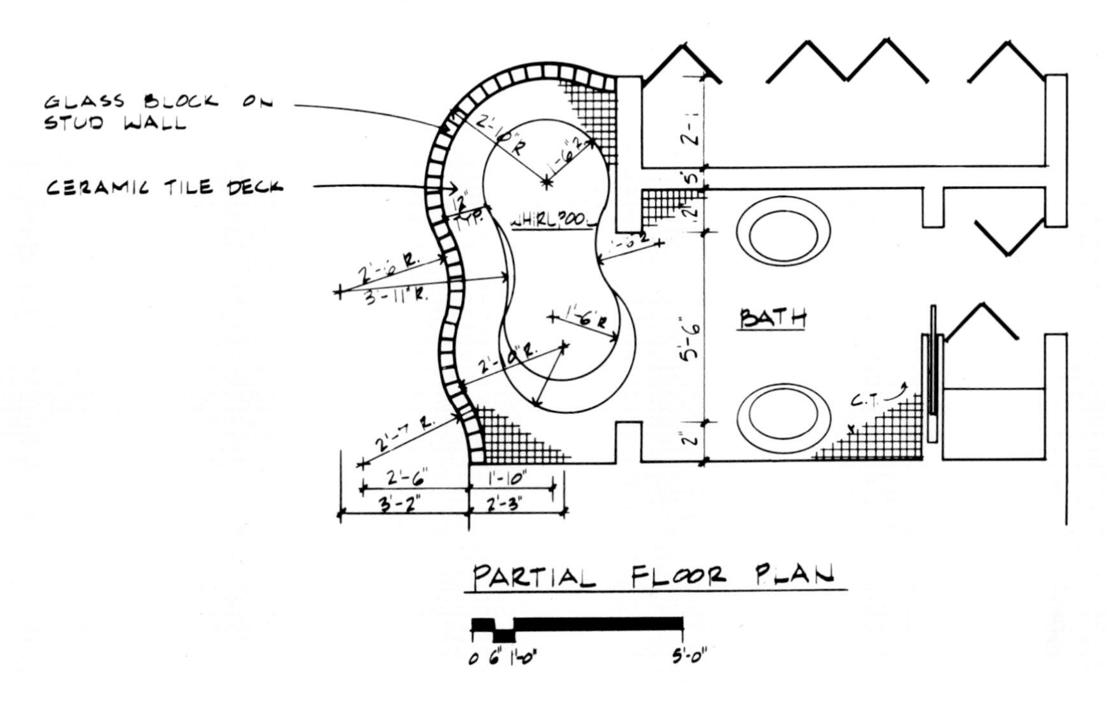
GLASS BLOCK ON STUD WALL
CERAMIC TILE DECK
WHIRLPOOL
BATH
C.T.
2'-6"
3'-2"
1'-10"
2'-3"
5'-6"
PARTIAL FLOOR PLAN
0 6" 1'-0" 5'-0"

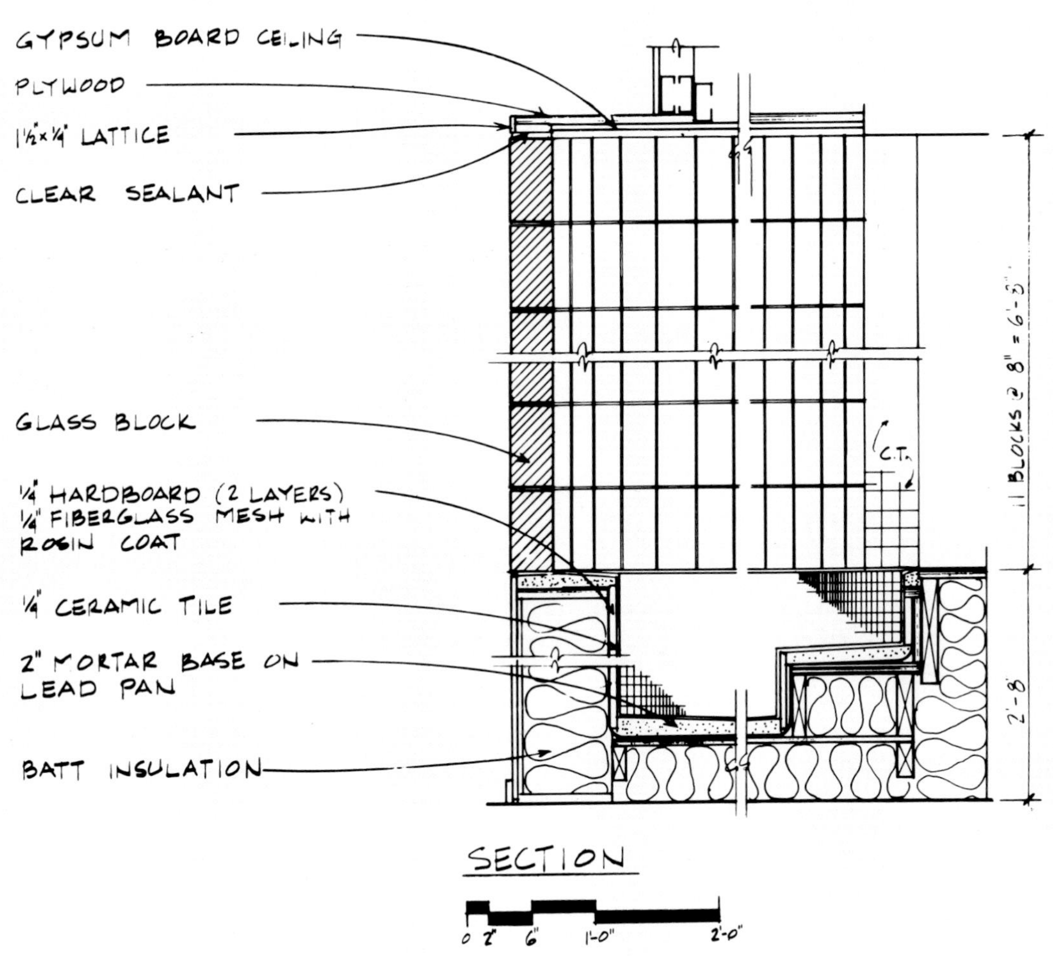
GYPSUM BOARD CEILING
PLYWOOD
1½"×¼" LATTICE
CLEAR SEALANT
GLASS BLOCK
¼" HARDBOARD (2 LAYERS)
¼" FIBERGLASS MESH WITH
ROSIN COAT
¼" CERAMIC TILE
2" MORTAR BASE ON
LEAD PAN
BATT INSULATION
C.T.
11 BLOCKS @ 8" = 6'-5"
2'-8"
SECTION
0 2" 6" 1'-0" 2'-0"

# Bookcases

## Chelsea Brownstone
*New York, New York*

**Architect**
Armstrong Cumming Architects

**Design Team**
Leslie Armstrong, AIA, Partner-in-Charge; Jeanette Young, Project Manager; Michelle Brewster, Interior Designer

**General Contractor**
Timothy Robertson, Octagon House Construction

**Fabricator**
Jim Luton and Julian Jackson, Octagon House Construction (cabinetwork)

**Photography**
© Norman McGrath

It is a courageous architect who agrees to tackle a renovation for clients who have undergone not one, but two previous renovation failures. But architects Armstrong Cumming were sanguine about their chances for the successful completion of a project where others had failed.

Originally from the South, the clients—a publisher and his wife, a literary agent—were determined to impose order on their cheerfully chaotic Chelsea brownstone "without imposing martial law." Their difficulty lay in opposing preferences for the allocation of the project budget: the husband wanted a capital improvement of the parlor floor; his wife wished to substantially refurnish the house. Both clients wanted more storage space for books so that other surfaces might be reclaimed from literary clutter.

After achieving a point of compromise on architectural improvements versus furnishings, the couple provided the architects with a budget of $100,000 for fees and finishes to rework the 600-square-foot space. Attention was primarily focused on the circulation hallway, already lined with bookcases that wrapped around a corner into the living room.

In order to emphasize a traditional differentiation between rooms, the wraparound bookcases were eliminated. The alcoves left by the previous shelving were furred out with gypsum board, slightly reducing them in width to receive shelves of either 12-inch or 24-inch depth. The 24-inch-deep shelves provide double-depth book storage capacity—or 60 percent more shelf space than is actually apparent—without impinging on floor space (*plan; section A*). A 12-inch-deep bookshelf unit was built into an alcove created by the living room corner. The hallway was thereby widened to 5′–0″, making it more a gallery than a traffic passage.

The cut-out shape of the cases carries its own aesthetic in keeping with the wife's desire for a traditional feeling. The architects designed a look for the cabinetry that is more evocative than authentic—one that includes, at the insistence of the architects, "clean white space" at the top in the form of solid, painted fascias. The solid panels emphasize that the books are set into the plane of the wall (*elevation*). By reintroducing carved stock trim and cornices from a casing catalog, Colonial allusion was achieved.

Adjustable brass shelf support sleeves provide subtle glitter, as the standard brass library rail does more forthrightly. Rollers on the rail foster easy movement of the ladder along the track, and from track to track (*section B*).

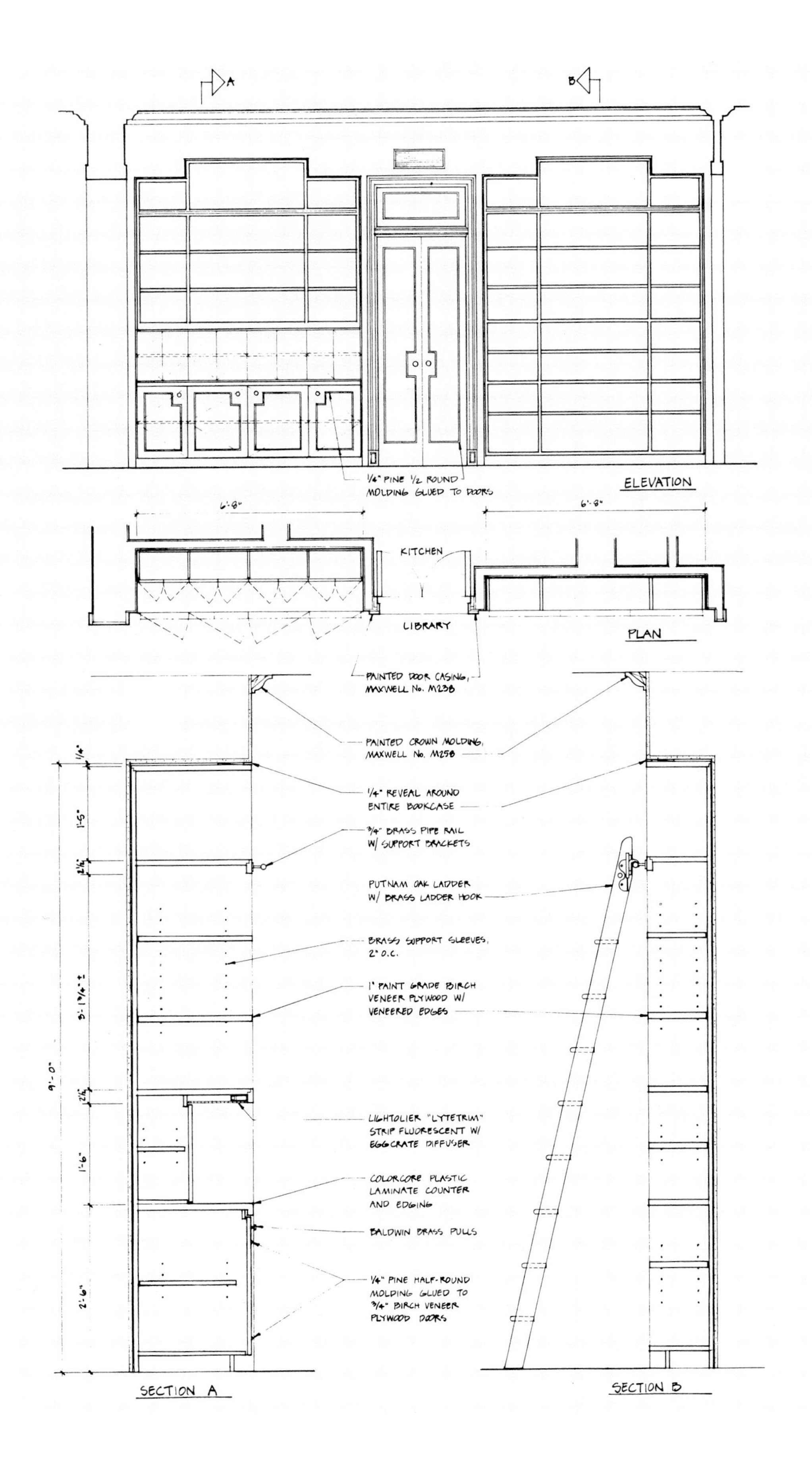
A
B
ELEVATION
1/4" PINE 1/2 ROUND MOLDING GLUED TO DOORS
6'-8"
6'-8"
KITCHEN
LIBRARY
PLAN
PAINTED DOOR CASING, MAXWELL No. M238
PAINTED CROWN MOLDING, MAXWELL No. M258
1/4" REVEAL AROUND ENTIRE BOOKCASE
3/4" BRASS PIPE RAIL W/ SUPPORT BRACKETS
PUTNAM OAK LADDER W/ BRASS LADDER HOOK
BRASS SUPPORT SLEEVES, 2" O.C.
1" PAINT GRADE BIRCH VENEER PLYWOOD W/ VENEERED EDGES
LIGHTOLIER "LYTETRIM" STRIP FLUORESCENT W/ EGGCRATE DIFFUSER
COLORCORE PLASTIC LAMINATE COUNTER AND EDGING
BALDWIN BRASS PULLS
1/4" PINE HALF-ROUND MOLDING GLUED TO 3/4" BIRCH VENEER PLYWOOD DOORS
1/4"
1'-5"
2 1/4"
3'-1 3/4" ±
9'-0"
2 1/4
1'-6"
2'-6"
SECTION A
SECTION B

# BOOKCASES

## SIMON–BELLAMY RESIDENCE
*Connecticut shoreline*

**Architect**
Centerbrook Architects

**Design Team**
Mark Simon, AIA, Partner-in-Charge;
Nick Deaver, AIA, Project Manager/Design

**Fabricator**
John Furness (cabinetry)

**Photography**
© Norman McGrath

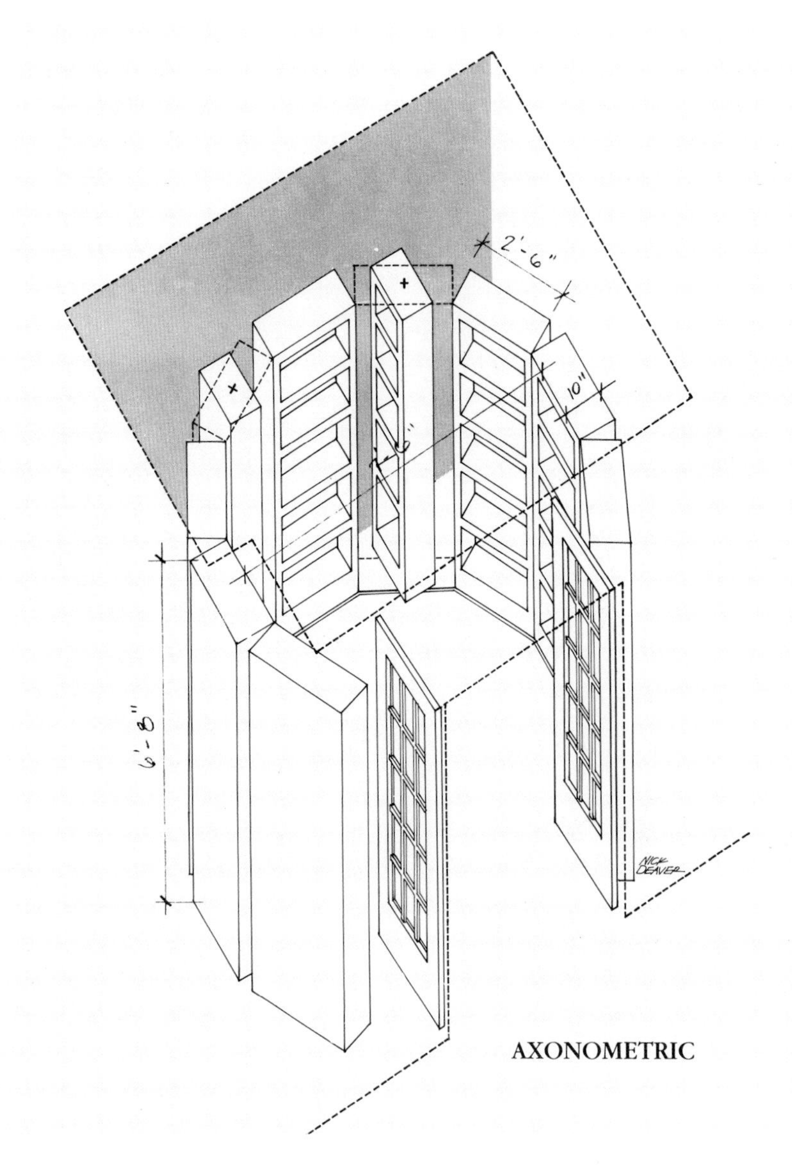

AXONOMETRIC

AT ONE TIME a man's home was deemed to be his castle; today, a man—or woman—is lucky to have even one room to call his or her own. Mark Simon, principal of Centerbrook Architects of Essex, Connecticut, is one of the more fortunate few. In search of privacy for himself, as well as for the other members of his family, Simon—who refers to his 2,000-square-foot house as "a small house with big dreams"—devised a number of first-floor rooms opening from a central corridor that are "alcovelike but not claustrophobic." Among them is an octagon-shaped library built out from rectilinear walls—a space just big enough to accommodate "tons" of books and one comfortable reading chair.

The visual impact of the library belies its conservative size. The octagonal configuration of the bookcases, as well as the faux ceiling dome that surmounts it, were designed to expand one's perception of the room's approximately 64 square feet. A similar manipulation of perception was obtained in financial terms: the apparently luxurious millwork and ceiling details were installed for a total cost, in 1983, of $2,000.

The bookcases were constructed of straightforward ¾-inch plywood, sanded and finished in two coats of warm "wood-tone" enamel. Structural stability of the bookcases was achieved by using three mutually supportive construction techniques: screwing and scribing flatbacked bookcases directly to the original walls; bracing pivoting, diagonal units (which provide access to corner storage) top and bottom with framing that is also affixed to flat units; and bolting all the units to the floor, "freezing" them in place with the weight of the joist-suspended and laterally braced dome (*axonometric*).

Thanks to the illusion created by a concealed cove light fixture, the dome appears to be a seamless structure floating above the bookcases. In fact, it is constructed of several pie-shaped wedges of ¼-inch drywall, the two layers of which have been screwed into sixteen jigsaw-cut and laterally wood-blocked plywood framing ribs. The segments of drywall were smoothed out with a skim coat of plaster, onto which two coats of sky blue paint were applied. Decorative dome detailing consists of glued-on bicycle reflectors that rise, in tiers of increasing density, from the base of the dome to surround an apex "ogee" fabricated of mundane and humorous materials—a joist-mounted retail-store security mirror, and glued-on highway reflectors.

AMERICA
REMBRANDT

## PRIVATE RESIDENCE
*New York, New York*

**Architect**
Steven Holl Architects

**Design Team**
Steven Holl, Principal-in-Charge;
Peter Lynch, Project Architect;
Ralph Nelson, Project Assistant;
Stephen Cossell, Project Assistant

**Fabricator**
Stefan Rohner (woodwork and cabinetry)

**Photography**
© Mark Darley/ESTO

THE MUSEUM TOWER CONDOMINIUM at the Museum of Modern Art is one of the more prestigious—and convenient—addresses a New Yorker can have; those lucky enough to possess apartments in the building tend to cherish them and, consequently, approach additions or renovations to the interior architecture with due respect. When a Japanese business student and his elder sister asked architect Steven Holl to develop a revised space plan and finish schedule for their 1,500-square-foot, forty-second-floor apartment, their only proviso, according to *Architectural Record*, was: "No chrome, no bright colors, and no shiny materials." (*see also* Door, page 80.)

During his first visit to the site, Holl devised a simple concept with which to guide the design of both the space and the furniture. The architect noticed that, because the tower's exterior walls rise directly up from the property line, standing in the apartment's corner window gives one the impression that the building is leaning out over the street. This impression intensified the vertical dimension of the apartment (as well as the vertical characteristic of the exterior cityscape), and added a third axis to the two horizontal axes controlling both the apartment's walls and the city's streets. The combination of these three dimensions suggested to Holl a composition based on X, Y, and Z axes.

Holl carried the X, Y, Z theme through the apartment in the imposition and coloration of the (occasionally freestanding) walls. Walls in the X axis are fabricated of charcoal-gray integral-color plaster; while those in the Y axis are finished in butterscotch-yellow plaster.

Holl noted the Z (vertical) axis episodically: a pole lamp near the corner window and vertical elements in the furniture. The steel vertical support of the dining room table creates a center for a set of X and Y axes that radiate out to an indefinite edge, while each of the three wool carpets elicits forms based on one of the three axes.

In Holl's plan, all of these objects relate to one another in a variety of ways: literal, poetic, systematic, and intuitive. They are not so much autonomous compositions as groupings that take on their meanings in relation to one another. It is Holl's belief that, by interconnecting and interacting with one another, the apartment's spatial relations become more fluid and entwined.

Corner formation was an important event in this scheme of axial dimensions. At one such juncture, Holl expanded upon the idea of corner-as-joint between two perpendicular planes—much as Scarpa does—by breaking down the single 90-degree angle into a number of such joints, and allowing the corner to repeat and become more complex.

Holl used one of the corners to impose a set of hinged, covered bookshelves, which transform the juncture into an "inverted" corner. Each of the cabinets opens and interlocks with the other (*sketch views in closed and open positions*), heightening the sense of interaction between X and Y axes. The corner is further dematerialized by the placement of an oil-finished wood door perpendicular to the cabinets.

Holl's Cartesian system allows the objects to pivot about vertical axes, emphasizing that rotation in the Z direction is the act that creates transition between the X and Y planes.

The cabinets are constructed of solid ash pieces painted yellow to a lacquer finish. The upper cabinet contains three 12-inch-high shelves set 5′–8½″ off the ground in a thick "wall" between dining room and master bedroom (*view from master bedroom hall*). The wall becomes thin again back in the corner where the bookshelves meet, allowing the cover of each shelf a "pocket" to pivot back into.

The cover of the upper cabinet, set on brass door hinges 12 inches in from the edge, contains a similar set of three shelves (*front view in open position*). On the bedroom side, the lower portion of the thick "wall" holds a stack of five 12-inch cabinets, each with double doors and 1-inch square ash pulls.

The lower set of cabinets is similarly constructed. The lower cover shelf, however, is not hinged to the lower cabinet; its hinges are instead attached from the back to the corner of the hollowed-out "pocket." Below the level of the lower cabinet, this pocket inverts and becomes a small projecting corner that supports the cabinets when open.

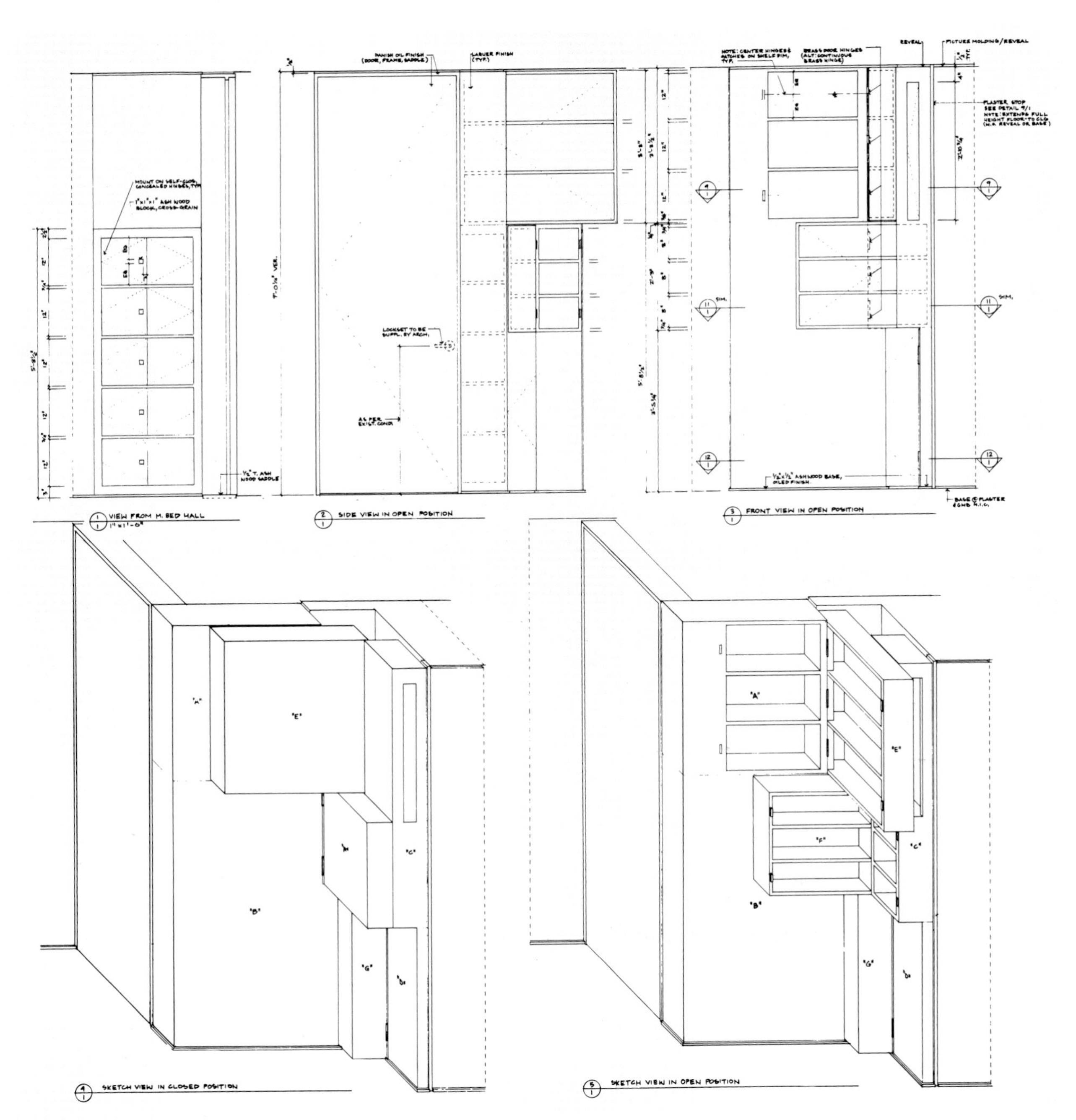

# Bookcases/Door Surrounds

**Harbor Country Residence**
*Sawyer, Michigan*

**Architect**
Tigerman/McCurry, Architects

**Design Team**
Margaret McCurry, AIA, Partner-in-Charge; John Holbert

**Fabricator**
Nelson Henderson

**Photography**
© Bruce Van Inwegen

In a compact country house of only 1,800 square feet, architect Margaret McCurry, of Tigerman/McCurry, nonetheless provided her clients with detailing that maximizes every square inch of available space.

Of particular note are the deeply recessed French door surrounds that punctuate the living room walls at symmetrically placed, and mirror-image, intervals. The door surrounds not only add picture framing perspective to the east/west outdoor views; they also, by their depth, suggest a "kinder, gentler" era of architecture—a client-directed conceptual prerequisite. Almost incidentally, the door surrounds serve a functional purpose, neatly storing an extensive collection of books.

The bookcase/door surround embrasures are constructed simply, and inexpensively, of ¾-inch finish plywood reinforced by wood blocking (*section*). Shelves are equidistantly fixed in place (*elevation*). The bookcase/door surrounds are painted (*plan*), as is all woodwork trim throughout the house. McCurry created the perception of craftsmanlike construction in the detailing by overscaling and matching the dimension of baseboards to the height, from floor to glass pane, of the door frame kick panel.

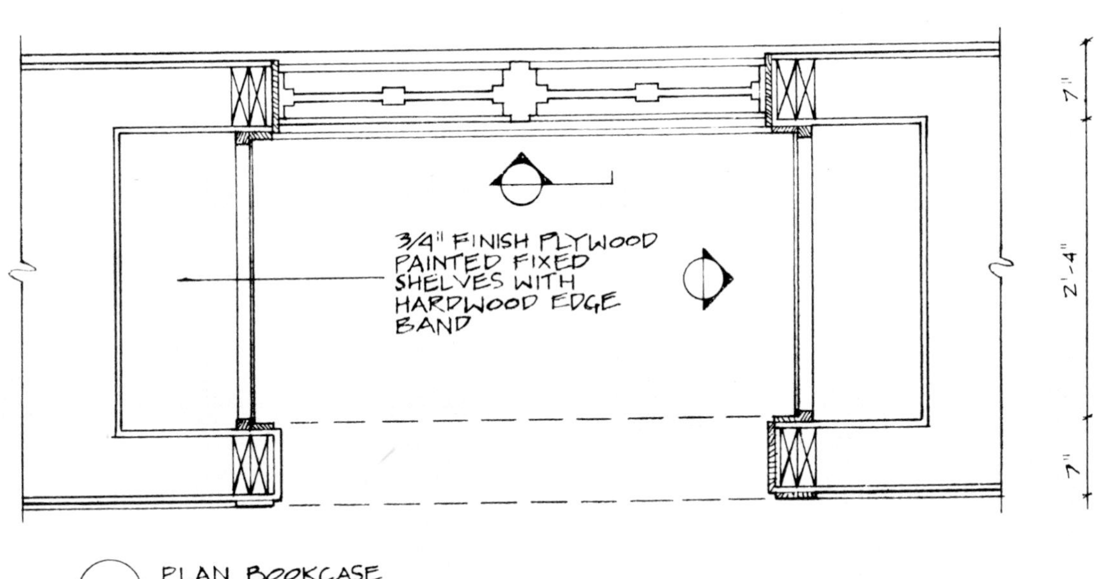


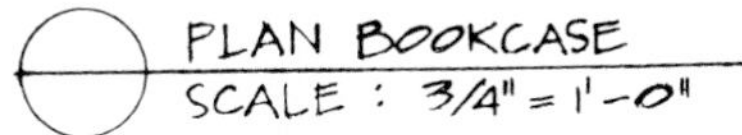


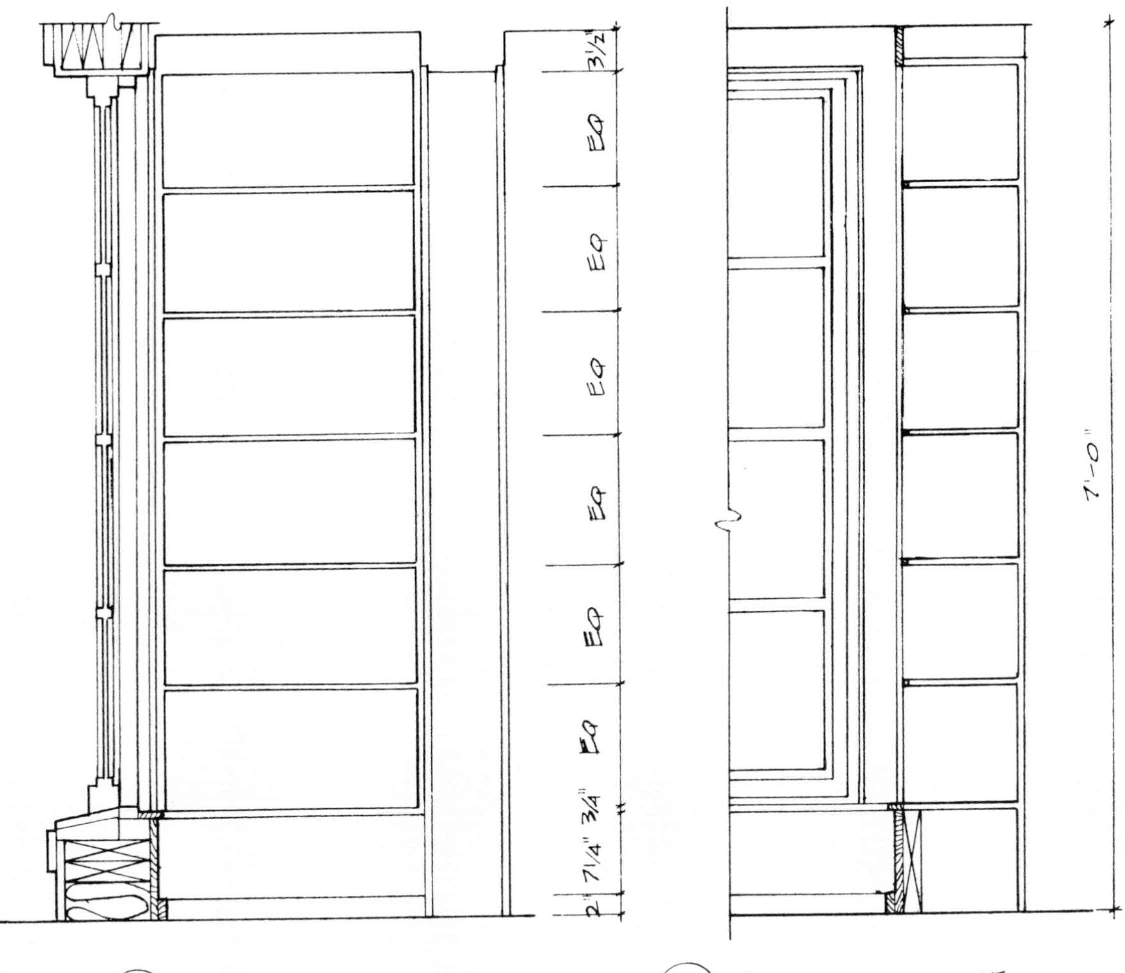


ELEVATION BOOKCASE
SCALE : 3/4" = 1'-0"

SECTION BOOKCASE
SCALE : 3/4" = 1'-0"

# Breakfast Nook

**Wharton Residence**
*Stamford, Connecticut*

**Architect**
Shope Reno Wharton Associates

**Fabricator**
Breakfast Millworks

**Photography**
© H. Durston Saylor

Like most New England houses dating from the 1790s, the former chicken farm residence in Stamford, Connecticut, that Bernard Wharton, of Shope Reno Wharton Associates, renovated for his own family was badly in need of repair and rejuvenation.

Within the low-ceilinged structure, according to the architect, "the kitchen was not only hideous to look at, but was also totally dysfunctional." Consequently, renovation of this essential space became the Whartons' highest priority (*see* Kitchen Cabinets, page 118).

Wharton and his wife, Caroline, wanted the kitchen to be "a gathering place" in which spending time with their two young sons, family, and friends could be as easily accomplished as the preparation of a serious, gourmet meal. The first decision the couple made, therefore, was to annex adjacent square footage from the original dining room to enlarge not only the kitchen's physical boundaries, but also its scope of possible activities.

Morning meals at the Whartons' now take place within the sheltering framework of a built-in breakfast nook that was intentionally designed to delight the couple's two children. Detailing forms that, to informed adults, allude to the Vienna Secessionist movement, suggest to children the towers of a magical city.

The breakfast nook consists of a table and two settle benches. Each bench back was constructed of a single ¾-inch plywood panel overlaid with a layer of gridded, hardwood fretwork. Curves and circular perforations were jigsaw cut; crown moldings and hardwood scraps were used to construct corner post caps; ½-inch round and scotia moldings were attached to baseboard panels. The table frame was similarly constructed of variously shaped and sized cut sections of solid hardwood, to which full round molding and perforated grillwork were nailed and glued. The clear maple tabletop was bolted to the base frame. With the exceptions of the tabletop, the arm rails, post colonnettes and grill perforations—which were finished in clear varnish—the entire breakfast nook was painted with industrial high-gloss enamel.

As a finishing touch, and thematically connective element between the eating and work areas of the kitchen, a wall-mounted cabinet, which contains an electrical panel, was detailed to match the table base, bench backs, and kitchen cabinets.

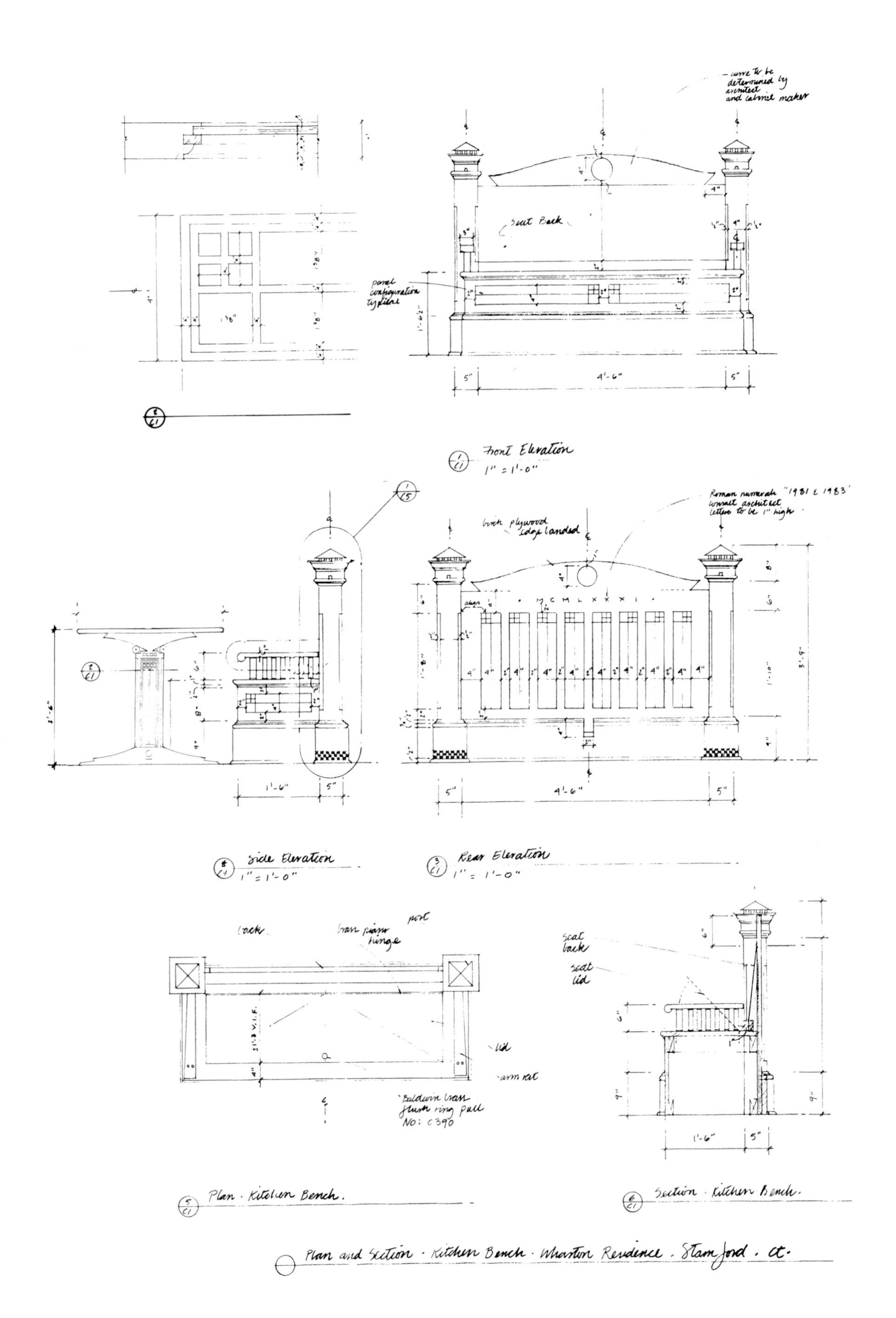
curve to be determined by architect and cabinet maker
Seat Back
panel configuration typical
Front Elevation
1" = 1'-0"
Roman numerals "1981 & 1983" cornice architect letters to be 1" high
birch plywood edge banded
M C M L X X X I
Side Elevation
1" = 1'-0"
Rear Elevation
1" = 1'-0"
back
brass piano hinge
post
lid
arm rest
Baldwin brass flush ring pull
NO: C390
seat back
seat lid
Plan · Kitchen Bench.
Section · Kitchen Bench.
Plan and Section · Kitchen Bench · Wharton Residence · Stamford · Ct.

# Breakfast Nook/Banquette

**Private Residence**
*Chicago, Illinois*

**Architect**
Quinn and Searl, Architects:
Linda Searl, Partner

**General Contractor/Fabricator**
Kissner Company

**Photography**
© George Lambros

Members of career couples—particularly those whose work involves different areas of concentration—often feel as if they are ships that pass in the night. With luck, or careful coordination, they may also meet in the morning, a factor that can make the kitchen a very important place.

In 1987, a Chicago couple—he, an investment banker and she, a counselor—asked Quinn and Searl to convert the two side-by-side, mirror-image townhouses they had purchased into a single-family home. The clients wanted an "open but private feeling" throughout the 3,500-square-foot space, with special emphasis on the kitchen as "common ground in which two people can work or relax together."

Because the twin townhouses were constructed in the 1970s with the ubiquitous low ceilings of that era, project architect Linda Searl encouraged the clients "not to try to decorate the undecoratable." Instead, she recommended using "form and color to relieve the rigidity of base building construction." With the clients' blessing, Searl developed a spare overall plan in which existing first-floor walls were demolished while both staircases were intentionally retained. One staircase now serves living space within the house; the other provides access to a professional office.

Spare space, form, and color were reiterated as thematic keynotes in new construction. An essentially open first-floor plan was enhanced by a curved partition wall (*see* Column, page 64) that divides the living and dining areas from the kitchen as it simultaneously forms the backbone of a breakfast nook/banquette.

The banquette's curve, a small radiused curve within the larger, 17′–0″ curve of the partition wall, was conceived as a sculptural object that would provide a sense of enclosure, as well as a sense of continuity in materials with adjacent kitchen cabinetry.

The large, outer wall was constructed of drywall screwed and glued onto studs placed 16 inches on center. The inside wall was fabricated by screwing two layers of ¼-inch drywall to stud framing placed 12 inches on center (*plan*). Both walls were taped, sanded, primed, and painted.

The banquette was fabricated by a millworker who utilized shipbuilding techniques in its construction. Three-quarter-inch plywood ribbing placed 12 inches on center created the banquette's curved frame; layers of ⅛-inch bending birch were used to form its "skin" (*section*). Formica's Cloud laminate was used as a finish on all surfaces (*elevation*) except the curved underbench skirt, which was painted to match. An adjacent desk and banquette end tables were built of the same materials.

The breakfast nook was constructed for $4,500—a modest portion of the modest total project budget.

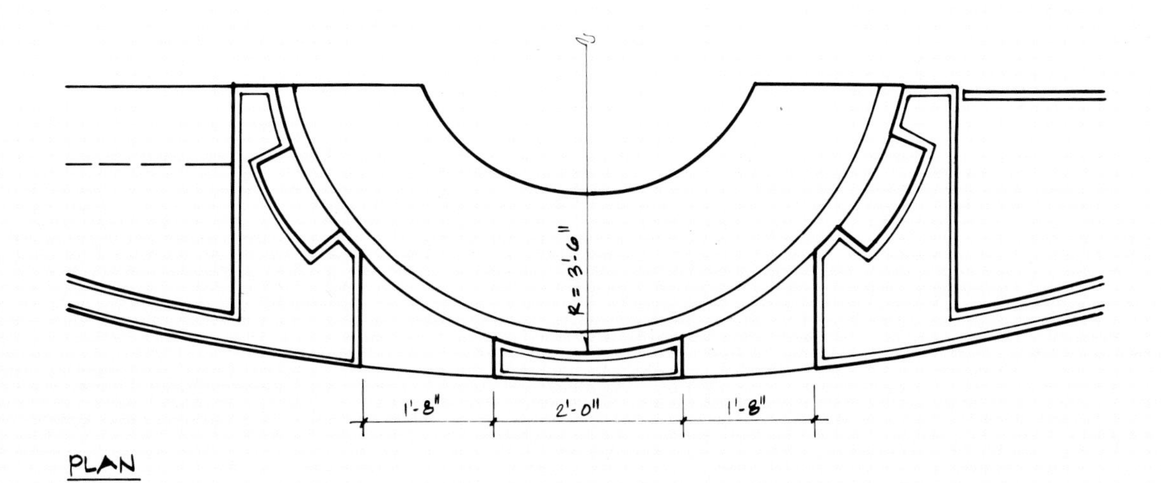
R = 3'-6"
1'-8"
2'-0"
1'-8"
PLAN

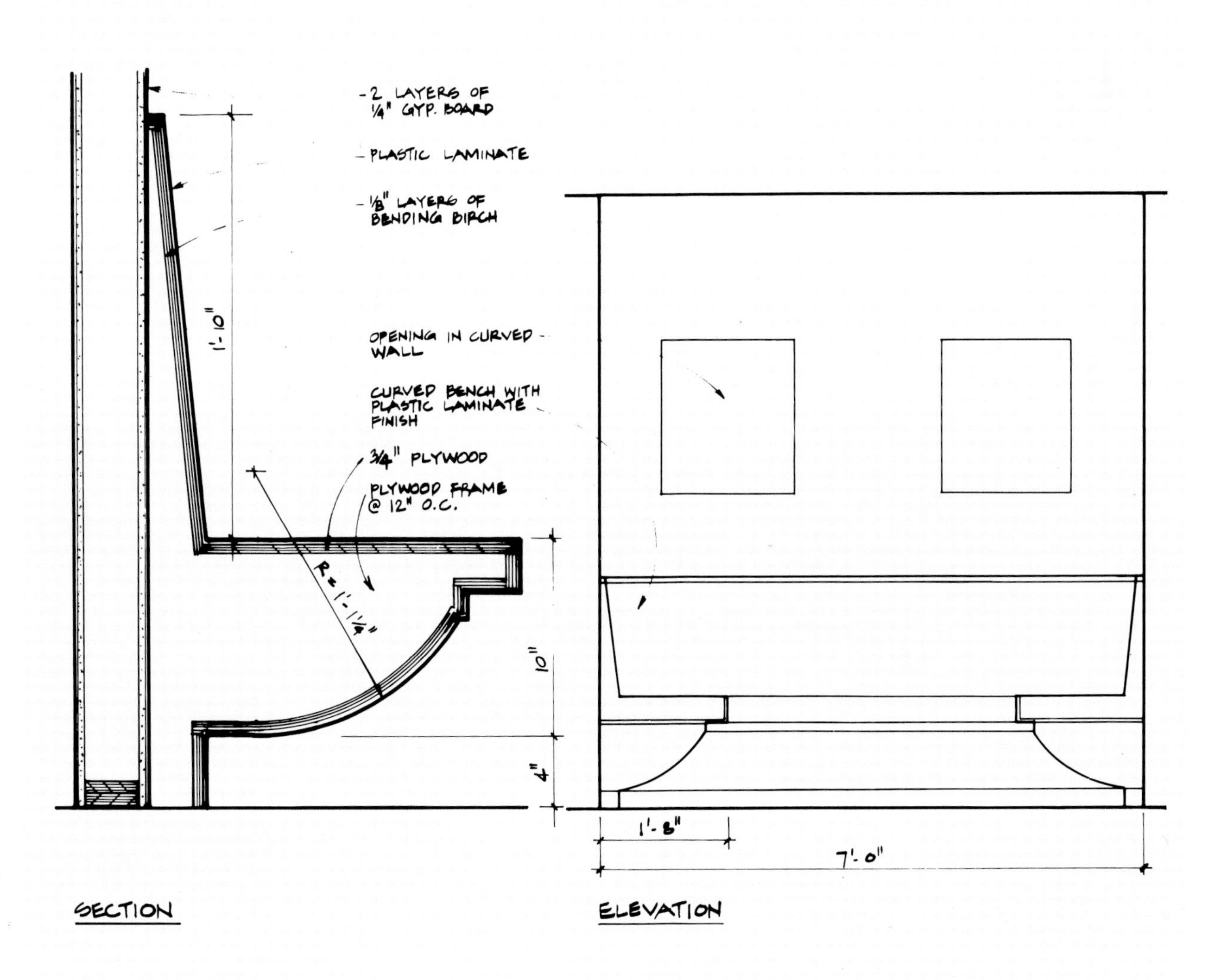
-2 LAYERS OF 1/4" GYP. BOARD
-PLASTIC LAMINATE
-1/8" LAYERS OF BENDING BIRCH
1'-10"
OPENING IN CURVED WALL
CURVED BENCH WITH PLASTIC LAMINATE FINISH
3/4" PLYWOOD
PLYWOOD FRAME @ 12" O.C.
R = 1'-1 1/4"
10"
4"
1'-8"
7'-0"
SECTION
ELEVATION

## PRIVATE RESIDENCE
*Washington, D.C.*

**Architect**
Hartman-Cox Architects

**Design Team**
George Hartman, Partner-in-Charge; William Grater; John F. Dale

**Lighting Consultant**
Claude Engle

**General Contractor/Fabricator**
E. A. Baker Company, Inc.

**Photography**
© Robert C. Lautman

A FULL-SCALE, bona fide ballroom was regarded as an essential space in the grand Washington, D.C., mansions constructed during the 1920s. But the couple who purchased and renovated this 22,000-square-foot house (*see* Staircase, page 196) in the 1980s had a different use in mind for the 1,204-square-foot room. They were interested in transforming the 28′–0″ × 43′–0″ space into both a reception and living area, as well as a private art gallery.

A ceiling/lighting plan that would adequately serve general ambient purposes as well as maximize the display impact of their art collection called for complex, flexible ceiling detailing. The plan was to incorporate natural, diffuse, and focused direct and indirect sources of illumination; a stereo/public address system; and a return air-circulation system.

A framed laylight ceiling detail is all that is visible of a multilayered, multifaceted design solution. The 10′–4″ × 26′–0″ laylight diffuses shafts of natural daylight that penetrate the room from a newly installed 8′–4″ × 24′–5″ hipped skylight, constructed of extruded aluminum reflective glass. The skylight rests on 2 × 6 wood posts that are bolted to new steel beams and saddles; they are mounted, in turn, on existing steel beams (*transverse section, ballroom*).

To make the skylight proportionally consistent with the exterior, hipped roof, and to make the laylight proportionally consistent with the room, Hartman-Cox deliberately designed the skylight to be about 26 percent smaller than the laylight. To mask this size difference and to avoid shadows from the wire hanging supports, the designers also included an unusual extra layer of diffused glass under the skylight (*transverse section, ballroom*).

The laylight itself is also a construction based on layering. Fluorescent light fixtures on the steel beams of the frame permit artificial lighting through the laylight. Successive layers of reflective and diffused laminated glass reduce total light transmittance to about 7 percent, sharply reducing harmful ultraviolet rays.

The lighting scheme is enhanced with forty light fixtures that have been recessed into the plaster beam soffit that surrounds the laylight. Each lamp can operate on high or low voltage and can be focused either on artwork or on the walls. Stereo/public address speakers are interspersed with the lights in the soffit (*reflected plan, laylight*). A ⅝-inch gap between muntin and crown molding allows return air to be drawn into the plenum above the joists (*muntin details*).

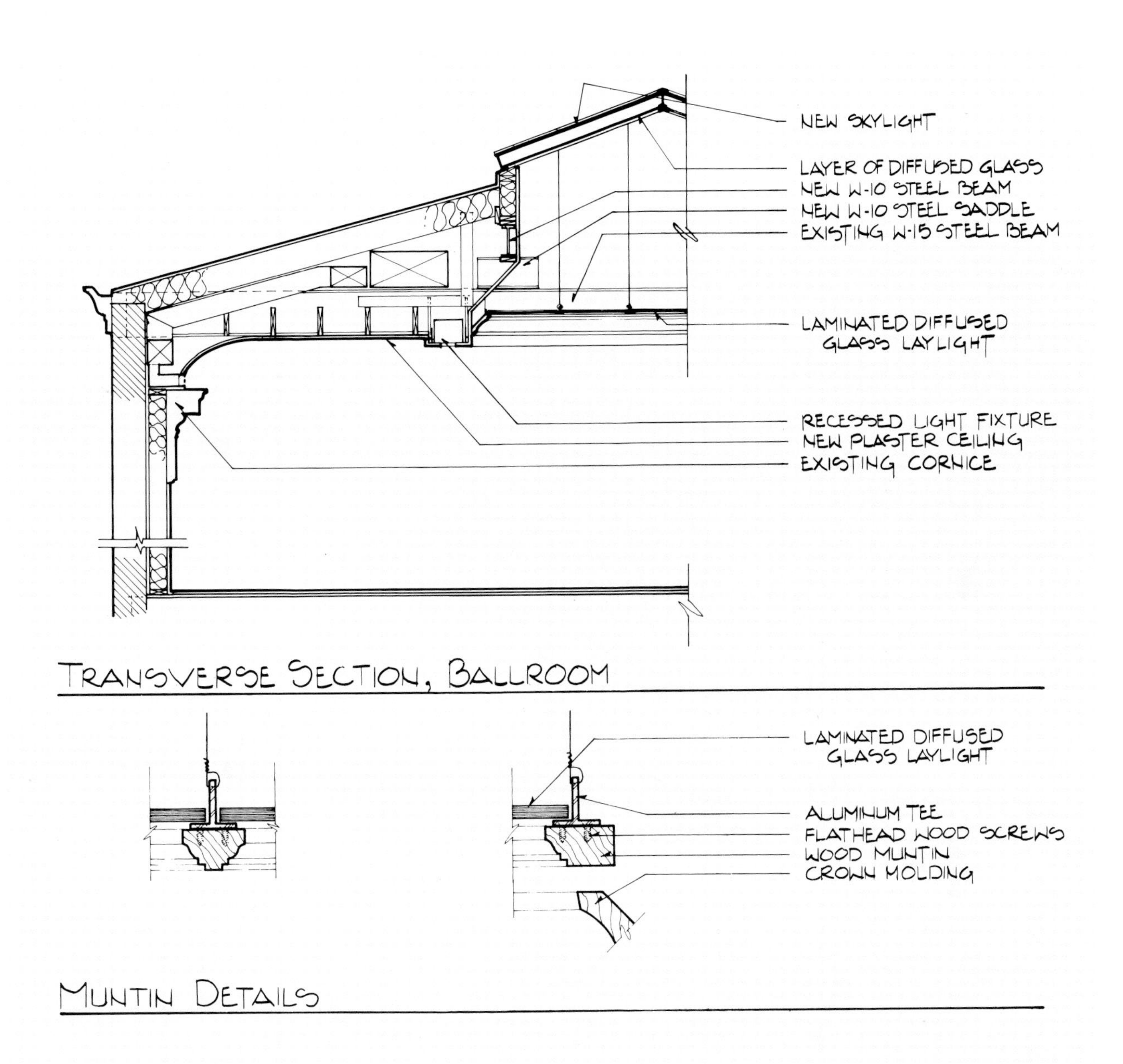
NEW SKYLIGHT
LAYER OF DIFFUSED GLASS
NEW W-10 STEEL BEAM
NEW W-10 STEEL SADDLE
EXISTING W-15 STEEL BEAM
LAMINATED DIFFUSED GLASS LAYLIGHT
RECESSED LIGHT FIXTURE
NEW PLASTER CEILING
EXISTING CORNICE
TRANSVERSE SECTION, BALLROOM
LAMINATED DIFFUSED GLASS LAYLIGHT
ALUMINUM TEE
FLATHEAD WOOD SCREWS
WOOD MUNTIN
CROWN MOLDING
MUNTIN DETAILS

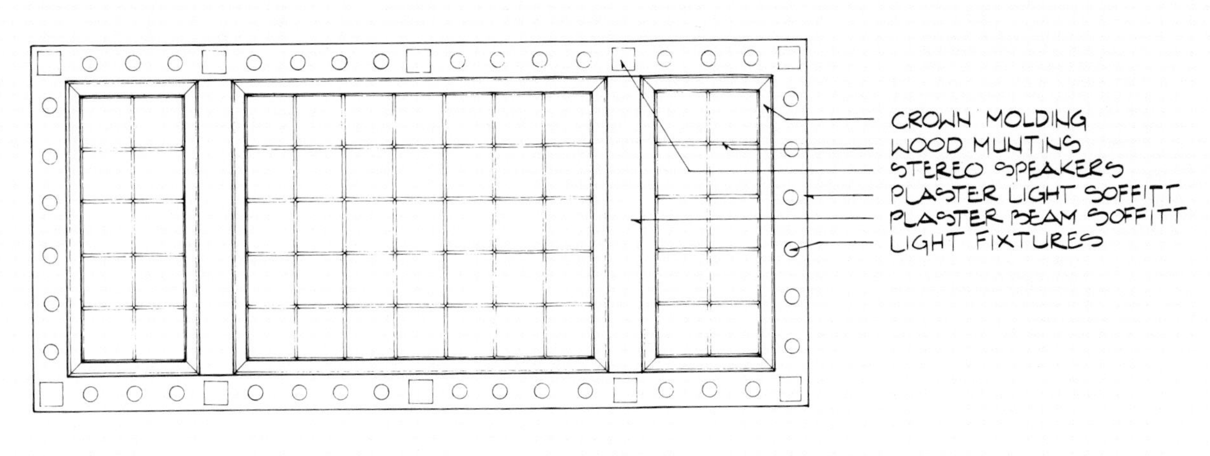
CROWN MOLDING
WOOD MUNTINS
STEREO SPEAKERS
PLASTER LIGHT SOFFITT
PLASTER BEAM SOFFITT
LIGHT FIXTURES

REFLECTED PLAN, LAYLIGHT

## PRIVATE RESIDENCE
*Kansas City, Missouri*

**Architect**
Roger Kraft: Architecture • Design

**Design Team**
Roger Kraft, Project Designer;
Mark Peters, Project Architect

**Fabricator**
Bob Falkenberg Company

**Photography**
© Mark Darley/ESTO

OPENING UP their residence to natural light was important to the owners of this 6,000-square-foot duplex apartment located on the tenth and penthouse floors of an Art Deco building in Kansas City (*see* Door, page 78; Radiator Cover/Closet Cabinetry, page 162).

Architect Roger Kraft imposed a number of specific finish materials throughout the space—reflective surfaces, white walls, and sandblasted glass doors, among them—to maximize the infusion, as well as the transfusion, of both natural and artificial light sources. But the most illuminating detail designed for the apartment is a skylight and diffusing grid that Kraft describes as "an exercise of intersected geometry."

The skylight was cut into the penthouse roof above the entry hall staircase as a secondary circle intersecting the primary circle of the entryway plan; like the stair, the skylight and diffuser are initially circular in form. However, directly above the point at which the stair straightens out, a concomitant, sloping rectangular panel intersects the circular diffuser. This cutaway panel allows the necessary increase in ceiling height for the stairway and completes the vertical sequence from circular entryway into the rectilinear interior of the second floor. The compounded-curve, cylindrical railing follows the semi helical twist curve of the stair.

Kraft designed the entire skylight assembly by referring to a traditional, two-part, nineteenth-century model: an "industrial" exterior light, for protection from the elements, that is masked on the interior by a separate and more refined glass element. In Kraft's version, an acrylic plastic dome serves as the outer light, which was affixed to a 9-inch insulated curb; the curb rests on a circular hole cut into the existing roof. Four incandescent fixtures resting on electric conduit frames provide nighttime illumination. The frames were set on concrete block bases and attached to existing exterior walls for stability.

Wooden blocking was attached to the interior, underside of the existing roof, to which a new gypsum board ceiling with a flanged 5′–8″-diameter opening was attached. The steel diffuser grid itself is independent of this assembly: it was hung from the new gypsum board and 2 × 4 stud walls, which extend up toward the ceiling hole.

The grid structure is primarily supported by its center axes: the ends of the two steel tees that cross at the circle's center hang by metal rods from four steel brackets. The brackets are nailed to the gypsum board wall well above the level of the diffuser grid. Like the stair, the grid appears to float from the wall (*section-elevation*).

The grid itself is made of steel T-sections, the outer rim by a curved steel angle. Connections were made by welding small steel angles to primary members and then bolting the angles to secondary members. The rectangular ceiling panel is attached to wood blocking above; a 1-inch closure reveal marks the joint where panel and grid meet (*plan*).

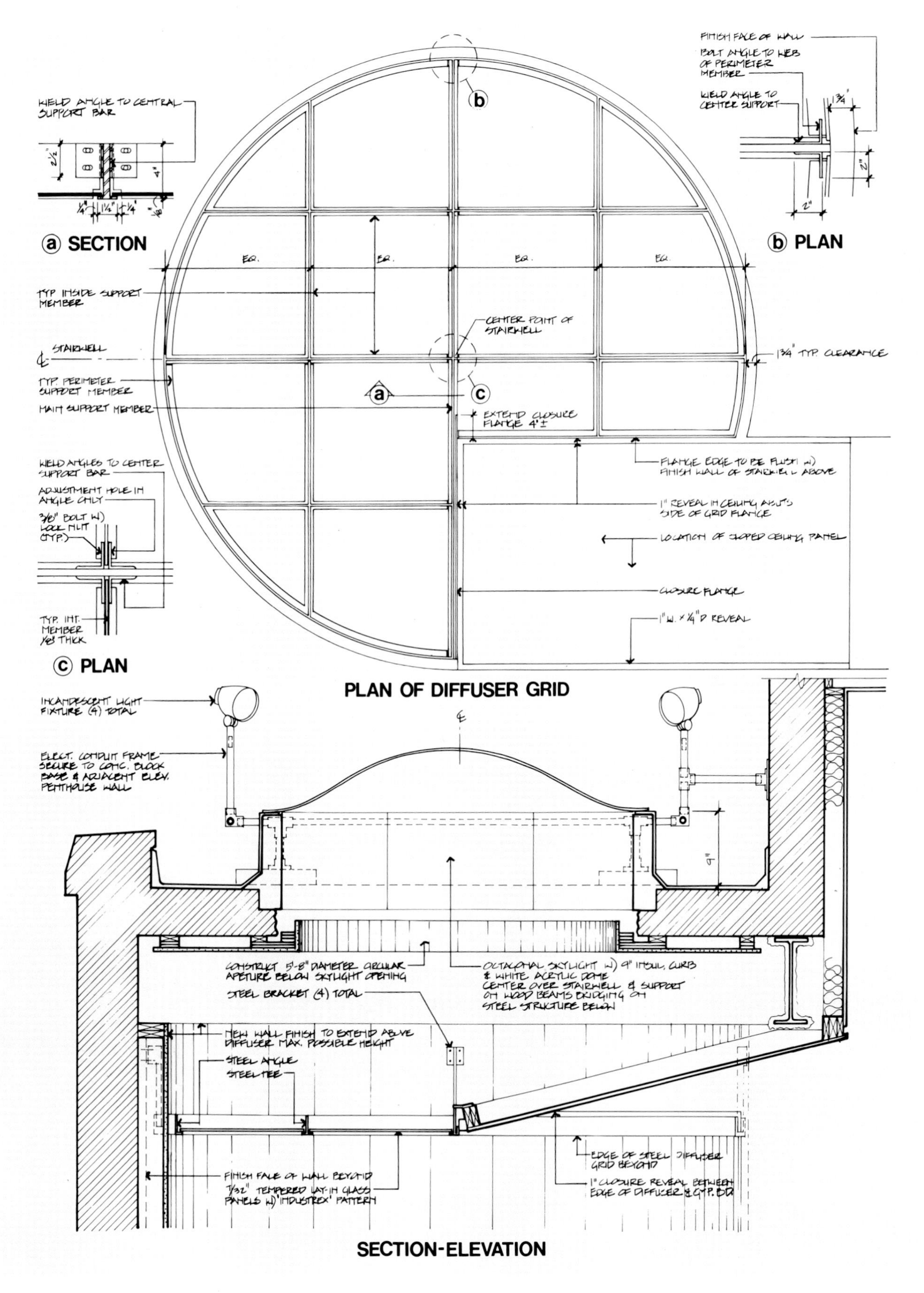

WELD ANGLE TO CENTRAL SUPPORT BAR
ⓐ SECTION
FINISH FACE OF WALL
BOLT ANGLE TO WEB OF PERIMETER MEMBER
WELD ANGLE TO CENTER SUPPORT
ⓑ PLAN
EQ.
EQ.
EQ.
EQ.
TYP INSIDE SUPPORT MEMBER
CENTER POINT OF STAIRWELL
STAIRWELL
1 3/4" TYP. CLEARANCE
TYP. PERIMETER SUPPORT MEMBER
MAIN SUPPORT MEMBER
EXTEND CLOSURE FLANGE 4'±
WELD ANGLES TO CENTER SUPPORT BAR
FLANGE EDGE TO BE FLUSH W) FINISH WALL OF STAIRWELL ABOVE
ADJUSTMENT HOLE IN ANGLE ONLY
1" REVEAL IN CEILING ABUTS SIDE OF GRID FLANGE
3/8" BOLT W) LOCK NUT (TYP.)
LOCATION OF SLOPED CEILING PANEL
CLOSURE FLANGE
TYP. INT. MEMBER 3/8 THICK
1"W. × 1/4"D REVEAL
ⓒ PLAN
PLAN OF DIFFUSER GRID
INCANDESCENT LIGHT FIXTURE (4) TOTAL
ELECT. CONDUIT FRAME SECURE TO CONC. BLOCK BASE & ADJACENT ELEV. PENTHOUSE WALL
CONSTRUCT 5'-8" DIAMETER CIRCULAR APETURE BELOW SKYLIGHT OPENING
STEEL BRACKET (4) TOTAL
OCTAGONAL SKYLIGHT W) 9" INSUL. CURB & WHITE ACRYLIC DOME CENTER OVER STAIRWELL & SUPPORT ON WOOD BEAMS BRIDGING ON STEEL STRUCTURE BELOW
NEW WALL FINISH TO EXTEND ABOVE DIFFUSER MAX. POSSIBLE HEIGHT
STEEL ANGLE
STEEL TEE
EDGE OF STEEL DIFFUSER GRID BEYOND
FINISH FACE OF WALL BEYOND
7/32" TEMPERED LAY-IN GLASS PANELS W) 'INDUSTREX' PATTERN
1" CLOSURE REVEAL BETWEEN EDGE OF DIFFUSER & GYP. BD.
SECTION-ELEVATION

## POOL HOUSE

*Beverly Hills, California*

**Architect**
Moore Ruble Yudell

**Design Team**
John Ruble, Principal;
Buzz Yudell, Principal-in-Charge;
Renzo Zecchetto, Project Architect;
Paul Nagashima, Staff Member;
Akai Yang, Staff Member

**Photography**
© Alex Vertikoff

IT SHOULD COME as no surprise that many actors enjoy performing in home movies and plays—those produced in the backyard with a supporting cast of family and friends—almost as much as they enjoy their professional work in films and television, and on Broadway. A well-known California actor became so enamored of this domestic medium that he asked architects Moore Ruble Yudell to incorporate an outdoor amphitheater and a recreation room into the new pool house construction planned for his family's Beverly Hills home.

The family asked that the pool house be sited on the property as unobtrusively as possible. The architects responded by setting the main space of the addition one-half level below the pool deck, and the rooftop terrace one-half level above—just high enough to create a separate "outdoor room" but with a close connection to the pool. The roof of the pool house was terraced and stepped to create amphitheater seating; the lower interior level houses the recreation room and changing rooms that open on the pool deck.

In designing the ceiling of the approximately 550-square-foot media room, the design team made an intentional asset of the stepped form created by the underside of the roof's amphitheater seating. The tiered ceiling was then punctuated, whimsically, with a star-shape detail, suggestive of the client's professional status within the industry.

The graphic impact of the star motif is accentuated by the architects' ratio of one down step into three in the ceiling (*section*). Each step was constructed simply; in keeping with the limited project budget, standard drywall was screwed into joists and nailers, and finished with a painted skim coat of plaster. To assure a smooth surface on the apron of the star-embracing circle (*reflected ceiling plan*), its curve was rendered in real plaster.

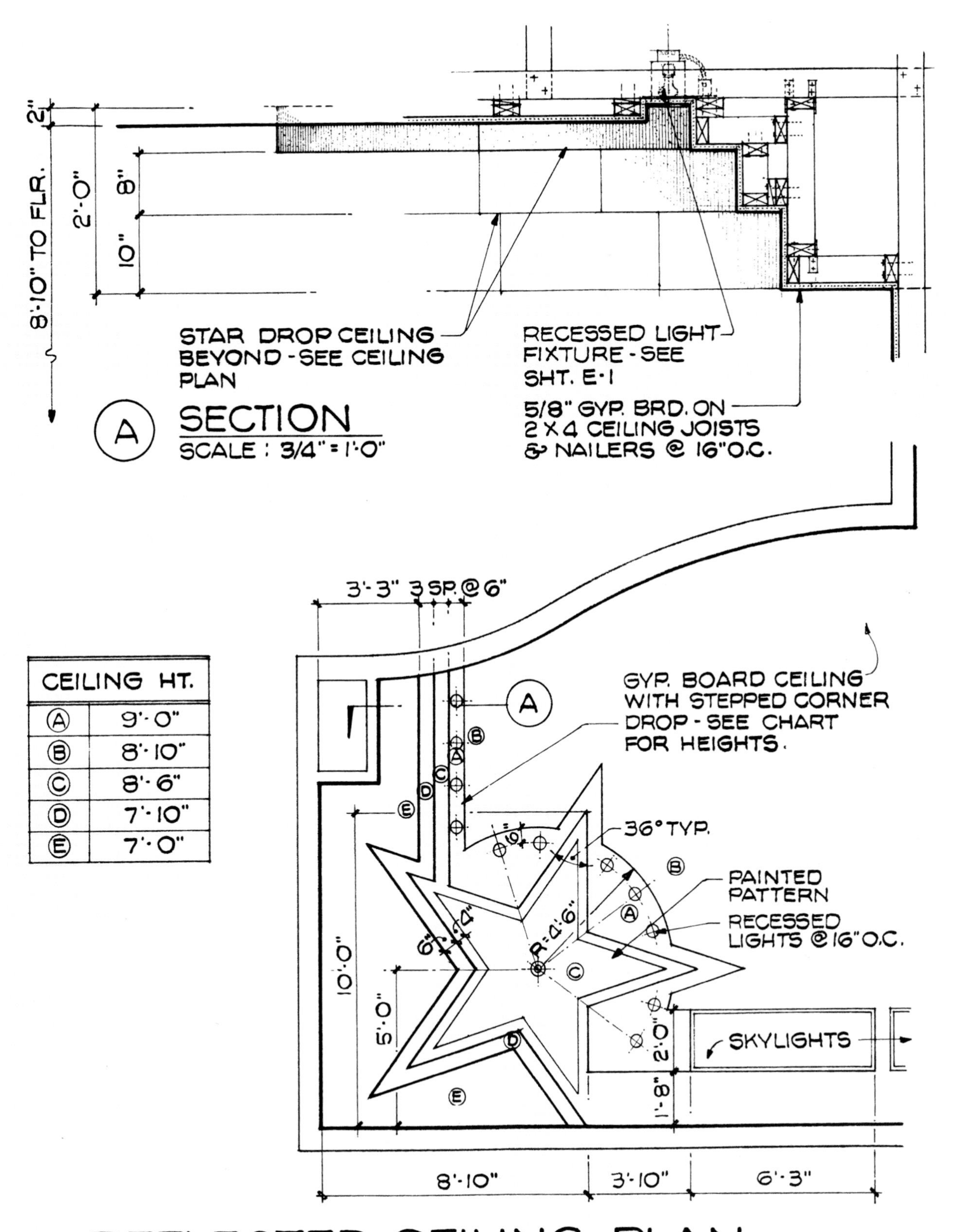


| CEILING HT. | |
|---|---|
| (A) | 9'-0" |
| (B) | 8'-10" |
| (C) | 8'-6" |
| (D) | 7'-10" |
| (E) | 7'-0" |

# REFLECTED CEILING PLAN

SCALE: 1/4" = 1'-0"

## LEA RESIDENCE
*Berwyn, Pennsylvania*

**Architect**
Architects Snyder • Snyder

**Design Team**
Susan Nigra Snyder, AIA;
James P. Snyder, AIA;
Nora Wren Kerr; Ann C. Geddes

**General Contractor**
C. I. Duncan Company, Inc.

**Photography**
© H. Durston Saylor

ARCHITECTS SNYDER • SNYDER is that rarity within the design profession—a young, energetic, talented partnership that has been known, resolutely, to turn away work. Time is, admittedly, a factor in the Snyders' decision-making process: Susan is a studio critic at the University of Pennsylvania's Graduate School of Architecture; Jim is a principal and designer for Geddes Brecher Qualls Cunningham. But time constraints are normal in the practice of architecture; what is unusual are the Snyders' self-imposed and exacting standards of ethics and excellence. In assessing potential clients and projects, both will assert: "Regardless of budget, if the job can't be done well, we won't do it at all."

Snyder • Snyder clients Susan and W. Bruce Lea III, as well as their two teenage daughters, have clearly profited from the architects' convictions. In 1987, the Leas decided to build an addition to their suburban Main Line home. In conferences with the Snyders it was decided that the addition would be intentionally "separated from the rest of the house as a retreat" and would, therefore, contain a transitional foyer/vestibule as well as a required music/family room. The Leas and the Snyders also agreed that the addition "should take full advantage of the wooded view."

Although program goals were relatively simple, corresponding design development and construction became matters of commensurate complexity. The design problem, according to Susan Nigra Snyder, was twofold: "Our objective was to bring both generous amounts of natural daylight and an enhanced perception of spaciousness to a new addition that would be substantially shadowed and spatially circumscribed by surrounding trees. We were also determined to minimize the number, while maximizing the quality, of details; because we were working on a fixed budget, with fixed labor costs, that meant utilizing a complete range of wood technology and stock trim components."

With admirable finesse, Snyder • Snyder developed a "home plate" footprint and concentric elevations that rise to meet in a complex, folded plane, fan ceiling and pentagonal roof—a free-span construction supported by high-stress, laminated beams (*plans at peak, dormer intersection, and window wall*). The angles of the folded plane ceiling break up light and sound waves within the 300-square-foot space, and thereby promote a sense of intimacy; in addition, kinetic, dancing light generated by the movement of trees outside pours through dormer set windows.

Due to the costliness of even stock windows, the architects specified windows that compensate, in quality and interest, for their limited number. Two side walls that are not fenestrated provide lateral privacy from neighbors; maximum-sized, double-hung windows framed in carefully proportioned, oversized trim provide unexpected drama, "projecting" the room into the wooded view beyond. The windows' multiple muntins add tangible, subtle grace to the hard-edged composition.

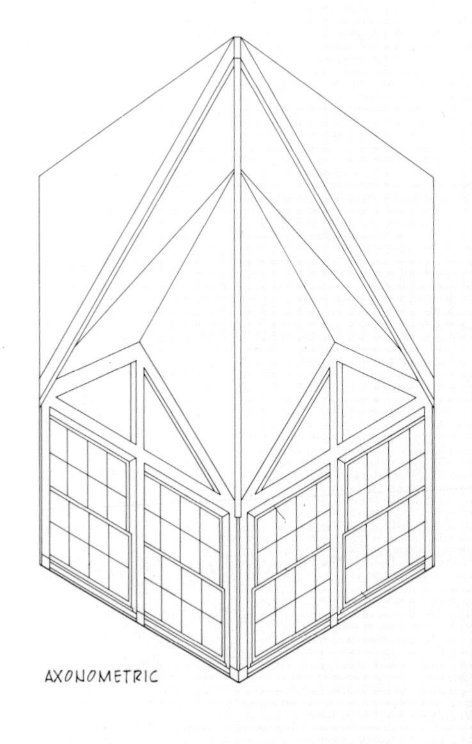

AXONOMETRIC

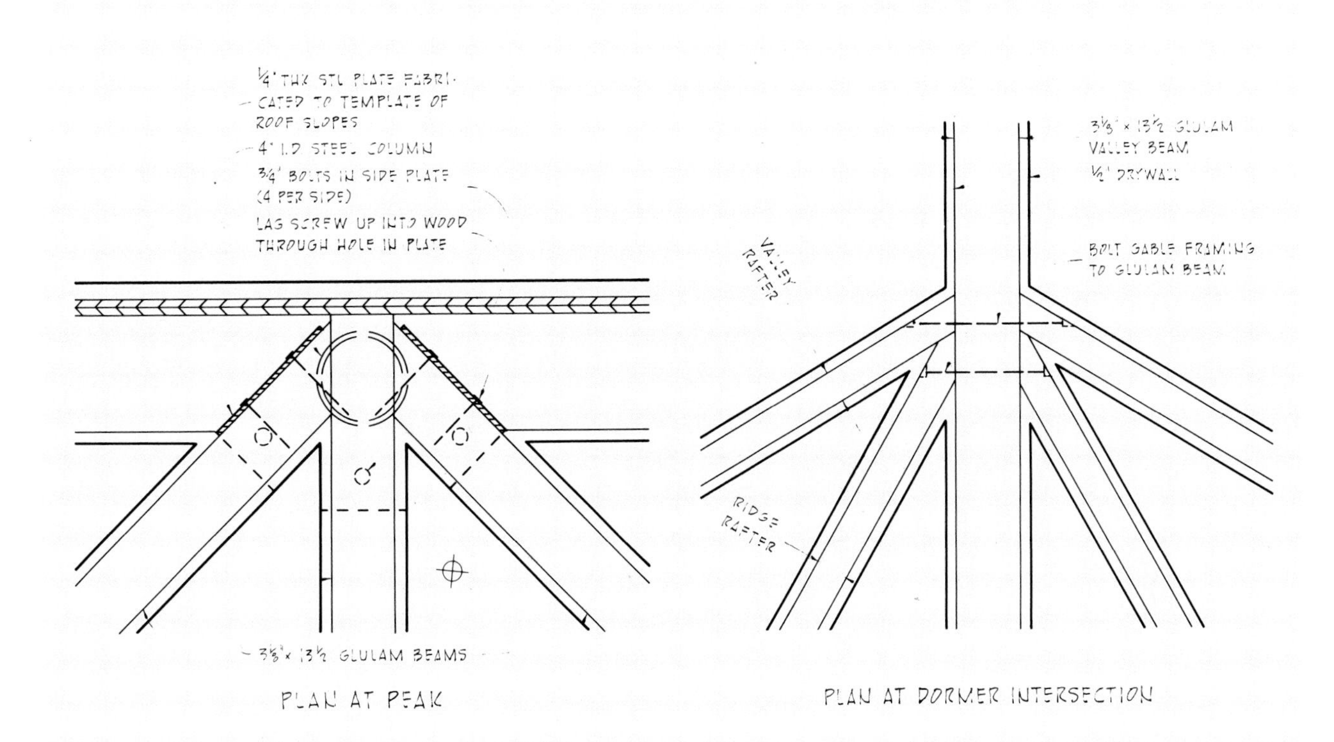
1/4" THK STL PLATE FABRI-
CATED TO TEMPLATE OF
ROOF SLOPES
4" I.D. STEEL COLUMN
3/4" BOLTS IN SIDE PLATE
(4 PER SIDE)
LAG SCREW UP INTO WOOD
THROUGH HOLE IN PLATE
3 1/8" x 13 1/2 GLULAM BEAMS
PLAN AT PEAK
3 1/8" x 13 1/2 GLULAM
VALLEY BEAM
1/2" DRYWALL
BOLT GABLE FRAMING
TO GLULAM BEAM
VALLEY RAFTER
RIDGE RAFTER
PLAN AT DORMER INTERSECTION

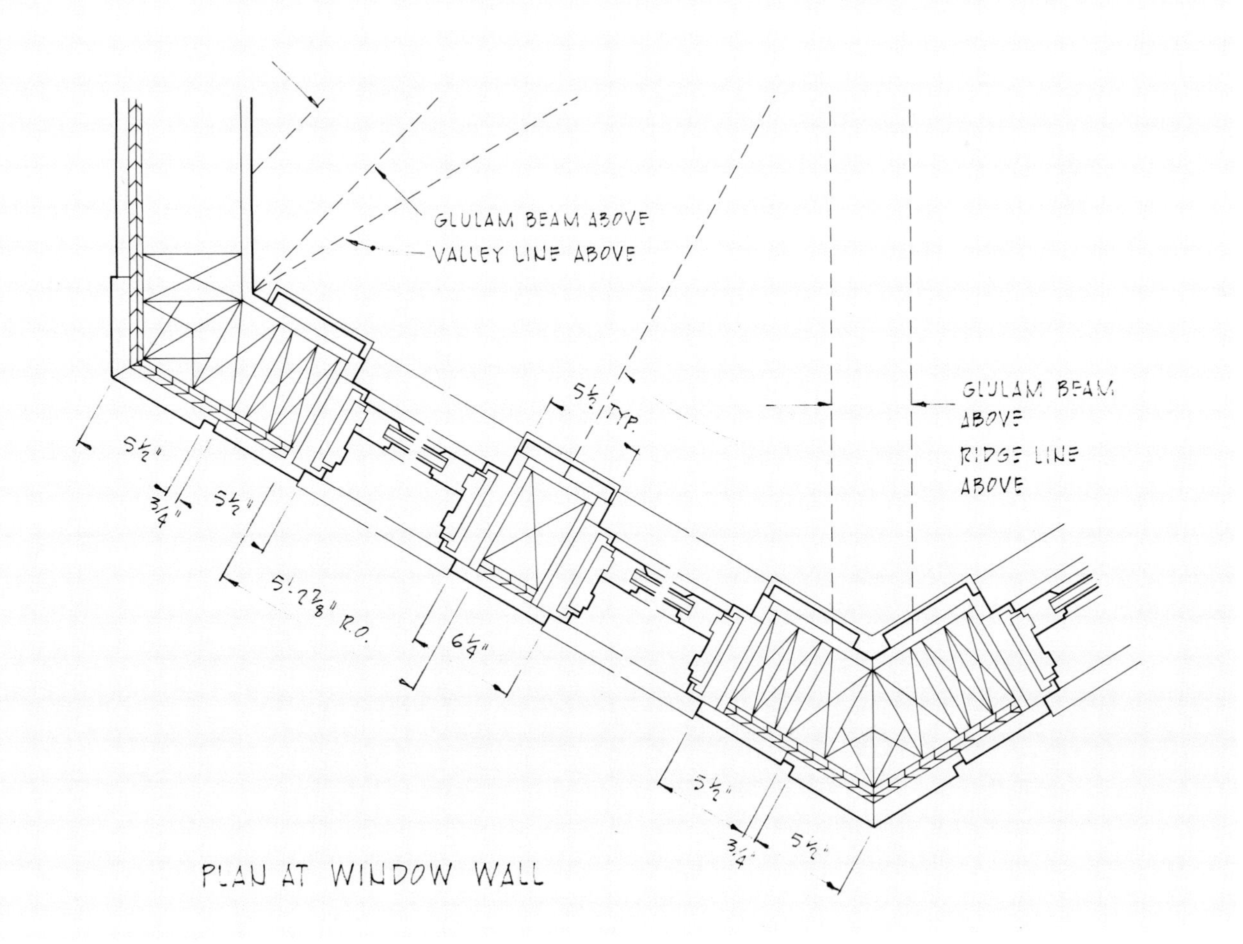
GLULAM BEAM ABOVE
VALLEY LINE ABOVE
5 1/2" TYP.
GLULAM BEAM
ABOVE
RIDGE LINE
ABOVE
5 1/2"
3/4"
5 1/2"
5'-2 7/8" R.O.
6 1/4"
5 1/2"
3/4"
5 1/2"
PLAN AT WINDOW WALL

# CEILING

## PRIVATE RESIDENCE
*Bethesda, Maryland*

**Architect**
Don A. Hawkins & Associates:
Don A. Hawkins, Architect

**General Contractor**
Clifford Stretmater, C.M. Stretmater Construction Company

**Photography**
© Maxwell MacKenzie

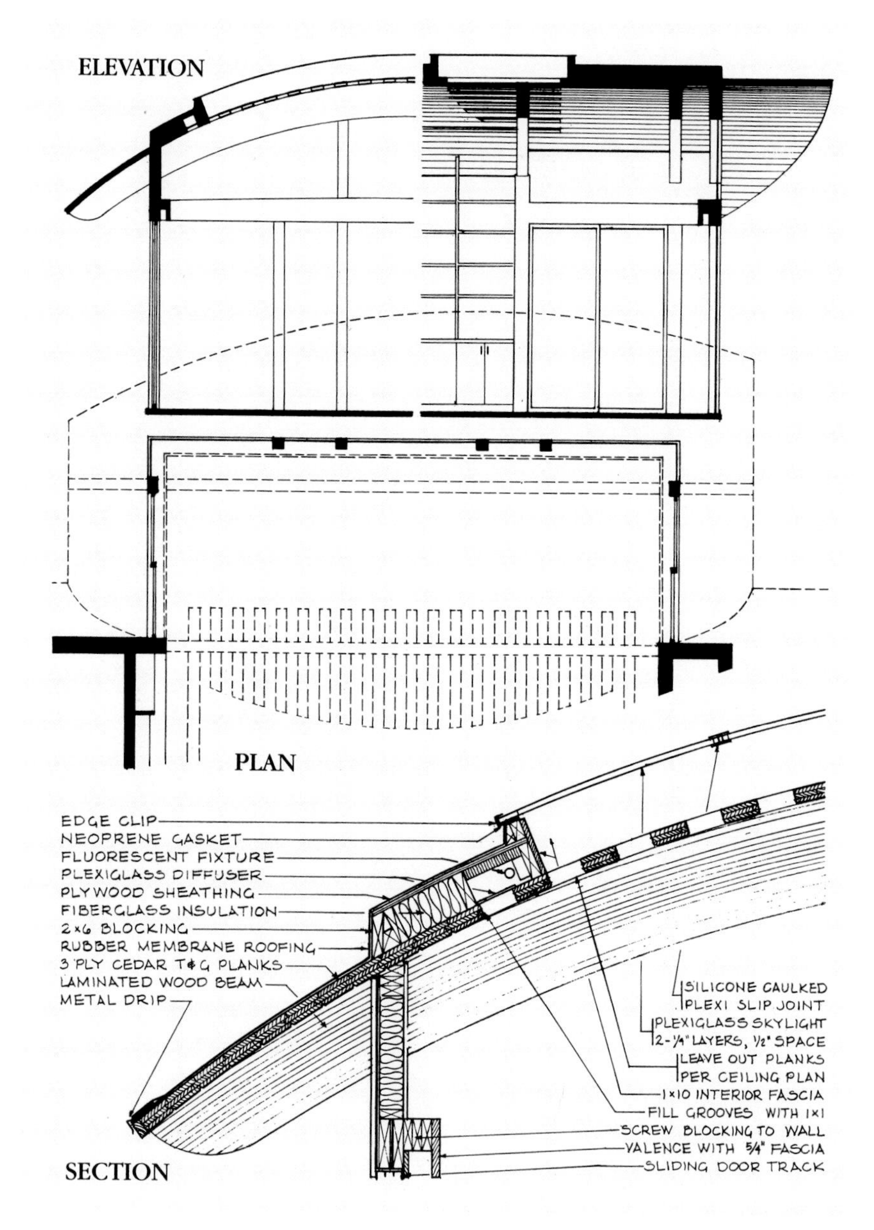


WHEN A BETHESDA, MARYLAND, psychiatrist and clinical social worker—both of whom maintained professional offices on the ground floor of the house they had lived in for twenty-two years—decided to remodel, they contacted the original architect, Joseph Miller, FAIA, who had retired. Through that contact the couple was referred to Don Hawkins, the architect's former student.

The owners liked the existing floor plan of the house and wanted to preserve it. Because both are music lovers, they wished to improve the acoustic quality of the space, and because both are avid bird-watchers, they wanted to increase the number and size of windows. The program was a comfortable one for Hawkins, whose admiration for his mentor's work made him reluctant to tamper with the integrity of the original design. Instead, it left him free to make one dramatic addition: to open the living room with a rectangular glass alcove.

The existing ceiling sloped down from a ridge beam in the direction of the new opening; Hawkins eliminated the spatial squeeze by cutting a barrel vault from the line of the ridge beam through the original roof and outward along the new alcove, revising the living room axis to point outward. The vault and new windows allowed Hawkins to transform the entire character of the room. Pushing back the living room wall 8′–0″ added 160 square feet; 240 square feet of glass were used.

The architect chose the barrel-vaulted ceiling form and the unpainted cedar planking from which it was constructed because the house belonged, stylistically, to "an architecture of restrained naturalism at the more refined end of the spectrum." A planked roof, curved over laminated beams, also had the strength to be cantilevered as much as 6′–0″ (*elevation*), permitting the deep overhang needed to diffuse light from the east-of-south exposure. Moreover, the resulting eave was thin enough to allow an outward arc in the overhang, making it wider to the west than to the east.

The system of alternating "necessary" and "unnecessary" planks in the ceiling not only eliminated glare, but also offered Hawkins the opportunity to create a slatted skylight, which runs across virtually the entire span of the ceiling. Similarly, omitting one long segment on either side of the skylight created openings for two fluorescent fixtures that were concealed in compartments that abut the skylight above the ceiling.

**PRIVATE RESIDENCE**
*Basking Ridge, New Jersey*

**Architect**
Shope Reno Wharton Associates

**Fabricator**
Lanidex Corporation

**Photography**
© H. Durston Saylor

IN THE MODERN WORLD of decreasing square footage per capita, one of the most valuable skills an architectural firm can offer its clients is the ability to make small spaces look larger. Since 1984, *House Beautiful* magazine has paid tribute to this talent by sponsoring an annual Best Small House competition. The 1986 winner—a Basking Ridge, New Jersey, house that was designed by Shope Reno Wharton Associates of Greenwich, Connecticut.

The program requirements outlined by the magazine called for "a small house that lives big, abounding in comfort, luxury and great style." Shope Reno Wharton Associates' winning design manifested all those requisite characteristics within just 1,500 square feet of what is, structurally, a straightforward, vertically oriented cube with a steep roof and broad overhang.

The house—built on a project budget of $250,000—was designed, according to the architects, "to enlarge one's perception of the space by manipulating both interior and exterior scale." That manipulation is primarily evident in a series of details, all of which were thoughtfully planned and beautifully executed.

Serpentine curved ceilings in the second-floor bedrooms exemplify the architects' adept, sleight-of-hand spatial control. A large cavity created by the steep pitch of the roof afforded the architects "an opportunity to enhance volumes, vertically, in a way that was not possible horizontally." The ceilings' curve is consistent with, if not concentric to, the roof pitch—like the roof itself, the highest plane of the ceiling is at the interior wall juncture beneath the roof peak; its lowest plane intersects the interior elevation of the exterior wall (*building section*).

The serpentine curved ceiling was created by nailing and gluing 3½-inch-wide lengths of tongue-and-groove wood to plywood gussets, which were cut to a pattern of the ceiling curve. In order to accommodate the room span, each gusset was constructed in two pieces and nailed to the joists above (*building section*). Crown moldings cover the juncture of ceiling and walls. The walls and ceilings were painted in two shades of white industrial enamel, a Shope Reno Wharton signature finish.

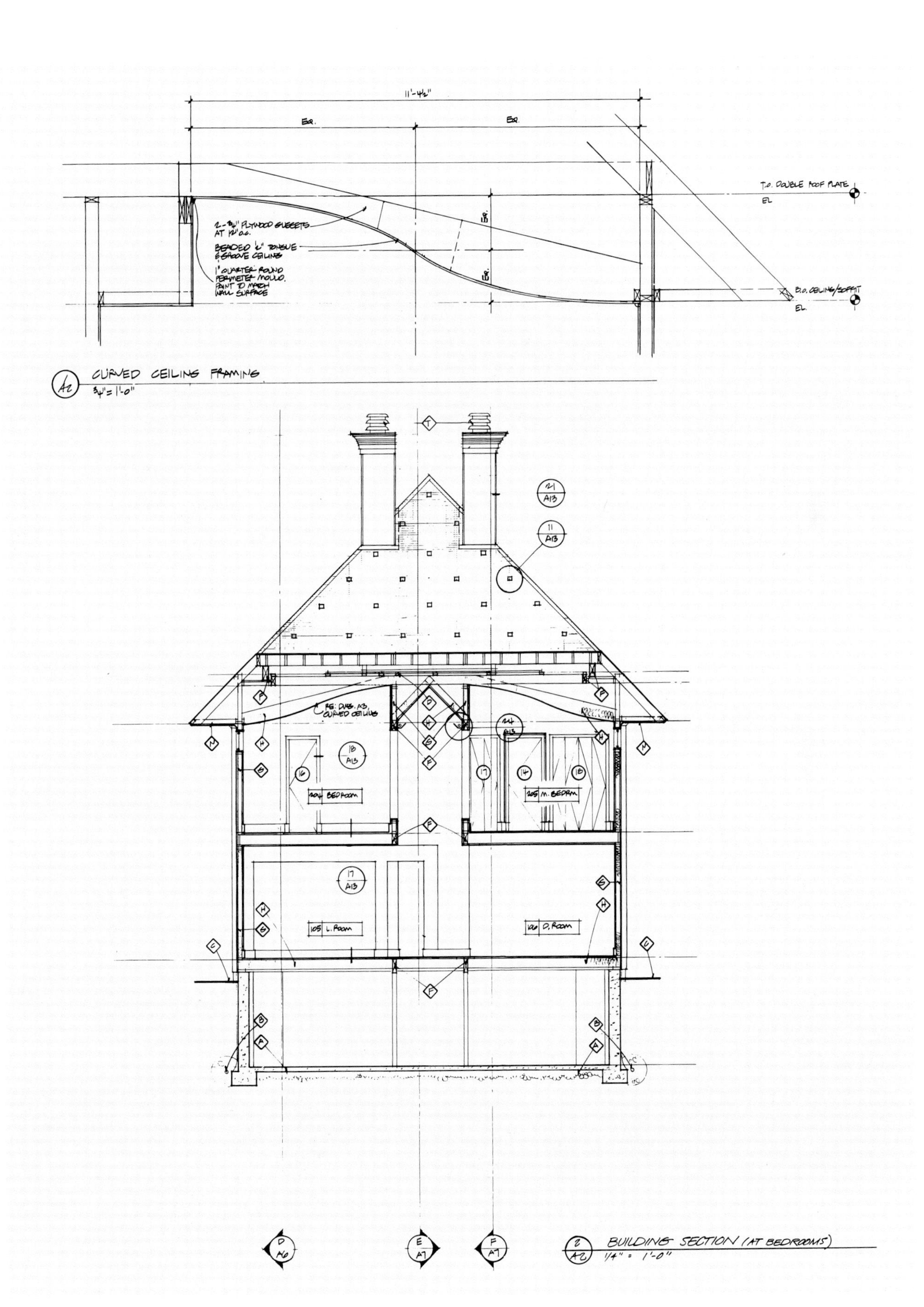
11'-4½"
EQ.
EQ.
T.O. DOUBLE ROOF PLATE
EL.
2-¾" PLYWOOD GUSSETS AT 12" O.C.
BEADED ¼" TONGUE & GROOVE CEILING
1" QUARTER ROUND PERIMETER MOULD. PAINT TO MATCH WALL SURFACE
B.O. CEILING/SOFFIT
EL.
CURVED CEILING FRAMING
¾" = 1'-0"
RE: DWG. A3, CURVED CEILING
204 BEDROOM
205 M. BEDRM
105 L. ROOM
106 D. ROOM
BUILDING SECTION (AT BEDROOMS)
¼" = 1'-0"

## Private Residence
*Westchester County, New York*

**Architect**
Peter L. Gluck and Partners, Architects

**Design Team**
Peter L. Gluck, Principal; Kent Larson, Partner; Cary K. Davis, Project Architect

**Construction Manager**
William A. Kelly & Co.

**Fabricators**
Hudson Valley Acoustical & Plastering, Inc. (plastering); Treitel-Gratz (bronze metalwork)

**Photography**
© Jeff Goldberg/ESTO

A middle-aged couple who enjoys entertaining dreamed of a house overlooking Long Island Sound. In 1986, they decided that their dream should be actualized. Their priorities for the house included creating a formal environment, but one not so formal that it would discourage visits from their grown children and attendant families; maximizing the magnificent Sound view; and offering the kind of amenities that would be conducive to entertaining.

Architect Peter Gluck responded with a 9,000-square-foot plan that is essentially one room in width, a footprint maneuver that provided a full view of the Sound from each room in the house. Gluck's design, an exercise in form simplicity, is centered by a large entry foyer that is square in plan (*key plan 5*). From this entryway, access is provided to the pool, the living room, and the dining room.

Narrowing the house to gain full views of the Sound meant putting some traditionally first-floor rooms on the second floor. Gluck situated the informal sitting room above the entry foyer, then sought to devise a way in which to link the house vertically as well as horizontally.

In order to connect the sitting room and the foyer, Gluck began by imposing an oculus at the apex of a dome. In spite of the generous dimensions of the house, he lacked the space for a true dome; instead, he constructed a pendentive dome formed by the union of four pendentives, cast in plaster. Thus, the ceiling may also be described as a groin vault.

Whereas in the Pantheon (for example) the mysterious light effects of the oculus are derived from sunlight focused through the aperture, in Gluck's design a system of artificial lighting was contrived in which a spotlight in the sitting room ceiling is focused through a lens. The light passes through the glass top of a "coffee table" which straddles the oculus in the sitting room, and then passes through the oculus itself. Finally, it strikes and diffuses in the circular pane of sandblasted glass which is suspended in the foyer as its ceiling fixture. The result is appropriately elusive: the fixture glows without revealing its light source (*section 3*).

The glass pendant is set in a bronze frame. It is tied by four bronze screeds to the bottom of the coffee table. The bronze legs that support the glass top of the table thin out as they continue down to the bronze strips that are inlaid into the plaster dome and support the fixture below (*partial elevation 1; detail 2*).

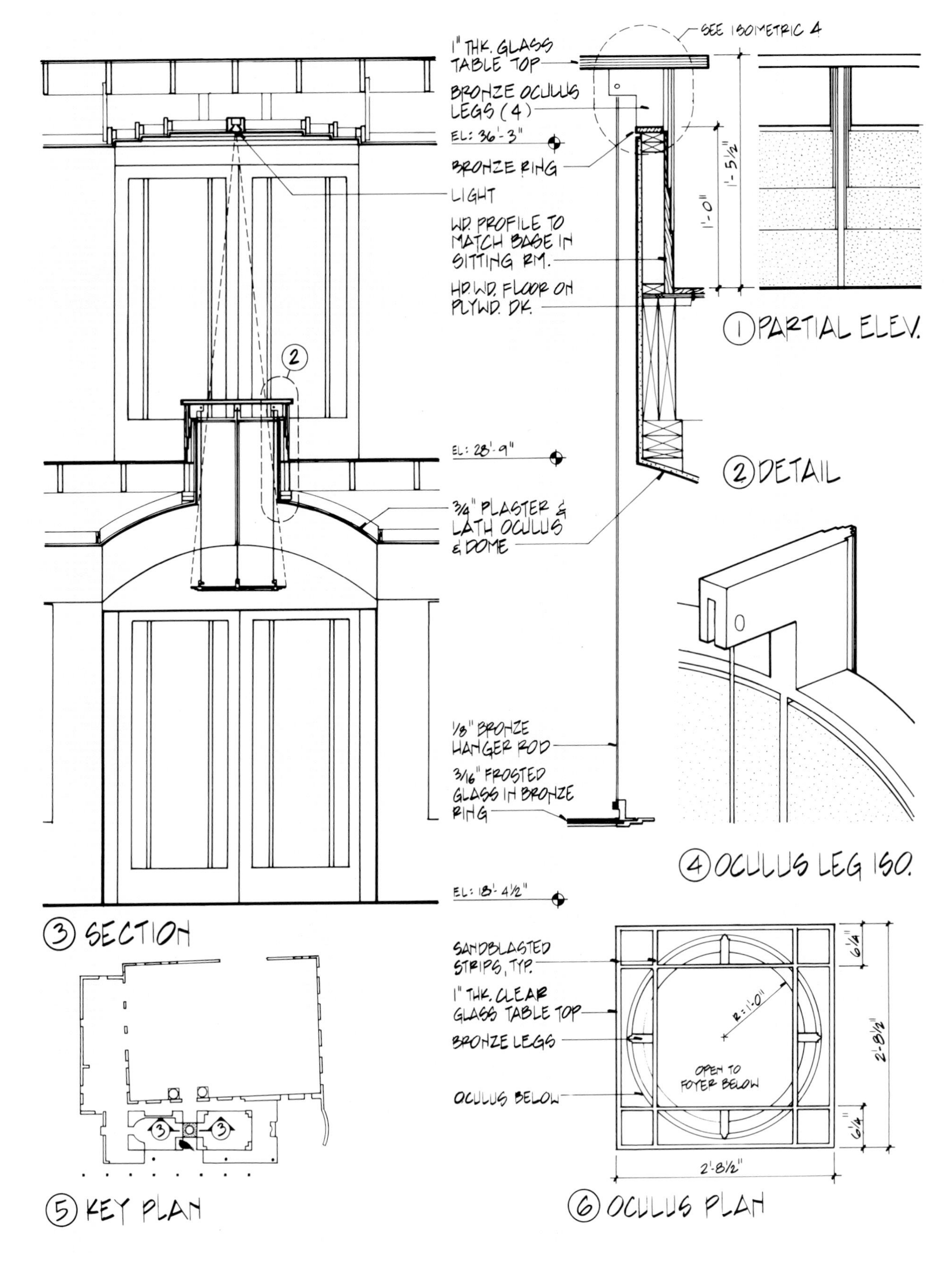
SEE ISOMETRIC 4
1" THK. GLASS TABLE TOP
BRONZE OCULUS LEGS (4)
EL: 36'-3"
BRONZE RING
LIGHT
WD. PROFILE TO MATCH BASE IN SITTING RM.
HD.WD. FLOOR ON PLYWD. DK.
1'-5½"
1'-0"
1 PARTIAL ELEV.
2
EL: 28'-9"
2 DETAIL
¾" PLASTER & LATH OCULUS & DOME
⅛" BRONZE HANGER ROD
3/16" FROSTED GLASS IN BRONZE RING
4 OCULUS LEG ISO.
EL: 18'-4½"
3 SECTION
SANDBLASTED STRIPS, TYP.
1" THK. CLEAR GLASS TABLE TOP
BRONZE LEGS
OCULUS BELOW
R=1'-0"
OPEN TO FOYER BELOW
6¼"
2'-8½"
6¼"
2'-8½"
3
3
5 KEY PLAN
6 OCULUS PLAN

## Private Residence

*Beverly Hills, California*

**Architect**
Moore Ruble Yudell

**Design Team**
Charles Moore, Principal;
John Ruble, Principal;
Buzz Yudell, Principal-in-Charge;
Peter Zingg, Project Architect;
Stephen Harby, Project Architect

**Photography**
© Tim Street-Porter

Getting an investment foot in the door in the Beverly Hills real estate market normally requires, quite simply, the availability of phenomenal amounts of cash. But a particularly astute, young couple landed a Beverly Hills house of their own by purchasing, within those renowned city limits, a small Spanish-style bungalow with "lots of potential."

The existing house was a dismal prospect composed of small, choppy rooms. To make room for themselves and their young children, the couple commissioned Santa Monica architects Moore Ruble Yudell to renovate the existing spaces and add, on one side, a wing containing kitchen/family room spaces on the ground floor and a master bedroom and bath suite on the second.

Between the old and new sections of the house, a transitional element was called for. The architects conceived a grand, bold gesture: a central gallery that would join the two structures together, tie the back garden to the front entrance, and open up the entire house to light and air.

As drawn during the initial design development phase of the project, the gallery was to have been constructed as an angular and unelaborated space—its singular amenity a bank of skylights in a sloped ceiling. But unornamented angularity did not quite provide the desired dramatic gesture; the slant of the ceiling tended to subordinate one portion of the house to the other. Moreover, a filtering device for the diffusion of direct sunlight had not yet been devised.

The design team's solution was to suspend, within the gallery's structural shell, a secondary "ceiling" consisting of perforated metal sheeting, bent to form over bowed framing, that simulates a structural barrel vault. *Simulate* is the operative word in referring to the detail: not only is the curved vault not structural, but also, in almost Cubist fashion, it is irregularly segmented both longitudinally and transversely, its sections actually gradated in height above the floor.

Moore Ruble Yudell's faux vault solution permitted simple and economical construction. Linear framing was fabricated of welded, stock steel tubes; transverse tubular segments were bent into semicircles. The spacing of the frame's transverse segments was determined by the location of the various doors that open into the corridor. Each end of a transverse tube was bolted into wood blocking built into the wall. The light-filtering, perforated-steel baffle sections, which were welded to the linear frames, were painted to match the gallery's wall (*section*).

At night, the translucent vaults become veils of light, illuminated by custom-made sconces that also function as capitals for pilasters along the walls.

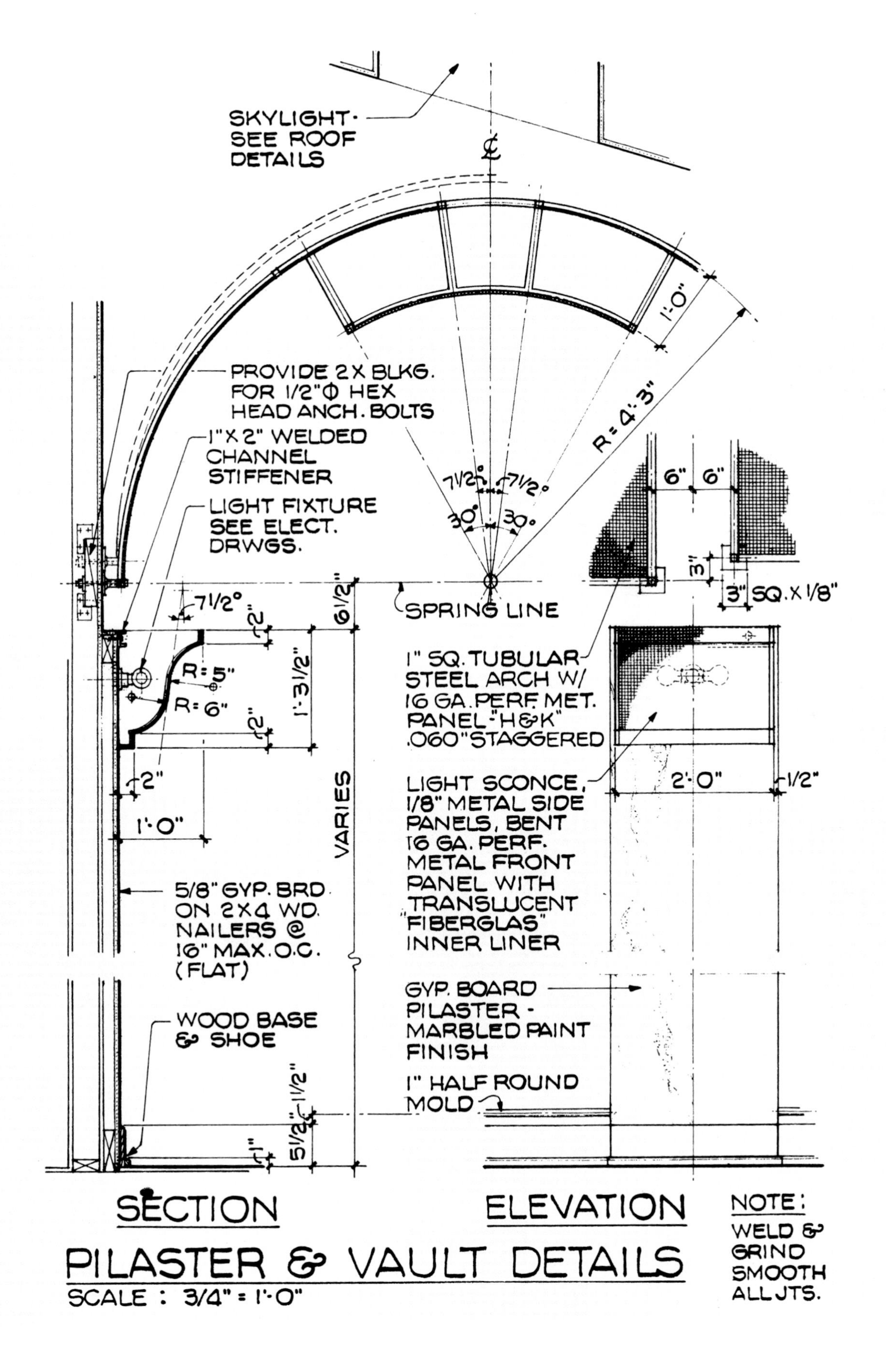
SKYLIGHT-
SEE ROOF
DETAILS
PROVIDE 2X BLKG.
FOR 1/2"Φ HEX
HEAD ANCH. BOLTS
1"X 2" WELDED
CHANNEL
STIFFENER
LIGHT FIXTURE
SEE ELECT.
DRWGS.
1'-0"
R=4'-3"
7 1/2°
7 1/2°
30°
30°
6"
6"
3"
3" SQ. X 1/8"
SPRING LINE
7 1/2°
6 1/2"
2"
R=5"
R=6"
1'-3 1/2"
2"
2"
1'-0"
VARIES
1" SQ. TUBULAR
STEEL ARCH W/
16 GA. PERF. MET.
PANEL-"H&K"
.060" STAGGERED
LIGHT SCONCE,
1/8" METAL SIDE
PANELS, BENT
16 GA. PERF.
METAL FRONT
PANEL WITH
TRANSLUCENT
"FIBERGLAS"
INNER LINER
2'-0"
1/2"
5/8" GYP. BRD.
ON 2X4 WD.
NAILERS @
16" MAX. O.C.
(FLAT)
GYP. BOARD
PILASTER -
MARBLED PAINT
FINISH
WOOD BASE
& SHOE
1" HALF ROUND
MOLD
1 1/2"
5 1/2"
1"
SECTION
ELEVATION
NOTE:
WELD &
GRIND
SMOOTH
ALL JTS.
PILASTER & VAULT DETAILS
SCALE: 3/4" = 1'-0"

# COLUMN

**PRIVATE RESIDENCE**
*Chicago, Illinois*

**Architect**
Quinn and Searl, Architects:
Linda Searl, Partner

**General Contractor/Fabricator**
Kissner Company

**Photography**
© George Lambros

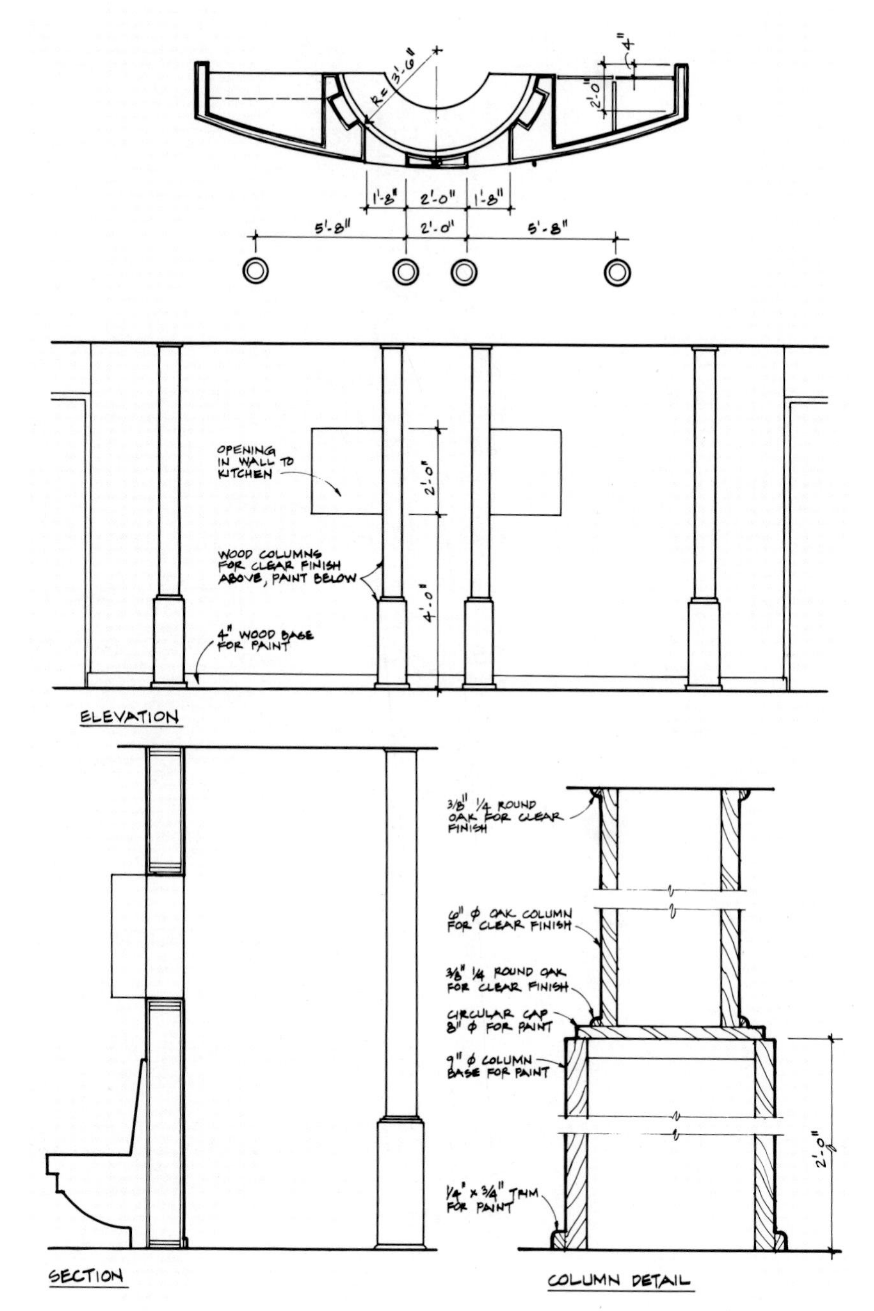


CHICAGO'S LOOP is famous for its number of important public buildings; it also boasts several very interesting private houses. This townhouse residence, renovated by Quinn and Searl, Architects, is a prime example of the latter, prime real estate category.

The primary objective of the renovation was to join two modern, identical townhouses into one. Secondary considerations were to create an open living and dining area and an adjacent, but more private, eat-in kitchen. The clients requested, however, that "privacy in the kitchen not interfere with views of the rear garden."

The turning point in the development of the renovation occurred when project architect Linda Searl designed a 17′–0″-radius, curved-wall partition to separate the kitchen from the living and dining areas (*see* Breakfast Nook/Banquette, page 46). The partition has two shadowbox openings—"windows" that frame depth-of-field shots of the garden.

Conversely, the curved wall and its windows are viewed from the living room through a course of four slender columns (*elevation*). The columns establish a similar field of vision, as they define the preferred circulation pattern from the stairs and between rooms (*section*).

Shipbuilding techniques that were utilized in the fabrication of the breakfast nook/banquette are also evoked by the smooth finish quality of the handsome wood columns. Shop-milled, with dowels inserted between vertical strips of clear finished oak, the almost ascetic columns rest on simple painted bases that accentuate their streamlined form (*column detail*).

The curved wall was constructed in 1987 for just over $1,000; columns were fabricated for $750 apiece.

## Private Residence
*Llewellyn Park, New Jersey*

**Architect**
Robert A. M. Stern Architects

**Design Team**
Anthony Cohn, Project Architect;
Ethelind Coblin, Assistant;
Gavin Macrae-Gibson, Assistant

**General Contractor**
Len Van Builders

**Photography**
© Peter Aaron/ESTO

Because appropriate scale is of particular importance to architect Robert A. M. Stern, his details, whether large or small, are almost invariably "right" for their respective applications. In 1982, when two successful attorneys—with a family of five active children—commissioned him to renovate their 1929 Georgian-style house and add an indoor swimming pool, Stern was given the opportunity to prove that even monumental scale can be manageable in a comparatively small space.

Sited at the sub-basement level of the house, and built forward of an existing terrace on the face of a slope, the roof of the new 1,500-square-foot pavilion—of glass, concrete, tile, and steel—is structurally supported by a series of columns. The design, according to the architect, "epitomizes the intersection of abstracted traditional imagery and modern technology"—an ideological intersection that is characteristic of Stern's "Modern Traditionalism."

Columnar support takes three forms: brass-clad freestanding columns, inspired by the palm-tree columns of the Brighton Pavilion; faux stone pilasters built out from the interior wall (*interior elevation*); and stone columns that penetrate the exterior glass window wall (*exterior elevation*). It is the last of these column applications that is of special note: the simplified columns on the exterior wall not only provide primary support for the glass roof; their capitals also support, behind a stepped soffit, a trough-channeled gutter (*sections*).

The exterior wall columns are encased in polished Kasota stone, quarried in Minnesota. Their massive scale and simplified profile suggest, according to Stern, "that realm between architecture and nature—the grotto." The grottolike character of the space is further enhanced by glistening tile, glass, and metal-clad surfaces.

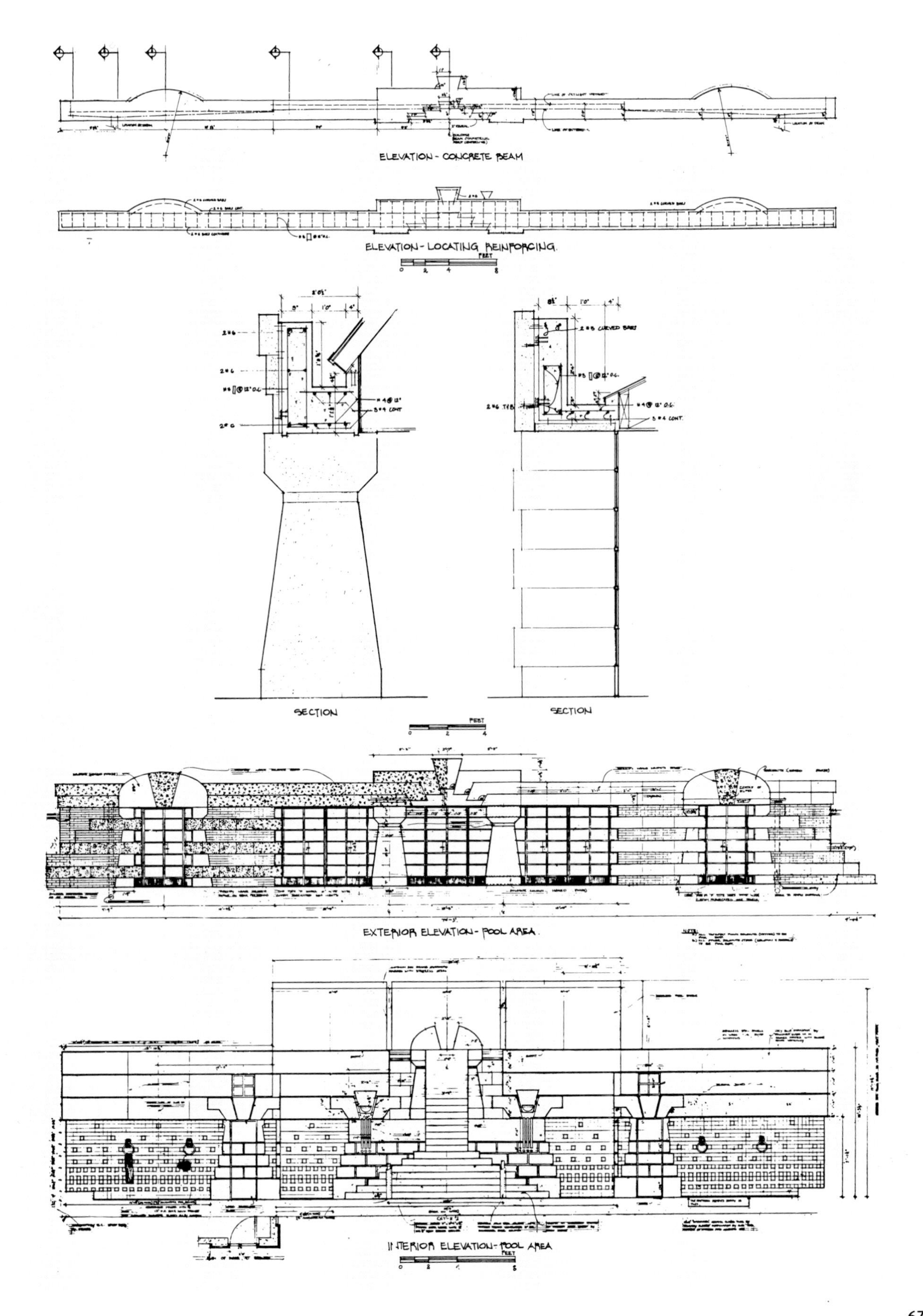
ELEVATION - CONCRETE BEAM
ELEVATION - LOCATING REINFORCING
FEET
0 2 4 8
SECTION
SECTION
FEET
0 2 4
EXTERIOR ELEVATION - POOL AREA
INTERIOR ELEVATION - POOL AREA
FEET
0 2 4 8

# Column/Desk

**Loft Apartment**
*New York, New York*

**Architect**
Lee H. Skolnick Architecture + Design

**Design Team**
Lee H. Skolnick, AIA, Principal;
Kurt Ofer, Assistant

**Fabricator**
Townhouse Finishings

**Photography**
© Antoine Bootz

According to experts, the transition from "family with children" to "empty nest couple" can be a rugged emotional experience, if viewed within the context of loss. A more positive, energizing approach was taken by clients of architect Lee Skolnick, who, in purchasing a SoHo loft, shut the door on an uptown family apartment in order to open some new doors in life.

Shutting down the uptown apartment, however, did not eliminate the inevitable accumulation of family belongings. Therefore, the clients—on a $20–30,000 budget—asked Skolnick to provide "plenty of storage, a home office, and an extra guest bedroom" without spoiling the open character of the 2,600-square-foot space.

The existing loft offered plenty of walls on which to display the owners' art collection, as it provided their prerequisites of "openness and light." Skolnick's task, therefore, became a space planning/detailing problem that he answered with considerable flair.

To define the boundaries of an office within the preferred open plan, Skolnick designed a platform that, together with a low wall, two screens and an eclectic palette of materials, is tied into an anchoring column. The result is an elevated home office composition in which each component is treated as a separate, and respected, element. The architect made a point of "asserting each material in its natural form": fiberglass is used in its natural color; steel is only primed; a tin ceiling (which is new) is sealed to avoid oxidation, but not painted. The ceiling floats away from walls, to expose the nineteenth-century building's original wood joists.

Maximizing the office's access to the light and air of the surrounding space, but at the same time emphasizing its separate identity, the desk nook thrusts a rounded prow into the living room. This 54″-high partition, which curls around the solid oak desk (*axonometric*), consists of an outer skin of corrugated fiberglass over a wood frame, and an inner face finished in drywall. The fiberglass is held to the frame with oak strips affixed through the fiberglass with brass screws. The line of the strips is continued beyond the ends of the wall into oak shelves.

Solid oak drawers for the desk are built into the 18″-diameter column, a detailing device that further enhances its usefulness. Although the column is not structural, it does

support the right end of the desk. The column is a standard construction-grade sonotube, which has been coated with plaster and painted.

In vivid contrast to the stark, industrial-strength wall and column are the romantic sliding screens, "a distant takeoff from shoji screens," according to Skolnick. While these serve the purpose of a shoji screen in both transmitting light and dividing space, they are relatively massive. Constructed of welded steel members that enclose panes of textured, iridescent glass, each of the two panels hangs from rollers mounted on a steel track. The track itself is suspended by three steel dowels that pass through the tin ceiling and are bolted to wood joists. The panels do not dangle; each rolls on a rubber plumb. Sliding one or both panels changes the geometric pattern of the panes and mullions. The screens also open or close the corner of the space when it is used as a sitting area; they provide privacy screening when the area doubles as a sleeping niche.

In addition to the column drawers and the shelves extending from the curved wall, the clients' storage needs were addressed by a series of wooden shelves cantilevered out from the wall with steel dowels drilled into the brick. As the final expression of Skolnick's aim to make all parts of the office ensemble answer storage requirements, a large cabinet was built into the platform itself.

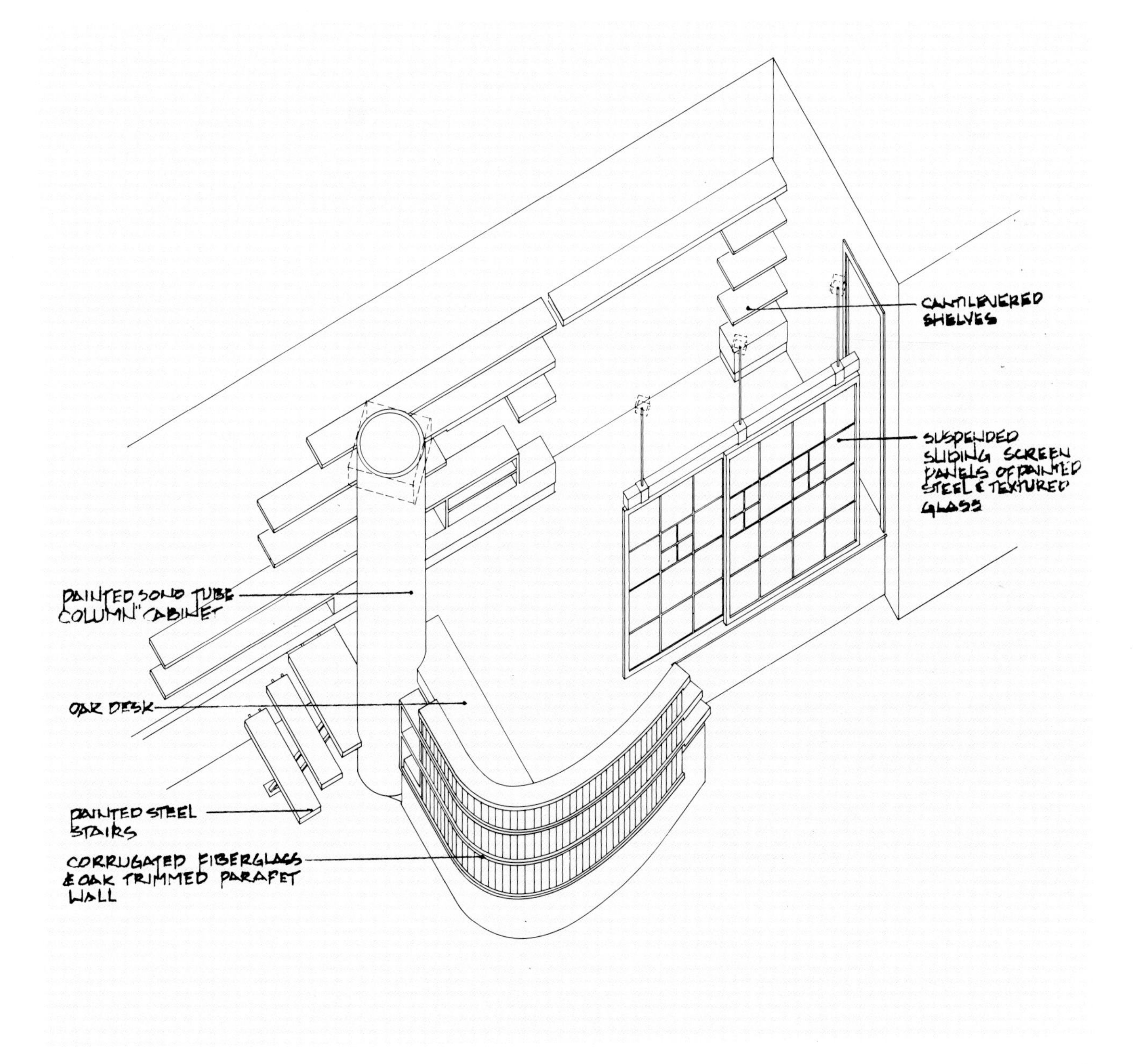

# Display Cabinet

**Strite Residence**
*Haverford, Pennsylvania*

**Architect/Interior Designer**
John M. Strite, IBD, FIDC,
AIA Affiliate

**Fabricator**
Carl W. Guckelberger

**Photography**
© John M. Strite

John M. Strite is a man of many interests and talents. In addition to his national and international practice as an architecture and interior design consultant, he is a college instructor of architectural history, a connoisseur of opera and classical music, and a self-confessed "Collector, with a capital C." Among his many collections are those of African masks, architectural relics, contemporary art and sculpture, and over one hundred one-of-a-kind chess sets.

Strite is, consequently, a believer in "a place for everything, and everything in its place." In 1973, having run out of places within spaces for his possessions, he bought a classic, if dilapidated, Philadelphia stone carriage house that boasted 3,600 square feet of potential "living, storage and display space." The renovation of the house and property, which is situated on Philadelphia's legendary Main Line, has been, according to the architect's understated description, "a sixteen-year busman's holiday."

The house and land Strite now shares with his wife (owner of ArtSouth, a corporate fine-arts research and acquisition firm) and son bears little resemblance to the "paved yard, dank, dark tack room, haylofts, and horse stalls" the architect took over in 1973. Today, the yard is a beautifully landscaped Japanese garden; the tack room—outfitted with individual compartments for stereo equipment and thousands of indexed tapes—has been converted to a literal and figurative "control center"; while haylofts and horse stalls have been replaced by a sun-drenched, two-story living room overlooked by a foreshortened loft. Only one equine reminder remains—a massive track-mounted barn door that is pragmatically used to close off the serious cook's kitchen.

It was on the living wall underneath the overhanging loft that Strite chose to store and display his chess sets "without ostentation." Although acquiring the collection has been a consumer's pursuit for the architect, displaying the chess sets might now be construed as a religious experience; the wall-to-wall, floor-to-ceiling display cabinets were built out with crown moldings 1′–11″ from an existing bearing wall to suggest "the deep portals of late Gothic cathedrals."

The detail of the display cabinet was intentionally designed to be modest in cost and simple in construction. To accommodate a change in elevation from the hall to the living room, the original plaster wall was blocked out and then drywalled, on the hall side, to match the dimension of one of two stair treads. On the living room side, the original wall was covered in fabric-wrapped panels of homosote, from which vertically applied 2 × 4 blocking was brought forward for two purposes: to accommodate the second stair tread dimension, and to frame out the actual display cabinet cavity. At the staircase archway, compounded crown moldings serve as both transitional and depth-of-composition elements. The cabinet fascia was constructed of clear white pine boards; piano-hinged cabinet compartment doors are fabricated of crown molding frames over clear panes of ⅛-inch glass. Chess sets displayed within the cabinet compartments rest on 3⁄16-inch plate-glass shelves, which may be slipped in and out of cross-cut slots that are notched into the wood blocking. As a final fillip, Strite fitted full-height, low-voltage halogen light strips into vertical grooves that are notched in the blocking (*axonometric*).

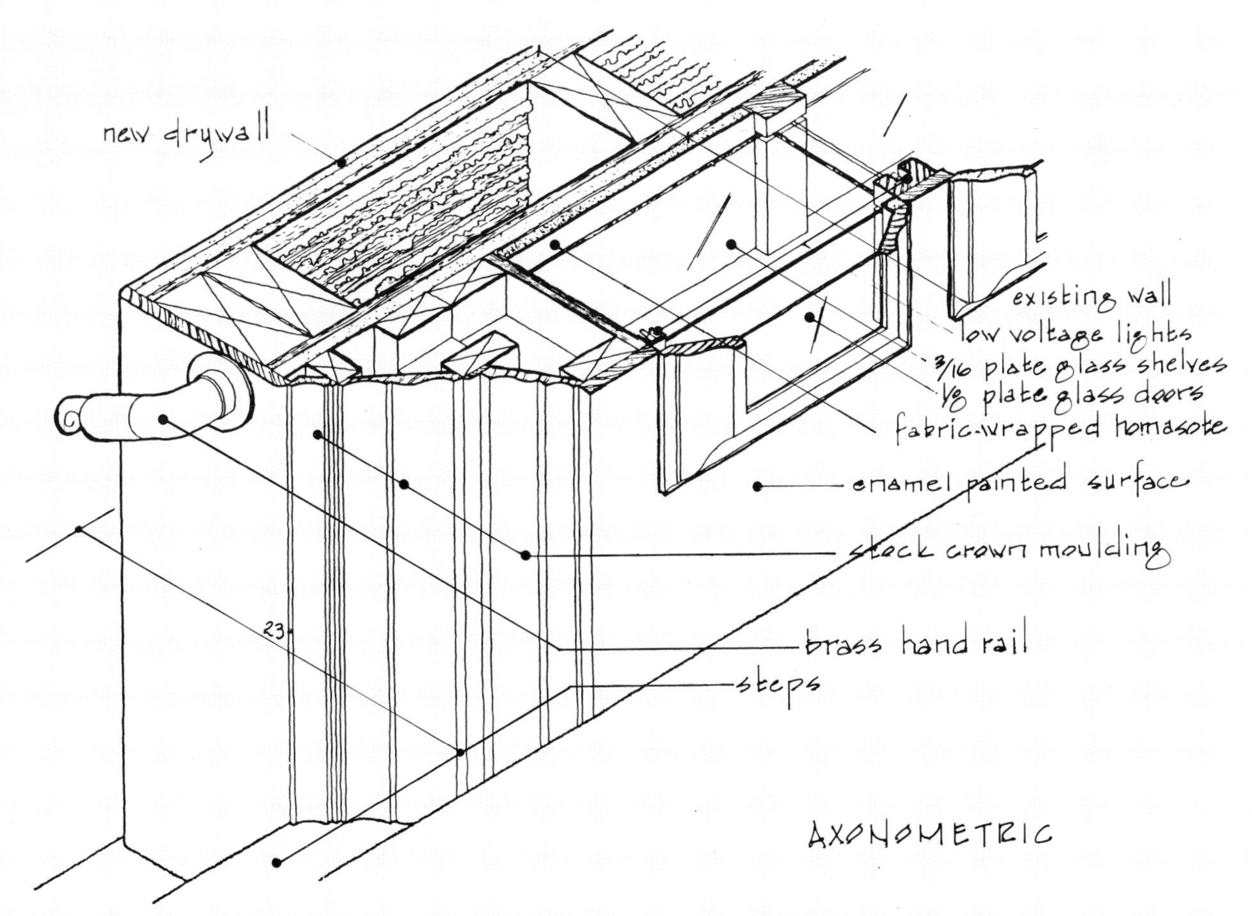
new drywall
existing wall
low voltage lights
3/16 plate glass shelves
1/8 plate glass doors
fabric-wrapped homasote
enamel painted surface
stock crown moulding
brass hand rail
steps
23
AXONOMETRIC

# Display Niche

**Riverside Drive Penthouse**
*New York, New York*

**Interior Designer**
Claudia Librett Design Studio

**Design Team**
Claudia Librett, Design Principal;
Gayle Kenigsberg, Design Associate

**Filing Architect**
Michael Sapinsky, AIA

**Construction Consultant**
John Deak, Jr., Deak Construction, Inc.

**Contributing Artists**
Charles Chamot, (wall art);
Lanie and Marek Cecula (ceramic art)

**Photography**
© H. Durston Saylor

The conversion of a shabby 650-square-foot, one-bedroom/one-bath penthouse apartment—with a 900-square-foot terrace—to an elegant 1,000-square-foot, two-bedroom/two-bath pied-à-terre was not, according to interior designer Claudia Librett, an easy task. Librett completed the project in a year that was "more often than not, a living nightmare," caused by "a bureaucratic building management company" and, during the weeks when the new living room extension was not yet under roof, "weather that was wetter than Noah's flood." Librett can laugh—now—about "several nocturnal rooftop vigils" that she spent operating a bilge pump.

The serene, sophisticated mood of the completed renovation gives no sign that ongoing chaos control was required to create it. What is evident is a combination of thoughtful space planning and fine detailing that was rendered in sumptuous, if inexpensive, materials (*see also* Bathtub Enclosure, page 31).

An example of that combination of qualities is to be found in the new entrance foyer, which was spatially developed after the designer conferred with the artists whose work was to be displayed there. The new foyer was then created by gutting existing walls, enlarging the area, and breaking its rectilinear rigidity with a curved partition—a partition that at once hides a plumbing stack, leads the eye to an important piece of art hung at the end of the corridor, and contains an eye-level, recessed, and shelved niche for the display of a collection of fine pottery.

The front elevation of the curved partition/display niche is constructed of two ¼-inch drywall layers screwed to 2″ × 4″ studs, set 9 inches on center. Two-inch by four-inch ledger strips were screwed to the right-angle walls behind the curved partition to support the weight of a smooth, polished slate display shelf mounted to a sheet of ¼-inch plywood. From the ceiling, the curved partition façade drops down well below the structural niche framing so that a block-mounted track light may be completely hidden from view (*entry hall niche detail*).

Allusion to stone materials is not limited to the slate shelf itself: ¼-inch-deep terrazzo floor tiles, cast from stone and acrylic aggregate, were laid in a checkerboard pattern in a 1-inch-deep setting bed to impart a feeling of substance and permanence to the space. Additional graphic punch and textural variety are subtly provided by an ebonized baseboard and solid-core cherry doors.

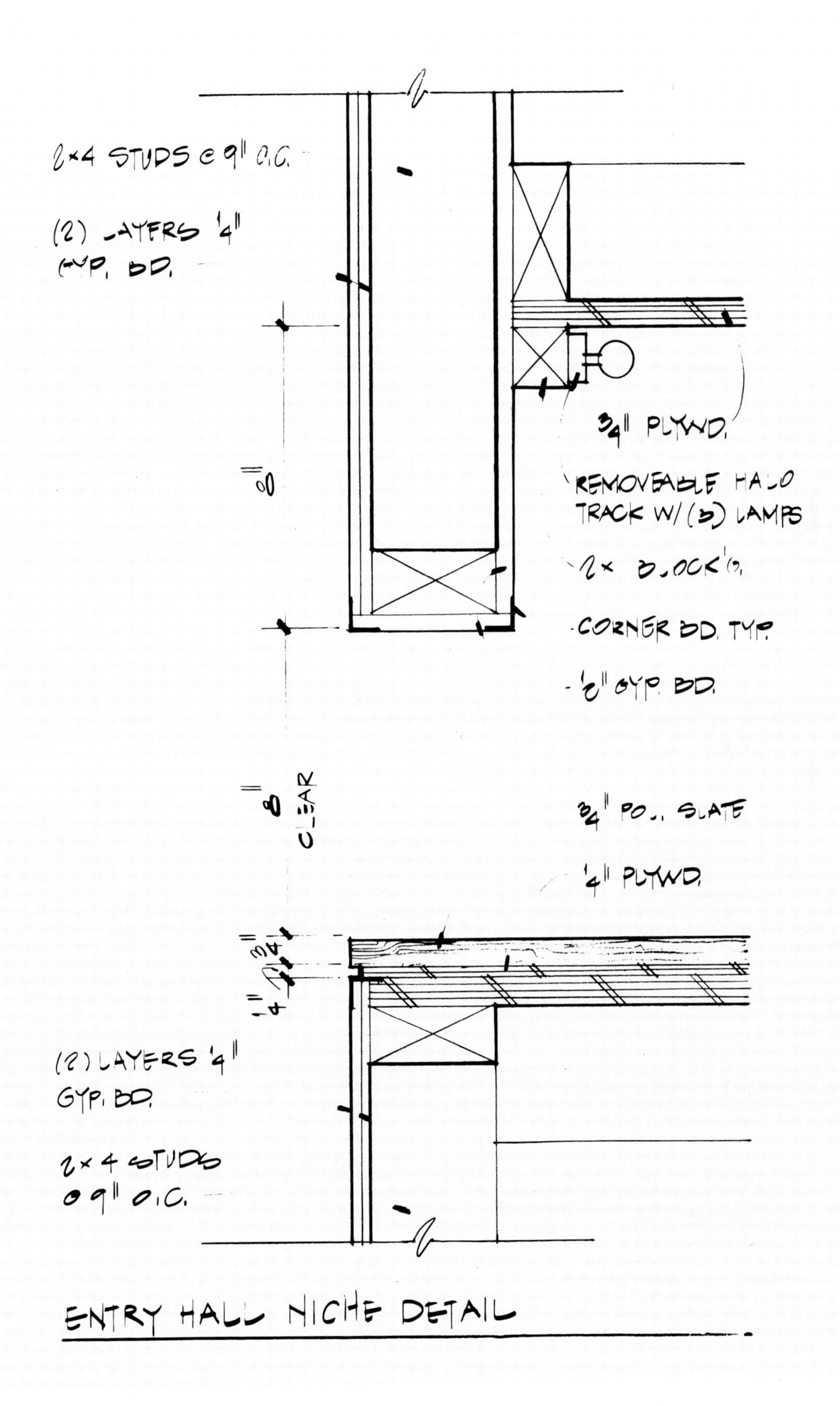
2×4 STUDS @ 9" O.C.
(2) LAYERS 1/4" GYP. BD.
8"
3/4" PLYWD.
REMOVEABLE HALO TRACK W/ (3) LAMPS
2× BLOCK'G.
CORNER BD. TYP.
1/2" GYP. BD.
8" CLEAR
3/4" POL. SLATE
1/4" PLYWD.
3/4"
1/4"
1"
(2) LAYERS 1/4" GYP. BD.
2×4 STUDS @ 9" O.C.
ENTRY HALL NICHE DETAIL

# Display Niche

## Kramer Residence

*New York, New York*

**Architect**
Machado and Silvetti Associates, Inc.

**Design Team**
Rodolfo Machado, Project Designer;
Jorge Silvetti, Project Designer;
Robert Miklos, Project Manager

**Fabricator**
Warren Pearl, Swim Construction Corporation

**Photography**
© Norman McGrath

An argentine diamond dealer who planned to spend two years in New York purchased a 2,000-square-foot apartment in the upper two stories of a Beaux Arts townhouse on the East Side of Manhattan. Ironically, although the grand style and impeccable detailing of the building's façade and public spaces reminded him of his "classical, French" home in Buenos Aires, his own apartment consisted of former servants' quarters and, therefore, lacked any detailing character.

The temporary expatriate asked Machado and Silvetti to undertake a renovation of the space that would, according to Machado, "capture the essence of the façade and main lobbies of the building without mimicking their language exactly." Because the client planned to be in New York for such a short time, he asked that the renovation work be completed without incurring undue cost.

Machado's solution, executed in 1980, responded forthrightly to the demands of the client's situation. While it clearly recalls the themes of classicism, whether of the Beaux Arts or other venues, it is spare, stripped to essentials, and of modest scale.

The trompe l'oeil success of Machado's design solution is most readily demonstrated within the 18′–0″ × 35′–0″ living/dining area on the apartment's main floor. By creating an axis running across the room from the centered fireplace on one wall to the sculpture niche on the other, Machado was able to use the articulation of a pair of columned walls to suggest the division of the room into separate living and dining areas.

The display niche for sculpture is the centerpiece of a wall more open than solid, in which the four capitalless columns (quasi pilasters) support a rectangular lintel that is the main unifying horizontal element. Centered between the two middle columns, and introduced by two planes slanting back from the lintel, the semicircular niche is carved out between a marble-topped cabinet (for dining room storage) and a ceiling lowered to the level of the lintel.

The entire detail, with the exception of the columns themselves, was constructed of standard plasterboard over wood framing; the columns are of shaped wood, finished in plaster. The statue in the niche is a copy of a famous Hellenistic Psyche.

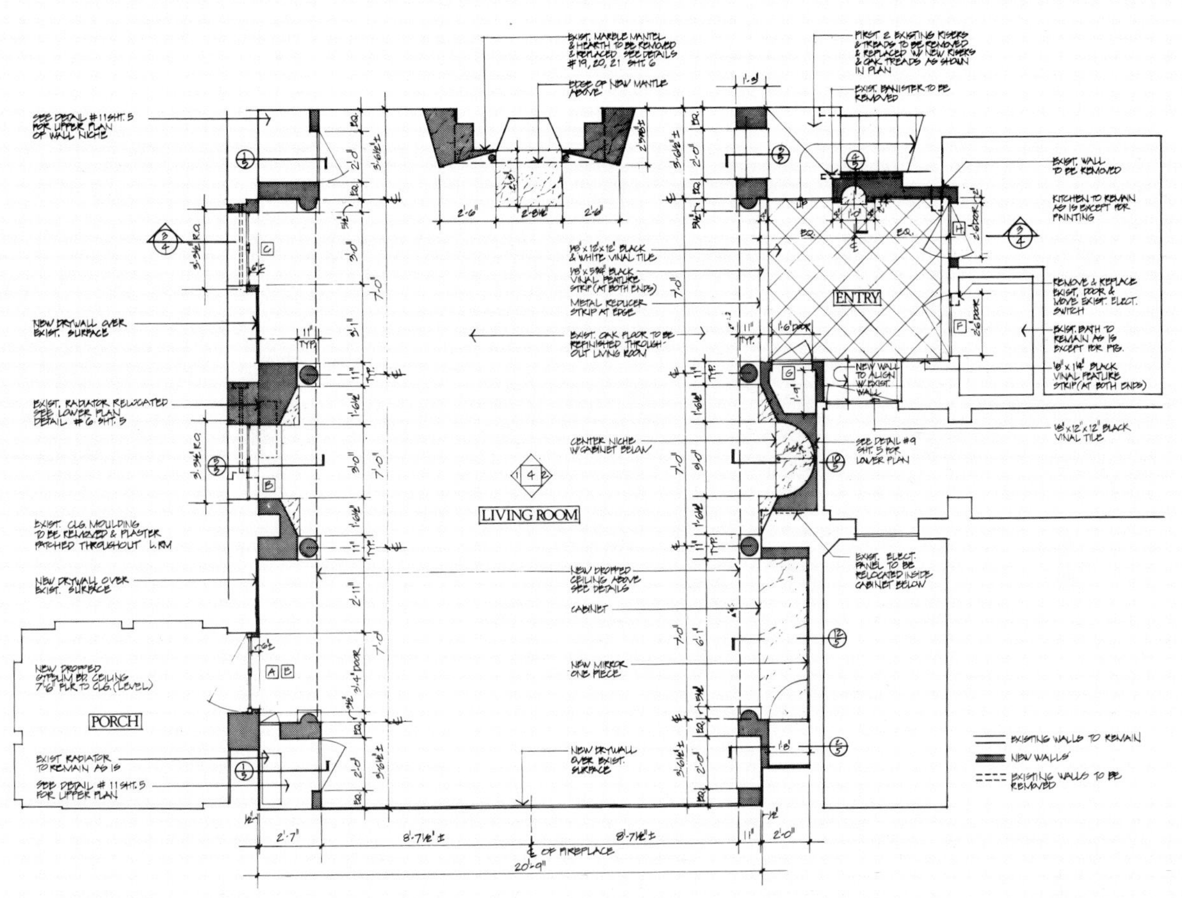


FIRST FLOOR PLAN
SCALE: 1/2" = 1'-0"

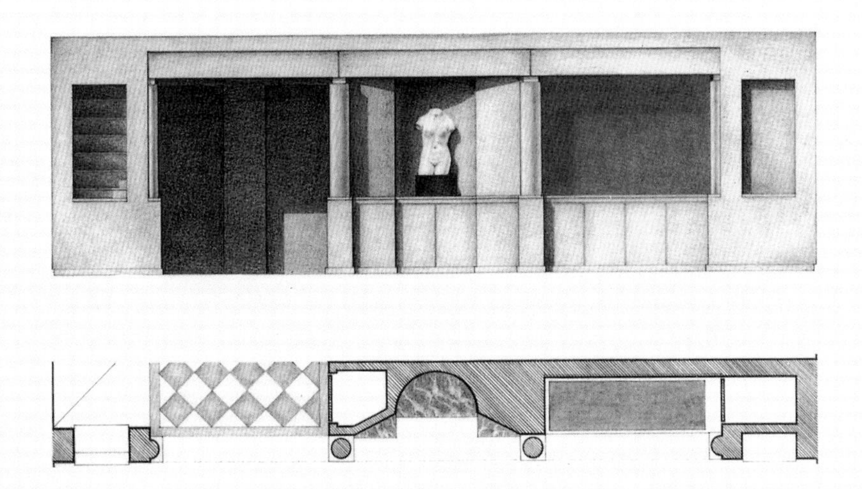

NICHE ELEVATION
SCALE: 1/2 = 1'-0"

# DOOR

### BLAIR RESIDENCE
*Fayston, Vermont*

**Architect**
David Coleman Architecture

**Design Team**
David Coleman, Architect;
Astrid Riemer, Project Assistant;
Craig Davis, Project Assistant

**General Contractor**
C.S. Construction

**Photography**
© Greg Hursley

BOB AND SUSAN BLAIR first met in Switzerland, where they fell in love with each other as well as with the simplicity and elegance of vernacular architecture. In particular, they were captivated by the French influence manifest in the local architectural tradition. Years later—after they had married and had had three children—the couple commissioned architect David Coleman to renovate their Vermont house in European fashion, integrating into the design a more refined Scandinavian flavor, appropriate to Vermont's own building traditions.

Coleman responded with a design he dubs a "Nordic-romantic" interpretation, one influenced by Scandinavian wood buildings of the 1920s. The wide, shallow arch he introduced as a motif throughout the dwelling is a graceful, fluid shape that relates to the bend of the brook on the property. The architect "hinged" the existing house and the new addition with an entryway/rotunda so that the house itself meanders slightly, like the brook.

The French doors the client requested were installed in the master bedroom leading onto a deck (*plan*). The arched doors were conceived as a picture frame; consequently, the color scheme within the room is basically neutral, a subtle articulation intended to enhance interaction with the picturesque landscape.

Coleman's French doors, which arc from 9′–2″ at the outside edge to nearly 12′–0″ at the center, were fabricated of Douglas fir, specified for its rigidity (*elevation*). Insulated glass panes are divided by muntins. The doors fit into a vault, the arch of which is supported from above by a plywood diaphragm (*section*). Lever handles, as well as the remaining hardware, are of polished brass.

Torch sconces accent the edges of the door. The fixture consists of an enameled white frame with a milk-glass lens.

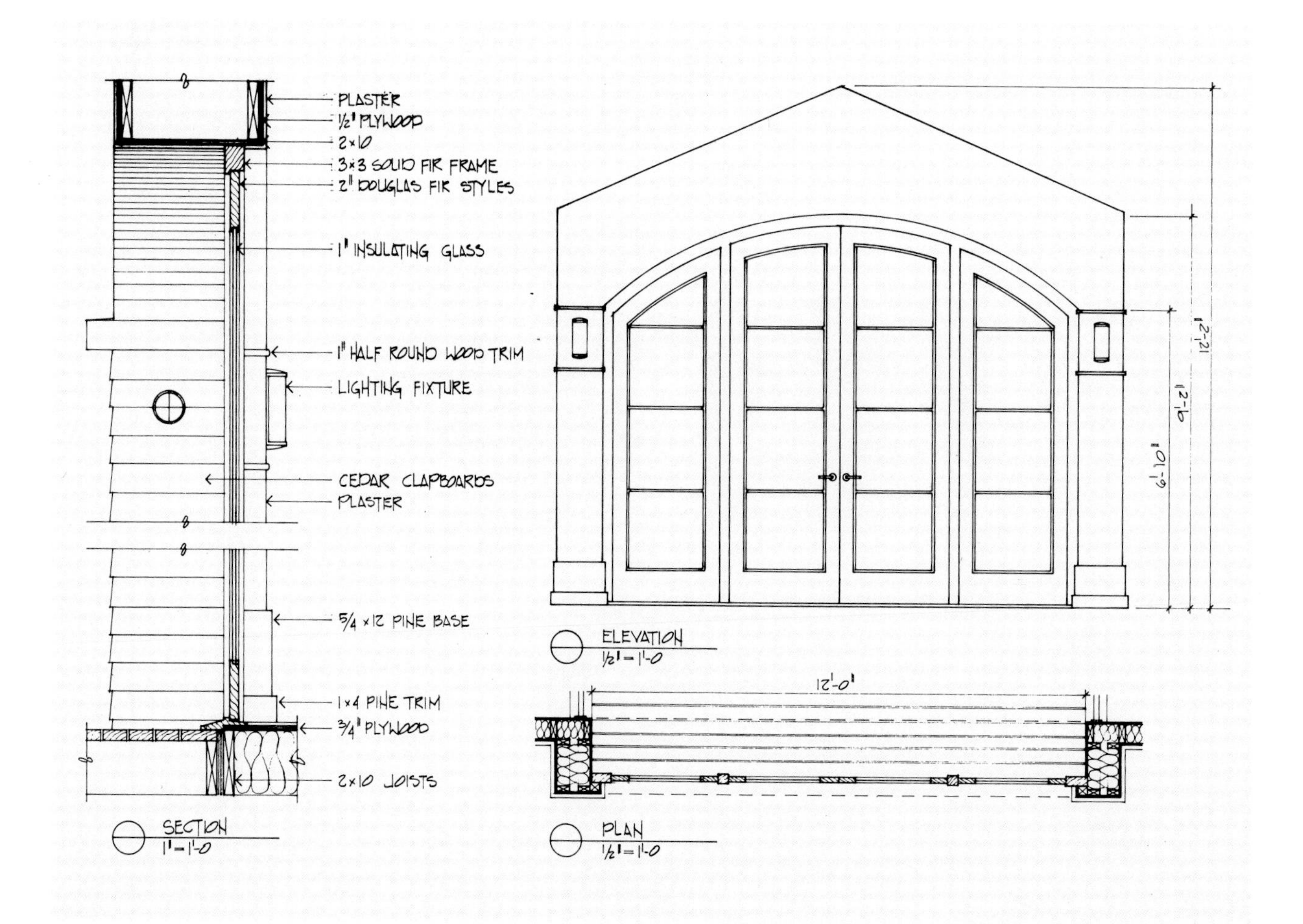

# Door

**Private Residence**
*Kansas City, Missouri*

**Architect**
Roger Kraft: Architecture • Design

**Design Team**
Roger Kraft, Project Designer;
Mark Peters, Project Architect

**Fabricator**
Bob Falkenberg Company

**Photography**
© E. G. Schempf (top);
© Mark Darley/ESTO (bottom)

An urban aerie was desired by an art dealer and her husband who, in 1985, decided to renovate a 6,000-square-foot apartment in a Kansas City complex comprised of three 1930s high rises. The couple commissioned Roger Kraft to design and oversee the project (*see* Ceiling, page 50; Radiator Cover/Closet Cabinetry, page 162).

The apartment occupies the entire tenth floor, and one-third of the building's penthouse level. According to Kraft: "The clients had one specific goal for the terraced apartment—to develop an environment that would reflect a level of taste commensurate with the art they collect and which would enhance the artwork through the understatement of the design." Kraft fulfilled this request with a series of gallery-like spaces finished in contrasting forms and materials that work together "to surprise and focus attention."

The two-story living room was given a new parquet floor to intentionally contrast with the tone of restored original wood paneling. The rich color value of the paneling against the naturally finished floor offsets displayed artwork as effectively as white walls against granite floors do elsewhere in rhythmic applications throughout the space.

Providing a prelude to the living room and creating a transition from the elevator, however, posed an interesting problem for the designer. He resolved both considerations by developing a circular plan that gives the entry hall (which also provides stair access to the penthouse) a sense of formal strength and independence. Glass doors, framed in black steel, with lockable bronze levers provide a sense of separation between spaces, a framed view of the artwork inside, and a bright counterpoint to wood surfaces.

Successfully juxtaposing two polar opposite rooms created a special challenge in designing the joint between the circle of the entry plan and the square of the existing wall. Kraft broke the new curved wall 5½ inches before the door opening, imposing a 180-degree metal bullnose to allow the wall to curl back on itself and create a reveal. The door frame is flush with the reveal surface (*plan; plan detail C*).

At 7′–4″, the door is the same height as the ceilings in all circulation areas; major rooms have higher ceilings. Kraft felt strongly about the quality of the door, using refined, visually light steel sections instead of aluminum. (Installation tolerances were so small that the need for caulked joints was entirely eliminated.) The door's clear glass contrasts with the sandblasted glass of the overhead light fixture.

As a preface to the rest of the apartment, Kraft took advantage of the need for a radiator in the middle of the vestibule wall to break the curve and create a display shelf for an art object.

Above the radiator, separated by another piece of 1¼-inch wood trim, a 1′–5″-high clear glass door opens onto a display shelf. The interior of the display area is finished in painted wood; at the top a removable Plexiglas light diffuser, supported by the display case's back and sides, separates the art piece from an incandescent light fixture above. The fixture is covered by a painted wood panel curved to match the wall and outlined by a ½″-wide by ⅛″-deep reveal set in 1¼ inches from the edges (*section detail A*).

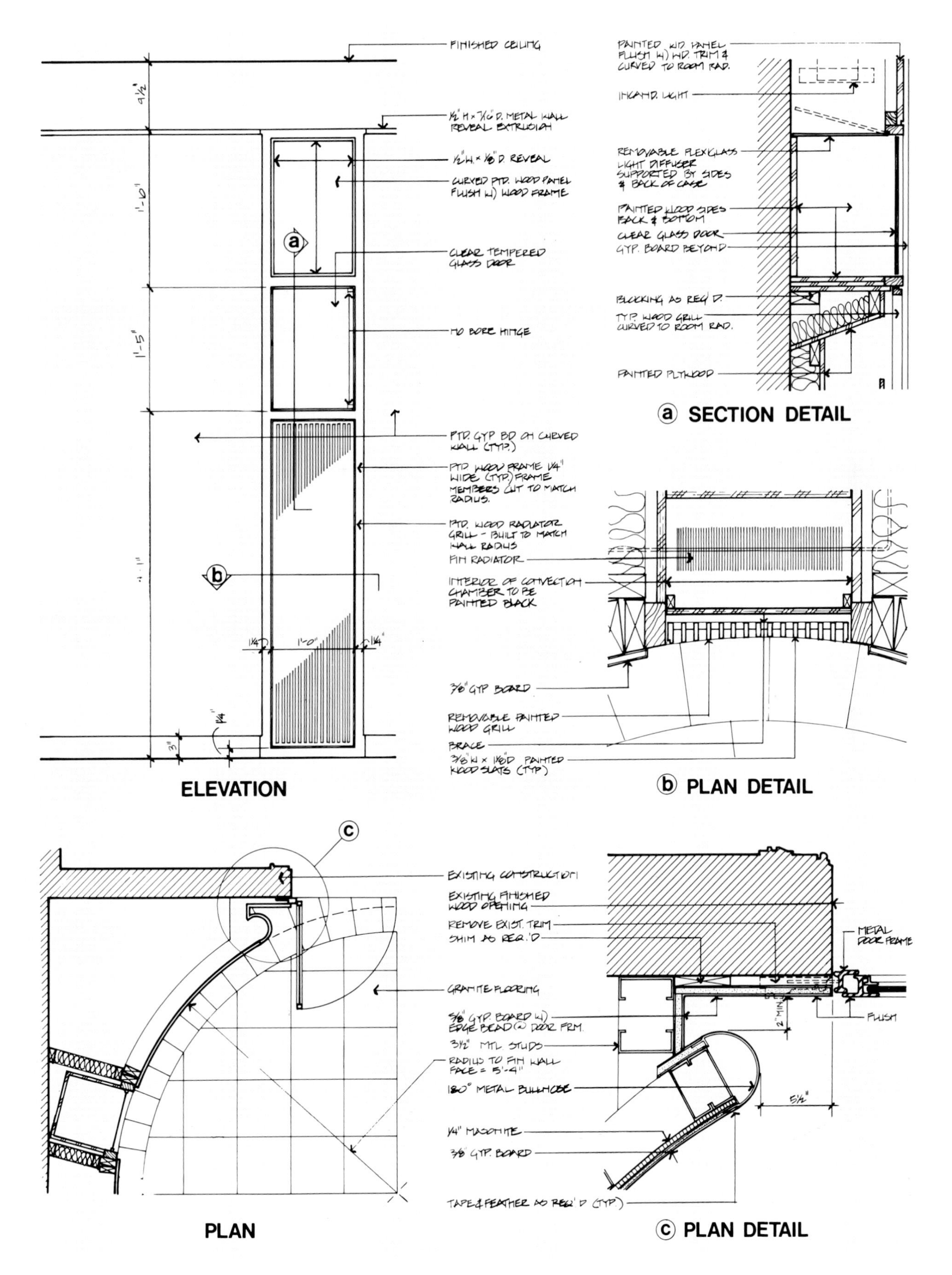
FINISHED CEILING
1/2" H x 7/16" D. METAL WALL REVEAL EXTRUSION
1/2" H. x 1/8" D. REVEAL
CURVED PTD. WOOD PANEL FLUSH W/ WOOD FRAME
CLEAR TEMPERED GLASS DOOR
NO BORE HINGE
PTD. GYP. BD. ON CURVED WALL (TYP.)
PTD. WOOD FRAME 1/4" WIDE (TYP.) FRAME MEMBERS CUT TO MATCH RADIUS.
PTD. WOOD RADIATOR GRILL - BUILT TO MATCH WALL RADIUS
PAINTED WD. PANEL FLUSH W/ WD. TRIM & CURVED TO ROOM RAD.
INCAND. LIGHT
REMOVABLE PLEXIGLASS LIGHT DIFFUSER SUPPORTED BY SIDES & BACK OF CASE
PAINTED WOOD SIDES BACK & BOTTOM
CLEAR GLASS DOOR
GYP. BOARD BEYOND
BLOCKING AS REQ'D.
TYP. WOOD GRILL CURVED TO ROOM RAD.
PAINTED PLYWOOD
FIN RADIATOR
INTERIOR OF CONVECTION CHAMBER TO BE PAINTED BLACK
3/8" GYP BOARD
REMOVABLE PAINTED WOOD GRILL
BRACE
3/8" W x 1 1/8" D PAINTED WOOD SLATS (TYP)
EXISTING CONSTRUCTION
EXISTING FINISHED WOOD OPENING
REMOVE EXIST. TRIM
SHIM AS REQ'D
METAL DOOR FRAME
GRANITE FLOORING
3/8" GYP. BOARD W/ EDGE BEAD @ DOOR FRM.
FLUSH
3 1/2" MTL. STUDS
RADIUS TO FIN. WALL FACE = 5'-4"
180° METAL BULLNOSE
1/4" MASONITE
3/8" GYP. BOARD
TAPE & FEATHER AS REQ'D (TYP)
2" MIN.
5 1/2"
9 1/2"
1'-10"
1'-5"
4'-1"
1 1/4"
1'-0"
3"
a
b
c

ELEVATION

ⓐ SECTION DETAIL

ⓑ PLAN DETAIL

PLAN

ⓒ PLAN DETAIL

# DOOR

## PRIVATE RESIDENCE
*New York, New York*

**Architect**
Steven Holl Architects

**Design Team**
Steven Holl, Principal-in-Charge;
Mark Janson, Project Architect;
Joe Fenton, Project Architect

**Fabricator**
Terry DeAngelis

**Photography**
© Mark Darley/ESTO

FOR THE YOUNG JAPANESE OWNERS of this 1,500-square-foot Museum Tower condominium at the Museum of Modern Art, architect Steven Holl developed a footprint and finish package based on the spatial relationship of one vertical and two horizontal axes, named by the architect X, Y, and Z. Holl emphasized the axis interaction with color standards developed for application on surfaces that pertain to each respective axis (*see* Bookcases, page 40).

A pivot is a key element in a composition based on Cartesian axes, as it allows rotation from one plane into another. One eye-catching element that incorporates all three axes of the overall composition is a multi-panel pivot door leading into a bedroom.

To emphasize this spatial transformation, Holl designed the door in three panels: two large overlapping panels that can open separately as "door" and "window," with a smaller "peephole" panel set into the latter. The first two pivot as "normal" doors—that is, about the Z axis—while the third pivots horizontally. All pieces are of the same color and thickness. When closed, the door appears a simple flat plane; when opened, the Cartesian geometry is "exploded" in all three directions. This multi-panel design underscores the basic idea of Cartesian geometry: that translation along, and rotation about, all three axes can describe all motion in three-dimensional space. A normal door, by contrast, would seem instead only to be "open" or "closed."

The entire door frame is 5′–6¾″ wide by 9′–1¼″ high. Constructed of ¾″-inch ash trim over gypsum wallboard, it reaches from the floor to a ½-inch reveal at the ceiling line. The doors are 1¾-inch-thick hollow-core ash construction. Both large doors are set on brass pivots mortised into both door and wood frame. The large vertical door's pivot is set 3¾ inches from the edge of the frame into an oiled ash saddle in the floor. At the pivot edge, a 1⅜″ × 5⅝″ piece of solid ash trim forms the frame, while also acting as a stop for the plaster on the outside of the bedroom wall.

The vertical door is 3′–6¾″ wide at the base, but a 2′–0″ × 2′–8″ cut is made into the upper corner to allow the 3′–2¼″-square "window panel" to overlap. Its pivot is set 10¼ inches back from its frame, or 3¾ inches from the joint with the large door.

The 9″ × 12″ vertical "peephole" window is set on the bottom edge of this square panel, 9 inches back from the joint between the two large doors. It rotates on a horizontal pin centered between its top and bottom edges.

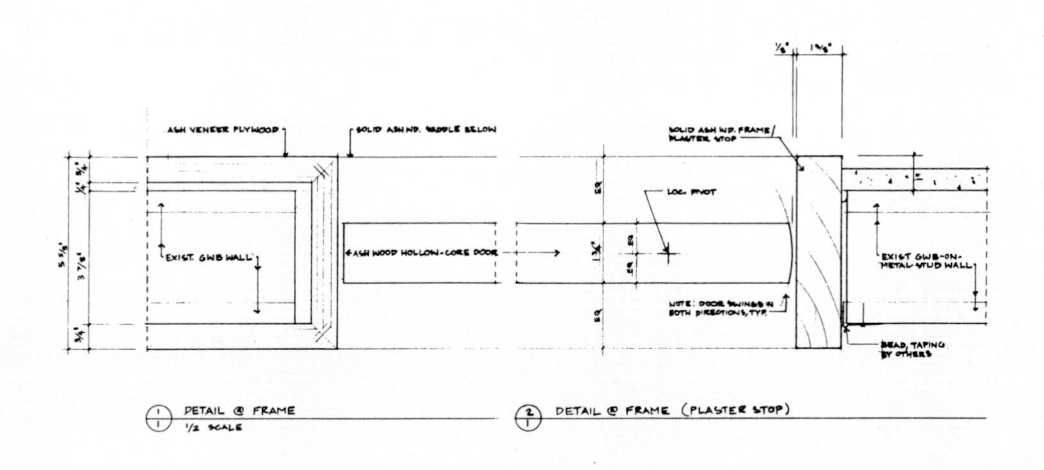

ASH VENEER PLYWOOD
SOLID ASH WD. SADDLE BELOW
EXIST. GWB WALL
ASH WOOD HOLLOW-CORE DOOR
5 5/8"
3 7/8"
3/4"
1/4"
LOC. PIVOT
EQ
1 3/4"
NOTE: DOOR SWINGS IN BOTH DIRECTIONS, TYP.
SOLID ASH WD. FRAME/ PLASTER STOP
1/8"
1 3/8"
EXIST GWB-ON-METAL-STUD WALL
BEAD, TAPING BY OTHERS
DETAIL @ FRAME
1/2 SCALE
DETAIL @ FRAME (PLASTER STOP)


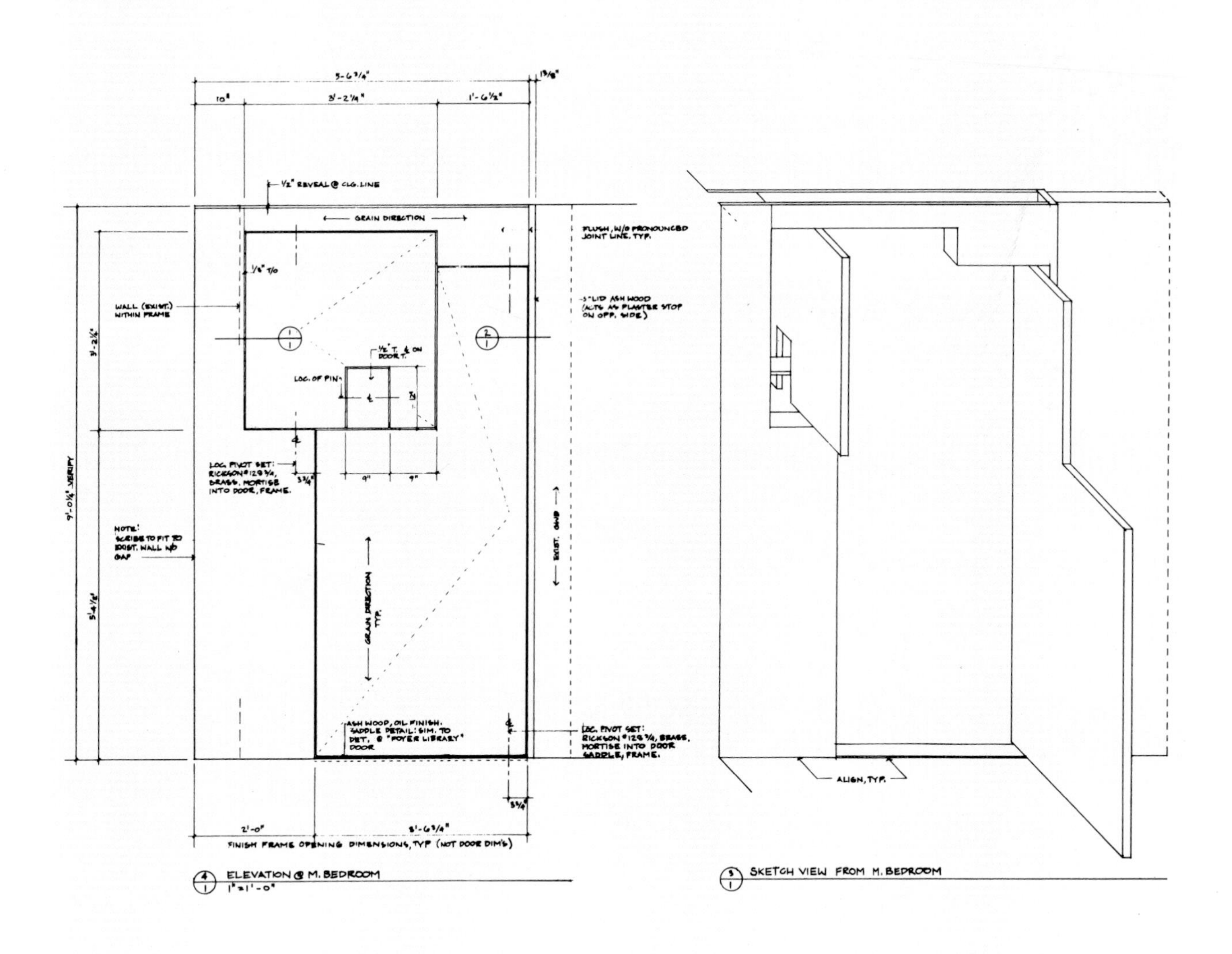

5-6 3/4"
1 3/8"
10"
3'-2 1/4"
1'-6 1/2"
1/2" REVEAL @ CLG. LINE
GRAIN DIRECTION
FLUSH, W/O PRONOUNCED JOINT LINE, TYP.
1/8" T/O
WALL (EXIST.) WITHIN FRAME
SOLID ASH WOOD (ACTS AS PLASTER STOP ON OPP. SIDE)
1/2" T. & ON DOOR T.
LOC. OF PIN
3'-2 1/4"
9'-0 1/4" VERIFY
LOC. PIVOT SET: RICKSON #128 3/4, BRASS, MORTISE INTO DOOR, FRAME.
3 3/4"
9"
9"
NOTE: SCRIBE TO FIT TO EXIST. WALL W/O GAP
GRAIN DIRECTION TYP.
EXIST. GWB
5'-4 1/2"
ASH WOOD, OIL FINISH. SADDLE DETAIL: SIM. TO DET. @ "FOYER LIBRARY" DOOR
LOC. PIVOT SET: RICKSON #128 3/4, BRASS, MORTISE INTO DOOR SADDLE, FRAME.
3 3/4"
2'-0"
3'-6 3/4"
FINISH FRAME OPENING DIMENSIONS, TYP (NOT DOOR DIM'S)
ELEVATION @ M. BEDROOM
1"=1'-0"
ALIGN, TYP.
SKETCH VIEW FROM M. BEDROOM

# Door

**Chelsea District Residence**
*New York, New York*

**Architect**
William McDonough Architects

**Design Team**
William A. McDonough, AIA, Principal;
Andrew Bartle, Project Assistant;
Joseph Vance, Drawings;
Daniel Radman, Drawings

**General Contractor**
Richard and Candy Harder,
Harder Construction

**Fabricator**
Will Parry Woodworking

**Photography**
© Christopher Little

A young business consultant and his graphic designer wife, constrained by a renovation budget of $30,000, were resigned to the prospect of only minimal architectural interest in their 1,000-square-foot penthouse loft in Manhattan's Chelsea district.

Architect William McDonough provided the couple with much, much more. Lucid spatial definition is enriched throughout the apartment by powerful, straightforward detailing that evokes the simple elegance of Zen calligraphy.

The new footprint of the loft is a loose variation of the classical nine-square plan. McDonough used the pattern of a gridded glass wall that forms one exterior edge of the square to derive a model for an interior wood and glass wall crossing the width of the apartment. Just as the exterior wall separates the exterior environment from the private apartment, the new wall, set on a smaller grid, separates the more public areas of the apartment from those that are private. Yet another grid of perforated metal light fixtures and exposed conduit intensifies this pattern in the plane of the ceiling (*axonometric*).

The patterns of both walls align with the grid of city streets outside. In deference to the twisted orientation of streets at Manhattan's southern tip, McDonough also introduced a line of walls, soffits, and counters on a true east-west orientation. This new plane provides a counterpoint to the geometry of existing walls and new grids, while also directing one's attention to the exterior views.

The interior grid wall performs a number of functions: incorporating a door to the study, ventilating windows, and double doors for the bedroom. The wall also becomes the doors of the kitchen cabinets, and at the top becomes a clerestory, allowing light to filter into every crevice of the apartment.

Although McDonough, as a matter of conscience, normally eschews the use of mahogany—favoring, instead, "woods that are not indigenous to the world's vanishing rain forests"—he accepted its use in this case because the boat builder/cabinetmaker wanted to use leftover materials from his shop. According to McDonough: "One of mahogany's most attractive characteristics is its stability and resistance to warping, swelling, and shrinking; usually we specify basswood [Linden] when the wood will be painted and we need dimensional stability."

The wall itself is set in wooden scribed pieces that were screwed through the existing ceiling and walls to blocking beyond, which created a reveal or shadow joint to

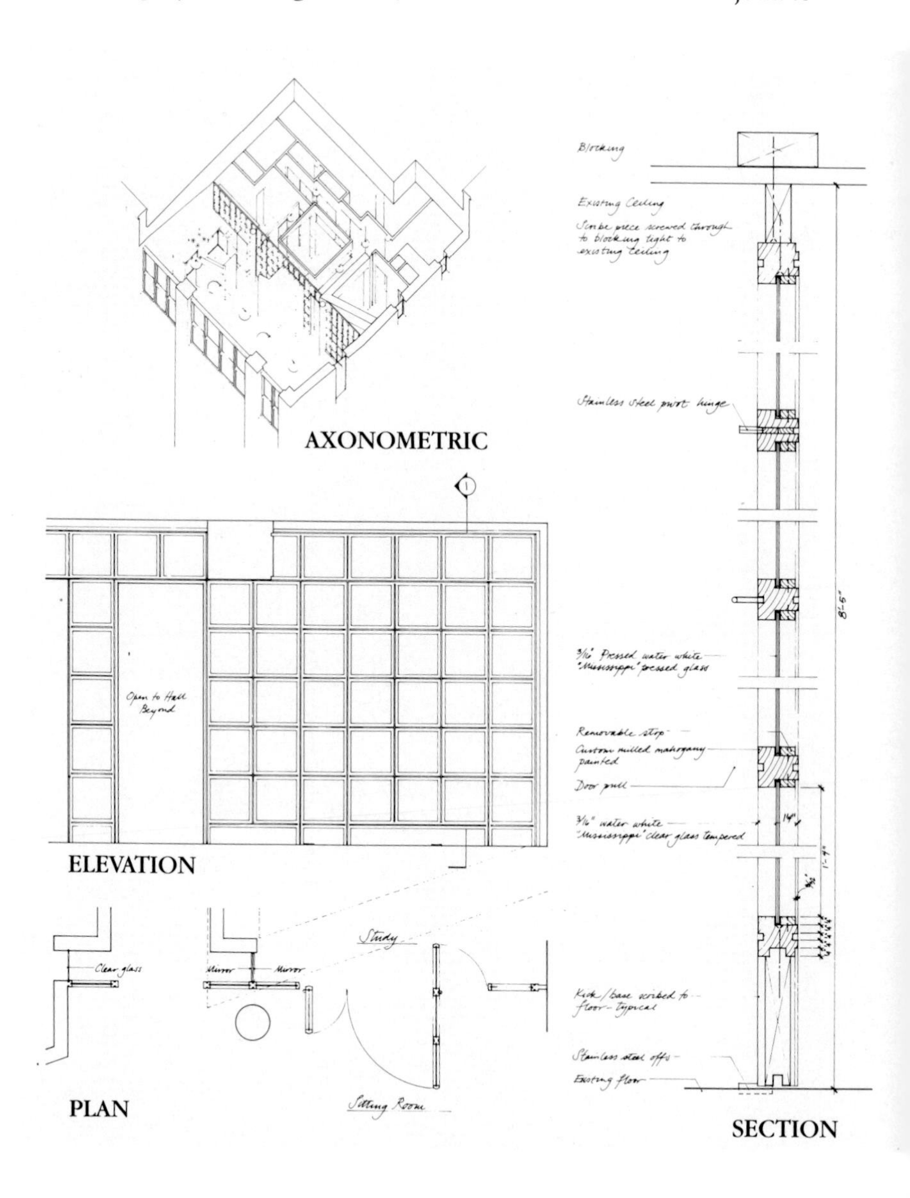

set the wall off from the surrounding architecture. The bottom of the wall was attached with screws to metal cleats that were themselves screwed into the wood floor.

The frame was constructed of custom-milled, painted mahogany, 1¼-inches square with rabbeted corners and reveals. The 3⁄16-inch pressed Mississippi white water glass panes are held in place with removable mahogany stops screwed to the frame. (McDonough is fond of this particular type of glass because it contains no iron and is, therefore, free of any green tinge.)

As in traditional Georgian architecture, in which consistent scale breaks down to smaller and smaller levels, the wall's wood detailing is larger on the living room side of the wall, smaller on the side of the smaller rooms. At the point where the wall divides the study from the living/dining room, the clients asked for an opening large enough to move their desk out of the study so that the space could be used as a guest bedroom as well. The size of the desk dictated an opening three panels wide; McDonough matched a single-panel door with a triple-panel pivot door to provide the appropriate clearance. Since the pivot rests on the one-third point of the larger door, the whole assembly is counterweighted with much more finesse than it would have been by a pair of double-panel doors. The clients view the detail solution somewhat more romantically—as "a ballerina performing a pirouette." The door's pivot hinges are stainless steel, inset flush with the floor on the bottom and set within the wood frame one panel from the top.

The sixteen center panes were fabricated of obscure glass to provide a degree of privacy and separation for the study, while the clear glass panes at the top, bottom, and sides allow a perception of the continuity of the apartment's volume.

## Michigan Avenue Apartment
*Chicago, Illinois*

**Architect**
Rudolph & Associates, P.C.

**Design Team**
Christopher H. Rudolph, AIA, Principal;
Lawrence M. Pettiti, Architect

**Fabricators**
Torben Jensen Woodcraft Co.;
Giannini & Hilgart
(stained glass)

**Photography**
© John Hollis Enterprises, Inc.

Doctors have precious little time to themselves; consequently, most feel that whatever time and privacy they have is precious. In discussing renovation plans for their 3,500-square-foot residence—located on Chicago's Michigan Avenue (*see* Floor Pattern, page 108)—two doctors who are also the parents of three children asked architect Christopher Rudolph to include a private library "sanctuary" within their home, an inner sanctum that could be either "open" to family conviviality or "closed" for much-needed solitude.

The clients and the architect agreed that floor-to-ceiling library cabinetry and shelving should be built out from three interior walls of the designated 20′–0″-square room, access to and from which was already established and limited to an existing archway on the fourth, hallway wall. The clients and architect further agreed that the Prairie School layered aesthetic endorsed for detailing throughout the entire residence should be rendered with particular freedom in the library.

Rudolph resolved the "open and closed" space problem in a single stroke by designing a stately pair of sliding stained and leaded glass doors that are mounted in front of the library entrance. The doors represent not only an outstanding adaptation of the Prairie School's approach to geometry and craftsmanship, but represent, when closed, a definitive but non-threatening barrier to intrusion.

The strikingly unornamented 6′–11″ × 3′–6″ door frames were constructed of solid 2¼-inch stained and hand-rubbed cherry (*library doors, 3*). Because each door frame weighs approximately 600 pounds, segments were joined together with dowels to achieve extra rigidity and strength. Double sets of ornamental rails were fabricated of platinum-stained white oak.

For the construction of the glass door panes, Rudolph enlisted talented craftsmen from Giannini & Hilgart—an authorized assembler of Tiffany-made glass, as well as the primary stained and leaded glass source for Louis Sullivan, George Elmslie, and Frank Lloyd Wright. Rudolph's pattern of custom-colored glass panels from Germany and domestic clear glass was carefully assembled with lead caming, then wrapped in soldered brass.

The sliding doors roll on sheaves that rest on a brass track, which is routed into the hardwood floor (*library door, 2*). No rollers or glides are used at the tops of the doors, which slide between blocking bolted to the inner surfaces of the soffits in effortless motion.

One step beyond the doors lies a granite threshold, enigmatically highlighted with a single dark granite square (*library doors, 3*). One or more steps beyond Prairie School allusion is the library ceiling, designed and rendered "to deceive the eye into perceiving a greater expanse through open, or behind closed, doors."

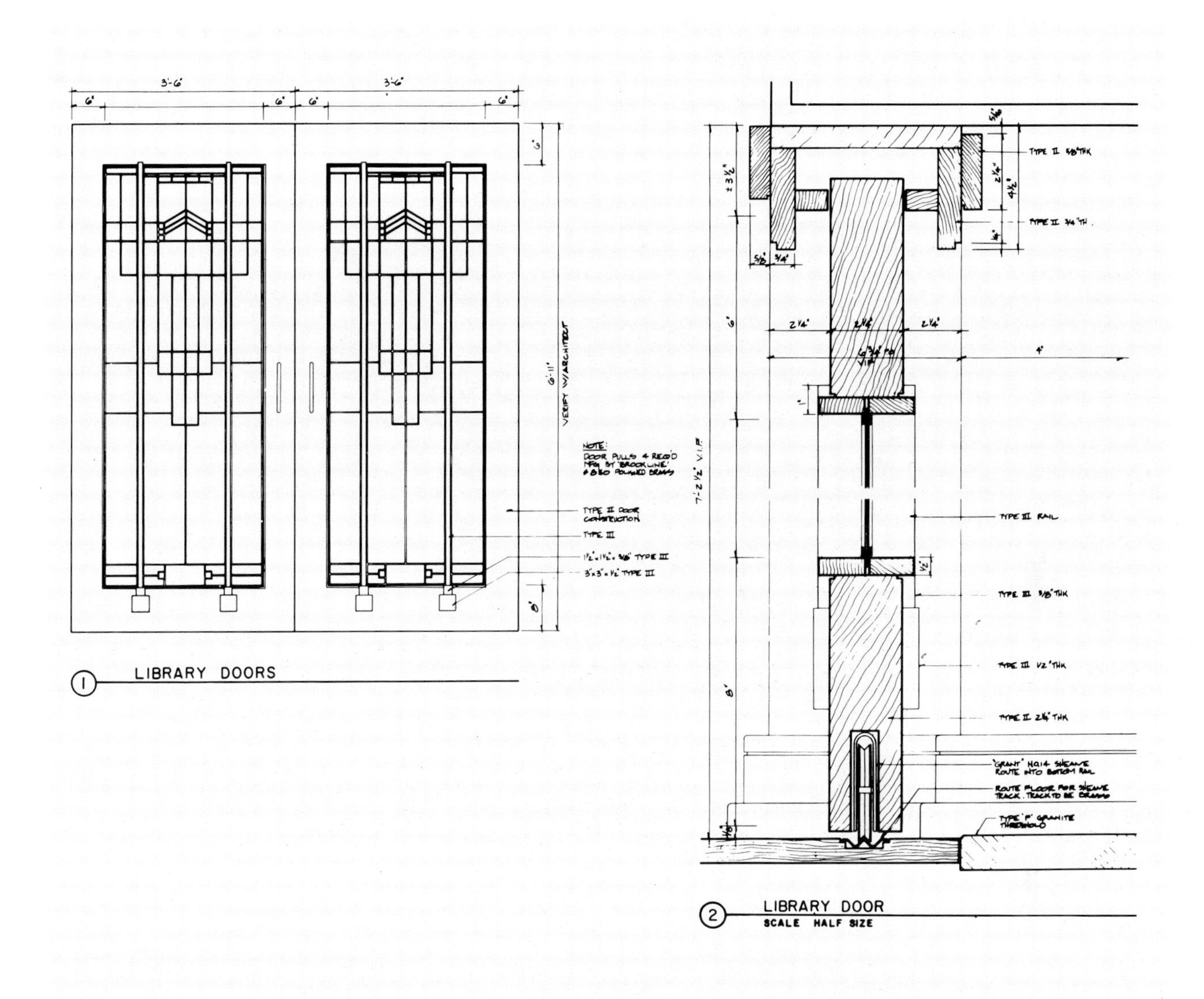
LIBRARY DOORS
LIBRARY DOOR
SCALE HALF SIZE
TYPE II DOOR CONSTRUCTION
TYPE III
TYPE III RAIL
TYPE II 2¼" THK
ROUTE FLOOR FOR SHEAVE TRACK. TRACK TO BE BRASS
TYPE 'F' GRANITE THRESHOLD

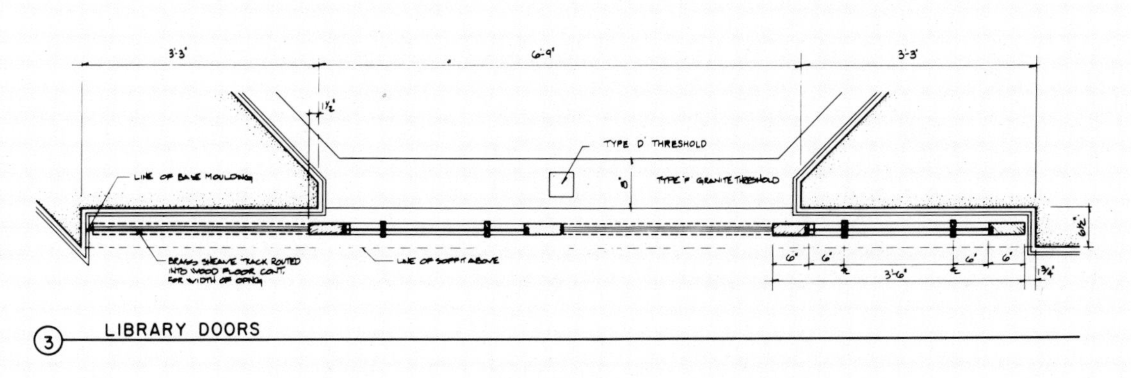
LIBRARY DOORS
TYPE 'D' THRESHOLD
TYPE 'F' GRANITE THRESHOLD
LINE OF BASE MOULDING
LINE OF SOFFIT ABOVE

# Door

## Harborside Residence

*Baltimore, Maryland*

**Interior Designer**
Rita St. Clair Associates, Inc.

**Design Team**
Rita St. Clair, FASID,
Principal-in-Charge;
Ted Pearson, ASID, Project Assistant

**Fabricators**
Kardell Studios (leaded and stained glass); Hough Woodworks (millwork and cabinetry)

**Photography**
© Tim Fields

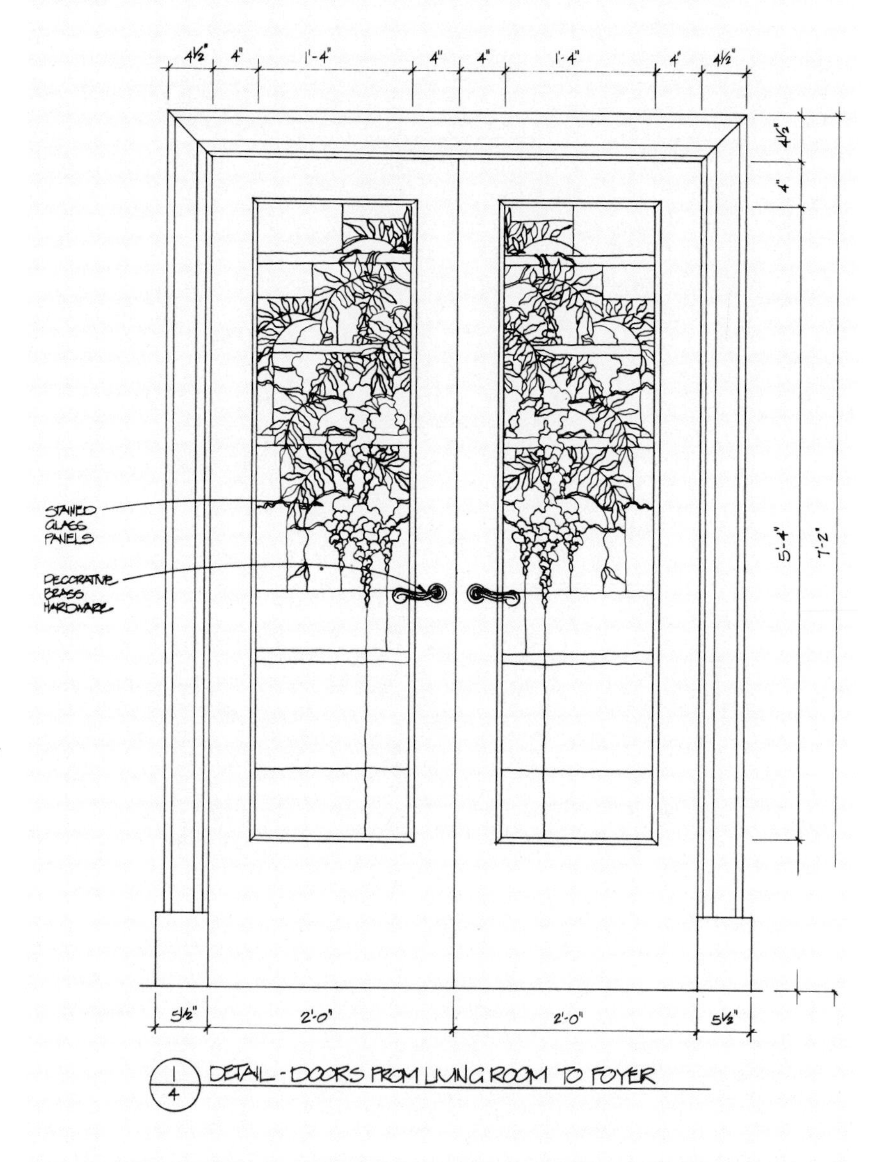


UPON ENTERING this Baltimore waterfront townhouse, one looks across a long entry foyer and stair hall to a handsome set of double doors that lead to the library. Because the library receives strong western sun in the afternoon, interior designer Rita St. Clair designed doors of stained glass that diffuse light as they illuminate the end of the foyer and create a focal point opposite the entry.

The doors' 4-inch stiles (1′–0″ at the base) were fabricated of cherry, as were the 4½-inch jamb and head moldings. Handsome as these elements are, attention is grabbed by two 1′–4″ × 5′–4″ leaded glass panels that depict wisteria foliage in natural colors, lending a Tiffany touch to the doors themselves and to the interior as a whole. The panels are possessed of a modern graphic design twist, however; the wisteria leaves and blossoms penetrate the compositional margins to drape over the lead and glass bands that divide one panel from the next. Decorative solid brass levers complete the door composition.

Other elements within the foyer composition include an antique brass light fixture on the ceiling, stock-patterned encaustic English floor tile, and a set of arched closet doors with trompe l'oeil niches painted on them. The doors, which conceal coat and firewood closets and a water heater, appear to contain niches for books, model ships, and other memorabilia beloved by the owners.

St. Clair designed a number of other details for the house that were rendered with similar attention to quality (*see* Bathroom Cabinets, page 28; Railing, page 168; Storage Cabinets, page 208).

## Private Residence

*Englewood, New Jersey*

**Architect**
Norman Jaffe, AIA, P.C., Architects

**Design Team**
Norman Jaffe, AIA, Architect;
Keith Boyce, Project Associate;
George W. Bradley, Project Associate

**Fabricator**
Ebner Woodwork Corporation

**Photography**
© Jeff Heatley

An eclectic assortment of turn-of-the-century mansions in Bergen City, New Jersey, provided the setting for a new 14,000-square-foot "traditional" house by Norman Jaffe.

The clients' priorities were essentially contradictory: although the house was to relate to the immediate architectural environment, it was to be a strictly contemporary environment. Other client considerations included large, quasi-public areas for entertaining, and private areas for teenage children.

Jaffe resolved the apparent dichotomy by allowing the local prevalence of masonry construction (brownstone, limestone, and brick), sloping roofs, and large gardens to influence the more modern forms.

As a parallel to this contrast between old and new, Jaffe juxtaposed massive walls finished in limestone with lighter, smaller elements—columns, doors, railings, and panels—made of redwood, teak, mahogany, and other woods.

Wood detailing allowed Jaffe to develop, in his modern forms, a richness usually associated with more traditional building techniques. The door Jaffe created as a standard for this project is framed by wood-paneled walls with solid wood trim; five horizontal mahogany boards, set back from the wall above, form the door's head. The jointed tongue-and-groove boards were set over ⅝-inch gypsum board supported by two 2x header beams. Right-angle joints were mitered and glued; a ½″ × 2⅛″ piece of solid wood trim, mitered to the panel on one side of the header, formed the stop. The edge of the jamb—similarly constructed except that it was supported by 2 × 4 studs with leveling shims—was set back ½ inch from the face of the header.

The door itself was constructed of mahogany veneer over a conventional solid core. The core was joined to 2¼″-thick × 7″-wide solid mahogany stiles on both sides with a ½″ × 2″ continuous oak spline. The spline, the joint between the "traditionally" constructed solid oak spline and the more contemporary core-and-veneer panel, is visible through a ¼-inch reveal.

The veneer panels were flush-jointed together, with 1″ × 3″ × ¼″ deep reveals at the base of each of the eight joints. Horizontal reveals, ½″ × ¼″ deep, mark the top of the upper set of veneer panels and the bottom of the lower set. The arrangement of the panels is reminiscent of traditional door construction.

Jaffe's door sits on pivots top and bottom; the centerline of its oil-rubbed brass Schlage hardware—a 6¼-inch plate with 3/12-inch lever—was set 3′–0″ off the floor. The plate was epoxied flush to the door surface by rabbeting out the wood rail.

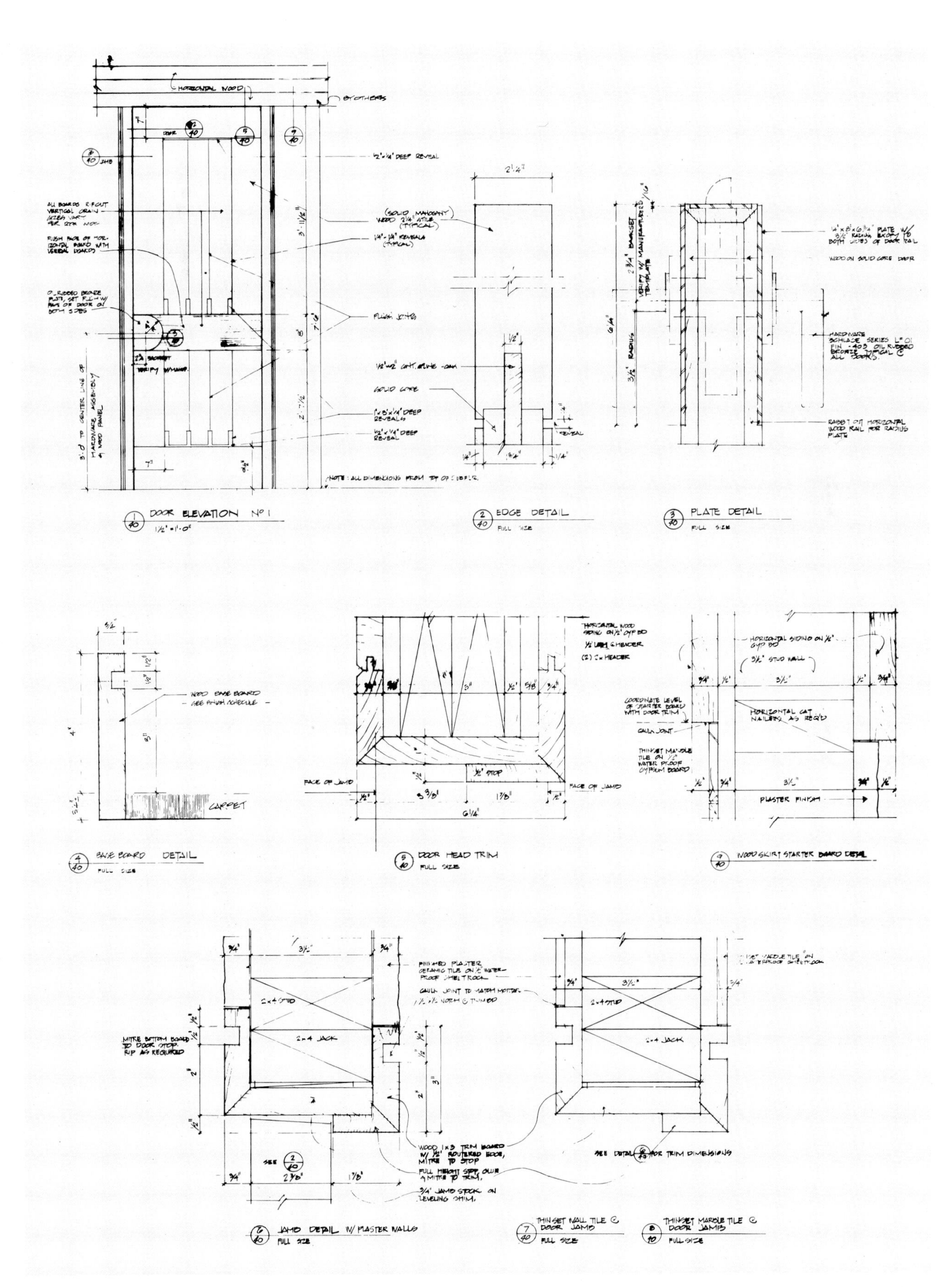
DOOR ELEVATION Nº 1
1½" = 1'-0"
EDGE DETAIL
FULL SIZE
PLATE DETAIL
FULL SIZE
BASE BOARD DETAIL
FULL SIZE
DOOR HEAD TRIM
FULL SIZE
WOOD SKIRT STARTER BOARD DETAIL
JAMB DETAIL W/ PLASTER WALLS
FULL SIZE
THIN-SET WALL TILE @ DOOR JAMB
FULL SIZE
THIN-SET MARBLE TILE @ DOOR JAMB
FULL SIZE
HORIZONTAL WOOD
FLUSH JOINTS
SOLID CORE
CARPET
PLASTER FINISH
2×4 STUD
2×4 JACK

# Door Surround

## Greenwich Village Residence
*New York, New York*

**Architect**
William McDonough Architects

**Design Team**
William A. McDonough, AIA, Principal;
Carl Finer, Project Assistant;
Joseph Vance, Project Assistant

**General Contractor**
Romac Construction

**Fabricator**
Mison, Inc. (steelwork)

**Photography**
© H. Durston Saylor

A MANHATTAN COUPLE—both of whom are well known in the worlds of publishing, fashion, and design, and who are jointly the parents of four children—commissioned architect William McDonough to renovate their four-story Greenwich Village townhouse. The existing space and its decor were surprisingly, and intentionally, unglamorous—the clients—originally from England—prefer their home to be an understated, comfortable environment in which their children may enjoy equal rights.

An important functional consideration in planning the renovation was to foil the drafts of cold air that persistently penetrated the building shell during winter months. The architect responded with a no-nonsense, door surround detail that, in conjunction with the existing entry door, creates an airlock.

Working with an average budget, McDonough developed a simple and serviceable—yet refined—door/door surround that is as unobtrusive as it is direct in problem solving. The appeal of a Georgian house, he felt, lay in its consistent features at all levels of detail. According to the architect: "A previous renovation had included the insertion of raw steel square tube columns and beams in the parlor space. Because the new door surround would mark the entry to an updated nineteenth-century townhouse, its design had to provide consistency within a new architectural language."

The architect placed a painted wood door, similar to the existing entry door, within a frame of glass and steel—the door becoming the only solid object in a transparent, ephemeral setting. The placement of the frame's members was determined by the door's outer dimensions, as though the frame was merely an extension of the borders of the object it contains. The frame is set into mirrored recesses within the wall; the brief reflections from these create an infinite perspective reminiscent of the visual layering apparent in John Soane's house in London.

The steel frame of the door surround was constructed of cold-rolled ½″ × 2″ square bar stock. Glass panels are held in place with ⅜-inch removable square stops (*plan section; section*). The steel sections, which also create the doorstop in the head of the door frame, are held in place with flush head

screws to minimize the perception of the frame's parts.

The frame is supported by wood blocking in the walls and ceiling: four 2 × 4s in the ceiling and the wall that support the hinge and smaller 1x blocking in the opposite wall. The ⅝-inch cuts in the ceiling and walls were finished with metal L-bead wrapped around each corner. One-eighth-inch-thick strips of mirror polish stainless steel form the "lining" of the 3-inch-wide recesses, their reflective surfaces allowing the frame to "disappear" into the wall. These thin strips were screwed from the back into 1¾" × ½" painted steel bar stock, which was then counterscrewed back into the wood blocking. On the wall with 1x blocking, the screws pass through the blocking into the brick wall beyond.

The inside face of this "primary frame" is now flush with the original wall surface. The frame serves as a ½-inch spacer, separating it from the wall and giving it the sense of an independent, detached object.

Another length of slightly wider 2" × ½" bar stock, with ⅜-inch square steel stops for one side of the glass already welded into place, was then screwed into the primary frame. Laminated safety glass was set into this "secondary frame," and the removable ⅜-inch steel stops were screwed into place.

The standard door matches the outside door and is constructed of solid wood stiles 9 inches wide at the base of the door, which surround four plywood panels with ¾-inch solid wood molding trim. The door rests on pivot hinges—the top hinge is attached to the steel frame, the bottom hinge to the floor. A brass olive knob completes the door hardware.

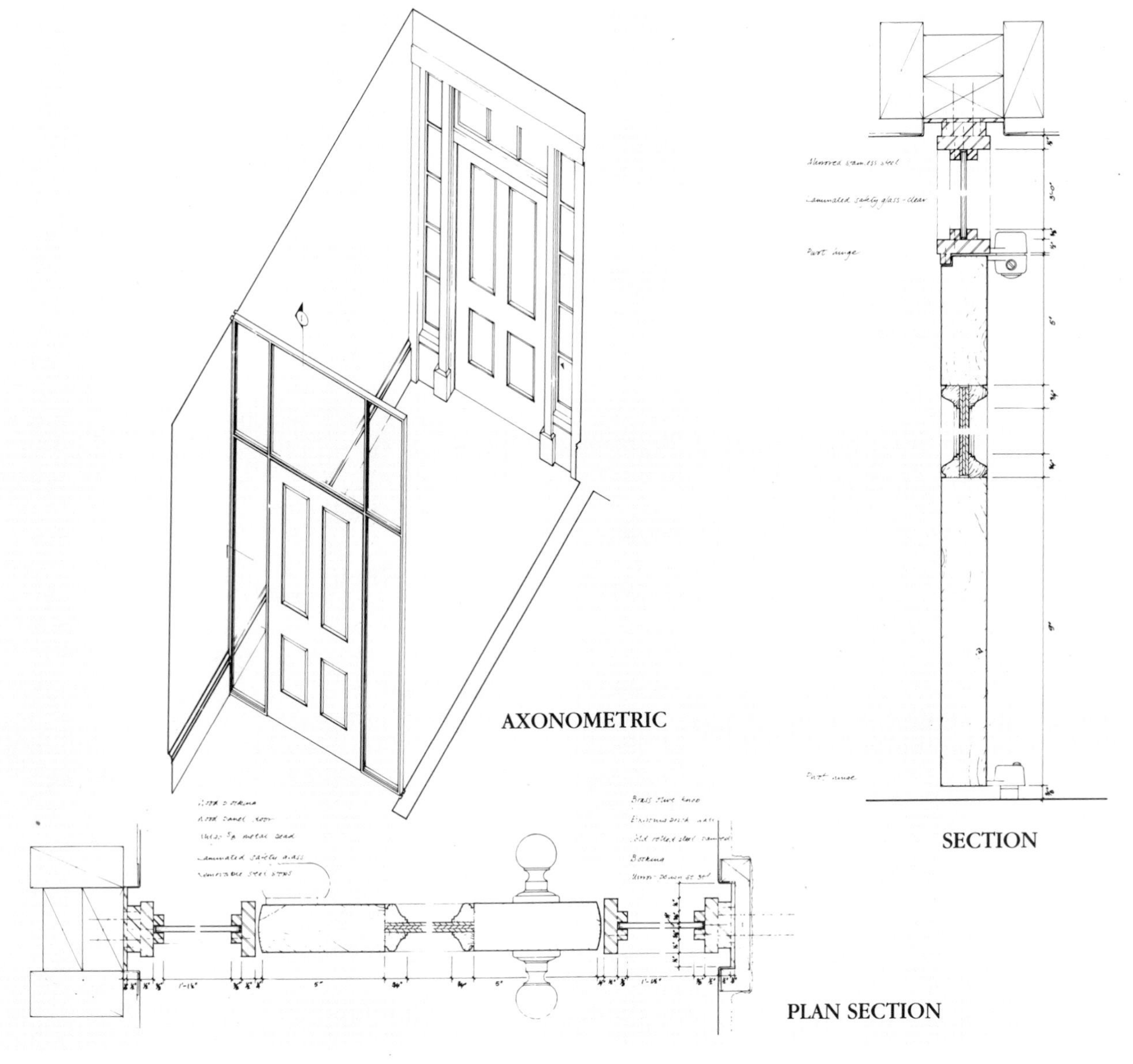

# Entertainment Center

**Takami Takahashi Residence**
*Kahala, Oahu, Hawaii*

**Interior Designer**
Sally Sirkin Interior Designs

**Design Team**
Sally Sirkin Lewis, Senior Designer; David Wheat, Project Designer/Coordinator; Ken Newman, AIA, Project Architect; James Picotte, Assistant

**Fabricators**
Banner Construction Company (general contractor); Audio Command Systems (audiovisual equipment); Amsco (doors)

**Photography**
© Peter Vitale

The luxury of almost limitless space is the primary impression derived from a quick perusal of this expertly composed and edited living room. But truth is often stranger than fiction: this elegant, "clean sweep" interior is part of a Hawaiian condominium that contains, in its entirety, only 2,000 square feet. Los Angeles–based interior designer Sally Sirkin Lewis created the illusory spaciousness of the apartment for a sophisticated Japanese client who desired "a contemplative environment of simplicity and serenity," and, on a more pragmatic level, wanted to "view the ocean and watch television, simultaneously."

Sirkin initially faced an inviolate building standard shell "overwhelmed by too many doors and long, sacrosanct windows." The imposition of an entertainment center containing a wet bar, a large screen television, stereo equipment, and appropriate storage shelves, therefore, necessitated the development of an interior wall storage cabinet.

The generic entertainment center concept pales in comparison to Sirkin's urbane rendition. The 12′–0″ × 2′–6″ cabinet was constructed of pedestrian plywood subframing, over which—thanks to a generous budget allocation—a number of custom components and sleek finish materials were applied. When closed off, the client's entertainment center now glows with the richness of burnished stainless steel doors; when open, it glitters with refractions from glass, mirror, and lacquer surfaces (*elevation*).

Attention to detail is a Sirkin hallmark; consequently, details within the detail are worthy of note. Flush-fitted doors open smoothly on pivot hinges bolted into the floor and into the headers (*pivot and jamb details*); the television picture tube is recessed into the wall (*plan*), while a touch-latch panel beneath the screen allows projection components to roll forward; the bar countertop is fabricated of back-painted glass; and all glass shelves are 1-inch thick. The interior of the cabinet is evenly washed, without flare spots, by 1-inch tubular strip lamps.

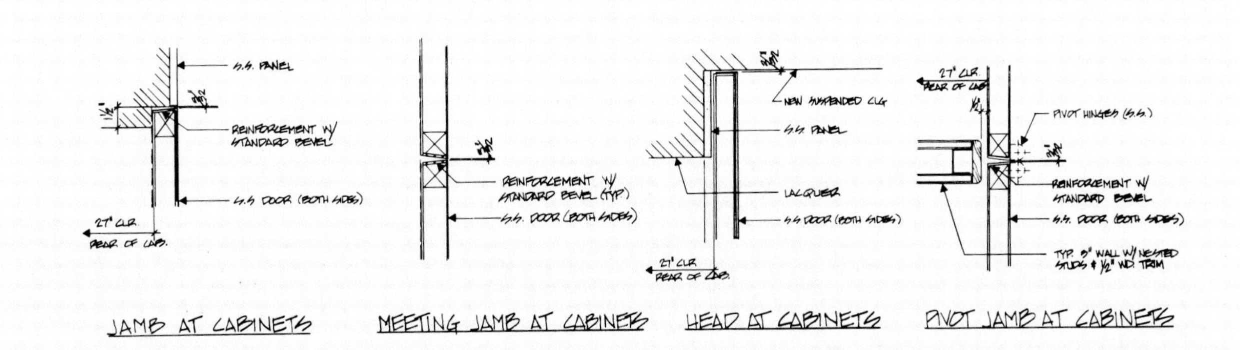
S.S. PANEL
REINFORCEMENT W/ STANDARD BEVEL
S.S. DOOR (BOTH SIDES)
27" CLR. REAR OF CABS.
REINFORCEMENT W/ STANDARD BEVEL (TYP)
S.S. DOOR (BOTH SIDES)
NEW SUSPENDED CLG
S.S. PANEL
LACQUER
S.S. DOOR (BOTH SIDES)
27" CLR. REAR OF CABS.
27" CLR. REAR OF CABS.
PIVOT HINGES (S.S.)
REINFORCEMENT W/ STANDARD BEVEL
S.S. DOOR (BOTH SIDES)
TYP. 5" WALL W/ NESTED STUDS & 1/2" WD. TRIM
JAMB AT CABINETS
MEETING JAMB AT CABINETS
HEAD AT CABINETS
PIVOT JAMB AT CABINETS

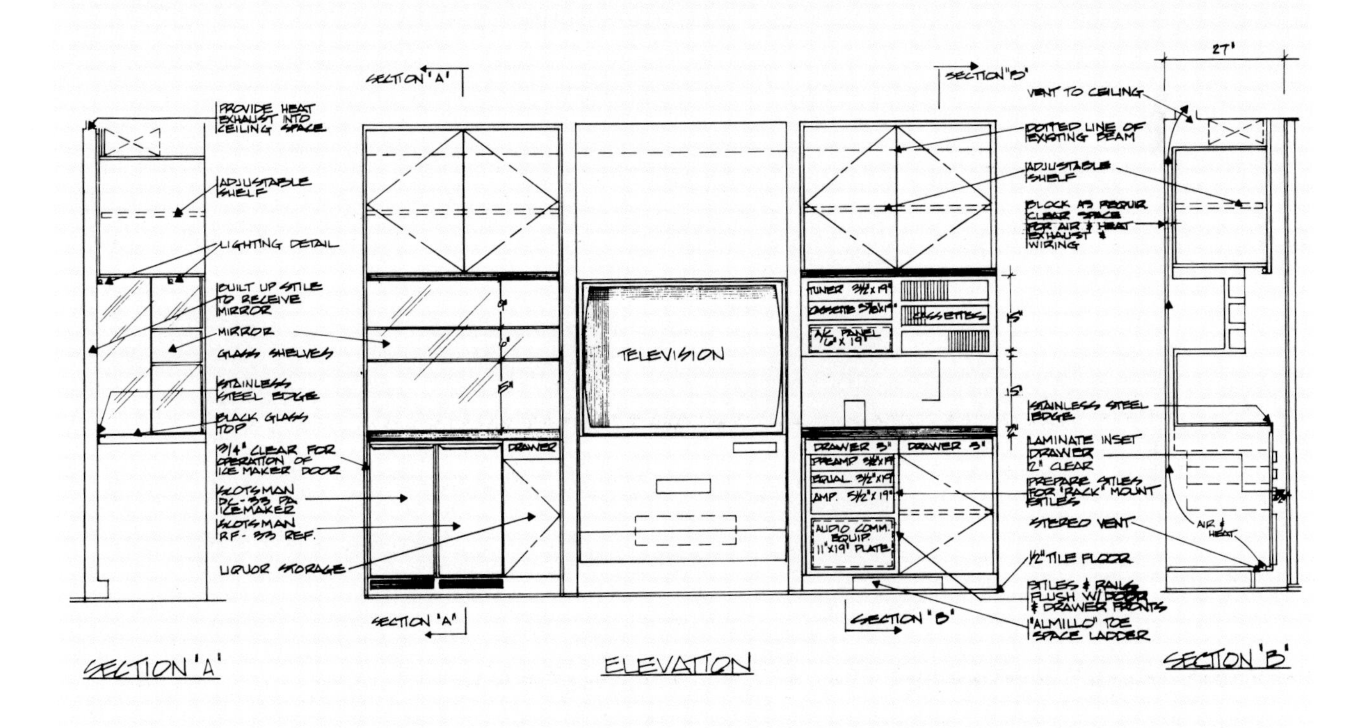
SECTION 'A'
SECTION 'B'
PROVIDE HEAT EXHAUST INTO CEILING SPACE
ADJUSTABLE SHELF
LIGHTING DETAIL
BUILT UP STILE TO RECEIVE MIRROR
MIRROR
GLASS SHELVES
STAINLESS STEEL EDGE
BLACK GLASS TOP
13/4" CLEAR FOR OPERATION OF ICE MAKER DOOR
SCOTSMAN DC-33 PA ICEMAKER
SCOTSMAN RF-33 REF.
LIQUOR STORAGE
DRAWER
TELEVISION
TUNER 3½x19
CASSETTE 5¾x19
A/C PANEL 12 x 19
CASSETTES
DRAWER 3"
DRAWER 3"
PREAMP 3½x19
EQUAL 3½x19
AMP. 5½x19
AUDIO COMM. EQUIP. 11x19 PLATE
VENT TO CEILING
DOTTED LINE OF EXISTING BEAM
ADJUSTABLE SHELF
BLOCK AS REQUIR. CLEAR SPACE FOR AIR & HEAT EXHAUST & WIRING
STAINLESS STEEL EDGE
LAMINATE INSET DRAWER 12" CLEAR
PREPARE STILES FOR "RACK" MOUNT STILES
STEREO VENT
1/2" TILE FLOOR
STILES & RAILS FLUSH W/ DOOR & DRAWER FRONTS
"ALMILLO" TOE SPACE LADDER
AIR & HEAT
27"
15"
SECTION 'A'
ELEVATION
SECTION 'B'

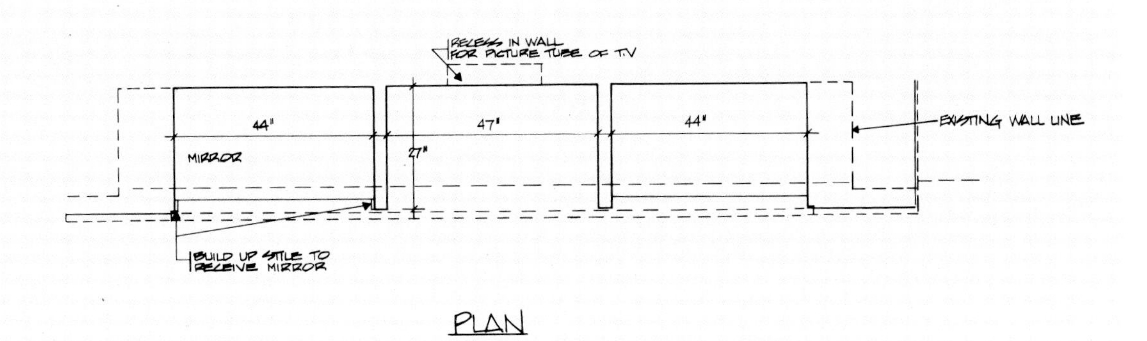
RECESS IN WALL FOR PICTURE TUBE OF T.V.
44"
47"
44"
27"
MIRROR
EXISTING WALL LINE
BUILD UP STILE TO RECEIVE MIRROR

PLAN

## ELLIOTT–GRUEN RESIDENCE
*Western Pennsylvania*

**Architect**
Centerbrook Architects

**Design Team**
Jefferson B. Riley, AIA, Partner-in-Charge; Julia Miner, AIA, Project Manager

**Fabricator**
Nicely and Nicely (general contractor and millworker)

**Photography**
© Norman McGrath

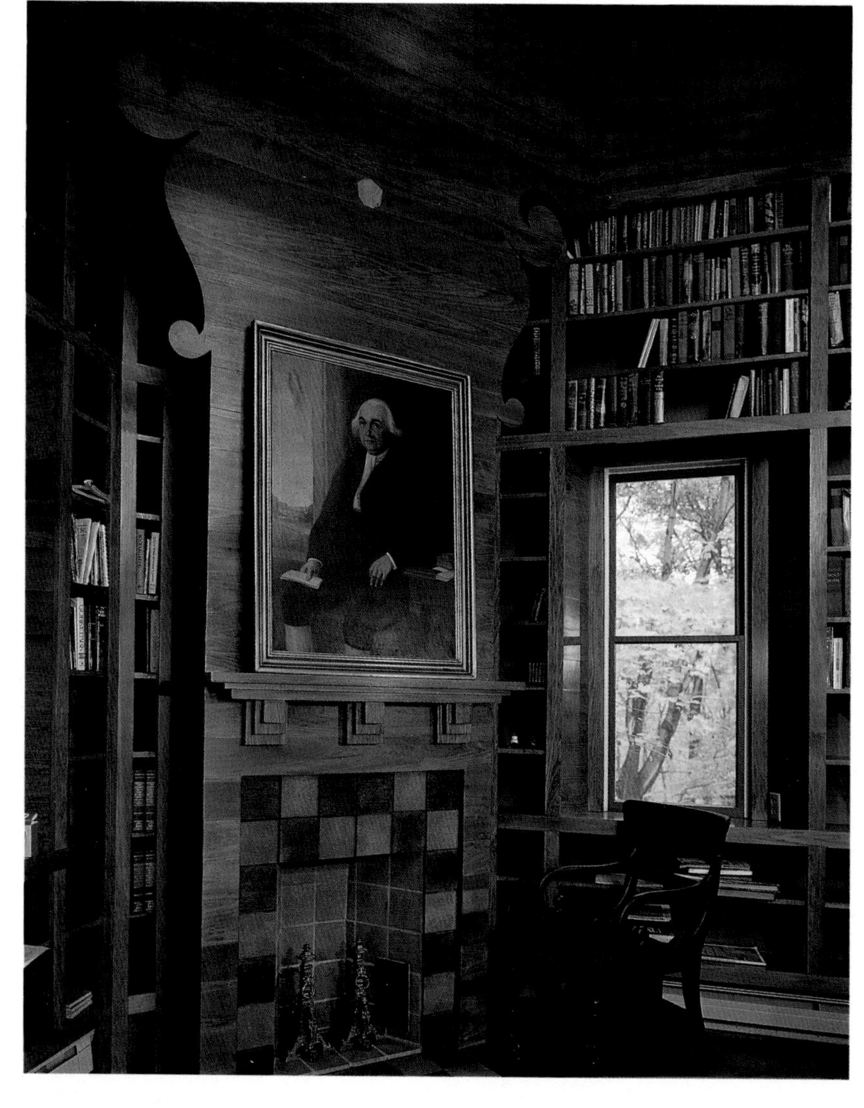

NON-READERS TEND TO "DECORATE" their libraries with books that are either indiscriminately purchased in lots at auction, or bought from dealers who sell books by the running foot. Such a cold-blooded approach was anathema to author Peter Gruen and artist/sculptor Anne Elliott, who developed the concept for their country house library quite differently.

In addition to offering Centerbrook of Essex, Connecticut, personal ideas on design direction, Gruen and Elliott allowed a few of their many all-time favorite books to "speak for themselves." In meetings with the project design team, the clients read passages from the works of, among others, Dashiell Hammett, Cicero, and selected Tibetan philosophers. "The quotes," according to Centerbrook's Jeff Riley, "gave us real direction as to the size and mood and color that this room should be."

Because Centerbrook already had designed individual, private studios for the clients, the joint library in the main house was developed in just 225 square feet. Although the dimensions of the room are small, Centerbrook devised—on a "very modest" project budget—a library that is rich in both textural quality and literary allusion.

Per Centerbrook's specifications, the project millworker, Glenn Nicely, used 1 × 6 boards of solid poplar to construct all the paneling sections, ceiling segments, and bookcases. A feeling of permanence and solidity emanates from the installed millwork because dimensioning of elevation elements is overscaled; horizontal headers, vertical casings, and shelf aprons are all more generously proportioned than those found in more standard constructions. Bookshelves extend floor to ceiling; accessibility to higher shelves is provided by a library ladder that glides on casters around the circumference of the room on a continuous track attached at the soffit line.

To achieve the seamless, integrated appearance of the paneled walls and ceiling, individual paneling boards were laid horizontally, attached with wood screws to studs placed 16 inches on center; all corner joints were mitered. The paneling was alternately cherry stained and sanded, then finished with wax/polyurethane.

The focal point of this handsome tray-ceiling library is a freespirited fireplace façade, which was designed and drawn—on-site and freehand—by Jeff Riley. The blithe, sensuous curve of the overmantel expresses, abstractly, the uplifting sense of delight that contact with good prose can bring. The serendipitous form was jigsaw-cut, by Nicely, from a full-scale paper template that was taped to extended paneling boards.

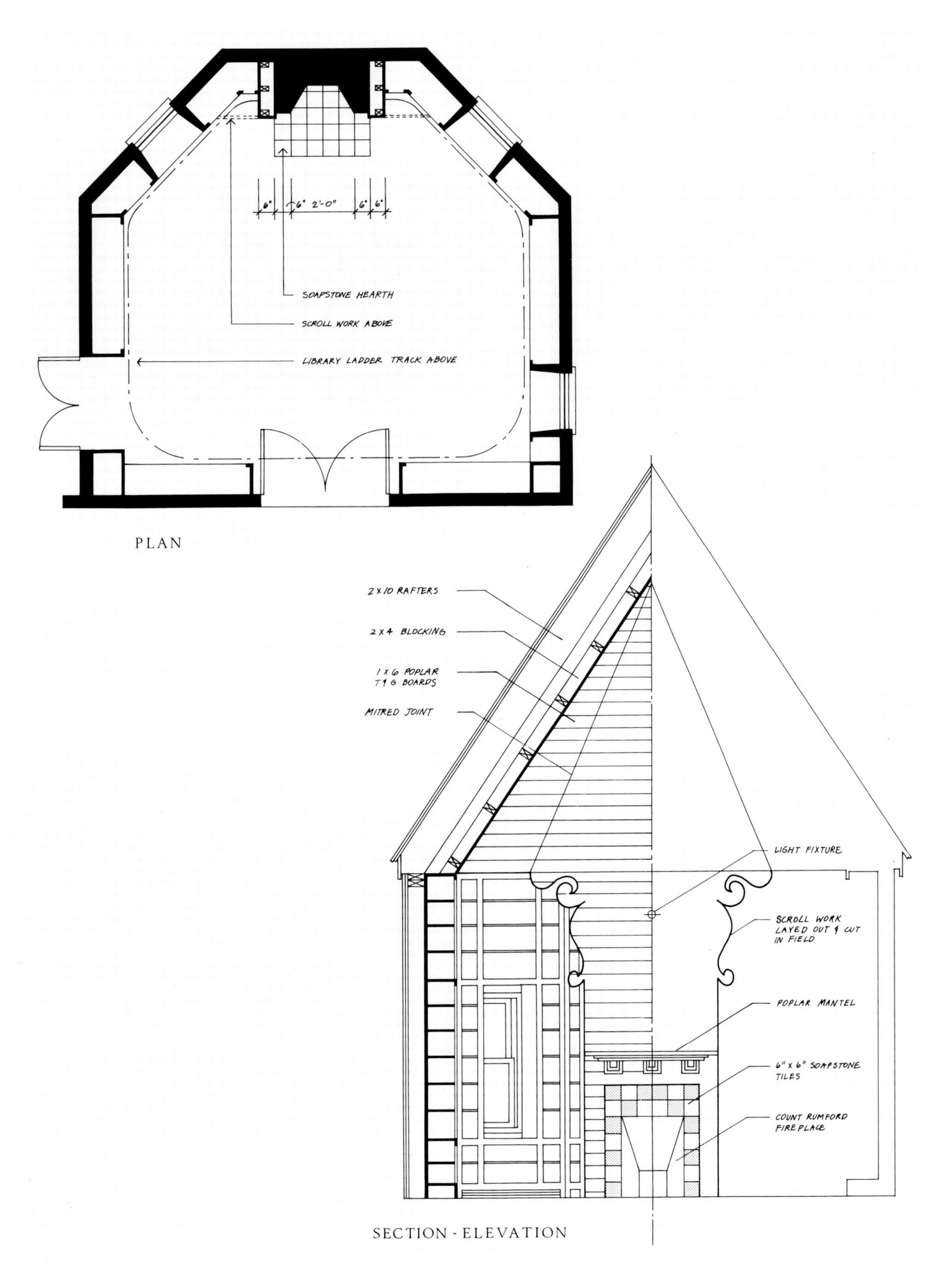
6"
6"
2'-0"
6"
6"
SOAPSTONE HEARTH
SCROLL WORK ABOVE
LIBRARY LADDER TRACK ABOVE
2 x 10 RAFTERS
2 x 4 BLOCKING
1 x 6 POPLAR
T & G BOARDS
MITRED JOINT
LIGHT FIXTURE
SCROLL WORK
LAYED OUT & CUT
IN FIELD
POPLAR MANTEL
6" x 6" SOAPSTONE
TILES
COUNT RUMFORD
FIREPLACE

PLAN

SECTION - ELEVATION

# FIREPLACE

## PRIVATE GUEST HOUSE
*Seattle, Washington*

**Architect**
James Cutler Architects

**Design Team**
James Cutler, AIA, Principal;
Bruce Anderson, Project Architect

**General Contractor**
Charter Construction

**Fabricators**
H. P. Frisch (masonry);
Charter Construction (concrete);
Mastro Woodworking (cabinets);
Northeastern Trawl Systems, Inc. (andirons)

**Photography**
© Peter Aaron/ESTO

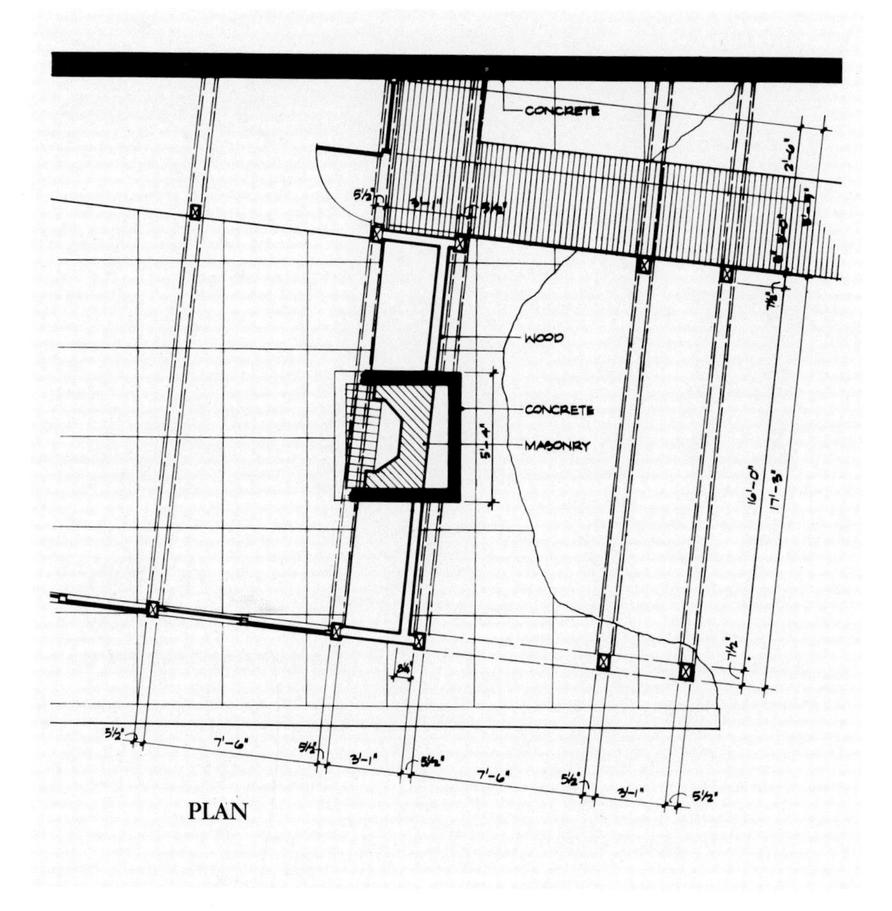


PLAN

LONG VISITS from out-of-town family and friends are events to be looked forward to and enjoyed, yet few people would dispute the fact that separate guest quarters simplify and enhance the experience. This, at least, was the opinion of a northwestern couple who in 1987 commissioned architect James Cutler to design a 1,800-square-foot guest house close—but not next to—their home.

Per client request, the architect situated the new structure "out of the direct line of vision from the main house, with as little impact on the surrounding forest as possible." Cutler accomplished what might otherwise have been something of an architectural conjuring trick, by digging the building into a topographical depression that occurred naturally on the property. The significant concrete retaining wall that was necessitated by Cutler's solution led to his description of the project as one consisting of heavy concrete "earth" elements juxtaposed against light wood "house" elements. Each primary element, according to the architect, "exists on its own discrete orthogonal axis." He adds: "Earth elements are an immutable, preexisting condition; house elements are a new, ephemeral response to that condition."

Cutler's elements take final form as a thoughtfully, and cerebrally planned, guest house that is—on its exterior—sensitively sited in concrete and clad in fir siding, while the interior walls of the house—spatially divided between a cluster of private bedrooms and a communal living room—are faced in finished fir paneling.

Because the two orthogonal axes are only 3–4 degrees apart, the guest house fireplace is the only point within the house where earth and house elements meet (*plan*). Consequently, the architect detailed the shallow, Rumford fireplace to reflect that special relationship, utilizing broken concrete and fir paneling in its mantel design (*interior elevation*).

The construction of the fireplace mantel was, according to the architect, "simple to build and difficult to refine" (*section*). The difficulty lay in the malleability of the concrete. In order to present a fractured, organic appearance to complement the exterior form of the fireplace (*exterior elevation*), the masonry had to be attacked by hand with a hammer; however, because the concrete had set "too long," the subtle shaving and shaping Cutler had envisioned was difficult to achieve. Cutler offers a word of wisdom to any craftsman attempting a similar effect: "Sculpt the concrete within a day and a half instead of waiting, as we did, for a week."

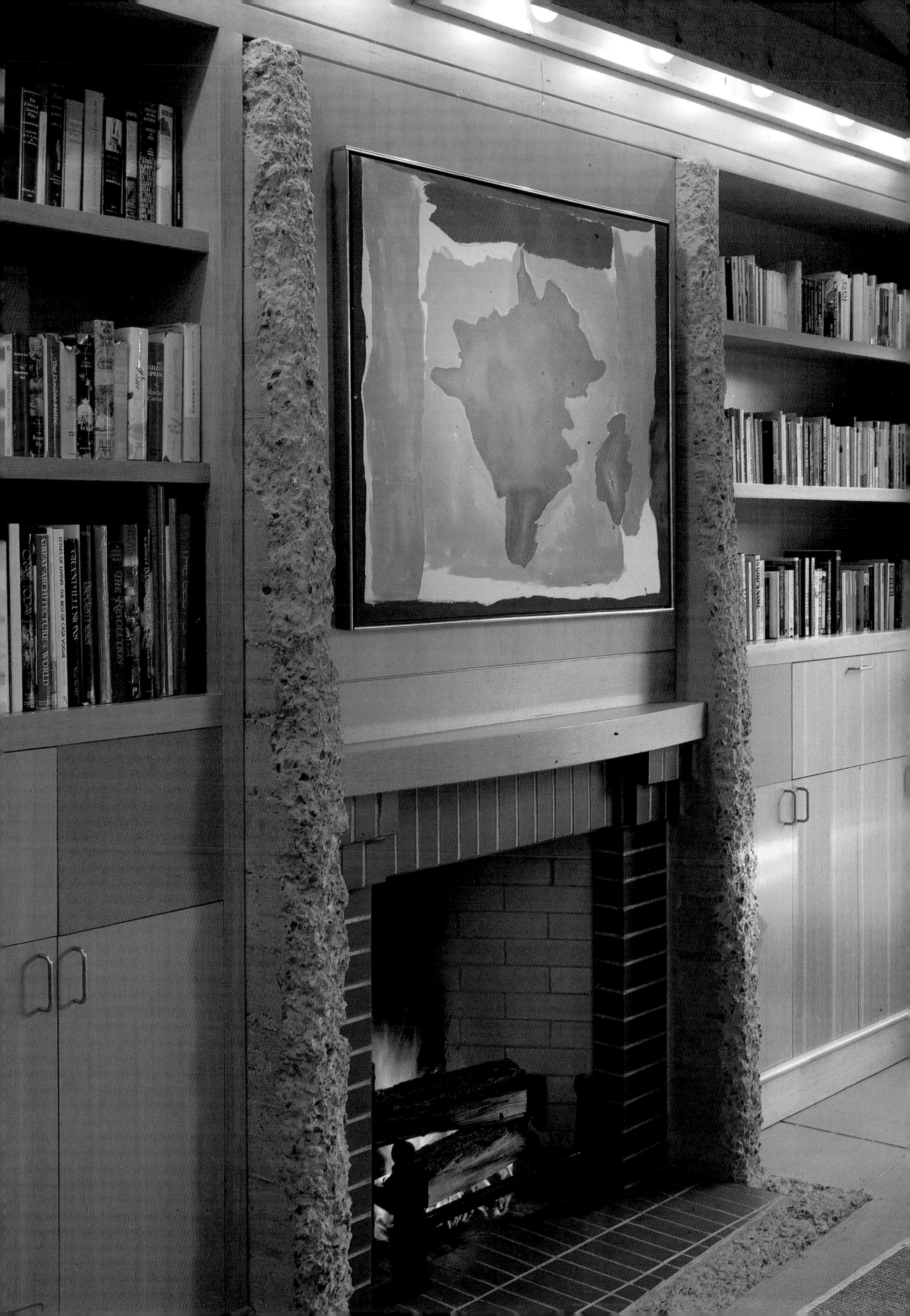
The Double Helix
Silent Spring
Rachel Carson
CRAFT TODAY
GREAT ARCHITECTURE of the WORLD
STYLES OF LIVING THE BEST OF CASA VOGUE
GRANDILLUSIONS
Biedermeier
THE REVOLUTION
IMAGINARY PLACES

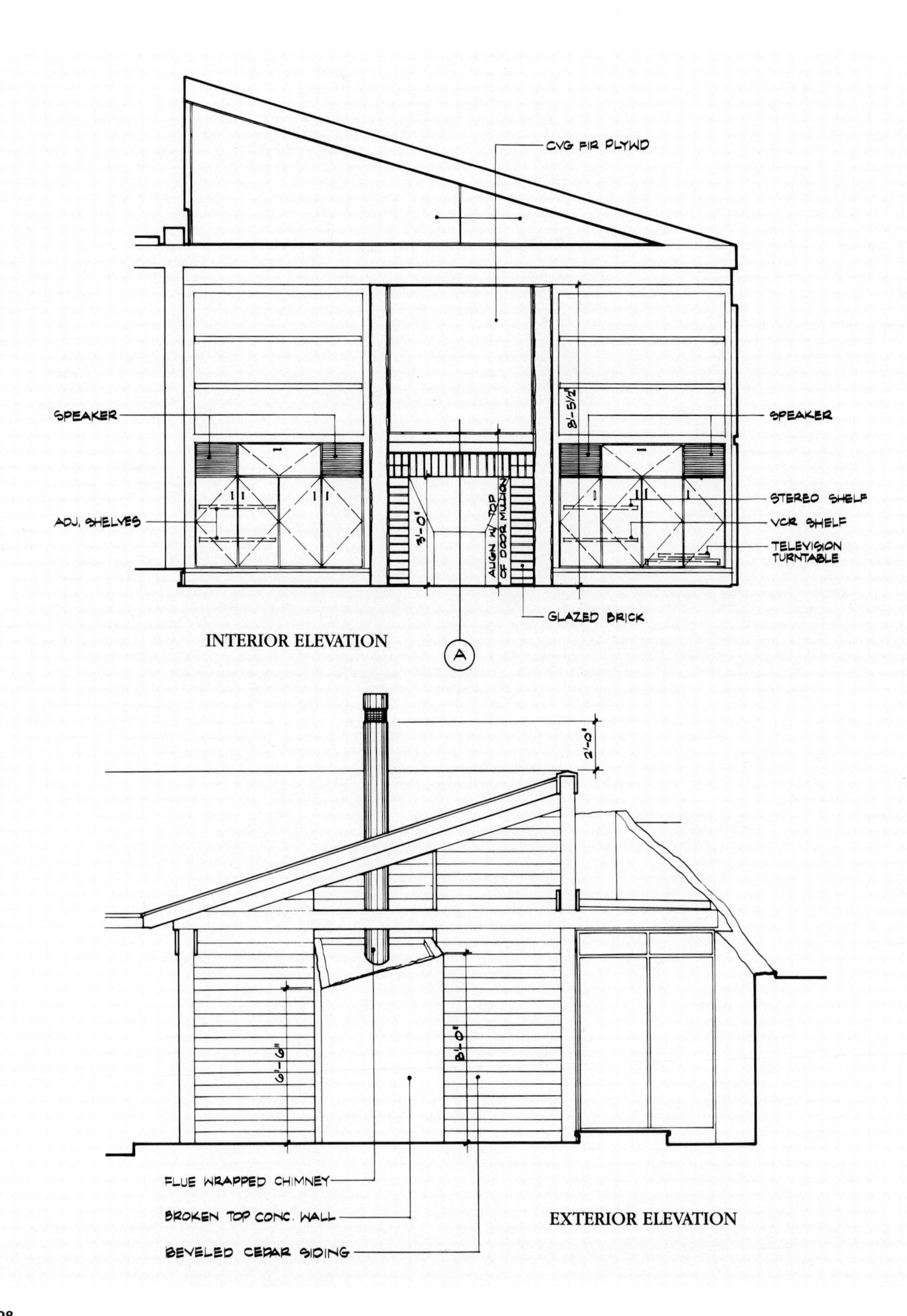


INTERIOR ELEVATION

EXTERIOR ELEVATION

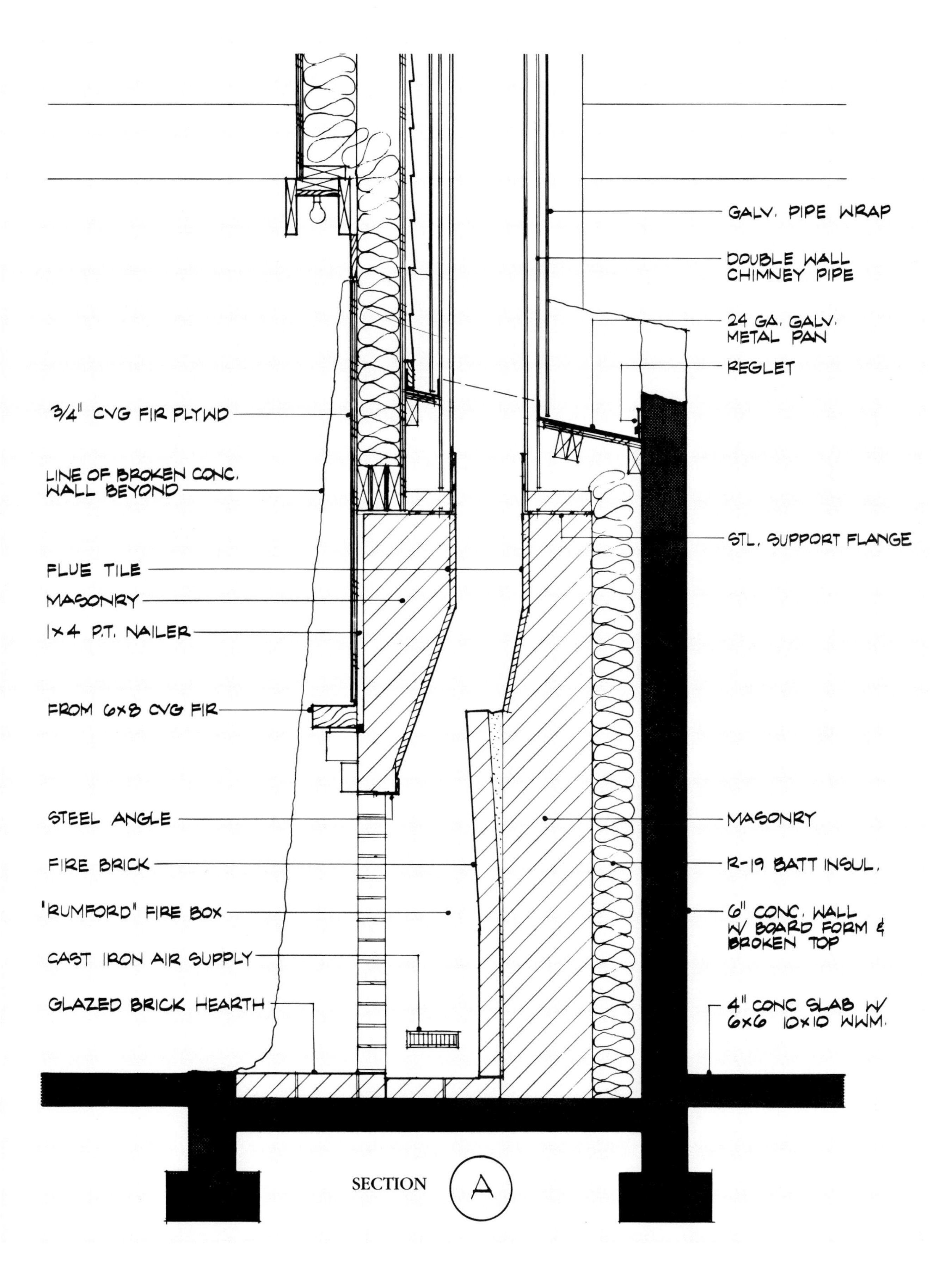
GALV. PIPE WRAP
DOUBLE WALL CHIMNEY PIPE
24 GA. GALV. METAL PAN
REGLET
3/4" CVG FIR PLYWD
LINE OF BROKEN CONC. WALL BEYOND
STL. SUPPORT FLANGE
FLUE TILE
MASONRY
1×4 P.T. NAILER
FROM 6×8 CVG FIR
STEEL ANGLE
MASONRY
FIRE BRICK
R-19 BATT INSUL.
"RUMFORD" FIRE BOX
6" CONC. WALL W/ BOARD FORM & BROKEN TOP
CAST IRON AIR SUPPLY
GLAZED BRICK HEARTH
4" CONC SLAB W/ 6×6 10×10 WWM.
SECTION
A

## LACKEY–LEHN RESIDENCE
*Kansas City, Missouri*

**Interior Architect**
Thomas Lehn, Principal, Kelly and Lehn

**Fabricators**
American Laminates (shelving);
Zahmer Sheet Metal (shelf frames)

**Photography**
© E. G. Schempf

INFUSING A STRAIGHTFORWARD 1930s Colonial house with enough visual interest to suit the sophisticated tastes and graphic sensibilities of an interior architect and an artist—without breaking a modest budget—were the chief priorities of interior architect Thomas Lehn and his artist wife, Jane Lackey, who undertook the renovation of their home in 1981.

The couple wanted to create a home environment and, in particular, a fireplace focal point that would stimulate their imaginations. They began the project by gutting every room of the house; they then redesigned the rooms to create a direct relationship between the existing spaces and their own personalities. The original oak floor was preserved for a specific reason: the juxtaposition of the old with the new served as a basic transitional device for redesigning the rest of the interior elements.

The living room fireplace had fallen into disuse—in part because its position in the room was off center and, in part, because its off-center placement caused an uncomfortable distance from the room's main seating area. Lehn hoped to restore the symbolic importance of the fireplace, without resorting to moving its position. He decided to develop the fireplace as a display area, filling the entire 14′–0″ wall with a tripartite system of fireplace, cabinetry, and shelving.

The tripartite composition rectifies the hearth's asymmetrical placement, as it provides display space for the Lehn's collection of folk art and travel memorabilia—a "humanizing" contrast to modernist detailing. Lehn began the fireplace wall transformation by building the fireplace out from the wall with a structure of tiles on a frame of water-resistant gypsum board. The actual fireplace sits behind brass-framed glass doors at the back of the hearth.

The 12″ × 12″, ½-inch-thick tiles—glazed ceramic on the surfaces perpendicular to the back wall, granite flame on the surfaces parallel to it—were held in place with a concrete mixture over wire mesh. The grout for both matched the granite tiles, creating dark bands that extend into the lighter ceramic surfaces. Both were set off from the floor by a 2½-inch flush-set base molding of verde antique marble.

The 1′–3″-deep white-oak mantel was capped with a 2½-inch half-round of ebonized oak trim. At the end of the mantel, the trim turns toward the back wall on a 2′–0″ radius to wrap a quarter-circular patterned glass shelf. The wood molding stops its turn at 1′–3″ out from the back wall to continue to face a second oak shelf; the glass shelf's painted metal frame completes the quarter-circle around to the back wall. A smooth transition was created between the mantel and shelf, while the glass panel provided an ethereal joint between the two elements.

The ebonized half-round continues to the room's end wall, providing space for a recessed incandescent fixture that lights the counter below. Above the mantel-level shelf, two more 1′–3″-deep shelves, made of plastic laminate with Colorcore edges, are supported by steel angles concealed in the ⅝-inch fiberboard back wall.

Underneath the three shelves, a cabinet with perforated metal doors conceals a television screen and speakers. The face of the cabinet begins flush with the outer face of the fireplace—set off from the floor by a reveal matched in height to the fireplace's base molding. Where the upper shelving completes its turn in toward the back wall, the lower cabinet begins a more subtle curve out into the room.

The 2′–2″-high cabinet top was constructed of black laminate edged in Colorcore. The custom metal frame doors, built of ¾″ × ¾″ steel tubing, have black-painted perforated faces and rest on pin hinges. Touch-latch closures were used to maintain a continuous surface.

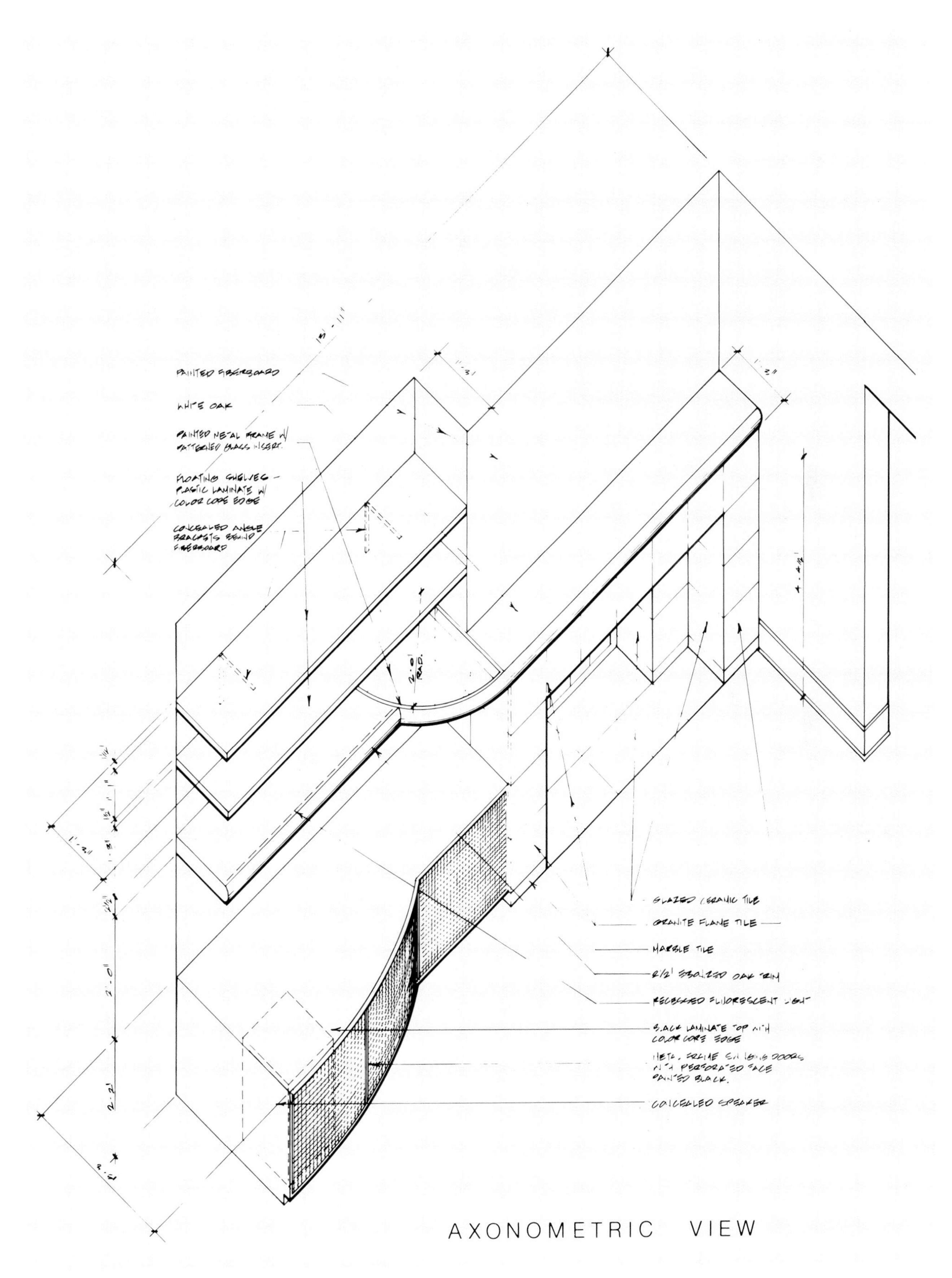
PAINTED FIBERBOARD
WHITE OAK
PAINTED METAL FRAME W/ PATTERNED GLASS INSERT.
FLOATING SHELVES - PLASTIC LAMINATE W/ COLOR CORE EDGE
CONCEALED ANGLE BRACKETS BEHIND FIBERBOARD
GLAZED CERAMIC TILE
GRANITE FLAME TILE
MARBLE TILE
2 1/2" EBONIZED OAK TRIM
RECESSED FLUORESCENT LIGHT
BLACK LAMINATE TOP WITH COLOR CORE EDGE
METAL FRAME SWINGING DOORS WITH PERFORATED FACE PAINTED BLACK.
CONCEALED SPEAKER

AXONOMETRIC VIEW

## GILBANE RESIDENCE

*Providence, Rhode Island*

**Architect**
Machado and Silvetti Associates, Inc.

**Design Team**
Rodolfo Machado, Project Designer;
Jorge Silvetti, Project Designer;
Gregory Conyngham, Project Manager

**General Contractor**
Joe Sussa, BT Equipment

**Fabricators**
Moliterno Stone Sales, Inc. (marble);
Castellucci Stone, Inc. (granite);
Modern Industries (cabinetry)

**Photography**
© Paul Warchol

IN 1984, Boston architects Machado and Silvetti Associates designed an unusually urbane basement apartment for the executive of a construction company. The 1,000-square-foot apartment—part of a 1790s house situated in Providence, Rhode Island—was in need of complete refurbishing in order to be habitable; the design team responded to that need by designing a completely outfitted environment.

Machado and Silvetti were faced with incorporating into their design two masonry piers, each about 7′–0″ square in plan, that support the chimney cores of the upper house. Turning a liability into an asset, the architects used each pier as the organizing point for a sector of the apartment. Following the lead of the upper floors, with their traditional quadripartite layout, Machado and Silvetti relied on a loose four-zone arrangement—living, bath, kitchen, and sleeping areas—in what remains essentially one open space.

Each pier was then clad in a distinct finishing material; one in white tile; the other, containing the fireplace, in granite. In constructing the new fireplace, the architects took advantage of the fact that they were building into an existing chimney. The fireplace fit into a niche in the pier, as the new flue connected to one already in place. The pier was then sheathed with a wooden frame that served as the support for blueboarding. The mantelpiece frame and the chimney cladding are made of the same white granite, flame-finished on the chimney face and polished around the fireplace proper. The ⅞-inch-thick granite slabs, as well as the mantelpiece frame, were then set in a bed of mortar.

The basement interior draws attention to the quality and level of detailing. According to Machado: "In such a small and almost windowless space [there are French doors along one wall, which face the fireplace and lead out into the garden], refinement of detail was essential in order to avoid claustrophobia."

The architects' palette of materials elsewhere in the apartment is consistent with this refinement: custom-built mahogany cabinetry and cherry floors with inlays of polished black granite.

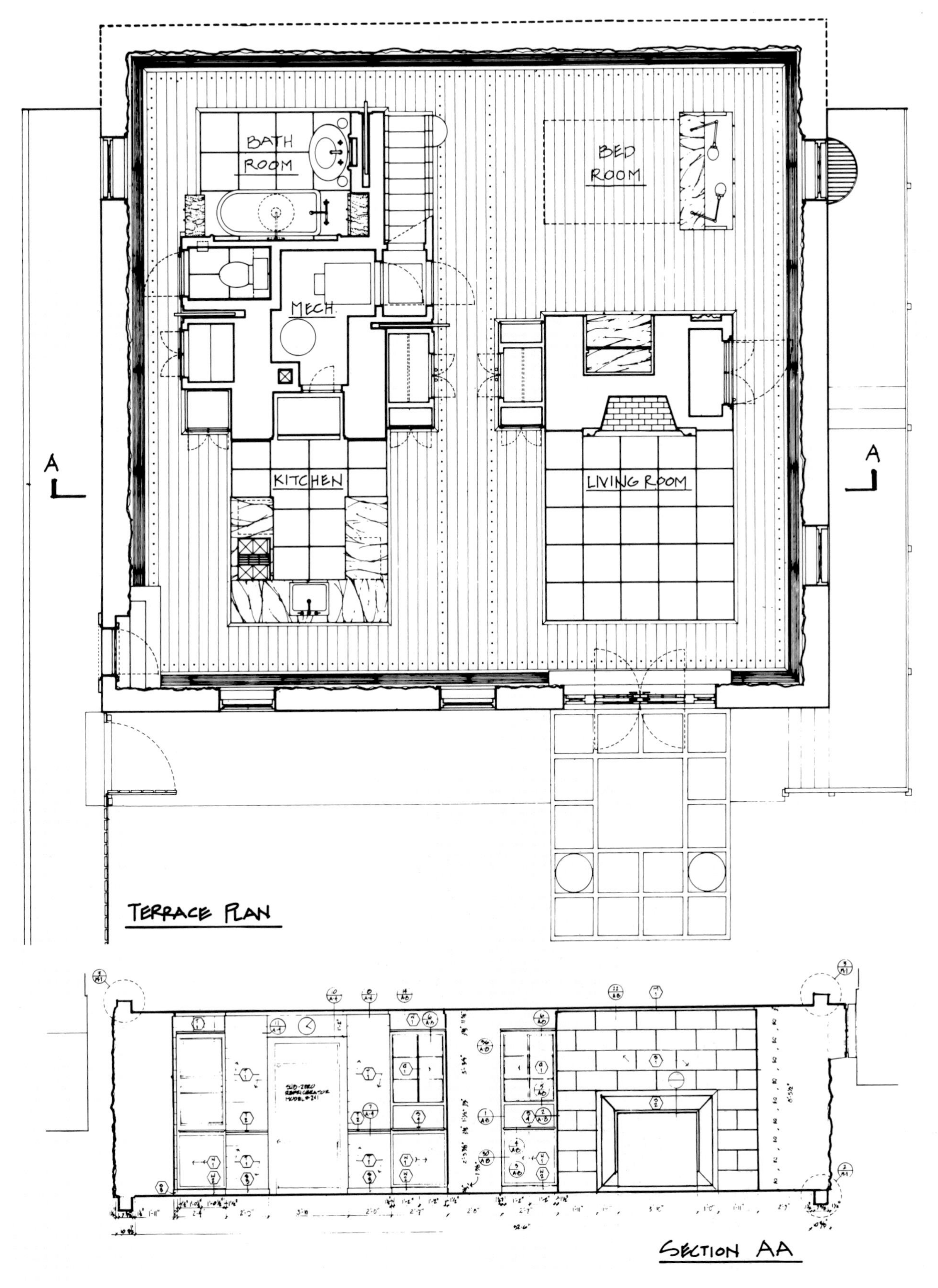
BATH ROOM
BED ROOM
MECH.
KITCHEN
LIVING ROOM
A
A
TERRACE PLAN
SECTION AA

## PRIVATE RESIDENCE

*Chicago, Illinois*

**Architect**
Quinn and Searl, Architects

**Design Team**
Linda Searl, Partner;
Kathryn Quinn, Partner;
Polly Hawkins, Architect;
Jihad Harik, Intern Architect

**General Contractor**
E & L Shilo Company

**Fabricator**
Steven Ethridge (electrical work)

**Photography**
© George Lambros

WHEN A HUSBAND AND WIFE have definitive, but very different, tastes—tastes that converge only in the contemporary art they collect—designing a house that will genuinely please both parties can be problematic. Which is precisely why a Chicago couple commissioned Quinn and Searl, Architects, to mastermind, as well as masterplan, a total renovation of their 4,000-square-foot Chicago townhouse.

The clients—one a bond trader and the other the owner of a needlepoint shop—asked the architects to come up with a "consensus" solution that would be "modern, but homelike and warm in feeling." To emphasize their art collection, the clients agreed that the space should be "neutral, but not bland." The completely vertical orientation of the house in conjunction with its 19′–0″ width posed additional, structural constraints.

Quinn and Searl resolved all the major program requirements at once by inserting a dramatic three-in-one vertical detail—that consolidates a fireplace; an "art object" flue shroud/light fixture; and a sculptural, open, three-story stair—into the center of the open, gallerylike plan. The staircase, which is rotated 15 degrees from the orthogonal to visually extend the axis, occupies 144 square feet on three of the four floors; the stair and fireplace together occupy 176 square feet on the living room floor.

According to Linda Searl: "The fireplace, which projects out from a screen wall punctuated by small square perforations, partially encloses the stair and enhances its figural character" (*elevation*). The fireplace flue "pins down" the center of the house, as it also rises 33′–0″ through the upper stories (*plan; section*). Because the architects wished to conceal the flue's ribbing, a smooth covering sleeve was fitted onto the flue itself. For further sculptural impact, a curved sheet metal "shroud" was wrapped around the flue cover and attached to the screen wall. The shroud houses a concealed neon light fixture, which, as it uplights the shroud curve, adds a playful and colorful fillip (*light detail*).

The stock metal firebox of the fireplace was framed in with wood and sheathed in ⅝-inch drywall. Colors of the marble tiles, in two thicknesses, define surfaces and volumes: ¼-inch-thick tiles were glued to the wall with latex adhesive; ¾-inch-thick hearth and mantel were thinset into place. All tile edges were polished at the corners.

The flue shroud was fabricated of ⅛-inch sheet metal and painted. Color emanating from the interior of the shroud is not paint, but rather the reflected glow of a concealed neon tube.

The fireplace and flue shroud were constructed in 1987 for $7,000.

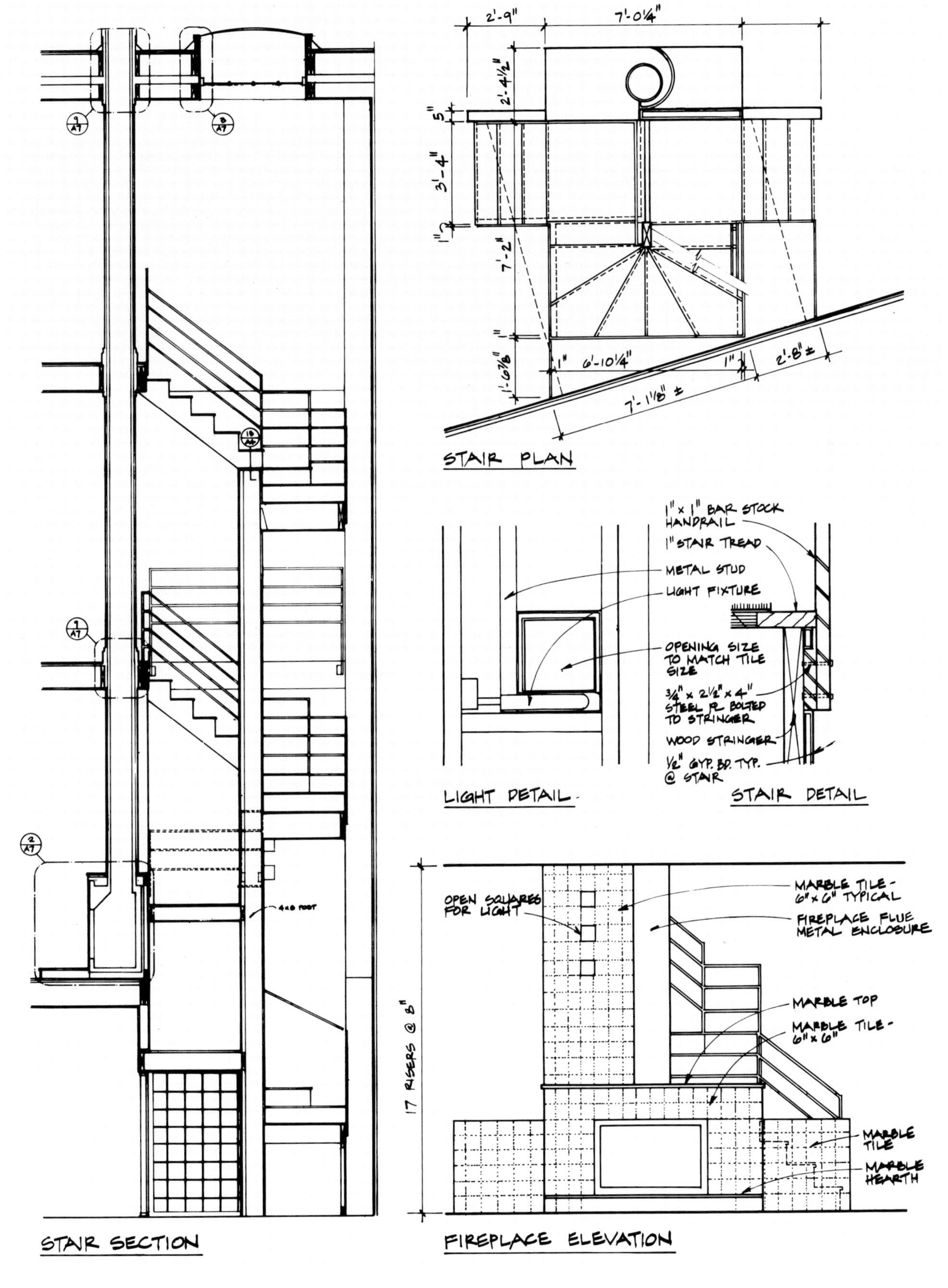

STAIR SECTION
4x8 POST
2'-9"
7'-0¼"
2'-4½"
5"
3'-4"
1"
7'-2"
1"
1'-6⅞"
1"
6'-10¼"
1"
2'-8" ±
7'-1⅛" ±
STAIR PLAN
1" x 1" BAR STOCK HANDRAIL
1" STAIR TREAD
METAL STUD
LIGHT FIXTURE
OPENING SIZE TO MATCH TILE SIZE
¾" x 2½" x 4" STEEL PL BOLTED TO STRINGER
WOOD STRINGER
½" GYP. BD. TYP. @ STAIR
LIGHT DETAIL
STAIR DETAIL
OPEN SQUARES FOR LIGHT
MARBLE TILE - 6" x 6" TYPICAL
FIREPLACE FLUE METAL ENCLOSURE
MARBLE TOP
MARBLE TILE - 6" x 6"
MARBLE TILE
MARBLE HEARTH
17 RISERS @ 8"
FIREPLACE ELEVATION

## WITHERSPOON RESIDENCE

*Marin County, California*

**Architect**
William Turnbull Associates

**Design Team**
William Turnbull, Jr., Principal;
Paul Lobush, Project Architect

**General Contractor**
P. D. Associates

**Structural Consultant**
Ray Lindahl

**Photography**
© Norman McGrath

ANNE WITHERSPOON'S HOUSE, designed in 1985 by William Turnbull, is located on the Point Reyes Peninsula in Marin County, California. The lovely natural setting on which the house is sited includes, on one side, panoramic water views of Tomales Bay and, on the other, a wooded creek.

The client wanted a house with a large communal space that would take advantage of the magnificent views. The architect, provided with a generous budget, designed the structure to maximize exposure to the views: the entrance was positioned on the bay orientation of the house, and a large deck was constructed on the sunny creek side, which is protected from constant winds.

Inside, Turnbull created a soaring "great room" so that the client, her children, and friends might gather for shared meals and conversation at any time of the day. Windows, placed on the diagonal, create a sense of movement, enhance the expanse of the views, and draw in abundant natural light. Scissor ceiling trusses serve as a link between the large scale of the room and the human scale of doors and windows; shadows cast by the trusses support the play of natural light.

The great room is anchored, as it is balanced, by two massive fireplaces that occur at either end of the space. Each of the two plastered (over cement block) fireplaces rises the entire height of the room—their long, sloping sides as well as the height of the firebox openings are designed to reflect heat. Cement blocks, which compose the foundation material of the firebox, rise up to the roof where the chimney itself is rendered in brick.

Plaster, rather than brick, was specified as the interior finish surface of the fireplaces to avoid the distraction caused by extraneous materials. The exposed heat-reflecting surfaces of the opening, however, were constructed of fire brick. A granite fireplace surround, which frames the firebox opening, rests on a concrete hearth, which in turn rests on a concrete floor (*fireplace section typical*). Hot water pipes are exposed at the rear of the east firebox so that fires can preheat water for the water heater.

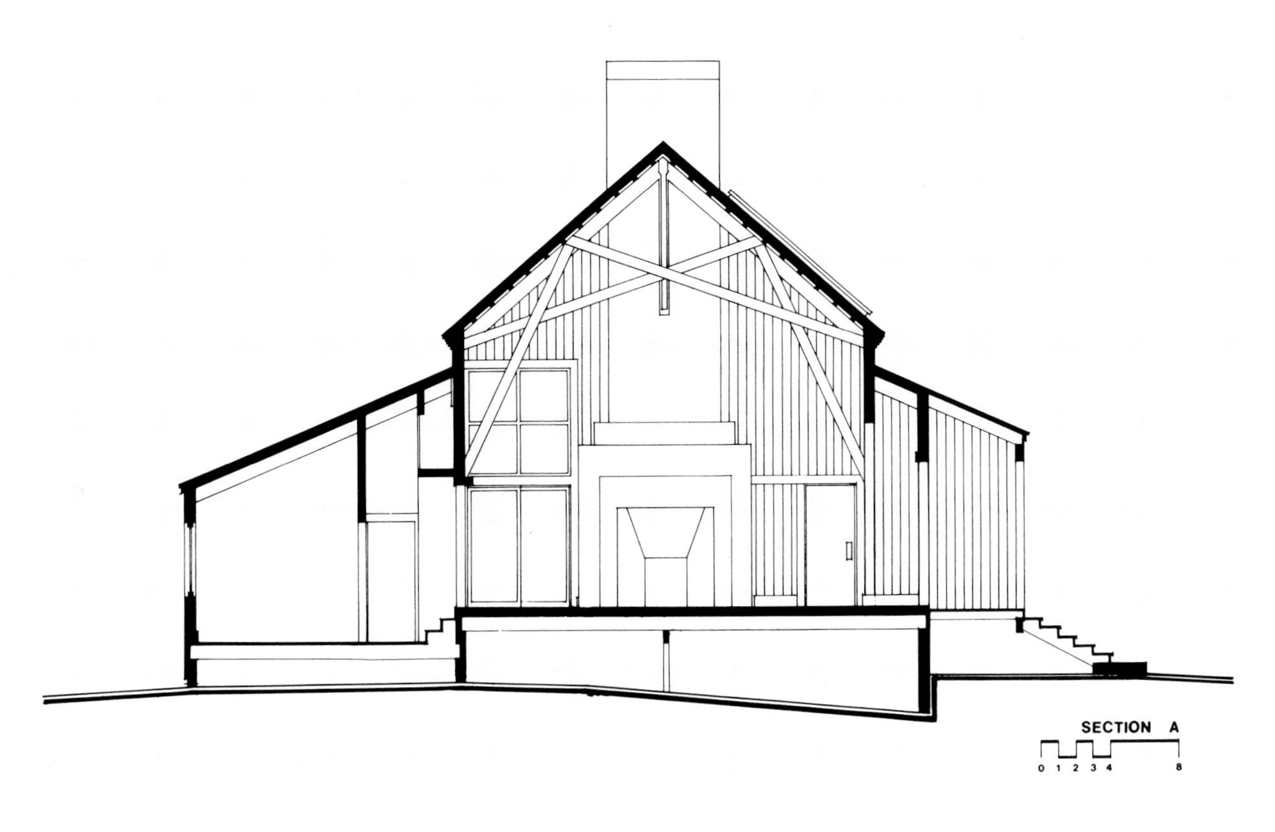
SECTION A
0 1 2 3 4 8

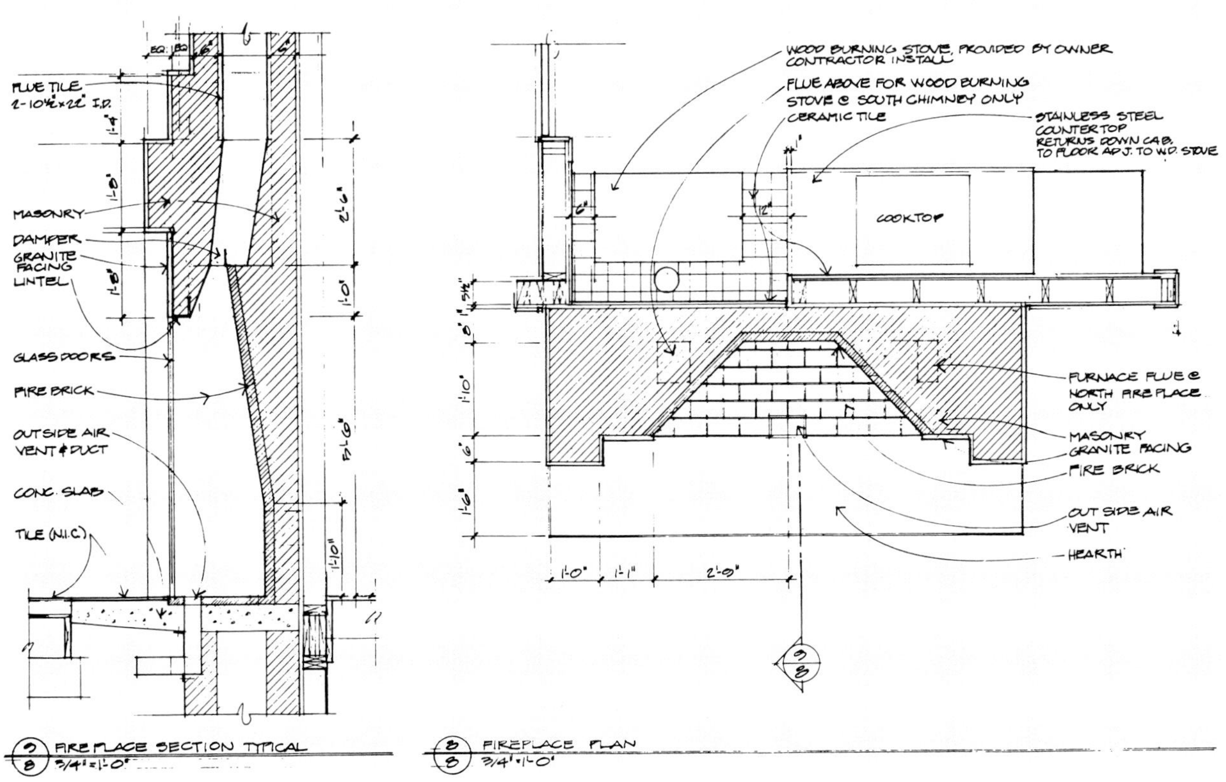
FLUE TILE
2-10½"x22" I.D.
MASONRY
DAMPER
GRANITE FACING
LINTEL
GLASS DOORS
FIRE BRICK
OUTSIDE AIR VENT & DUCT
CONC. SLAB
TILE (N.I.C.)
FIRE PLACE SECTION TYPICAL
3/4"=1'-0"
WOOD BURNING STOVE, PROVIDED BY OWNER
CONTRACTOR INSTALL
FLUE ABOVE FOR WOOD BURNING
STOVE @ SOUTH CHIMNEY ONLY
CERAMIC TILE
STAINLESS STEEL
COUNTERTOP
RETURNS DOWN CAB.
TO FLOOR ADJ. TO W.D. STOVE
COOKTOP
FURNACE FLUE @
NORTH FIRE PLACE
ONLY
MASONRY
GRANITE FACING
FIRE BRICK
OUT SIDE AIR
VENT
HEARTH
FIREPLACE PLAN
3/4"=1'-0"

# Floor Pattern

**Private Residence**
*Chicago, Illinois*

**Architect**
Rudolph & Associates, P.C.

**Design Team**
Christopher H. Rudolph, AIA, Principal; Lawrence M. Petitti, Architect

**Fabricator**
Milwaukee Marble Co.

**Photography**
© John Hollis Enterprises, Inc.

Looking down becomes a way of life for enthusiastic high-rise inhabitants, to whom vertigo is an anathema and views are paramount. It therefore made perfect sense to two high-rise-dwelling clients of Christopher Rudolph to embellish their entry hall floor with an inlaid pattern that alludes to the architecture apparent in the urban landscape below.

The pattern for the entry hall floor was designed, as was the entire 3,500-square-foot apartment, by architects Rudolph & Associates—advocates of the art of ornamental detailing and fine craftsmanship, and connoisseurs, as well as accomplished interpreters, of Prairie School motifs (*see* Door, page 84). The finished entry foyer—with its elaborately framed interior window of ornamental glass and its linear floor pattern—immediately establishes a perception of quality, as well as a definitive Prairie School connection.

Rudolph employed thirty-two types of marble and granite to create the floor's "urban quilt" character. According to the architect: "Many pieces which seem similar actually differ, as the contents of a ragbag are transformed into a cohesive, formal design in traditional quilting." The use of subtle variations in both stone coloration and characteristic contributes to the layering effect of floor pattern, wall trim, and ceiling lines—all of which balance the foyer's formality.

Specialty fabricators in Milwaukee cut and polished each ⅞-inch-thick marble component, individually laminated to a base of 1¼-inch-thick travertine. The floor was shop-assembled in three large segments, which were shipped to the site and laid in a mud setting bed on the concrete subfloor. Travertine ("C") and verde antique ("G") marbles dominate the pattern, in contrast to bianco tassos, white cremo, and red carnelian granite.

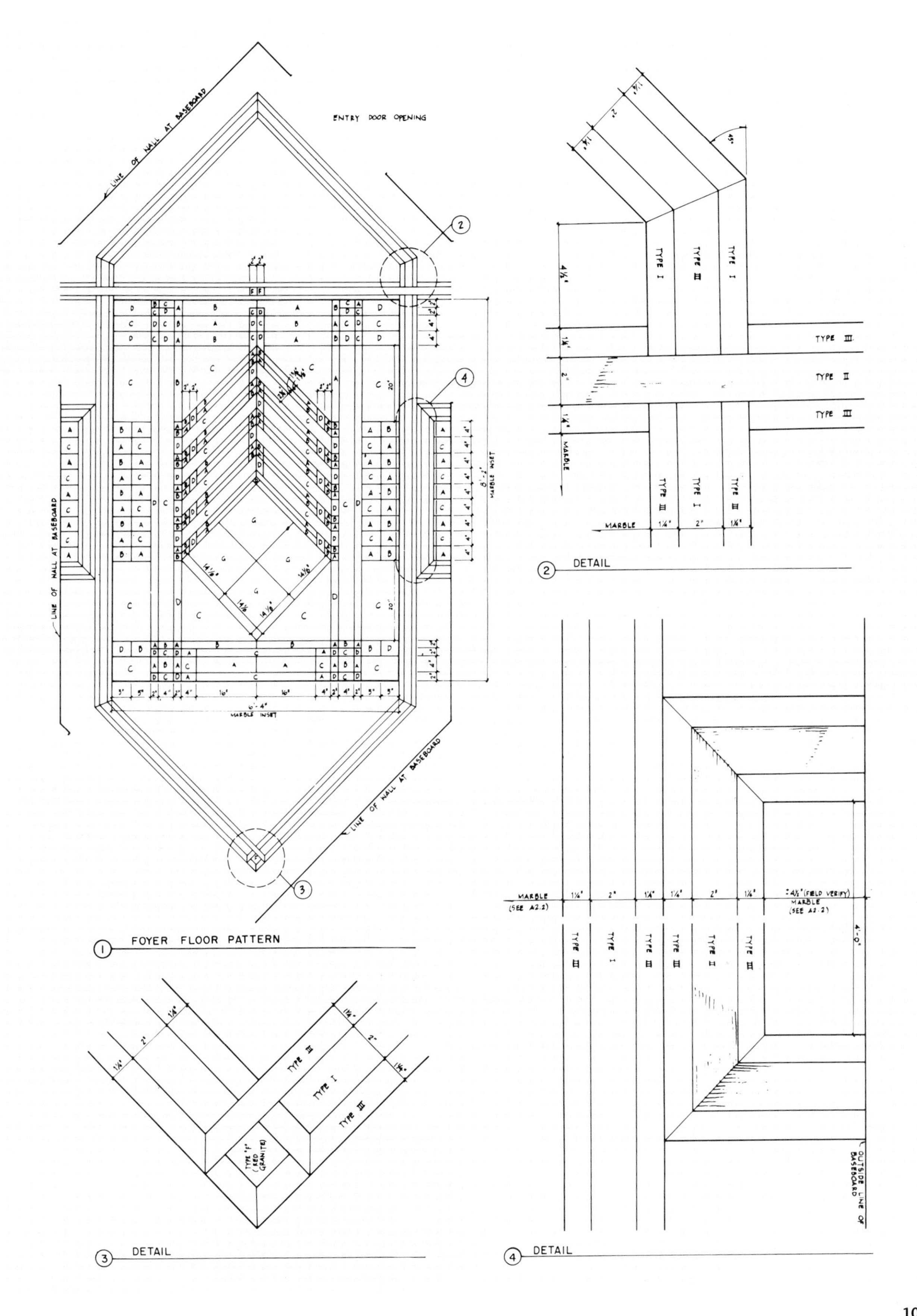
ENTRY DOOR OPENING
LINE OF WALL AT BASEBOARD
MARBLE INSET
FOYER FLOOR PATTERN
DETAIL
TYPE I
TYPE II
TYPE III
MARBLE
4'-0"
OUTSIDE LINE OF BASEBOARD

# FLOOR PATTERN

## PRIVATE RESIDENCE
*Boston, Massachusetts*

**Architect**
Graham Gund Architects

**Design Team**
Graham Gund, Design Principal;
David T. Perry, Principal;
Bill Ridge, Project Architect;
Donna Schumacher, Monica Sidor, Project Team

**General Contractor**
ZZI Construction Company, Inc.

**Fabricators**
Al Held (art), Andre Emmerich Gallery;
William Brower (floor installation)

**Art Consultant**
Aptekar Arts Management

**Photography**


**BOSTON'S BEACON HILL** is a historic district of townhouses. However, a Beacon Hill couple with twentieth-century preferences in regard to interior architecture, furnishings, and the display of their art collection wanted to integrate their preferences with those more prevalent in the immediate environment. Cambridge architect Graham Gund was commissioned to design for them "a contemporary apartment rendered with eighteenth-century craftsmanship." Gund was given a generous budget to complete the 2,200-square-foot renovation.

One of the most important tasks facing Gund, from an aesthetic point of view, was to design an entrance hall that would serve as a prelude and introduction to the apartment and the art collection. Gund created an elliptical foyer that opens onto several rooms, with the main view facing forward into the living room.

The entry hall also opens upward. A double-height space, the foyer allows views upward to a balcony, the gridded wood railing of which is bent to match the elliptical floor plan. Similar to other railings in the house, the balcony grid rests not on the floor of the upper level, but extends down across the face of cut floor and hangs below the ceiling line. The overlap gives the railing the sense of a free plane floating in space—one that is not specifically a part of the second floor but instead engages both levels of the space. The grid also relates to the gridded fenestration in the living room windows and to its linear coffered ceiling (*see* Partition, page 142).

Gund's main effort in making the entry foyer a presage to the owners' art collection was not in the walls or balcony, but rather in the floor. The architect decided that the floor itself should be a work of art, and hired Aptekar Arts Management, an art consultancy firm, to select an appropriate artist. Lucy Aptekar contacted painter Al Held, who created a watercolor maquette of the intricate, sinuous pattern he designed.

Held's design, a twisting, snakelike pattern, was inspired by the oval shape of the entrance. Its overlapping forms, juxtapositions of straight and curvilinear elements, contrasting light and dark panels, and linear forms that extend out of the foyer at several points create a three-dimensional effect that is heightened when seen from the balcony above.

Woodworker William Brower began construction of the floor by selecting, with Held's assistance, eight hardwoods: maple, shedua, walnut, wengé, white oak, ash, bubinga, and red birch (*plan*). The maple was to serve as a backdrop to the pattern created by the other seven woods, with the bubinga and red birch used for the dominant curvilinear forms.

Brower then interpreted and expanded Held's sketch to fit the exact dimensions of the room. In his shop, Brower constructed a floor as large as the entrance hall out of 4-inch-wide strips of maple and laid the full-scale drawing of the floor pattern on top. The pattern pieces were cut out and glued to the milled finish hardwoods; these were then

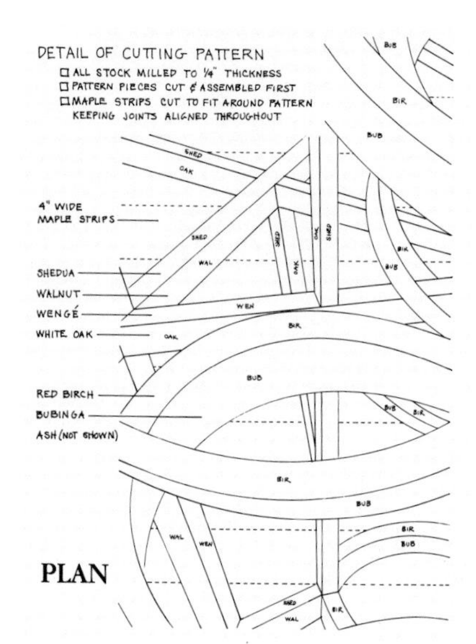


PLAN

rough cut with a bandsaw and sanded to the exact shape.

The finished pattern pieces were then laid back down on the maple "background floor" and their outlines traced onto the maple surface. The pieces were removed, the outlines knifed into the maple, and the final cuts made.

The floor was assembled into 4-foot sections, which were taped together and then transported from the shop to the site. The pieces were manipulated to fit the foyer and then glued to the plywood subflooring. No nails were used. To ensure total adhesion, 25-pound bags of lead shot weighted down the floor while the glue dried.

## Petal House
*West Los Angeles, California*

**Architect**
Eric Owen Moss • Architect

**Fabricator**
Howard Newhouse

**Photography**
© Tim Street-Porter/ESTO

In 1984 Brad and Maritza Culbertson made the decision to expand and renovate their 1,100-square-foot frame house in West Los Angeles.

In addition to creating a new master suite, guest room, studio and kitchen, the Culbertsons wanted to increase the size of their living room and add a roof-deck Jacuzzi (*see also* Kitchen Cabinets, page 116; Rotunda, page 172). Architect Eric Owen Moss delivered a delightfully idiosyncratic, original design package that has since won several merit awards from professional organizations; it was thoroughly documented by Pilar Viladas and Peter Cook in the June 1984 issue of *Progressive Architecture* (*exterior elevation*).

Moss's intent was to achieve a metamorphosis of the existing building into a picaresque series of discrete "events" which manifest and extend the essential characteristics of its neighborhood architecture. In the dining room, Moss has created one such event. Since the space exists only as an intermediary zone between living room and kitchen—the fireplace is the only divider between these areas—Moss used the wood joists in the dining room ceiling to give the room definition (*floor plan*).

The eleven joists stretching across the dining room have angled cuts removed from their bottom sides. The peaks of the cuts move from one joist to the next in the form of a slightly curved diagonal. This curve, in fact, takes the shape of a specific mathematical figure—a hyperbolic paraboloid—which gives the room a dynamic quality "whether," Moss says, "you understand it mathematically or not" (*ceiling plan*). The curve, along with the asymmetrically placed fireplace, creates a spatial movement from the living room through the dining room into the kitchen.

The joists are single 2 × 14 pieces of Douglas fir hung from the walls by heavy-duty joist hangers. The hangers were screwed through the drywall into the wooden studs (*section*).

Finish panels of ½-inch birch plywood were screwed into wood blocking between the joists, giving the entire ceiling a wood finish that provides a contrast to the white surrounding walls and the colorful furniture designed by Peter Shire.

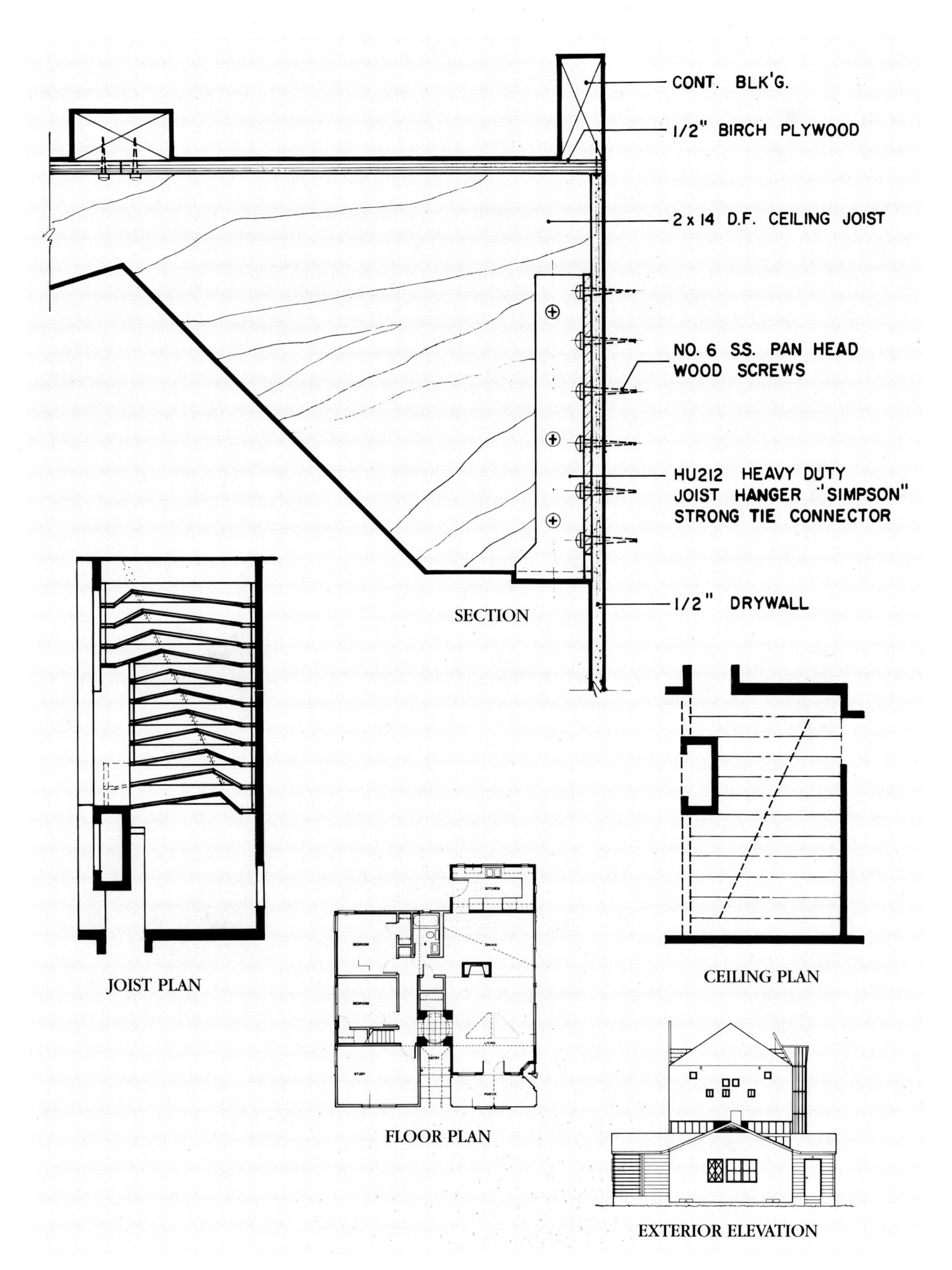

SECTION

JOIST PLAN

CEILING PLAN

FLOOR PLAN

EXTERIOR ELEVATION

## PANISH LOFT
*New York, New York*

**Architect**
Anderson/Schwartz Architects

**Design Team**
Frederic Schwartz, Partner-in-Charge; Marc L'Italien, Project Architect

**Lighting Consultant**
Clark Johnson, Johnson Schwinghammer Lighting Consultants

**General Contractor**
Alan Larivee, Alan Custom Building

**Fabricator**
Pell Gris Cabinets

**Photography**
© Anderson/Schwartz Architects

UNTIL ANDERSON/SCHWARTZ renovated the Manhattan SoHo loft of chef and restaurateur Larry Panish, the "hippest place in town" might well have been one of Panish's three restaurants: Moondance in SoHo; Lox Around the Clock in Chelsea; and the Pipeline in Battery Park City. Now, post-renovation, the most coveted invitations issued to favored patrons and friends are for private parties "chez Panish."

It was inevitable that the 300-square-foot kitchen would become the first area of concentration, as well as the focal point, of the phased 2,000-square-foot loft renovation project. Having requested the development of a "sizable preparation island," Panish, a certified master chef, asked only that the architects develop "an imaginative, as well as functional, solution."

The design team used the client's request for a serious preparation island as the literal departure point for their conceptual plan. By visualizing a massive, irregularly contoured island/counter as "a mineral landfall surrounded by a kitchen sea" (*see* Kitchen Island/Counter, page 136), the architects quickly realized that the upper cabinets—if spaced asymmetrically and suspended from the ceiling—could be perceived as "the cluster of floating clouds that hover over an actual sea island" (*plan*).

The cloud concept led, in turn, to the technical development of the cabinets as double-function details; the result—cabinets that serve not only as storage containers for kitchen equipment, but also as diffused, nonglaring light sources for the island/counter surface.

The frontal, or outward-facing, elevations of the rectilinear cabinets were covered by inclined fascia panels constructed of 2′–0″ × 4′–0″ panels of perforated, corrugated aluminum (*front elevation*). By slanting each aluminum panel 23 degrees from the bottom, a 7-inch reveal was created at the top of each cabinet, within which a fluorescent light fixture was screwed to mounting brackets (*detail*). Each cabinet doubles its lighting function with a linear, incandescent fixture screwed to its base (*detail*). The actual right-angle front wall of each rectilinear cabinet was covered in white Colorcore laminate over plywood framing so that light reflection might be maximized through the perforated aluminum. As an "expression of the reality of the material," the architects deliberately exposed the electrical conduits that supply power to the lighting fixtures in the cabinets. Other exposed surfaces of the cabinets themselves were faced in maple veneer.

Each cloud cabinet is suspended from ceiling rafters with two unpainted steel "C" brackets (*rear elevation*). On the back elevation of each cabinet, doors constructed of solid-maple-framed plate glass are hung from concealed hinges. The plate-glass panes were sandblasted to enhance the "ephemeral" character of the cabinets (*rear elevation*).

The Panish kitchen was completed in 1988.

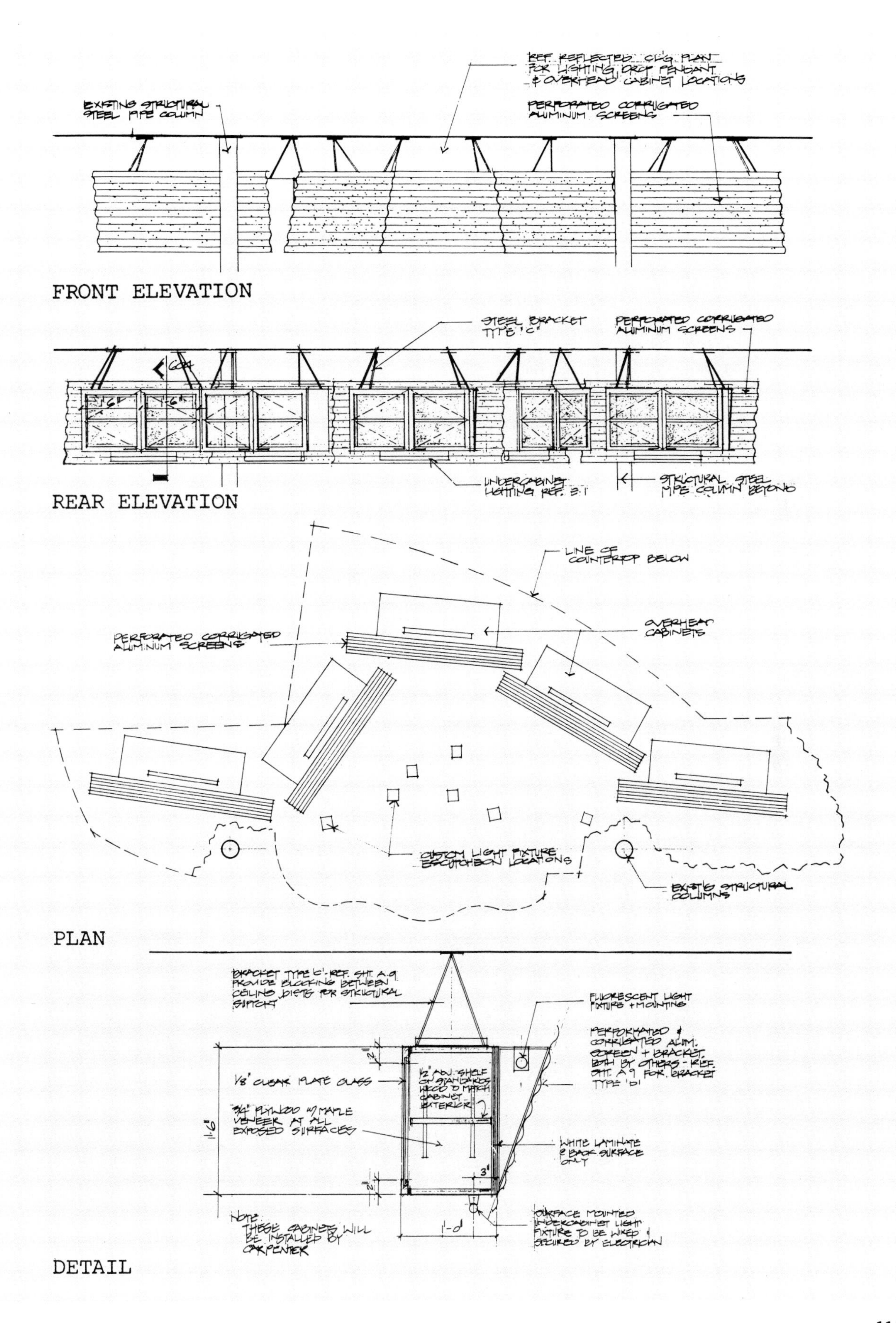
REF. REFLECTED CLG. PLAN FOR LIGHTING, DROP PENDANT & OVERHEAD CABINET LOCATIONS
EXISTING STRUCTURAL STEEL PIPE COLUMN
PERFORATED CORRUGATED ALUMINUM SCREENING
FRONT ELEVATION
STEEL BRACKET TYPE 'C'
PERFORATED CORRUGATED ALUMINUM SCREENS
UNDERCABINET LIGHTING REF. 3.1
STRUCTURAL STEEL PIPE COLUMN BEYOND
REAR ELEVATION
LINE OF COUNTERTOP BELOW
PERFORATED CORRUGATED ALUMINUM SCREENS
OVERHEAD CABINETS
CUSTOM LIGHT FIXTURE ESCUTCHEON LOCATIONS
EXISTG STRUCTURAL COLUMNS
PLAN
BRACKET TYPE 'C' - REF. SHT. A.9 PROVIDE BLOCKING BETWEEN CEILING JOISTS FOR STRUCTURAL SUPPORT
FLUORESCENT LIGHT FIXTURE + MOUNTING
PERFORATED & CORRUGATED ALUM. SCREEN + BRACKET, BOTH BY OTHERS - REF. SHT. A.9 FOR BRACKET TYPE 'D'
1/8" CLEAR PLATE GLASS
1/2" ADJ. SHELF ON STANDARDS WOOD TO MATCH CABINET EXTERIOR
3/4" PLYWOOD W/ MAPLE VENEER AT ALL EXPOSED SURFACES
WHITE LAMINATE @ BACK SURFACE ONLY
1'-6"
3"
1'-0"
NOTE: THESE CABINETS WILL BE INSTALLED BY CARPENTER
SURFACE MOUNTED UNDERCABINET LIGHT FIXTURE TO BE WIRED & SECURED BY ELECTRICIAN
DETAIL

# Kitchen Cabinets

**Petal House**
*West Los Angeles, California*

**Architect**
Eric Owen Moss • Architect

**Fabricator**
Howard Newhouse

**Photography**
© Tim Street-Porter/ESTO

Escalating land values in West Los Angeles persuaded Brad and Maritza Culbertson, in 1984, to renovate and expand their conventional 1,100-square-foot, post–World War II frame house, and to adjoin a studio to a detached garage. To enliven the property, and thereby maximize their investment, the couple commissioned iconoclastic architect Eric Owen Moss to design the renovations and additions. Moss is known for espousing the decidedly unconventional, even within the context of Los Angeles's quixotic architectural attitude (*see* Joist, page 112; Rotunda, page 172).

The kitchen was designed as an experience independent from other rooms of the house, its form mirroring a porch added to the opposite side of the existing structure. Moss emphasized the intersection of old and new by allowing the roof overhang of the existing house to penetrate into the kitchen addition, where it "shelters" the oven and refrigerator and provides an opportunity for hanging light fixtures.

This small piece of "old" roof was given further emphasis by dematerializing the new roof with a skylight. The existing rafters of the old roof protrude into the kitchen, where they are left exposed underneath and covered on top with black fiberglass shingles. Lengths of ½-inch-diameter rigid conduit are attached to several rafters to supply power to the vaporproof light fixtures attached to the rafter ends (*elevation-section, refrigerator wall*).

Holes were punched through two kitchen cabinets, so that, according to the architect: "Instead of the usual dog food concealed inside, there is a window opening with a view to the garden outside." The punched holes create an opening for an aluminum window and frame. The window head continues to form the bottom of the upper cabinet; the sill forms the top of the small band of cabinet below (*elevation-section, cabinet wall*).

The windowed cabinet that Moss created is a thought-provoking example of the varied ways in which stock cabinetry can be transformed into unique detailing. All the cabinets in the Culbertson kitchen were initially factory-fabricated; all but the windowed cabinets were installed conventionally, attached to blocking in the exterior wall and faced on the outside by 1x wood siding.

The Allmilmo cabinets are covered in corrugated white textured laminate—a soft, rounded, leather-like finish material that represents yet another Moss-inspired exercise in the presentation of the unexpected.

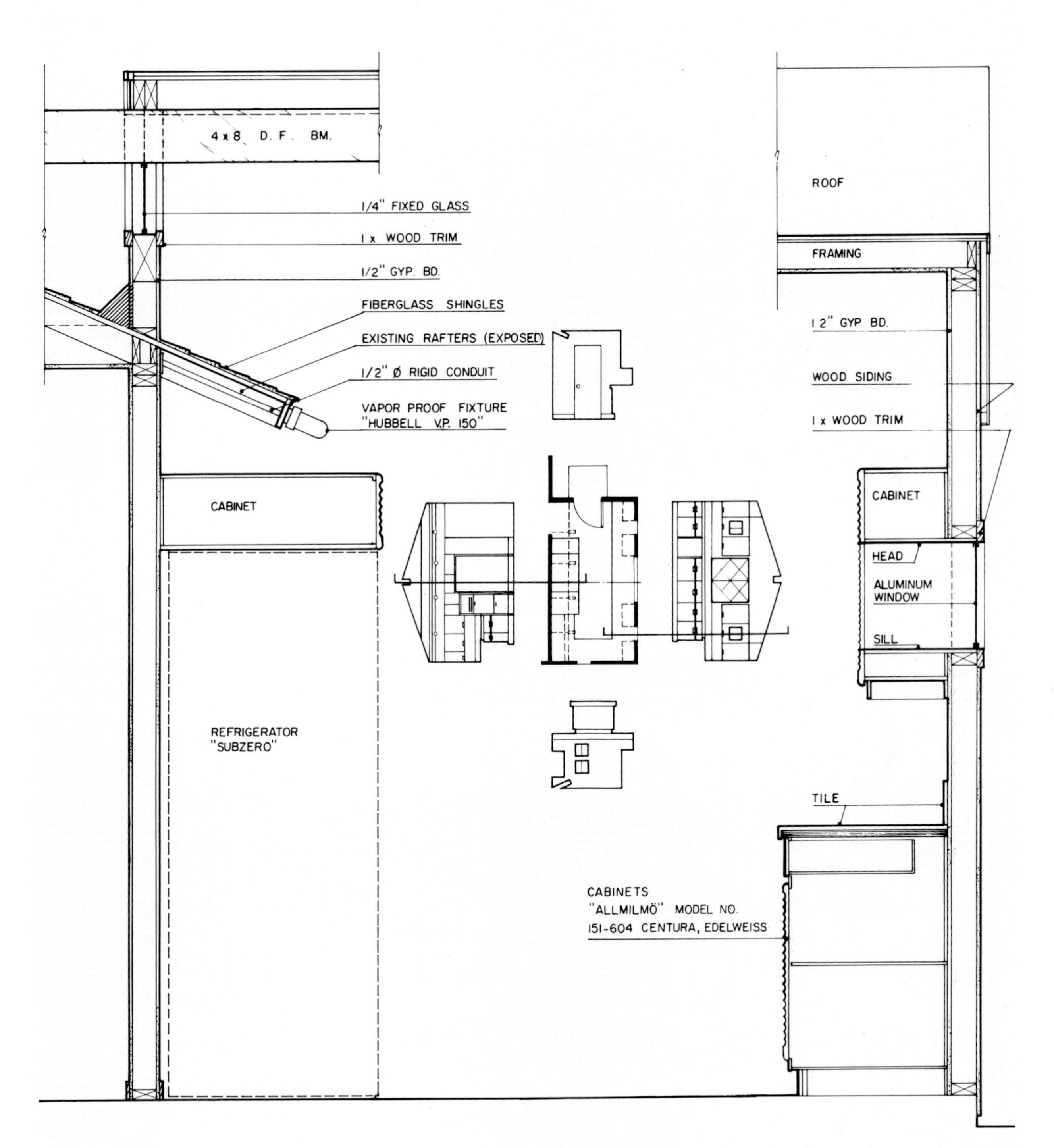
4 x 8 D. F. BM.
1/4" FIXED GLASS
1 x WOOD TRIM
1/2" GYP. BD.
FIBERGLASS SHINGLES
EXISTING RAFTERS (EXPOSED)
1/2" Ø RIGID CONDUIT
VAPOR PROOF FIXTURE
"HUBBELL V.P. 150"
CABINET
REFRIGERATOR
"SUBZERO"
ROOF
FRAMING
1 2" GYP BD.
WOOD SIDING
1 x WOOD TRIM
CABINET
HEAD
ALUMINUM
WINDOW
SILL
TILE
CABINETS
"ALLMILMÖ" MODEL NO.
151-604 CENTURA, EDELWEISS

ELEVATION—SECTION

# Kitchen Cabinets

**Wharton Residence**
*Stamford, Connecticut*

**Architect**
Shope Reno Wharton Associates

**Fabricator**
Breakfast Millworks

**Photography**
© H. Durston Saylor

Traces of the Vienna Secessionist movement are alive and well in current American architecture and interior design, as witnessed by this Stamford, Connecticut, kitchen, completed in 1986. Bernard Wharton, a principal of Shope Reno Wharton Associates, and his wife, Caroline Wharton, an interior designer, developed a number of details for their own kitchen (checkerboard floor, marble countertop, decorative horizontal band of semispherical tacks and gridded glass upper cabinet doors) that not only recall a Secessionist aesthetic, but also reflect their ideal of a "clean, white, and well-crafted" kitchen design (*see* Breakfast Nook, page 44).

Working with a project budget of $30,000, the couple began the renovation process by gutting the existing "dysfunctional" kitchen and annexing additional square footage from the adjacent dining room so that an L-shaped work area and informal dining space could be incorporated into 400 square feet.

Because the ceiling height of the Wharton's kitchen is only 6′–5″, the upper cabinets were carefully scaled to give the impression of normal dimensions, although they are, in fact, only 2′–0″ tall. Crown molding attached at the top of the upper cabinets beneath the actual ceiling plane further enhances a perception of height (*elevations 2 and 3*).

The upper cabinet doors were fabricated of glass panes clipped to ¾-inch hardwood frames. The glass panes are overlaid by hardwood grillwork that was installed ⅛ inch in front of the glass—a ploy that adds "Japanese shoji screen" depth to the cabinet door composition. Cabinet doors were inlaid with clear maple cube plugs after being shop-sprayed with industrial high-gloss enamel. Shiny porcelain knobs and pulls reinforce the concept of "clean white" space.

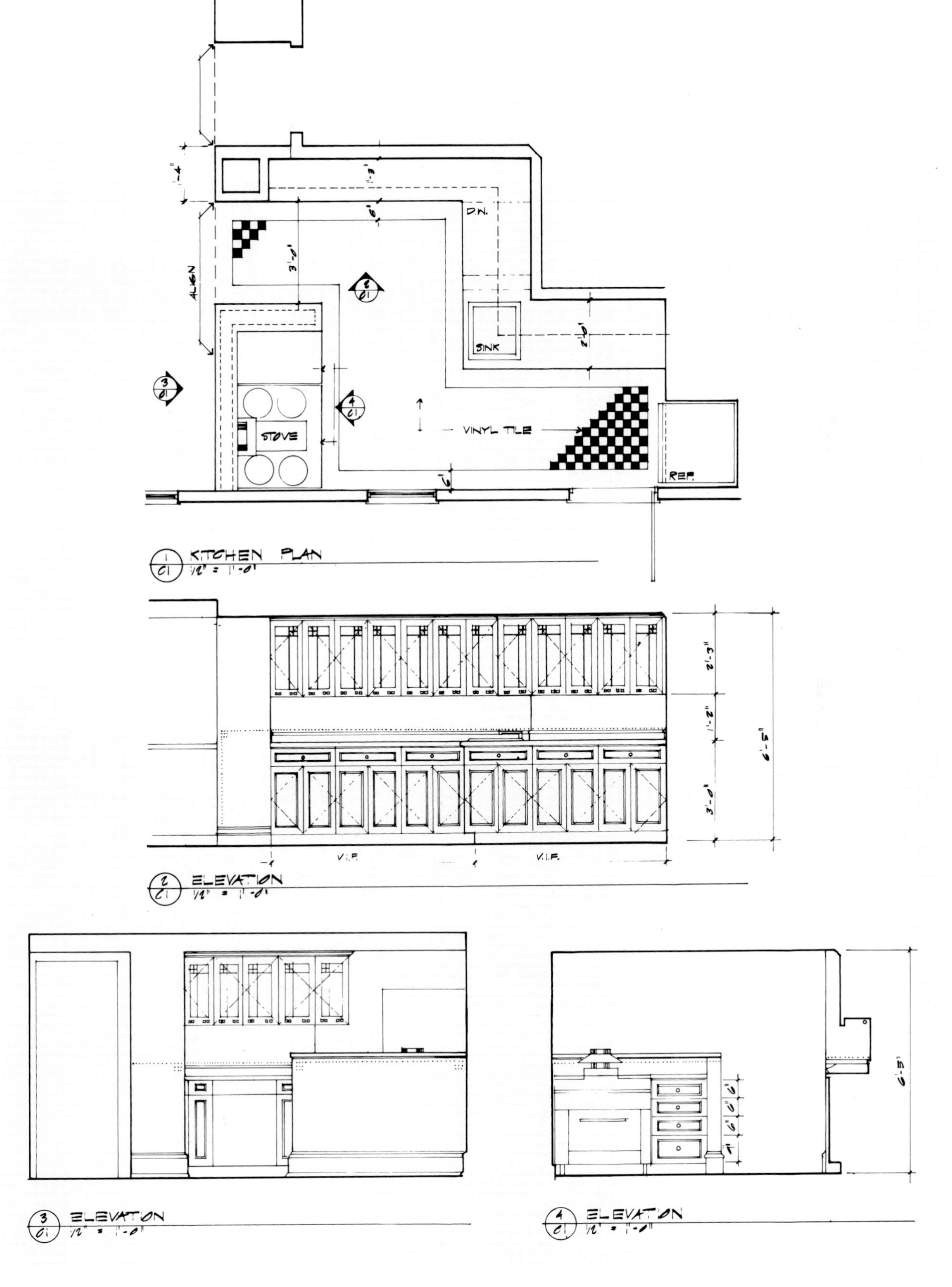
D.N.
ALIGN
1'-4"
1'-3"
1'-6"
3'-0"
2'-0"
SINK
STOVE
VINYL TILE
REF.
6"
1 C1 KITCHEN PLAN 1/2" = 1'-0"
2'-3"
1'-2"
3'-0"
6'-5"
V.I.F.
V.I.F.
2 C1 ELEVATION 1/2" = 1'-0"
6'-5"
3 C1 ELEVATION 1/2" = 1'-0"
4 C1 ELEVATION 1/2" = 1'-0"

**Private Residence**
*Southern Rhode Island*

**Architect**
Shope Reno Wharton Associates

**Fabricator**
Architectural Preservation Group

**Photography**
© H. Durston Saylor

A stultifying sameness can occur in kitchen planning, spaces in which viable layouts and essential storage elements—upper, lower, and full-height cabinets—are limited in both type and number. Add certain cyclical preferences in color and finish, and the generic kitchen can be a very predictable place.

Not so this summer house kitchen, designed by Shope Reno Wharton Associates, for a couple with grown children. This unusually long galley kitchen was intentionally developed to serve as both an "informal, efficient workspace" and "unobtrusive backdrop" to adjacent living and dining spaces that overlook southern Rhode Island's coastal waterfront.

The predominant feature of the workspace is a 24′–4¼″ bank of upper and lower cabinets that were aligned, in elevation, with a row of ceiling skywindows installed side-by-side between roof rafters (*elevation*). Because the rafters and supporting span beam precluded the installation of standard-height upper cabinets, the architects designed a 1′–4″ × 1′–0″ upper cabinet module to fit flush beneath the beam (*section at cabinet*). Covered in meticulously crafted glass-framed doors (*stile and panel details*), the cabinets, unlike standard-height cabinets, offer eye-level storage in which every cubic inch is completely accessible.

The kitchen occupies 300 square feet of the 6,000-square-foot, 1890s Shingle-style barn the architects renovated for the family in 1985.

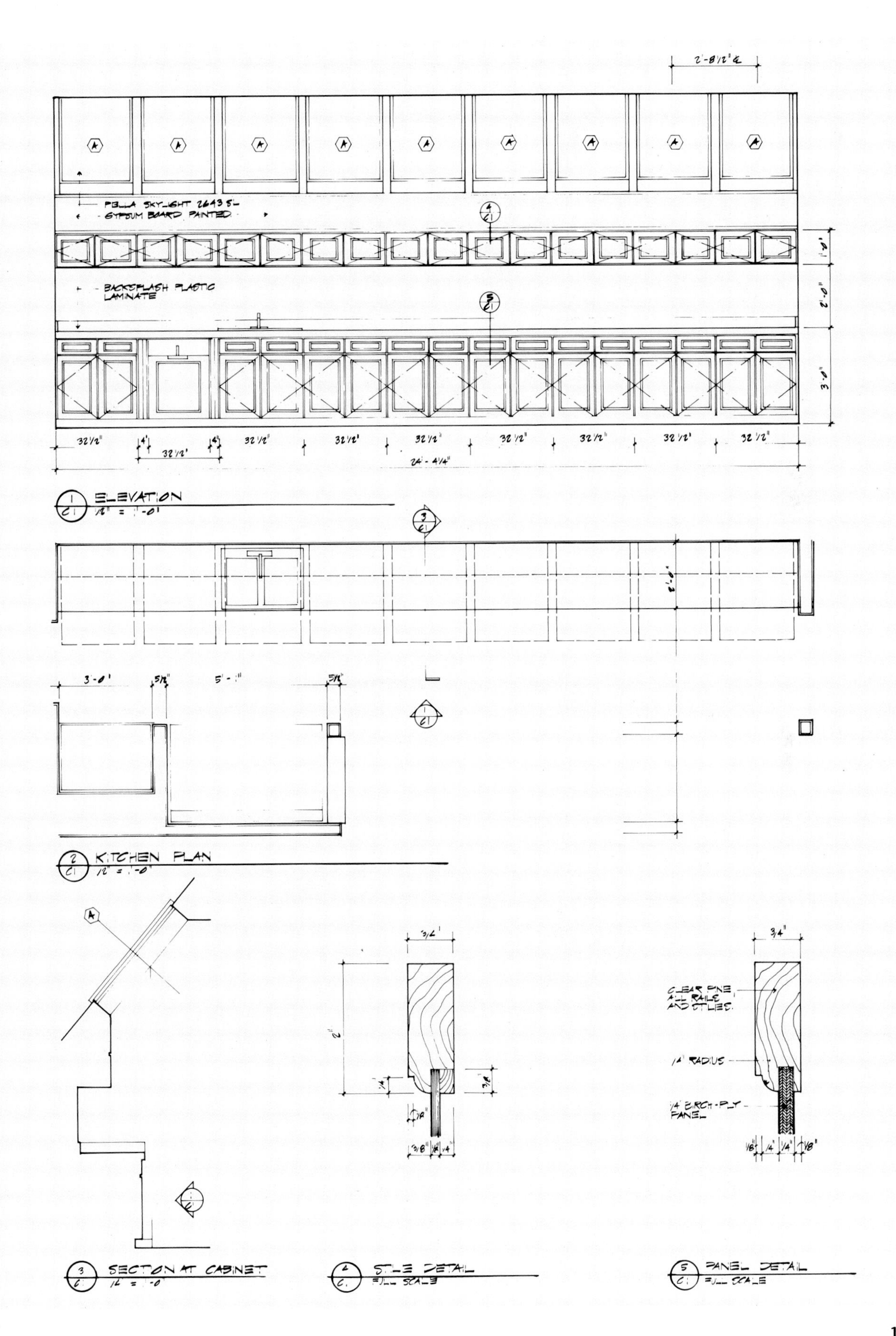
2'-8 1/2" C
PELLA SKYLIGHT 2643 SL
GYPSUM BOARD PAINTED
BACKSPLASH PLASTIC LAMINATE
1'-0"
2'-0"
3'-0"
32 1/2"
4"
32 1/2"
24' - 4 1/4"
1 C1 ELEVATION 1/2" = 1'-0"
3'-0"
5'-1"
2 C1 KITCHEN PLAN 1/2" = 1'-0"
3/4"
2"
CLEAR PINE ALL RAILS AND STILES.
1/4" RADIUS
1/4" BIRCH-PLY PANEL
3 C1 SECTION AT CABINET 1/2" = 1'-0"
4 C1 STILE DETAIL FULL SCALE
5 C1 PANEL DETAIL FULL SCALE

# KITCHEN CABINETS

## MOUNT RESIDENCE
*Atlanta, Georgia*

**Architect**
James Mount/Architect

**Design Team**
James Mount, AIA, Architect;
Sharon Mount, Interior Designer

**Fabricator**
Frank Zorc

**Photography**
© Hugh Loomis

ATLANTA-BASED ARCHITECT James Mount is a busy man—a principal of his own firm and an instructor at the College of Architecture at Georgia Institute of Technology. His wife, Sharon, is the vice president of interiors at Heery International. Together, the couple juggle their professional lives with the activities of their two teenagers and, more often than not, a flock of their own as well as their teenagers' friends.

Thus, when the family made the decision to renovate their 1920s house, a certain bizarre logic would have suggested that the Mounts hire a colleague, with more time to spare, to design it. But logic has little to do with a do-it-yourself bent, particularly when professional pride is involved. Accordingly, the Mounts undertook the project themselves: "We would have been terrible clients—opinionated and differing in our opinions, meticulous to the point of obsession and, because of our respective schedules, invariably unreachable for group discussion."

Before remodeling, the house was much as it had been since its 1929 construction. The couple wanted to lighten the house, to modernize it. The kitchen, in particular, required a total overhaul to update the space and improve its functionality.

The Mounts, as a matter of conscience and economy, recycled materials from the existing kitchen wherever possible. Layers of floor covering were removed until the original oak flooring was exposed; the floor was then sanded and waxed. The reclaimed floor symbolically linked the new cabinets to the antiquated structure, as it suggested a clean stylistic direction.

The new cabinets the Mounts designed for the kitchen serve two purposes—one practical, one aesthetic: they are used as standard storage receptacles, and as display cabinets for the glass and china the family collects.

The cabinets were constructed simply of solid basswood, according to the Mounts' ingenious, simplified design. In this system, an upper cabinet frame 2′–3″ × 3′–0″ with six 9-inch square openings was formed from rails in stiles of paint-grade wood in component pieces. This framework was backed with a full-size sheet of glass, held in place with snap-in plastic stops that allow easier cleaning.

The finish for wood cabinets and door frames began with a mixture of oil-based paint and mineral spirits in equal proportions. The dilution of the paint was intended to allow the wood grain to show through. (The paint was mixed with mineral spirits because, unlike turpentine, the fluid does not reduce the paint's sheen.) The cabinets were sealed with several coats of polyurethane. Concealed hinges allow the cabinets to read as smooth surfaces. Pulls—black neoprene rectangles—are minimal in scale and strongly graphic in impact.

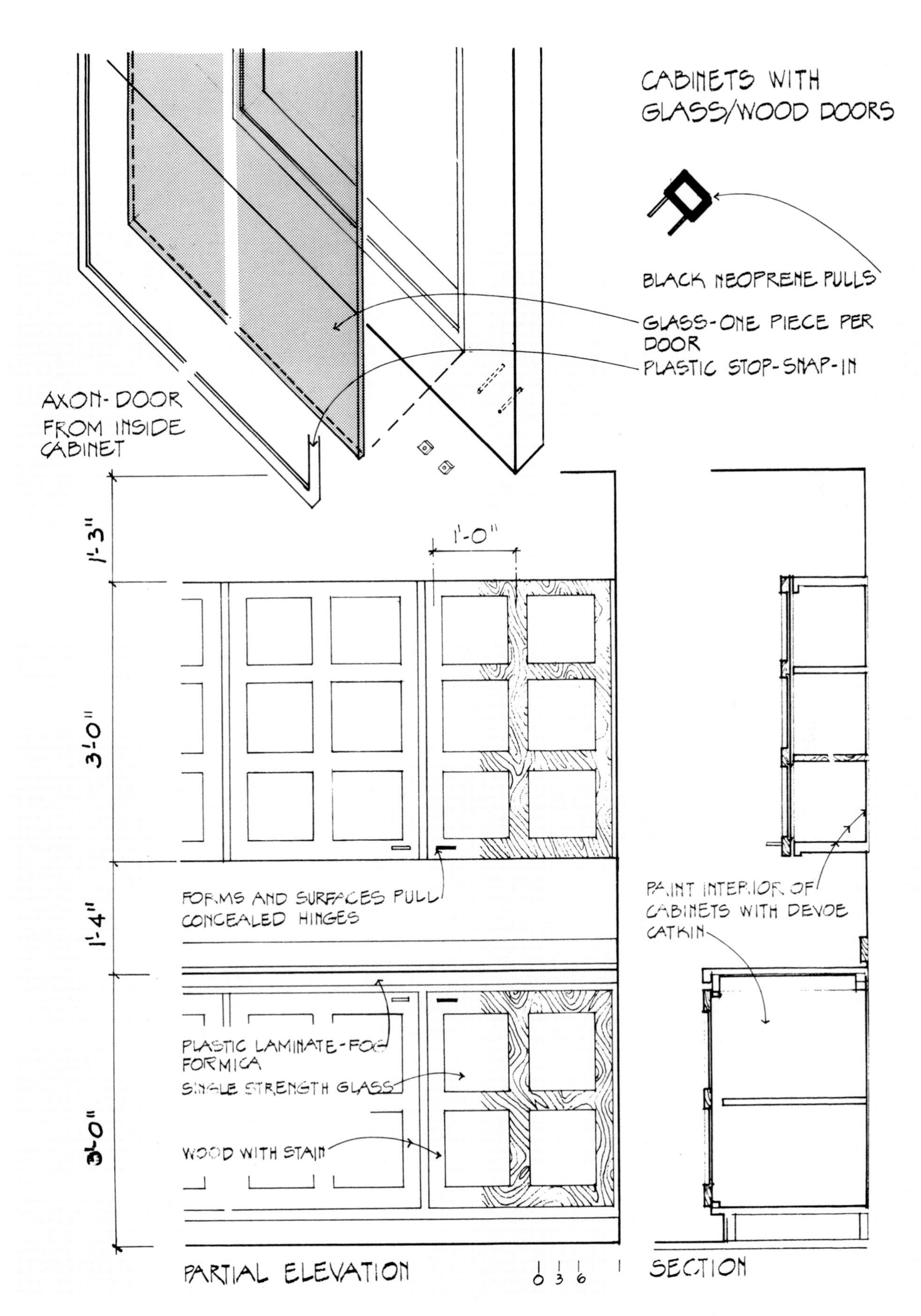
CABINETS WITH
GLASS/WOOD DOORS
BLACK NEOPRENE PULLS
GLASS-ONE PIECE PER
DOOR
PLASTIC STOP-SNAP-IN
AXON-DOOR
FROM INSIDE
CABINET
1'-3"
1'-0"
3'-0"
FORMS AND SURFACES PULL
CONCEALED HINGES
1'-4"
PAINT INTERIOR OF
CABINETS WITH DEVOE
CATKIN
PLASTIC LAMINATE-FOG
FORMICA
SINGLE STRENGTH GLASS
3'-0"
WOOD WITH STAIN
PARTIAL ELEVATION
0 3 6
SECTION

## FOREST DUNES RESIDENCE
*Covert County, Michigan*

**Architect**
Pappageorge Haymes Ltd.

**Photography**


TEM HORWITZ, a prominent Chicago developer by day, tries to lead his private life—at night and at weekends—on the Tai Chi principle of "ordered simplicity." Accordingly, he and his wife purchased a lakefront site in western Michigan, on which to build a "sun-drenched family getaway house in close contact with nature."

Pappageorge Haymes delivered the Horwitz "dream house" by developing an east/west oriented, 2,300-square-foot plan that was based, conceptually, on "an ordered informality in a progression of open spaces." The largest open space—a double-height living room, a dining area, and a kitchen—allows the couple, as well as their three children, to enjoy an informal flow of activity from one public "room" of the space to another.

The kitchen, although fully equipped with upper cabinets on its interior wall, is divided from the dining and living areas of the space by a 7′–3″ horizontal span of counter-covered lower cabinets. Consequently, the cook—"whomever that may be on any given day"—is able to enjoy spectacular and unobstructed views of Lake Michigan through a peninsular configuration of floor-to-ceiling gridded windows.

Pappageorge Haymes embellished the back and the exposed side of the room-dividing lower cabinets, in elevation, with a free-form stainless steel "skirt" that faces the dining area (*elevation; plan-stainless steel skirt*). The insouciant skirt reinforces the carefree mentality of the house without inhibiting access to the utility cabinets on the kitchen side.

Vertical plywood ribs that form the contour of the curved skirt were screwed to the cabinet frames. A fascia of thin, pliable stainless steel sheeting was then attached to the ribs, top and bottom, with stainless steel screws.

The stainless steel skirt works in tandem with the cabinets to support and stabilize an overlaid, oversized cantilevered counter (*plan*). The exaggerated, cloud-shaped form of the countertop, which was constructed of white laminate over particleboard, was drawn with a compass and cut with a jigsaw.

This moderately priced cabinet/skirt/counter detail was constructed on-site in just three days; the entire Horwitz house was constructed in 1985 on a project budget of $65 per square foot.

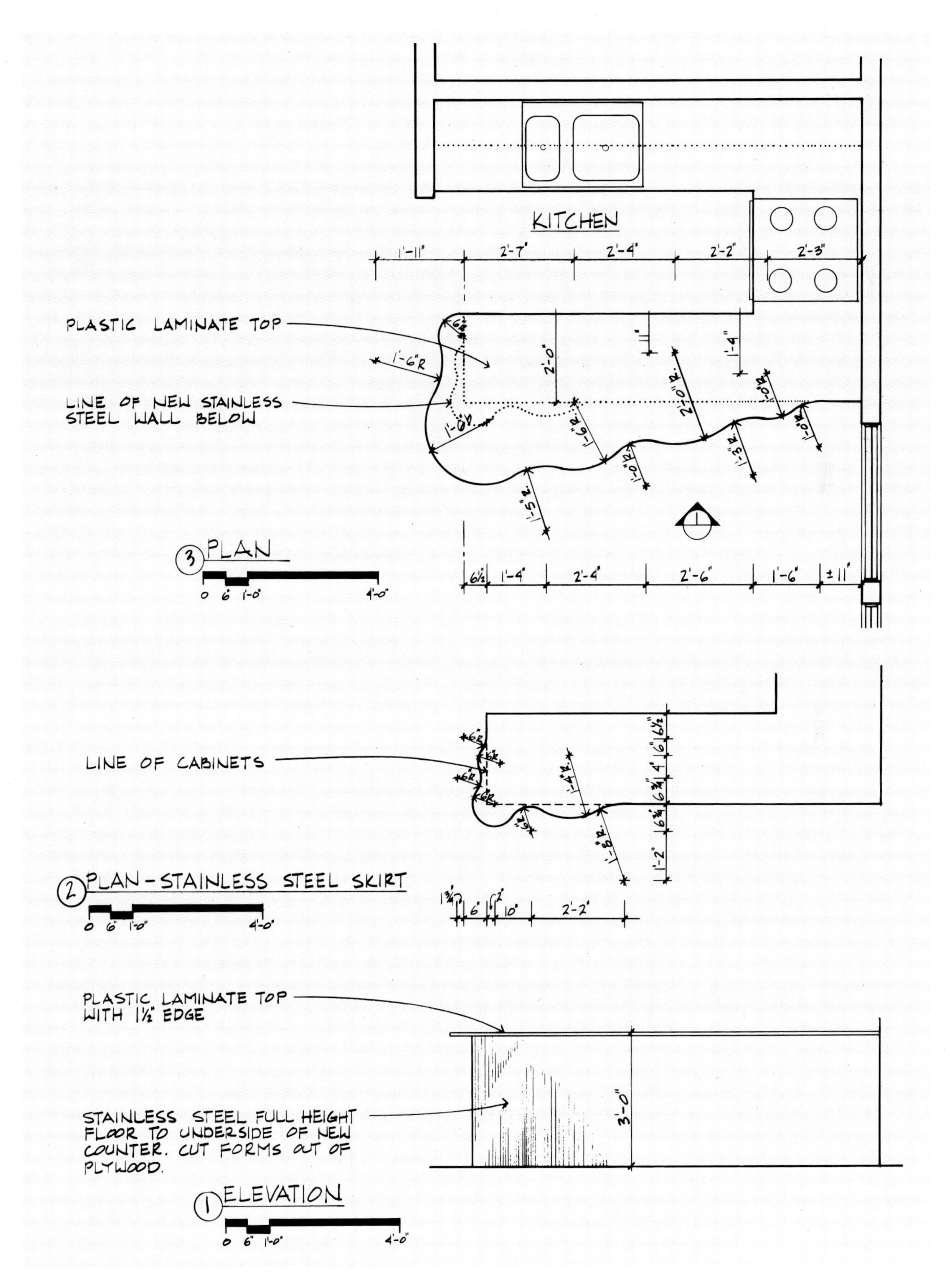
KITCHEN
PLASTIC LAMINATE TOP
LINE OF NEW STAINLESS STEEL WALL BELOW
3 PLAN
LINE OF CABINETS
2 PLAN - STAINLESS STEEL SKIRT
PLASTIC LAMINATE TOP WITH 1½" EDGE
STAINLESS STEEL FULL HEIGHT FLOOR TO UNDERSIDE OF NEW COUNTER. CUT FORMS OUT OF PLYWOOD.
1 ELEVATION

## PRIVATE LOFT
*New York, New York*

**Architect**
Haigh Space Architects

**Design Team**
Paul Haigh, AIA, Architect;
Barbara H. Haigh, IDSA, Designer;
Scott K. James, Architectural Designer;
Elizabeth Forcellini, Interior Designer

**General Contractor**
Martin Construction, Inc.

**Photography**
© Elliott Kaufman

THE RENOVATION of this 2,125-square-foot SoHo loft is a "tale of three surgeons." Both owners are surgeons—he, oral; she, gynecological. And Paul Haigh, not a surgeon but, rather, the project architect, adopted a "surgical" approach to the loft's interior design. According to Haigh, that meant that his method, metaphorically, was "to cut open and strip each architectural element to the point of exposing and displaying its structure and layers," the chief points of affinity between the two professions. (*See also* Pavilion, page 154).

Haigh's solution manifests not only careful thought but also high style, particularly evident in the 185-square-foot kitchen. There, the architect's aim of stripping away surfaces is most clearly realized; not only the stove ventilation pipe itself, but also water and drain pipes are exposed, with surfaces polished to hospital-lab hygienic standards. Two structural columns are similarly bare, and because light and sprinkler fixtures are suspended rather than recessed, the ceiling gives the appearance of having been pared back to the structural level above it. In the wall connecting the kitchen with the small study, an incisionlike opening lends the partition an organic character.

The range under the ventilating hood is a stainless steel Thermidor, set into the clients' preferred polished granite countertop above a Haigh-designed base cabinet. The cabinet brings the loft's ubiquitous quadrant curve into the kitchen, where it is also reflected on the ceiling (*axonometric*). The base functions as a storage cabinet for cooking ware.

The ventilating hood itself was fabricated of off-the-shelf 8-inch-diameter flexible aluminum duct; its weight is supported by a simple collar, the flange of which was sandwiched between two 1′–2″ square plates of 1/16-inch stainless steel (*section; plan*). The plates, in turn, were hung from the structural ceiling by 1/4-inch stainless steel rods, onto which stainless steel dome nuts were threaded (*section; plan*). The curvature of the duct resulted from the off-set locations of the range in conjunction with the building's existing ventilation ductwork, to which the kitchen hood had to be connected.

The range has its own built-in down-draft extractor, which functions as an auxiliary vent to the suspended tubular hood. Haigh recommends the solution as a change-of-pace ventilation detail; despite the absence of the usual broad hood feeding into an exhaust duct, this hood works extremely well.

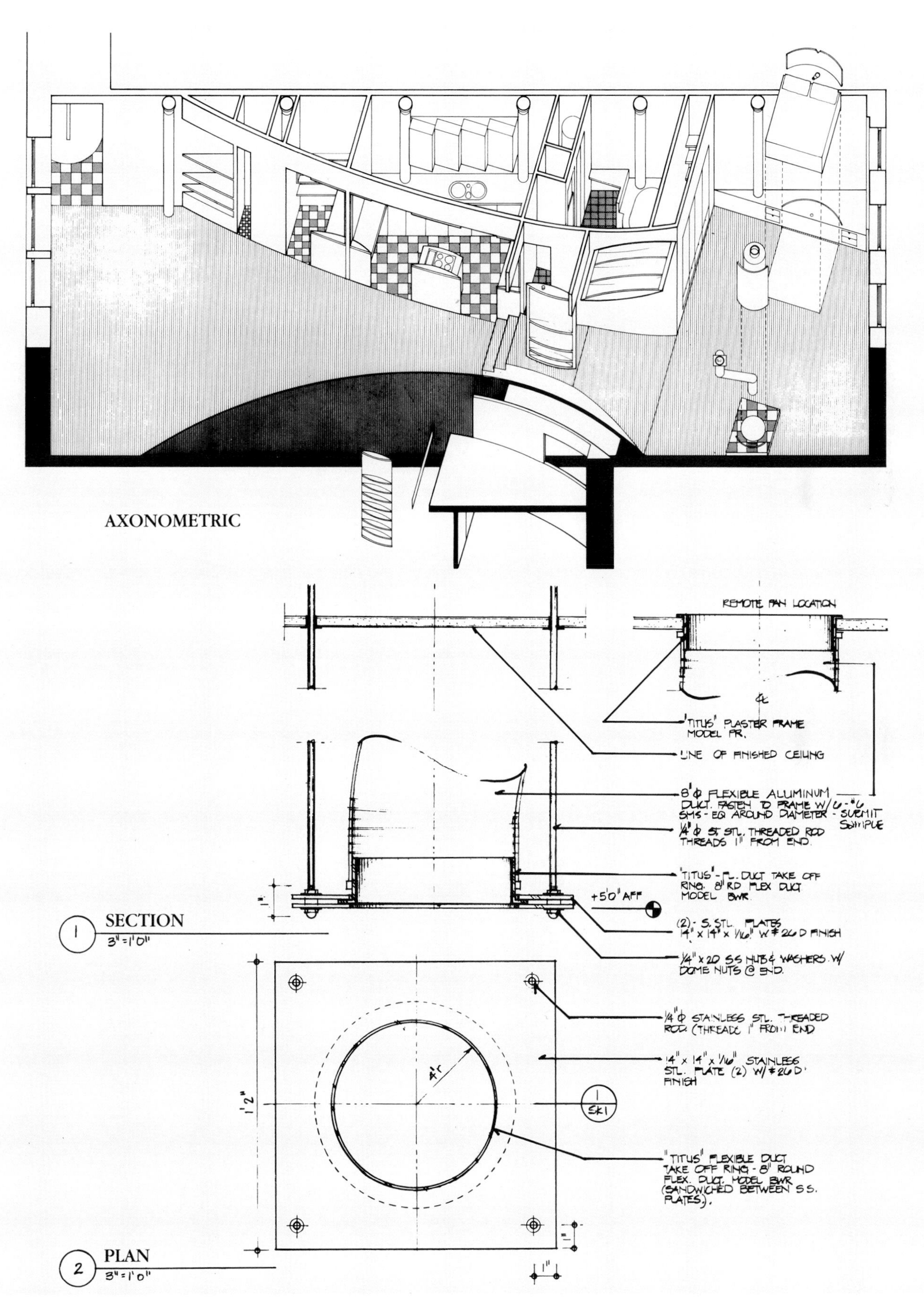
AXONOMETRIC
REMOTE FAN LOCATION
℄
"TITUS" PLASTER FRAME MODEL FR.
LINE OF FINISHED CEILING
8" Φ FLEXIBLE ALUMINUM DUCT. FASTEN TO FRAME W/ 6-#6 SMS-EQ AROUND DIAMETER - SUBMIT SAMPLE
1/4" Φ ST. STL. THREADED ROD THREADS 1" FROM END.
"TITUS"-FL. DUCT TAKE OFF RING. 8" RD FLEX DUCT MODEL BWR.
+5'0" AFF
(2)-S. STL. PLATES 14" x 14" x 1/16" W/ #26 D FINISH
1/4" x 20 SS NUTS & WASHERS. W/ DOME NUTS @ END.
1
SECTION
3" = 1'0"
1/4" Φ STAINLESS STL. THREADED ROD (THREADS 1" FROM END
14" x 14" x 1/16" STAINLESS STL. PLATE (2) W/ #26 D FINISH
4"r
1'2"
1
SK1
"TITUS" FLEXIBLE DUCT TAKE OFF RING - 8" ROUND FLEX. DUCT. MODEL BWR (SANDWICHED BETWEEN S.S. PLATES).
2
PLAN
3" = 1'0"
1"

# Kitchen Hood

**Lawrence Residence**
*Hermosa Beach, California*

**Architect**
Morphosis

**Design Team**
Thom Mayne, Principal;
Michael Rotondi, Principal;
Benjamin Caffey, Project Manager;
Frank Lupo, Project Manager;
Marlou Vengelers, Project Manager;
Kazu Arai, Project Manager

**Mechanical Consultant**
The Sullivan Partnership, Inc.

**Structural Consultant**
Erdelyi Moon Mezey

**Photography**
© Peter Aaron/ESTO

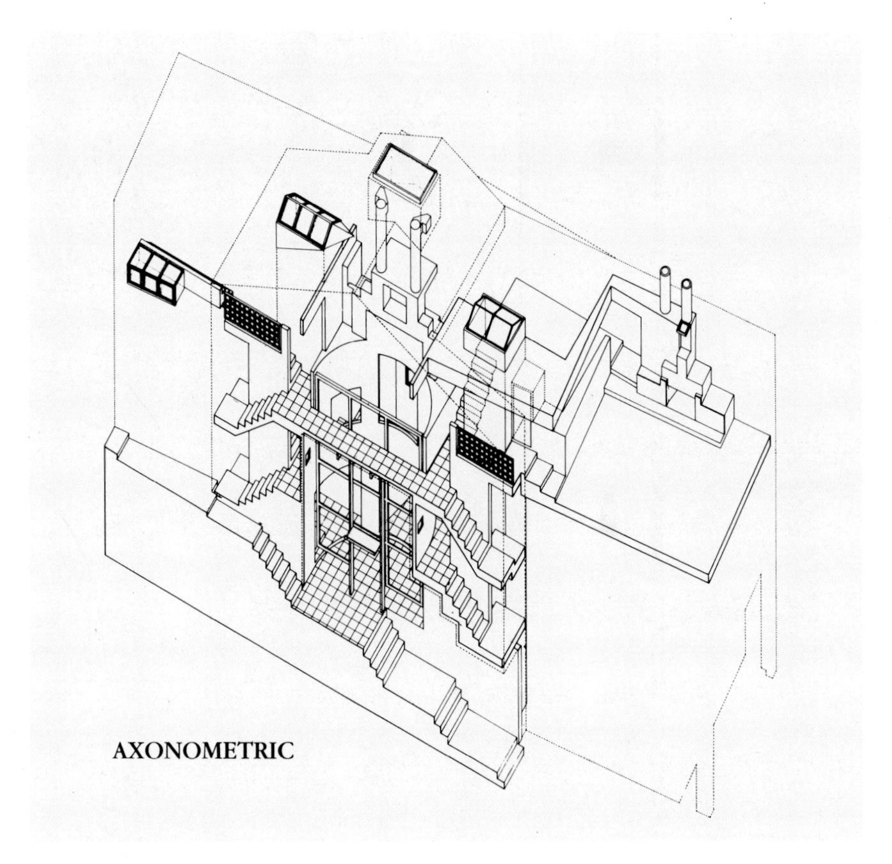

AXONOMETRIC

Viable building sites in proximity to Los Angeles that also overlook the Pacific Ocean are a rarity these days, and those lots that do remain tend to be problematic—they are apt to slide off into the ocean at the first earthquake tremor or be blocked from the magnificence of their view by a cloud of Los Angeles's yellow smog. But a semiretired lawyer and his wife were luckier than most: they found a narrow 30′ × 85′ lot with a 17-foot slope that overlooked the Pacific without pollution obfuscation. After sponsoring an informal architectural competition, they commissioned Morphosis, of Santa Monica, to design and oversee the construction of their house (*see* Storage Cabinets, page 207).

The program the clients presented to the architects was demanding—they aspired to "a piece of architecture, not just another building." Morphosis accepted the challenge, developing a concept that was original both in its approach to design and construction economy. The firm's careful attention to financial management resulted in a construction cost of $100–120 per square foot (cheaper, Morphosis believes, than if the project had been bid), of which about 20 percent was attributable to the difficult excavation and foundation work for the site.

The site ultimately determined not only the price, but also the layout of the house. The upper floor commands the best views of the ocean, and the only views up and down the coast. It seemed the appropriate location for the family's main focus: the wife's excellent cooking. Thus, the upper story is devoted entirely to the kitchen, the dining room, and a sun roof that doubles as an outdoor dining area.

The 4,200-square-foot house is relatively narrow (24 feet at the kitchen) and vertical (three full floors above the basement). Morphosis's organizing principle, therefore, was vertical: a semicircular air shaft or "public space," flanked by stairways and bridged between the second and third floors (*axonometric*). "One can stroll up, down, and around this space," says Morphosis principal Michael Rotondi, "and discover different aspects of the house at different times of day. No matter where the sun is during the day, the house is filled with it; but the sunlight varies in direction and character, and the home takes on many different moods."

The kitchen range, set into Colorcore laminate cabinets, was placed so that the cook can see across the top of the public space, as well as through the window beyond, to views along the coast.

Behind the granite counter rise two massive 3′–0″ square columns; from these the ventilation hood is cantilevered out 3′–0″ over the range. The columns and hood shell are standard wood-frame and plasterboard construction; inside the shell a custom inlay pan of welded stainless steel is bolted, as the motor and fans are bolted into the pan. These suck exhaust air into two sheet metal risers that vent at right angles into the open air through the plastic "parapets" of a large skylight cut through the redwood ceiling.

# KITCHEN ISLAND

**RANTA RESIDENCE**
*Mahapac, New York*

**Architect**
William M. Cohen, Architect

**Design Team**
William M. Cohen, Principal;
David Arnold, Associate

**Structural Engineer**
Joong Lee

**Construction Manager**
Edward Worthington
Construction Company

**Fabricators**
R & D Woodworking;
Sally Johnnes (trompe l'oeil)

**Photography**
© Norman McGrath

BARBARA AND RAYMOND RANTA lived happily for eight years in a charming eighteenth-century farmhouse in upstate New York. But charm tends to wear thin under an endless barrage of maintenance problems; consequently, in 1986 the Rantas commissioned architect William Cohen to design a brand-new, "no-maintenance" weekend getaway house that—to make occasional, yet year-round entertaining easy—was to include "a heated sunporch near an open kitchen."

The architect was given carte blanche to select an appropriate 8-acre building site from among the 56 acres the clients owned in Mahapac, New York. Cohen selected a high site that provides breathtaking views of nearby mountains.

As a first step in reducing maintenance, the design team developed a graveled courtyard plan, within which the main house, a garage, a pool, a pool house, and a 5-foot perennial border were enclosed. To maximize fuel economy and privacy as well, all major living spaces in the main house, including the master bedroom suite, are intentionally situated on the ground floor; guest room accommodations are contained on the second floor so that they may, when empty, be shut off from the rest of the house.

The Rantas are infrequent entertainers, neither of whom wishes to take time out from business or leisure pursuits to cook, particularly in isolation. Therefore, the design team developed a cruciform footprint for the first-floor plan, centered both symbolically and literally by an island kitchen that was positioned at the intersection of the two major axes.

Because the kitchen was built as a low-partitioned island, rather than a full-height partitioned room, social interaction with family or guests in the entry hall, living room, or dining room is unimpeded. Because the dividing partition extends 1′–4″ above standard counter height, kitchen clutter from outside the island is hidden from view.

The island was configured to function as a galley kitchen (*plan; interior elevations*) with open storage both inside and out (*north, east, west elevations*). The cabinetry was shop-built in seven sections so that stock dimensions of plywood, as well as red oak veneer and trim could be used. The design team reinvested those savings by developing a number of finish details for the island that were then fabricated in solid oak, including a radius-edge baseboard and a countertop apron. Red oak was specified to match the oak floors laid throughout the first floor, which blend, in turn, with the frame finishes of major furnishing pieces.

A full-size refrigerator, on axis with the entrance, is recessed into the full-height north wall immediately beyond the island. The refrigerator door was painted by a trompe l'oeil artist to simulate the screen door of the Rantas' original farmhouse, with a background suggestive of its romantic, landscaped view.

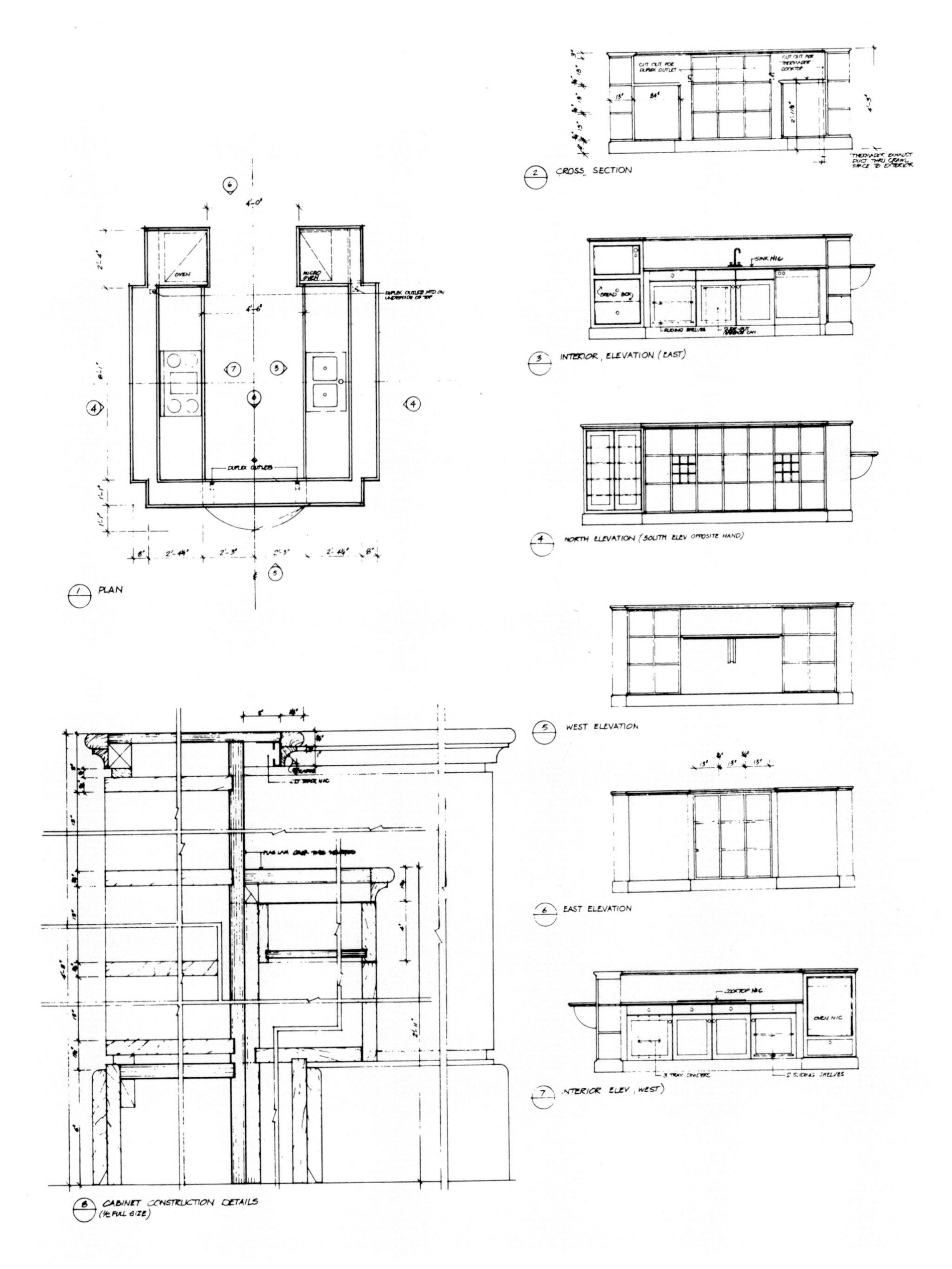

1 PLAN
OVEN
DUPLEX OUTLETS
2 CROSS SECTION
3 INTERIOR ELEVATION (EAST)
SINK N.I.C.
BREAD BOX
4 NORTH ELEVATION (SOUTH ELEV OPPOSITE HAND)
5 WEST ELEVATION
6 EAST ELEVATION
7 INTERIOR ELEV, WEST)
OVEN N.I.C.
8 CABINET CONSTRUCTION DETAILS
(1/2 FULL SIZE)

# Kitchen Island

**Private Residence**
*Greenwich, Connecticut*

**Architect**
Shope Reno Wharton Associates

**Fabricator**
Colonial Woodworking, Inc.

**Photography**
© H. Durston Saylor

Houses built in the 1930s are, more often than not, gracefully proportioned structures built of high-quality materials. Such houses are highly prized by their owners and prospective buyers, who philosophically accept necessary renovations as a price well worth paying.

In 1983 Shope Reno Wharton Associates began a $290,000 renovation of and addition to an elegant 1930s Pennsylvania-style farmhouse located in Greenwich, Connecticut. Their clients—a real estate developer and a writer, with two children—asked the architects to reorder space within the house; add modern, family spaces; and open the house inside and out to light and views of the grounds and small lake.

The kitchen was quickly designated as the new hub of the house, although in its existing condition it was too small to provide the integrated dining space the clients hoped for. The kitchen did, however, offer the advantage of access to the dining room, a home office, and an adjacent bedroom.

By tearing down a party wall between the kitchen and the original pantry, the architects annexed 500 square feet that now incorporate into the kitchen a new dining area with a fireplace, as well as an archway entrance to the pool house addition.

Circulation within the expanded kitchen is routed around an oval preparation island that separates the work area from the dining room space without causing obstruction. Conviviality is encouraged by the island, in which a kneehole notch was cut to accommodate pull-up stools (*island plan; elevation 1*).

The oval configuration of the island and the upper cabinet door frames was developed to reinforce the curved archway that leads to the pool. But the oval end cabinets are not dead space; each houses quarter-round shelves for extra storage (*elevations 2 and 4*).

The workspace elevation of the island was fitted with drawers rather than door-covered cabinets to simplify the cook's access to pots and pans (*elevation 3*). Variously sized drawers were fitted beneath a downdraft gas cooktop, surmounted by a heavy-gauge stainless steel hood that was rolled to achieve an appropriate curve (*island section*).

The oval island is constructed of a ½-inch birch plywood frame that was bolted to the floor with steel angles. Curved door panels are fabricated of steam-bent ¼-inch plywood, set into ¾-inch frames.

The entire island was shop-sprayed with industrial high-gloss enamel in a dustfree environment. New stained oak floors connect the kitchen thematically to old oak floors throughout the house.

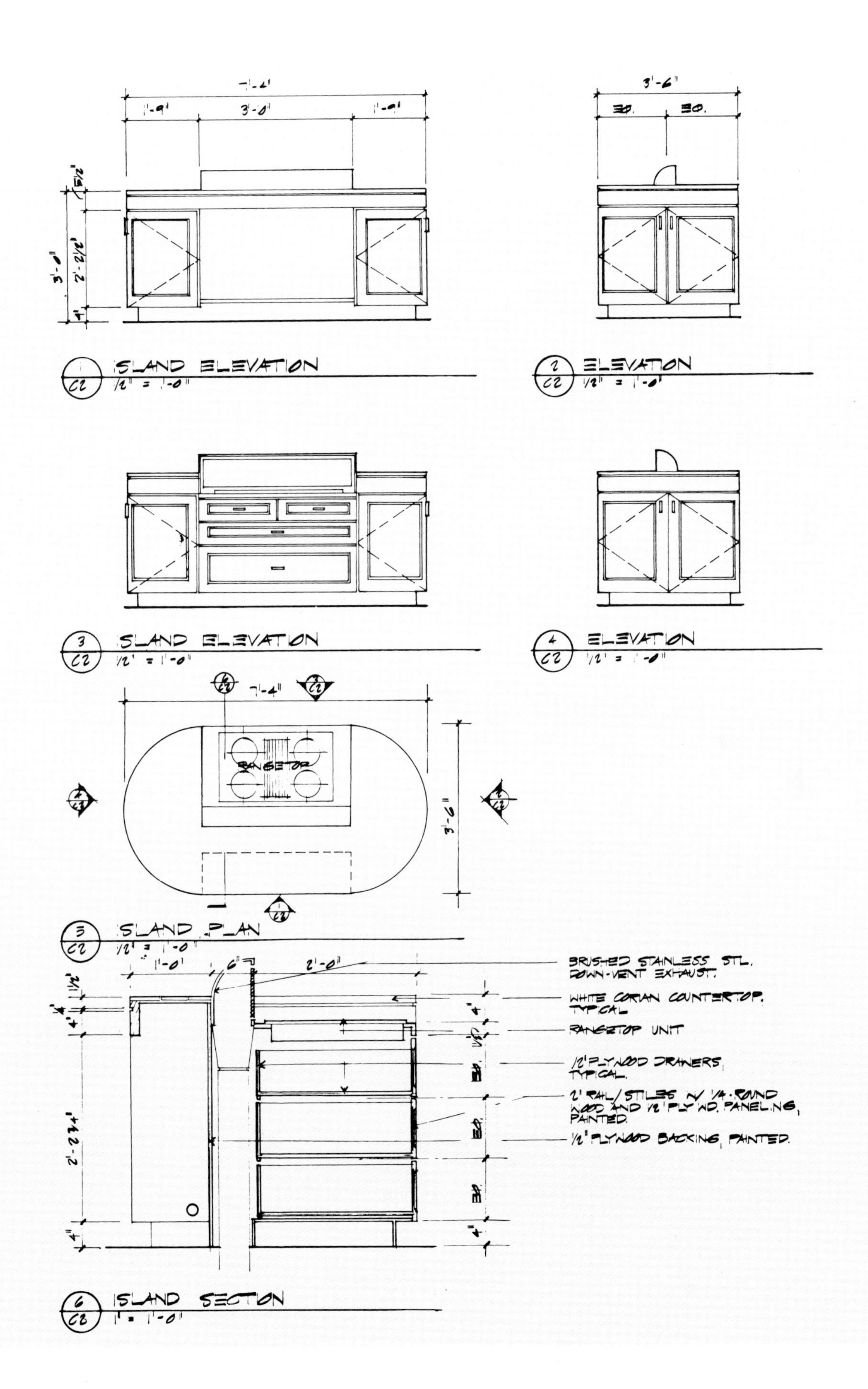
ISLAND ELEVATION
1/2" = 1'-0"
ELEVATION
1/2" = 1'-0"
ISLAND ELEVATION
1/2" = 1'-0"
ELEVATION
1/2" = 1'-0"
ISLAND PLAN
1/2" = 1'-0"
RANGETOP
ISLAND SECTION
1" = 1'-0"
BRUSHED STAINLESS STL. DOWN-VENT EXHAUST.
WHITE CORIAN COUNTERTOP, TYPICAL
RANGETOP UNIT
1/2" PLYWOOD DRAWERS, TYPICAL.
2" RAIL/STILES W/ 1/4-ROUND WOOD AND 1/2" PLY WD. PANELING, PAINTED.
1/2" PLYWOOD BACKING, PAINTED.

# KITCHEN ISLAND

**PRIVATE RESIDENCE**
*Kansas City, Missouri*

**Architect**
Roger Kraft: Architecture • Design

**Design Team**
Roger Kraft, Principal-in-Charge and Project Designer; Kathy Horstman, Project Architect

**Fabricator**
Bob Falkenberg Company

**Photography**
© Chris Kilmer

THERE IS AN ART to living well that consists, in part, of one's ability to transcend day-to-day problems by focusing instead on simple pleasures. A Kansas City couple who collect fine art as well as fine wine and liquors possess that special skill in full measure.

According to architect Roger Kraft, enhancing the pleasure his clients derive from their various collections quickly became the primary goal of the project. Details were developed throughout the house to establish "a clean, gallerylike space that draws attention to the collections, complementing rather than competing with them."

In the breakfast room, a streamlined island bar was designed to serve functional purposes, yet its sculptural form also serves the room as a primary piece of art. The island is a model of efficiency in cubic-storage planning—the every-inch-counts variety normally associated with the design of yacht fittings.

The island was constructed as a box within a box. Wood blocking and plywood framing provide structural support for the finish panels, doors, and countertop of Honduran mahogany plywood, as well as for interior compartments finished variously in painted wood, plastic laminate, or metal (*sections B and D*). The compartments house two concealed liquor cabinets, an icemaker, a refrigerator, adjustable storage shelves, and a recessed, pivoting television stand (*plan-section; front and rear elevations*). The countertop, banded in solid mahogany edging (*section C*), is punctuated by flush-fitted, metal-lined bottle wells, mahogany covers for electrical outlets, burners for coffee, a hot pad, a sink, and hatch covers for the liquor cabinets (*top plan*). The quarter-circle hinged mahogany hatches lift with fingerhole pulls to reveal bottle wells below. In elevation, at the opposite end of the island and facing the breakfast table, a curved mahogany sliding door—set ⅜ of an inch back from the bar edge on an interior track—opens 60 degrees to reveal the television (*elevation A*).

The island countertop is finished in Honduran mahogany veneer applied so that the grain runs lengthwise along the bar. All of the mahogany plywood was lightly stained to even out small discrepancies in wood coloration, and was then treated with several coats of satin polyurethane.

The oval shape of the 11′–6″ bar is accentuated concentrically on the ceiling plane by a recessed oval light fixture. Floor banding, rendered in black Andes granite, also reiterates the oval theme.

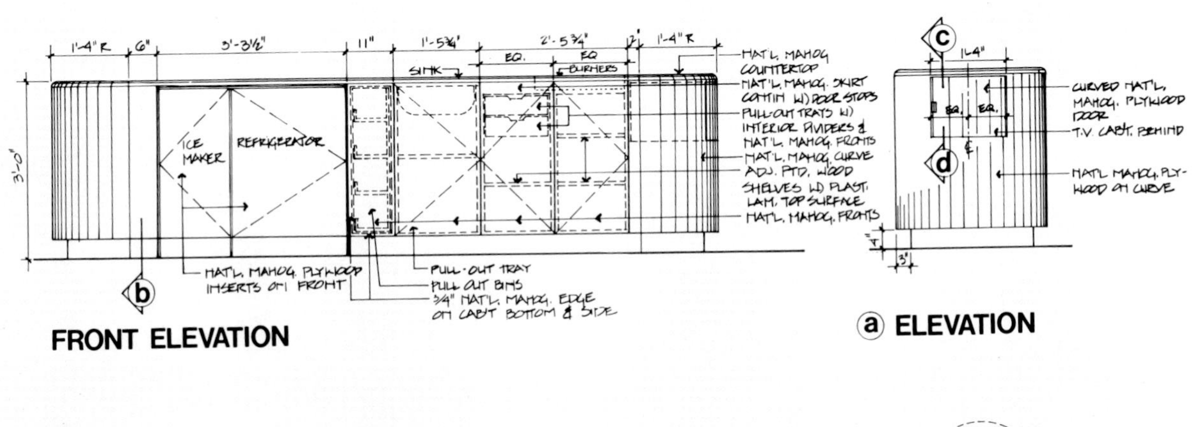


**FRONT ELEVATION**

ⓐ **ELEVATION**

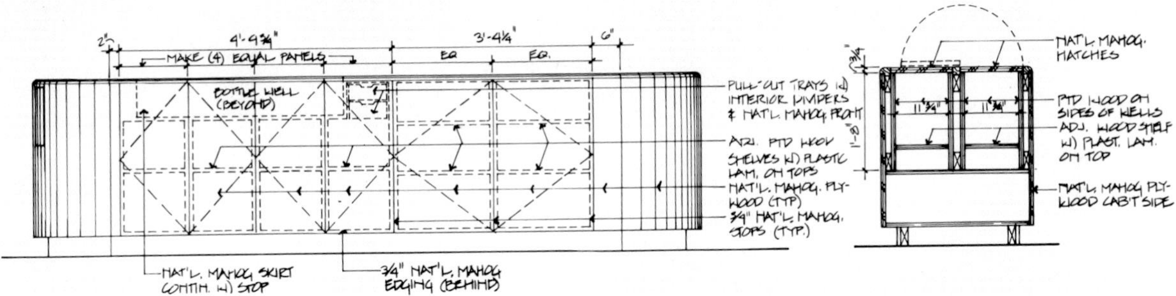


**REAR ELEVATION**

ⓑ **SECTION**

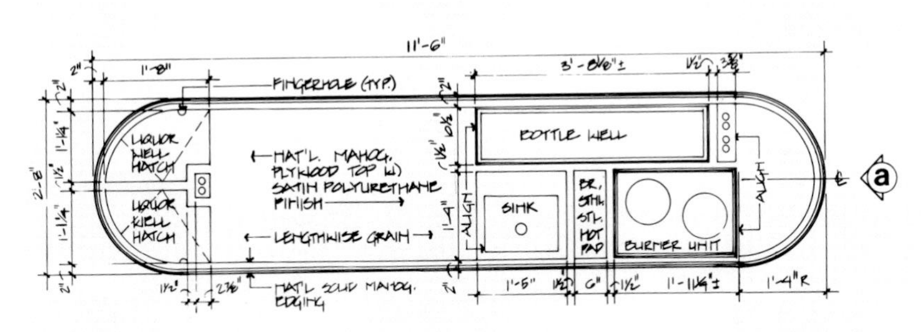


**TOP PLAN**

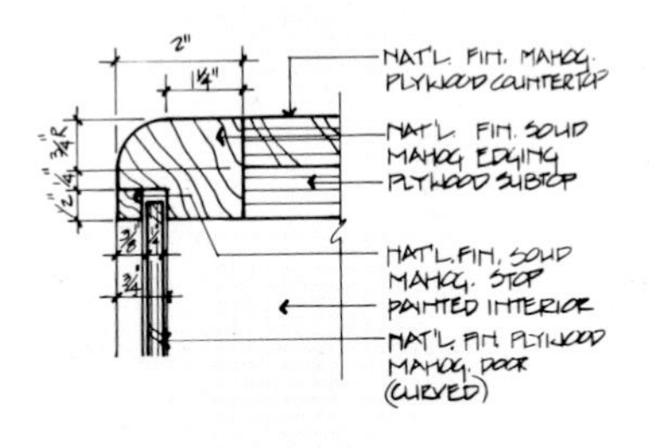


ⓒ **SECTION**

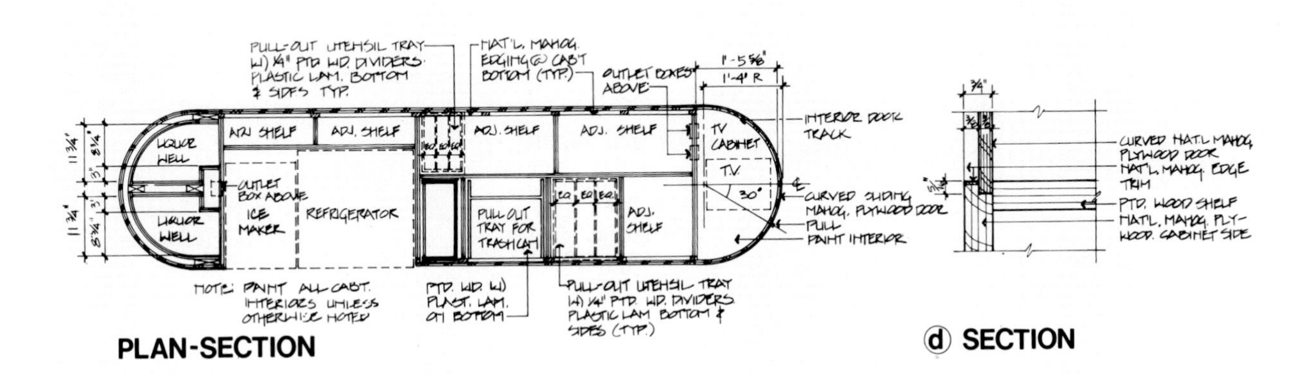


**PLAN-SECTION**

ⓓ **SECTION**

# KITCHEN ISLAND/COUNTER

**PANISH LOFT**
*New York, New York*

**Architect**
Anderson/Schwartz Architects

**Design Team**
Frederic Schwartz, Partner-in-Charge; Marc L'Italien, Project Architect

**Lighting Consultant**
Clark Johnson, Johnson Schwinghammer Lighting Consultants

**General Contractor**
Alan Custom Building

**Fabricators**
Peter Jevremov, Metal Forms Studio (base metal work); Henry Cook, (stainless steel)

**Photography**
© Anderson/Schwartz Architects

CENTER STAGE in the SoHo loft of Larry Panish—the master chef and restaurateur who routinely entertains from two to twenty-two guests—is one of the most captivating professional kitchens extant in a private residence. Architects Anderson/Schwartz developed the overall kitchen plan, as well as its one-of-a-kind island/counter detail, in response to a client request for "elegance combined with functionality, specifically expressed by sheer size in preparation area, and finish materials that not only work with stainless steel, but also make a design statement." The client left stylistic development entirely up to the imagination of the design team. His final directive: "Go for it."

The architects complied, with considerable panache. Moved, perhaps, by the expanse of the surface that their client demanded, architects Frederic Schwartz and Marc L'Italien carried the "island" metaphor used to describe a freestanding kitchen counter-cum-cabinet one step further into the realm of imagination: they decided to shape the pattern and edge of the surface irregularly, as if it were a map of a real island. Two existing structural columns (*photograph*) served as points of "reference and erosion," from which the "coastline" of the counter edge erodes (*island plan*).

About 40 percent of the surface area was executed in stainless steel; the balance was rendered in an artisan's palette of eleven different granites and marbles—materials that contribute to an overall quality of eccentric elegance. "We felt," says Schwartz, "that the contrast of qualities derived from juxtaposing many stones brought out and enhanced the inherent character of each."

The marble surface of the island was conceived as a topographical map. Anderson/Schwartz made precise, full-scale paper templates for each segment, selected specific marble slabs at the yard, and then entrusted the actual cutting work to proven craftsmen. The counter was fabricated off-site in three segments (identified in the *island plan* as abc, def, and ghijk), which were butt-jointed to one another, as well as to the already finished steel surface, on-site.

For such a broad surface with so many component pieces it was crucial to compensate for the expansion and contraction that normally occurs from temperature and humidity fluctuations. Therefore, instead of laying the ¾-inch marble directly on the ½-inch plywood subsurface, the fabricator was asked to cut and sandwich an intermediate layer of ⅜-inch white Carrera marble in between. The three sandwiched layers are bonded together with adhesive.

Frederic Schwartz refers to the island/counter detail as "the island of many marbles." (For another innovative detail from the same kitchen, *see* Kitchen Cabinets, page 114).

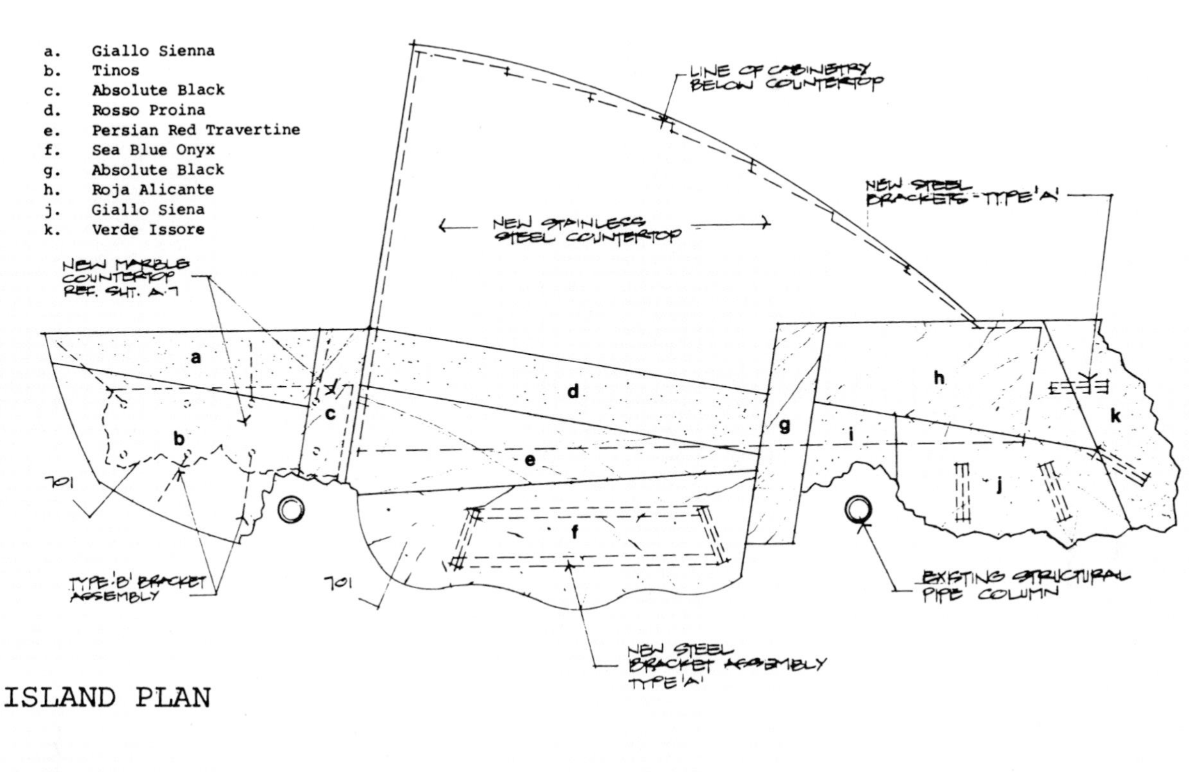


ISLAND PLAN

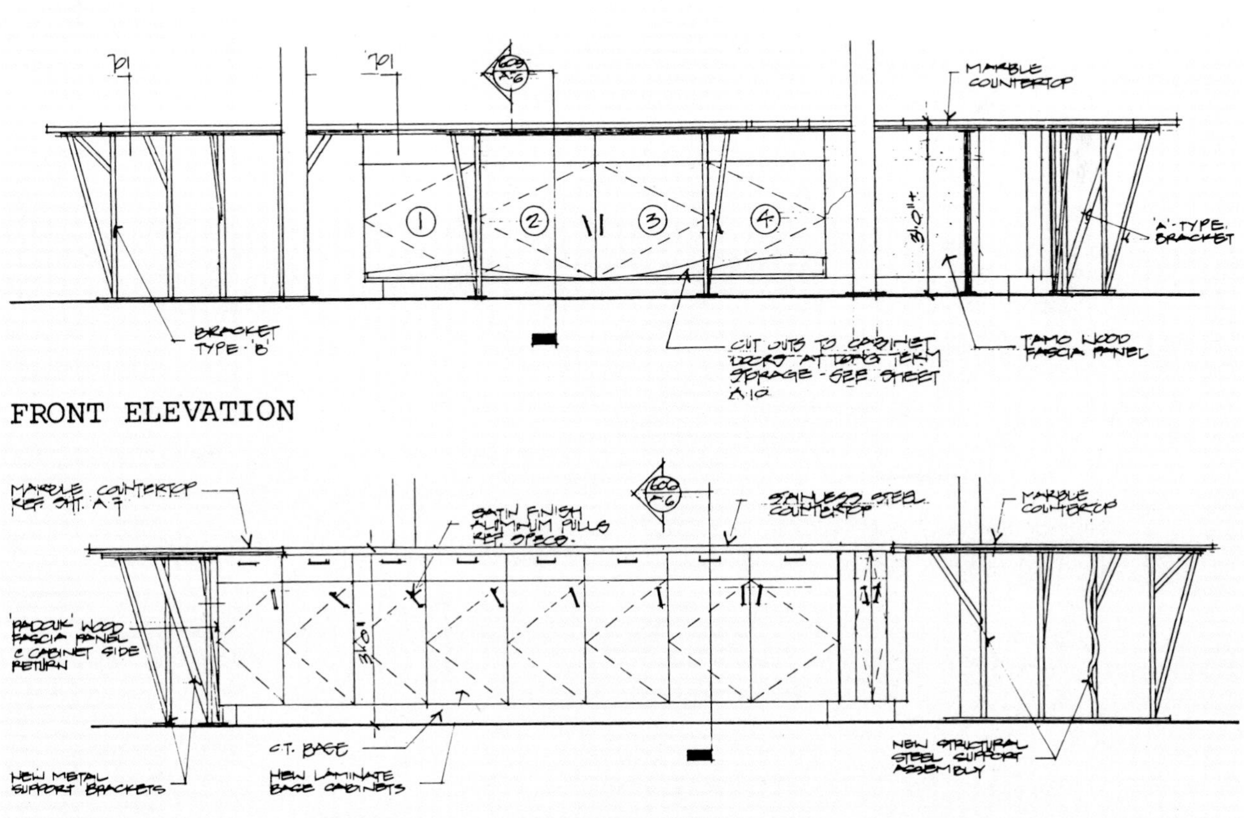


FRONT ELEVATION

# Molding

**Private Apartment**
*Chicago, Illinois*

**Architect**
Rudolph & Associates, P.C.

**Design Team**
Christopher H. Rudolph, AIA, Principal;
Lawrence M. Petitti, Architect;
Janet L. Steidl, ASID, Designer

**General Contractor**
Robert P. Schultz, Inc.

**Fabricator**
Torben Jensen Woodcraft Co.

**Photography**
© John Hollis Enterprises, Inc.

Small spaces call for design restraint; grand gestures, if incorporated into such interiors at all, must be handled and scaled with great care. Thus, a Chicago bachelor who collects antique prints confidently commissioned Christopher Rudolph—a creator of precise, elaborate detail on any scale (*see* Bathroom Cabinet, page 26; Door, page 84)—to redesign his 1,000-square-foot residence while keeping its character "quiet."

Rudolph transformed the apartment by stressing delicacy and restraint in his detailing solution, which consists of trim moldings that work with a subtle palette of colors (gray, silver, and gray-green, offset by pewter and zinc fixtures) to integrate the entire apartment. The molding not only stretches across the walls and ceilings of each room, but also connects one room to another.

Rather than attempting to impose a strict correspondence of wall and ceiling patterns to either locations or shapes of doors, windows or furnishings, Rudolph aimed for subtle surprise. The irregular molding grids and paints of six colors and two textures create their own logic—a subtle Mondrian-like surface pattern that succeeds in overcoming the apartment's inherent deficiencies without overwhelming the space (*reflected ceiling plan*).

The impact of the detailing was further enhanced by Rudolph's specification of several sizes and varieties of molding, all of which, although fabricated of stock sizes and shapes, contrast effectively (*details 8, 10, 13*). Rudolph used ceiling molding to lead the eye toward windows and doors, as well as wall molding to break the somewhat disproportionate height of the ceilings and to make the rooms appear wider.

All trim is paint-grade birch, glued and nailed to the existing plaster walls or, in the case of ceiling trim, to blocking that was pneumatically nailed to the ceiling.

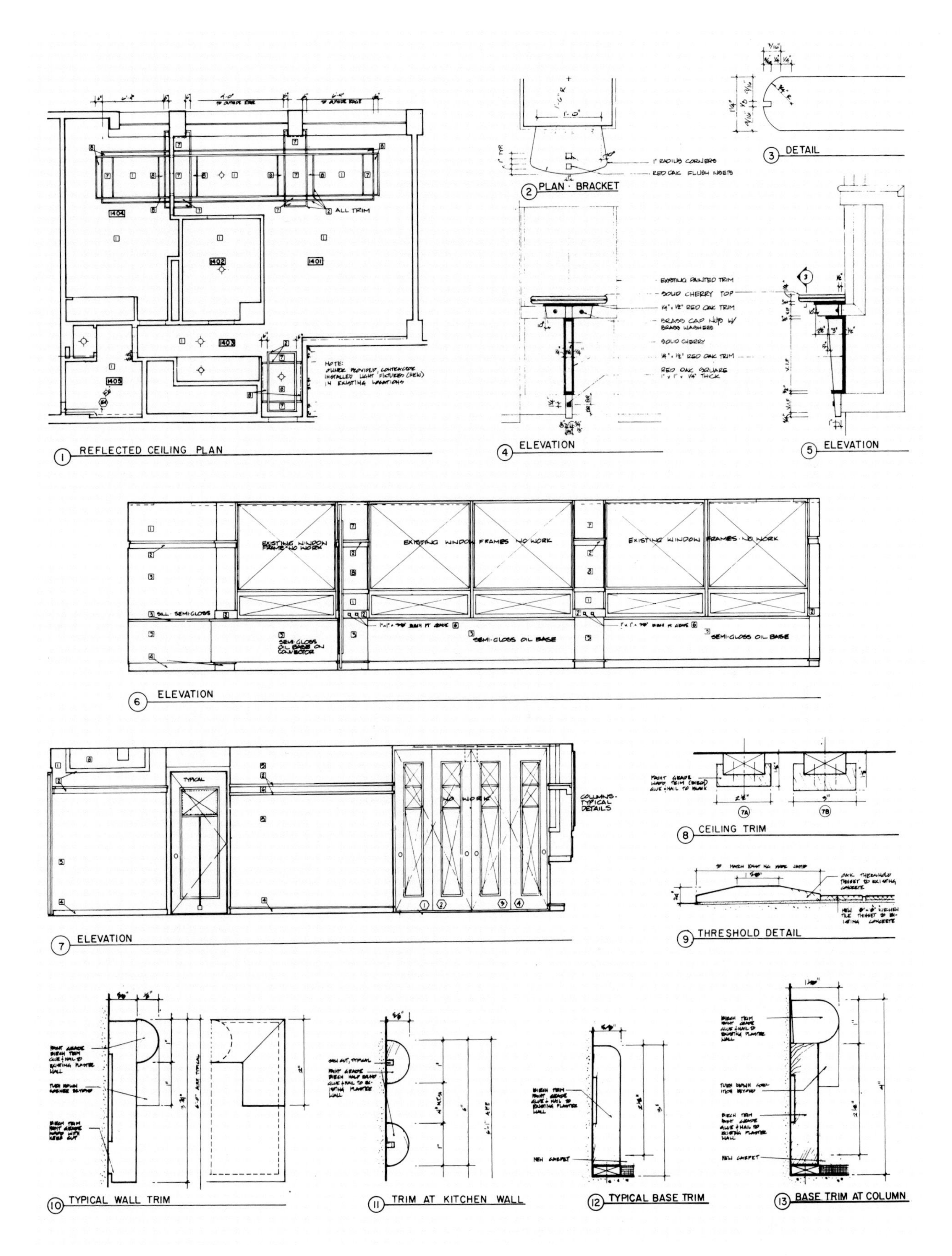
1 REFLECTED CEILING PLAN
2 PLAN · BRACKET
3 DETAIL
4 ELEVATION
5 ELEVATION
6 ELEVATION
7 ELEVATION
8 CEILING TRIM
9 THRESHOLD DETAIL
10 TYPICAL WALL TRIM
11 TRIM AT KITCHEN WALL
12 TYPICAL BASE TRIM
13 BASE TRIM AT COLUMN
EXISTING PAINTED TRIM
SOLID CHERRY TOP
BRASS CAP NUTS W/ BRASS WASHERS
SOLID CHERRY
EXISTING WINDOW FRAMES NO WORK
SEMI-GLOSS OIL BASE
NO WORK
COLUMNS - TYPICAL DETAILS

# Newel Post

**Payne Residence**
*Greenwich, Connecticut*

**Architect**
Shope Reno Wharton Associates

**Fabricator**
Hobbs, Inc.

**Photography**
© H. Durston Saylor

An urbanite who moves out of the city may love the novelty of new country surroundings, yet still feel a certain nostalgia for skyscrapers. Architects Shope Reno Wharton Associates designed a house for client Bruce Payne (a well-known manager of musical talent) in Greenwich, Connecticut, that reflects and respects Payne's affection for both "city and country, or the best of both worlds."

The 5,000-square-foot house—developed on "an average 1988 Connecticut budget"—revolves around a two-story, multi-windowed stair hall that was designed as an orientation element to define interior axes and maximize exterior views (*stair plan*). As the singular double-height space in the house (*section thru stair*), the stair hall, according to the architects, "required detailing that would emphasize its verticality."

The design team used Colonial, multi-paned windows on three levels to thematically connect the space to its "traditional New England horse-country" neighbors. Urban allusion was manifested by newel posts that romanticize recollections of Gotham (*elevation of newel cap*).

It is the newel posts of the staircase hall that command particular attention. Each 9′–0″-high newel post was built, at its cap, as a hollow light box suggestive of skyscraper towers. Standard lamps, screwed into porcelain sockets on plywood platforms concealed within each post, shine incandescent light upward through grilled translucent panels set into the cap (*section @ newel cap*). Newel post caps were assembled from bits and pieces of clear hardwood that were nailed and glued. All edges were chamfered to remove sharp edges; the entire newel post construction was then sanded and painted with high-gloss industrial enamel.

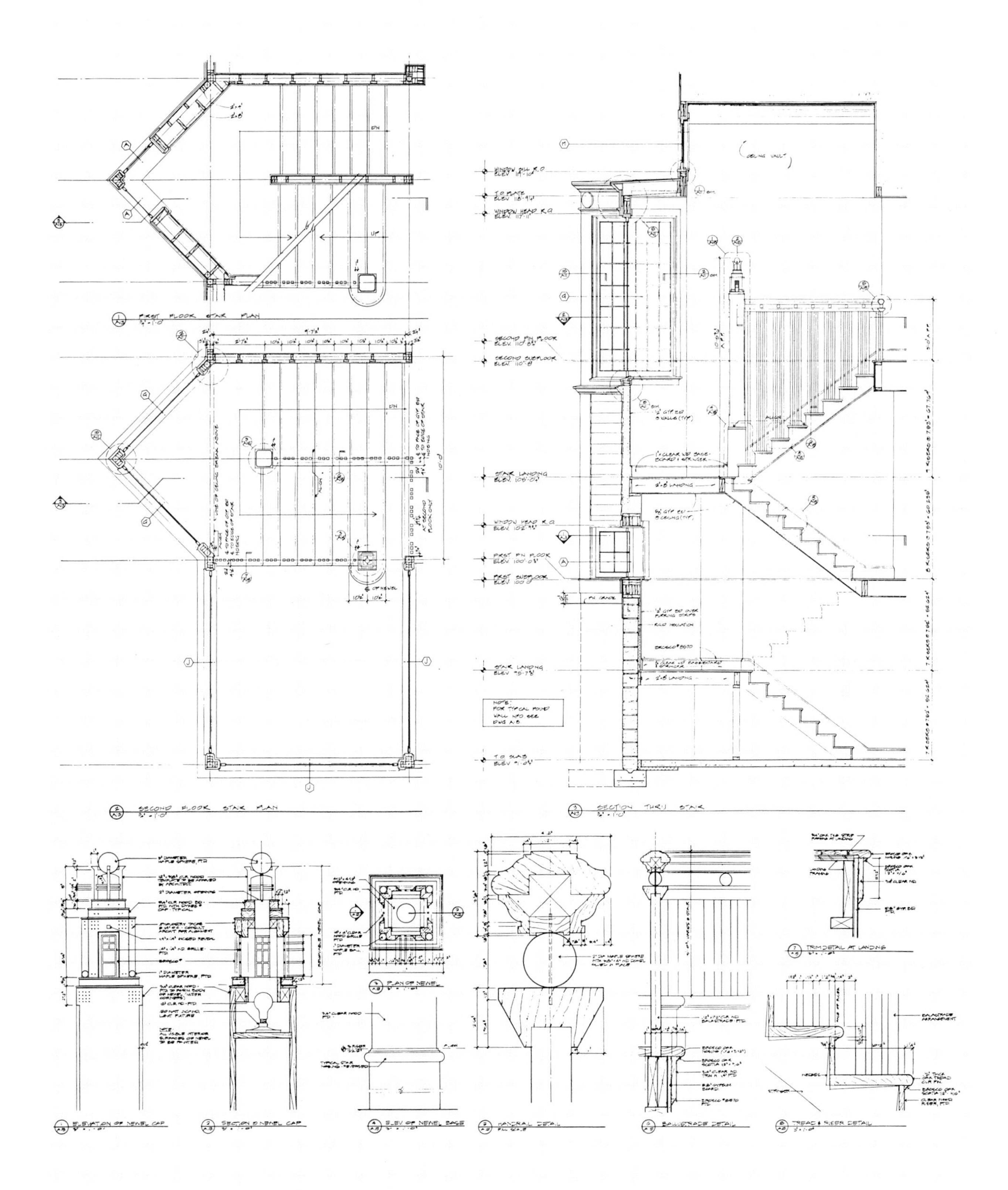
FIRST FLOOR STAIR PLAN
SECOND FLOOR STAIR PLAN
SECTION THRU STAIR
ELEVATION OF NEWEL CAP
SECTION @ NEWEL CAP
PLAN OF NEWEL
ELEV OF NEWEL BASE
HANDRAIL DETAIL
BALUSTRADE DETAIL
TRIM DETAIL AT LANDING
TREAD & RISER DETAIL

# PARTITION

**PRIVATE RESIDENCE**
*Boston, Massachusetts*

**Architect**
Graham Gund Architects

**Design Team**
Graham Gund, Design Principal;
David T. Perry, Principal;
Bill Ridge, Project Architect;
Donna Schumacher, Monica Sidor, Project Team

**General Contractor**
ZZI Construction Company, Inc.

**Fabricators**
Al Held (art), Andre Emmerich Gallery;
William Brower (floor installation)

**Photography**
© Warren Jagger Photography

WHEN ARCHITECT Graham Gund was commissioned to renovate a Beacon Hill townhouse in Boston, his mandate was to provide "a lively atmosphere for entertaining guests as well as provide a suitable display background for an extensive art collection." The clients also directed the architect to preserve the interior's existing sense of spaciousness and light, adding a proviso that the design team was to avoid the traditional detailing imagery common to the neighborhood (*see* Floor Pattern, page 110).

Gund was given a generous budget to remodel the 2,200-square-foot interior, which included an old ballroom. The ballroom was at once the best and most problematic feature of the space. The architect wanted to break down the overwhelmingly large volume into smaller, humane spaces without losing the room's original sense of monumentality.

Gund conceived a house within a house plan for the room. Maple veneer paneling, used throughout as a finish material, reinforces an intentionally staged sense of airiness; as light changes from the softness of morning to the strong shadows of afternoon, a sense of passing time is evoked.

Arched walls both define spaces and give them a more domestic scale. Specifically, a central freestanding arched partition wall was created to define an edge of the double-height living room. Because the architects needed to impose this detail without violating the remarkable sense of volume, the wall was punctuated and penetrated with openings that create vistas extending from space to space. Ebony diamond inlay detailing complements the maple paneling.

The wall, stabilized from behind by the balcony, was constructed of typical 2 × 4 wood studs, which were then covered by a layer of ½-inch plywood. The plywood became the nailer surface for the maple finish paneling and ebony diamond inlays.

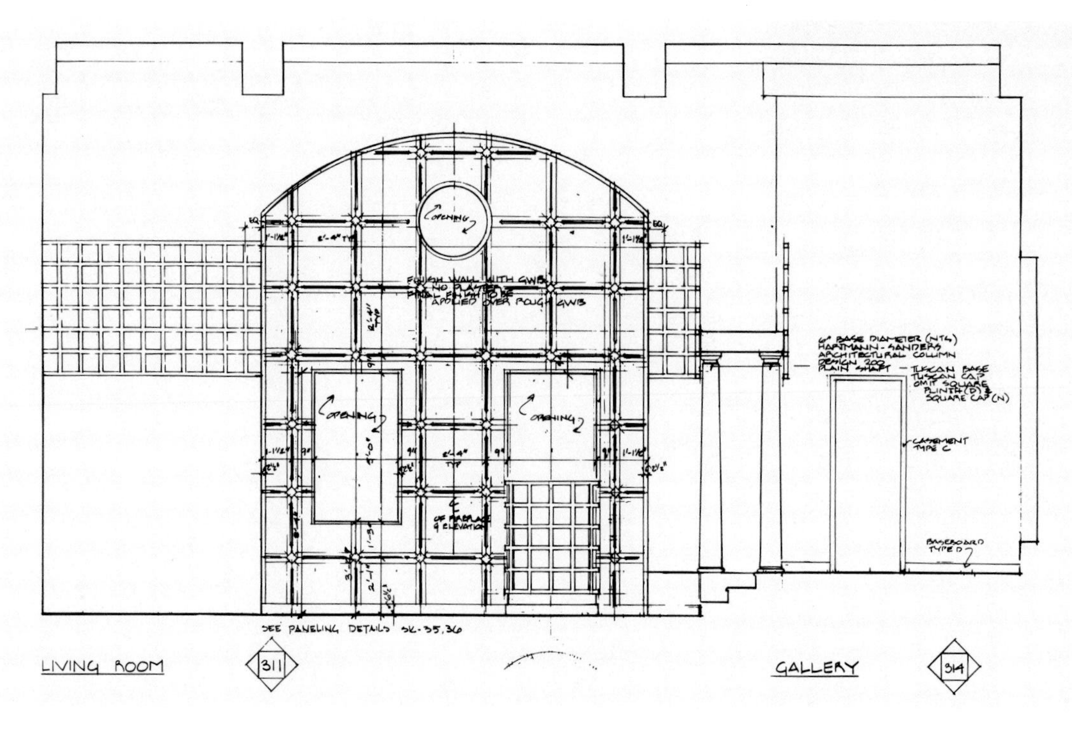

# Partition

## Park Avenue Penthouse

*New York, New York*

**Architect**
Peter L. Gluck and Partners, Architects

**Design Team**
Peter L. Gluck, Principal;
Kent Larson, Partner

**Fabricator**
Frank Vooris, The Homestead

**Photography**
© Norman McGrath

A PARK AVENUE COUPLE—he, an investment banker and she, a writer for fashion magazines—enlisted Peter L. Gluck and Partners to renovate their spectacular but somewhat dysfunctional prewar penthouse apartment.

The existing apartment consisted of a 1,200-square-foot ballroom on the third floor, 1,200 square feet on the second floor, and 1,500 on the first level, or bedroom floor. Although a few details, including the original honeycomb ballroom ceiling and the English paneling in the library, were to be left intact, the clients asked Gluck to devise a new, larger kitchen and breakfast area, and a new entry foyer with a lighter, more open ambience. Gluck was given a budget of approximately \$300–400 per square foot with which to implement the renovation, a generous allocation in most of the country, but only an average figure for the environs of Park Avenue.

The existing foyer was too tight, low, and awkward. The kitchen was too narrow and could be extended only into the foyer. There was only one window to the kitchen and none in the dining area, and it was dark at the top of the stairs. The designer's three-in-one solution was to divide the foyer with a clear ash and glass partitioning screen that annexes new square footage for a breakfast area and pantry, allows natural kitchen light to reach the foyer, and expands the foyer vertically so that light spills onto the landing.

The partition wall was constructed of solid ash muntins and glass panes, the complex pattern and right-angle geometry of which allude to the configuration of the honeycomb ceiling without reiterating its precise form. The wood members of the partition were lacquered and butt-jointed, conjoined in tongue-and-groove fashion on top and shimmed underneath.

Similar complexity is evident in tangential floor finishes: the hallway is checkered with 12″ × 12″ black and gray marble; the breakfast room incorporates both 2″ × 2″ and 6″ × 6″ gray and white tiles.

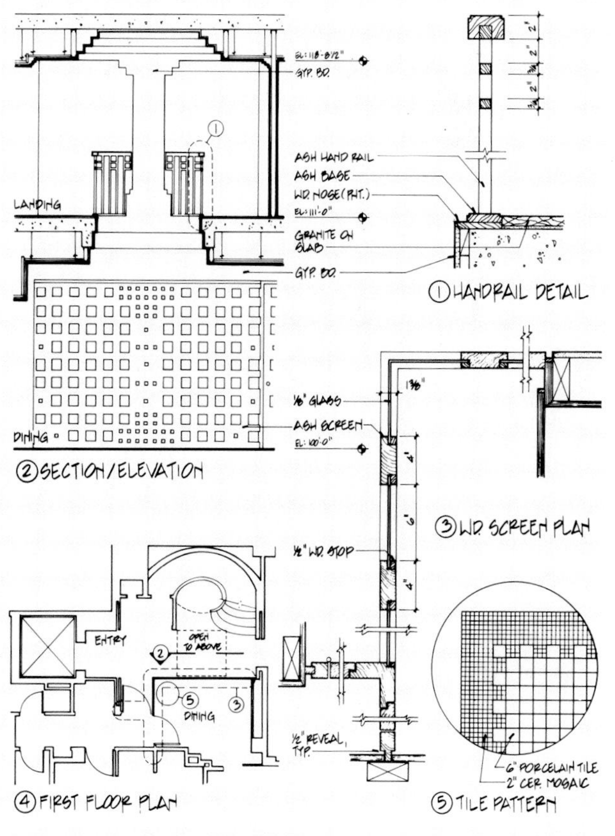

## ECKSEL RESIDENCE
*Franklin, Michigan*

**Designer**
Thomas Lehn, Principal, Kelly and Lehn

**Fabricators**
Francisco Perez (cabinetry);
Howard Crouch (cabinetry)

**Photography**
© Thomas Lehn

FOR THE DETROIT-BASED ECKSELS—a magazine publisher and an art-tour leader with grown children—opening their congested kitchen to the rest of the house and filling it with light both needed to be accomplished if their 1980 kitchen renovation was to be judged a success. Because the Ecksels have an interest in sculptural design and architectural detail, they considered $18,000 money well spent to achieve handsome detailing that would include plenty of storage space.

The designer, Thomas Lehn, chose to leave most of the existing ranch-house kitchen intact, except to create a stronger sense of light in the room by painting the pink ceilings and walls white, and by covering some of the existing metal cabinetry with white epoxy. Lehn's major move was to design a counter and cabinet that would serve as a more permeable divider between the kitchen, family room, and entry vestibule—opening up the kitchen while still defining its boundaries.

The designer wanted to create a sculptural piece that functioned both as architecture and as furniture; the counter and cabinet were therefore designed integrally with a set of closets built into the wall.

The 7′–0″ closets match the height of the doorway into the entrance vestibule, as the end of the closet curves 90 degrees to run flush with the inside face of the doorway, creating a smooth transition from one to the other. The other end of the 2′–4″-deep closet "intersects" the counter and slightly taller cabinet, which projects 5′–6″ out from the wall above the closet. The top of the closet runs flush with the underside of the top band of the cabinet, making the first seem to disappear into the second.

The outer end of the 3′–6″-wide counter is "radiused" into a semicircle, lending a sculptural quality to the piece and fostering a smoother channel of circulation through the narrow 3′–0″ gap between the counter end and the opposite wall. This semicircle is matched in the upper end cabinet; both relate back to the curved end of the closet wall, and all three elements work together to provide a transition from vestibule to family room to kitchen.

The curved ends of the counter and cabinet units each contain two storage shelves, enclosed by two quarter-circular doors. Each door is constructed of two pieces of ½-inch-thick preformed plywood that were laminated together. Doors are hung on custom steel-pivot pins that fit into the floor and rise up through hand-turned nylon bushings. A touch-latch mechanism was used instead of protruding pulls to preserve the sculptural continuity of the piece.

The lower counter also contains bookshelves and a liquor cabinet on the family room side, drawers and cabinets with recessed chrome pulls on the kitchen side. Separated from these components by a small reveal and a 3-inch band of epoxy painted wood, plastic laminate covers the countertop, set 3′–0″ above the floor.

The upper cabinet, 2′–0″ high by 2′–6″ deep and set 2′–0″ above the counter, contains two ¼-inch glass shelves with a recessed fluorescent cove fixture above to highlight display space. On the kitchen side, doors that match the profile of the original metal cabinet doors cover cabinet shelves, which provide additional storage space. Another recessed fluorescent fixture wraps the underside of the entire cabinet unit, providing illumination for the countertop below. A band of epoxy painted wood, similar to that which appears on the counter apron, caps the entire cabinet.

Sliding bifold closet doors were set on a track 1½ inches above the floor. The doors are 2-inch-thick pieces of masonite resting on a closet frame of poplar. The doors' custom chrome pulls were designed to match existing kitchen cabinetry hardware. Since all surfaces were a minimalist white, the architects used varying textures of vinyl on the cabinet surfaces to create a subtle differentiation among them.

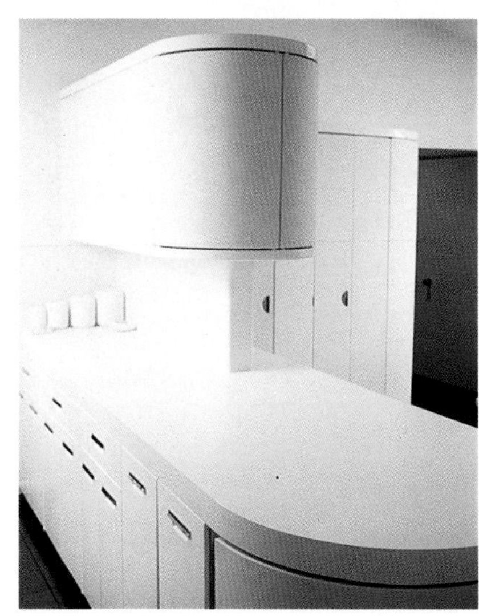

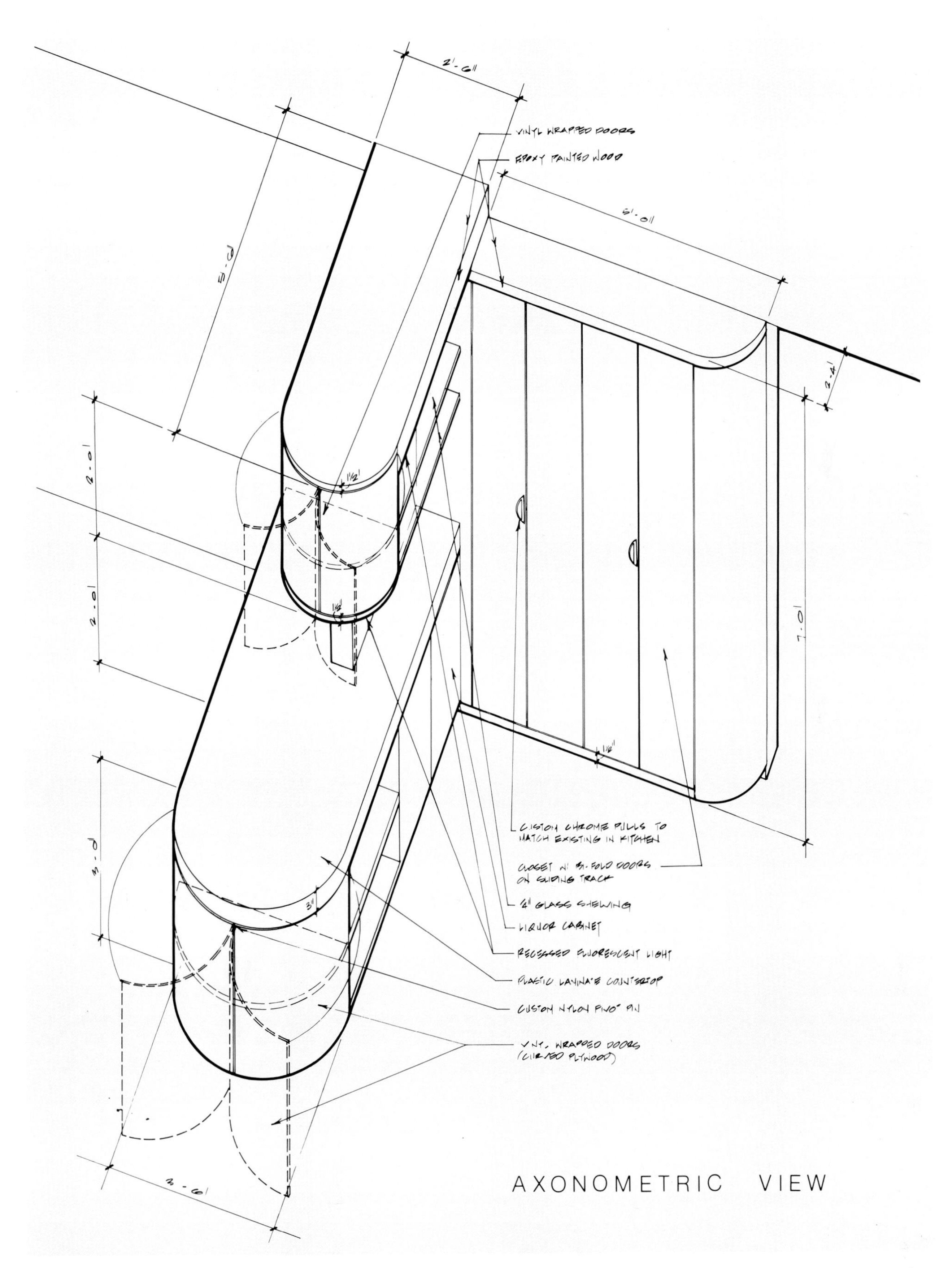

2'-6"
VINYL WRAPPED DOORS
EPOXY PAINTED WOOD
5'-0"
5'-0"
2'-0"
2'-0"
3'-0"
3'-6"
7'-0"
2'-4"
1 1/2"
1 1/2"
1 1/2"
3"
CUSTOM CHROME PULLS TO MATCH EXISTING IN KITCHEN
CLOSET W/ BI-FOLD DOORS ON SLIDING TRACK
1/4" GLASS SHELVING
LIQUOR CABINET
RECESSED FLUORESCENT LIGHT
PLASTIC LAMINATE COUNTERTOP
CUSTOM NYLON PIVOT PIN
VINYL WRAPPED DOORS (CURVED PLYWOOD)

AXONOMETRIC VIEW

**Private Apartment**
*New York, New York*

**Architect**
Charles Patten Architects

**Design Team**
Charles Patten, AIA, Principal;
Robert Rossi, Project Team;
Rich Oechsler, Project Team;
Maureen Cornwell, Project Team;
Paul Knapton, Project Team

**General Contractor**
Glenn Muller,
Metro Design, Inc.

**Fabricator**
Kitchen Solutions

**Photography**
© H. Durston Saylor

It was the issue of entry to a Park Avenue apartment that caused an investment broker and his family to enlist the aid of architect Charles Patten (*see also* Wall, page 218). Although their 1920s apartment boasted 4,000 square feet of floor space, its entry hall was dark and decidedly cramped; the clients asked for "a more generous space."

The architect found himself up against one of the basic characteristics of New York City apartment building design as rendered during the first half of the century: otherwise spacious dwellings were almost invariably accessed through narrow, closed spaces. Although the clients did not specifically cite it as a problem, the large dining room felt (again typically) claustrophobic and lacked adequate storage.

Although Patten was given a project budget of approximately $1,000,000, he saw no reason to spend money when imagination would suffice. His solution relied on a relatively simple alteration in the shape and structure of one wall—a maneuver which addressed all three problems, confirming Patten's belief in his overall design as a solution "of forms, not material."

Patten removed the solid wall between the dining room and the entry foyer, replacing it with three elements: a bowed wall—not quite semicircular—surmounted by a gridded glass panel above with cabinets below; and two flanking French doors, one of which was the existing door, since then relocated (*elevations; plan*).

The elegance of this solution lies in the fact that even though the wall actually encroaches on the floor space of the foyer, it nonetheless "opens" the entry to natural light, which passes through the windowed dining room and the grid wall panes. At the same time, the foyer is given a focus and more definition.

The bowed wall was constructed of standard drywall over wood stud construction. Glass windowpanes were set in wood mullions constructed of pine with a custom paint finish. To match the curve of the existing crown molding, Patten returned to the original building standards, casting new moldings in plaster.

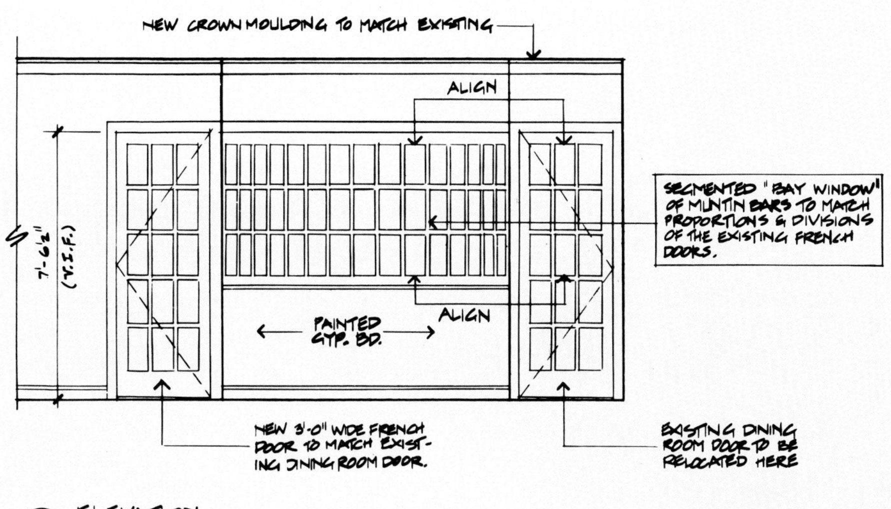
NEW CROWN MOULDING TO MATCH EXISTING
ALIGN
SEGMENTED "BAY WINDOW" OF MUNTIN BARS TO MATCH PROPORTIONS & DIVISIONS OF THE EXISTING FRENCH DOORS.
7'-6½" (V.I.F.)
ALIGN
PAINTED GYP. BD.
NEW 3'-0" WIDE FRENCH DOOR TO MATCH EXISTING DINING ROOM DOOR.
EXISTING DINING ROOM DOOR TO BE RELOCATED HERE

1 ELEVATION

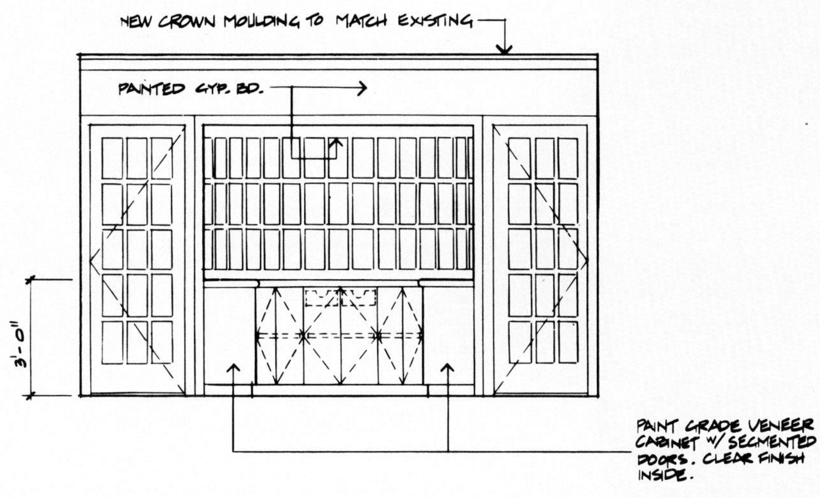
NEW CROWN MOULDING TO MATCH EXISTING
PAINTED GYP. BD.
3'-0"
PAINT GRADE VENEER CABINET W/ SEGMENTED DOORS. CLEAR FINISH INSIDE.

2 ELEVATION

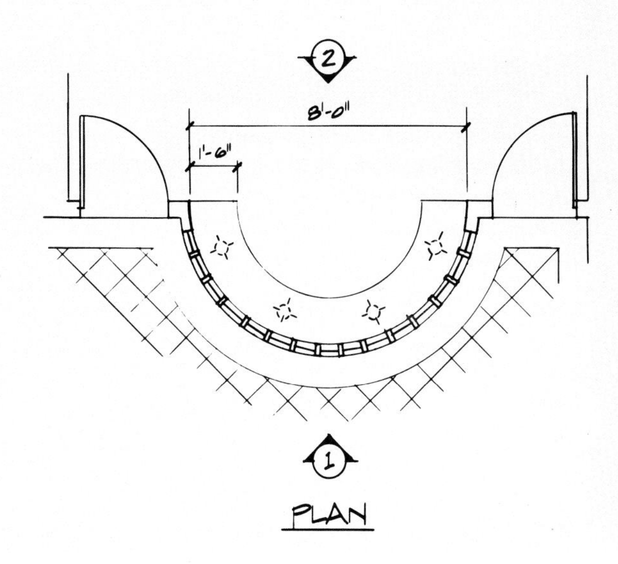
2
8'-0"
1'-6"
1

PLAN

# PARTITION

**PRIVATE RESIDENCE**
*Chicago, Illinois*

**Architect**
Pappageorge Haymes Ltd.

**Fabricator**
Interior Woodworking Corporation

**Photography**
© Wayne Cable

DETAILS THAT SERVE more than one function are usually developed for "economy-size" apartments, designed on economy budgets. But the double-function detail that architects Pappageorge Haymes designed for this posh penthouse apartment was developed in a space with relative room to spare and was funded by an enviable budget (*see* Shower Enclosure, page 182). Why, then, was this kitchen/dining-area cabinet partition made part of the plan? The simple answer, according to the architects: "Our client wanted a minimal, no-wall solution and had asked for a 'non-clichéd' buffet." By incorporating the kind of space-saving detail the architects might have designed for a smaller job into this 2,400-square-foot apartment—albeit, on a larger scale—they were able to accentuate the luxury of open space as they responded to client priorities; by rendering the detail in a one-of-a-kind finish, the architects were able to raise a straightforward piece of cabinetry to a sculpted and painted objet d'art.

The double-face cabinet is visually organized and functionally divided, in elevation, into fourteen bays and three tiers of 1′–4″-square panels, or compartments, on either side. Because tangential kitchen cabinetry was constructed and fitted, at a right angle, to the partitioning cabinet on the kitchen side (*kitchen plan; countertop detail*), some squares in either room are for storage; others are blind (*elevations 1 and 2*).

Pappageorge Haymes packed an impressive number of task-specific details within the overall cabinet. In the kitchen, an undercounter, side-by-side refrigerator/freezer unit occupies four 1′–4″ × 4′–2″ bays (*elevation 1; refrigerator section*); stacked microwave and conventional ovens occupy, tangentially, an additional two. In the dining room, a 1′–4″ × 8′–4″ pull-out buffet in the middle tier extends, horizontally, across six bays (*elevation 2; buffet section; buffet cabinet detail*). Other square compartments, some faced in black glass, open by touch latch to reveal stored china and crystal.

To accommodate the dimensions of the building's freight elevator, the cabinet was shop-built in four sections, then delivered to the site for assembly. The ¾-inch plywood frame is veneered, on the interior side, with 1⁄16-inch Kortron; in the dining room, a veneer of Medite was faux painted to simulate flamed, iridescent steel.

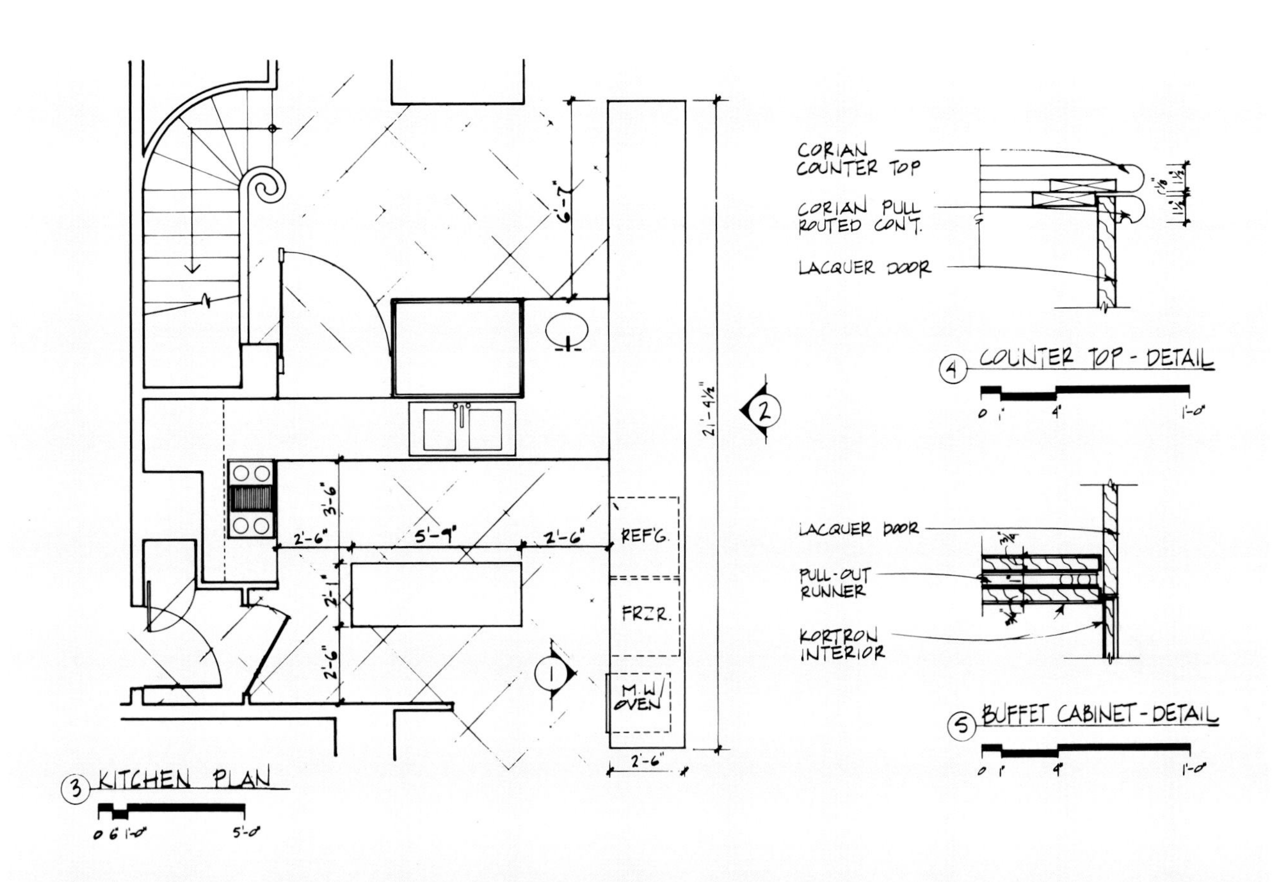
CORIAN COUNTER TOP
CORIAN PULL ROUTED CON'T.
LACQUER DOOR
4 COUNTER TOP - DETAIL
0 1" 4" 1'-0"
REF'G.
FRZR.
M.W/ OVEN
6'-7"
21'-4½"
3'-6"
2'-6"
5'-9"
2'-6"
2'-1"
2'-6"
2'-6"
LACQUER DOOR
PULL-OUT RUNNER
KORTRON INTERIOR
5 BUFFET CABINET - DETAIL
0 1" 4" 1'-0"
3 KITCHEN PLAN
0 6 1'-0" 5'-0"

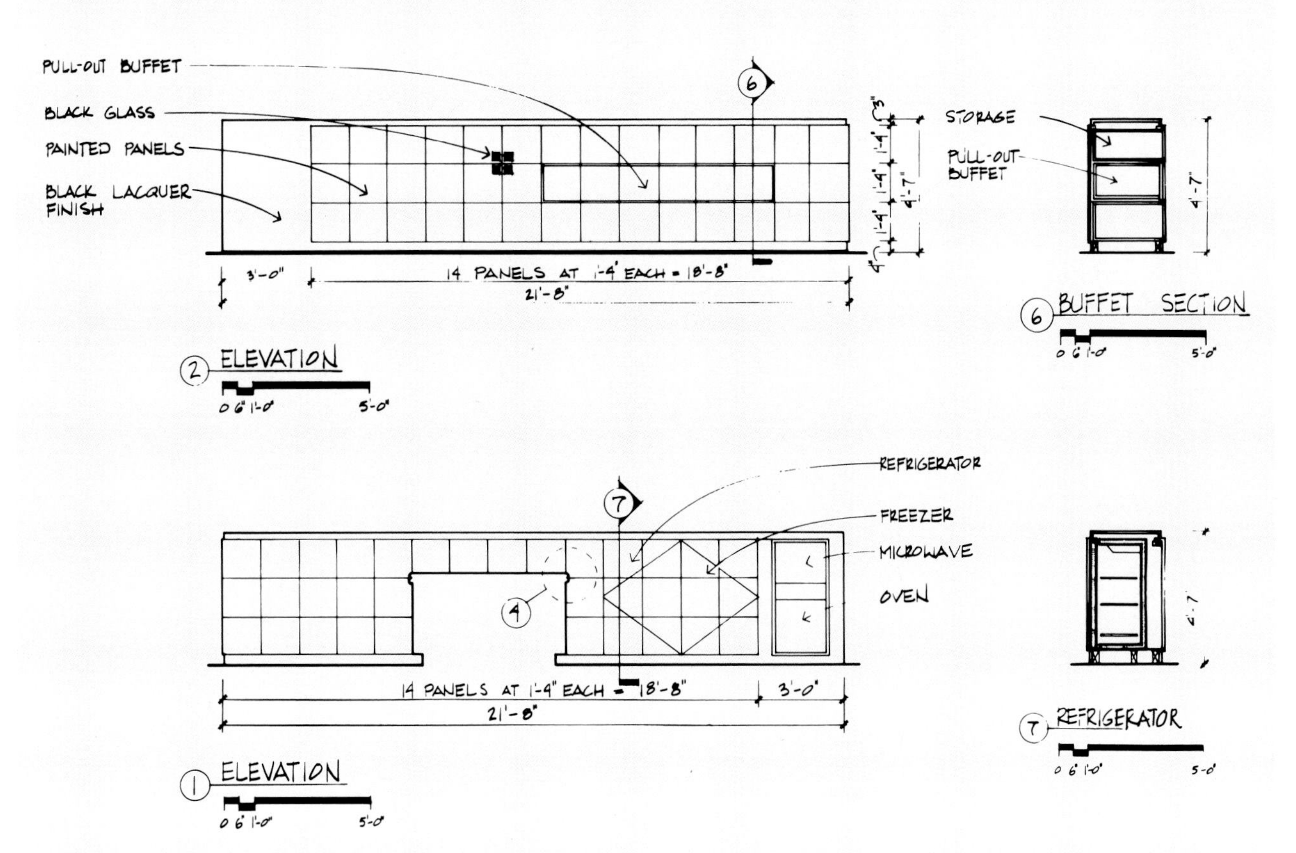
PULL-OUT BUFFET
BLACK GLASS
PAINTED PANELS
BLACK LACQUER FINISH
3'-0"
14 PANELS AT 1'-4" EACH = 18'-8"
21'-8"
1'-4"
4'-7"
STORAGE
PULL-OUT BUFFET
4'-7"
6 BUFFET SECTION
0 6" 1'-0" 5'-0"
2 ELEVATION
0 6" 1'-0" 5'-0"
REFRIGERATOR
FREEZER
MICROWAVE
OVEN
14 PANELS AT 1'-4" EACH = 18'-8"
3'-0"
21'-8"
4'-7"
7 REFRIGERATOR
0 6" 1'-0" 5'-0"
1 ELEVATION
0 6" 1'-0" 5'-0"

## BENNETT–NOVAK RESIDENCE
*Cincinnati, Ohio*

**Architect**
Michael Schuster Associates:
Michael Schuster, Principal/Designer

**General Contractor**
Jeff Stevens, J & B Construction

**Photography**
© Ron Forth

FOR THE THIRD, and top, floor of a nineteenth-century rowhouse renovation, the sky was just about the clients' limit for architect Michael Schuster in developing a space plan and finish details. Owners Jim Bennett and Mary Novak (now Bennett), asked only that the architect "flood the area with light" and "connect the floor thematically, if more informally," with details on the two floors below.

Schuster answered both form and function requirements at once by adapting a grid detail for the third floor that had already been designed for incrementally more formal applications elsewhere in the house. Whereas the articulated gridwork—a cruciform cross section, all edges of which are square cut in profile—was to be open filigree, as well as smaller in scale, for the large masonry openings on the first two floors (*see* Archway, page 18), for the third and more playful level, the grid was filled in with milk glass and exaggerated in scale (*section thru window @ stairs; detail plan of window @ stairs; elevation*).

On the top floor, the translucent glass grid was set into partitions rather than walls because floor-to-ceiling privacy on the "adults-only" level was not a concern. In addition to allowing a free flow of diffused light throughout the space, the 9′–0″ height of the partitions resolved a potential disparity in cornice detail caused by the third floor's slanted ceilings.

The partitions are constructed of painted drywall on studs placed 16 inches on center. Millwork for grid panels and the cornice was rendered in painted, finely grained poplar.

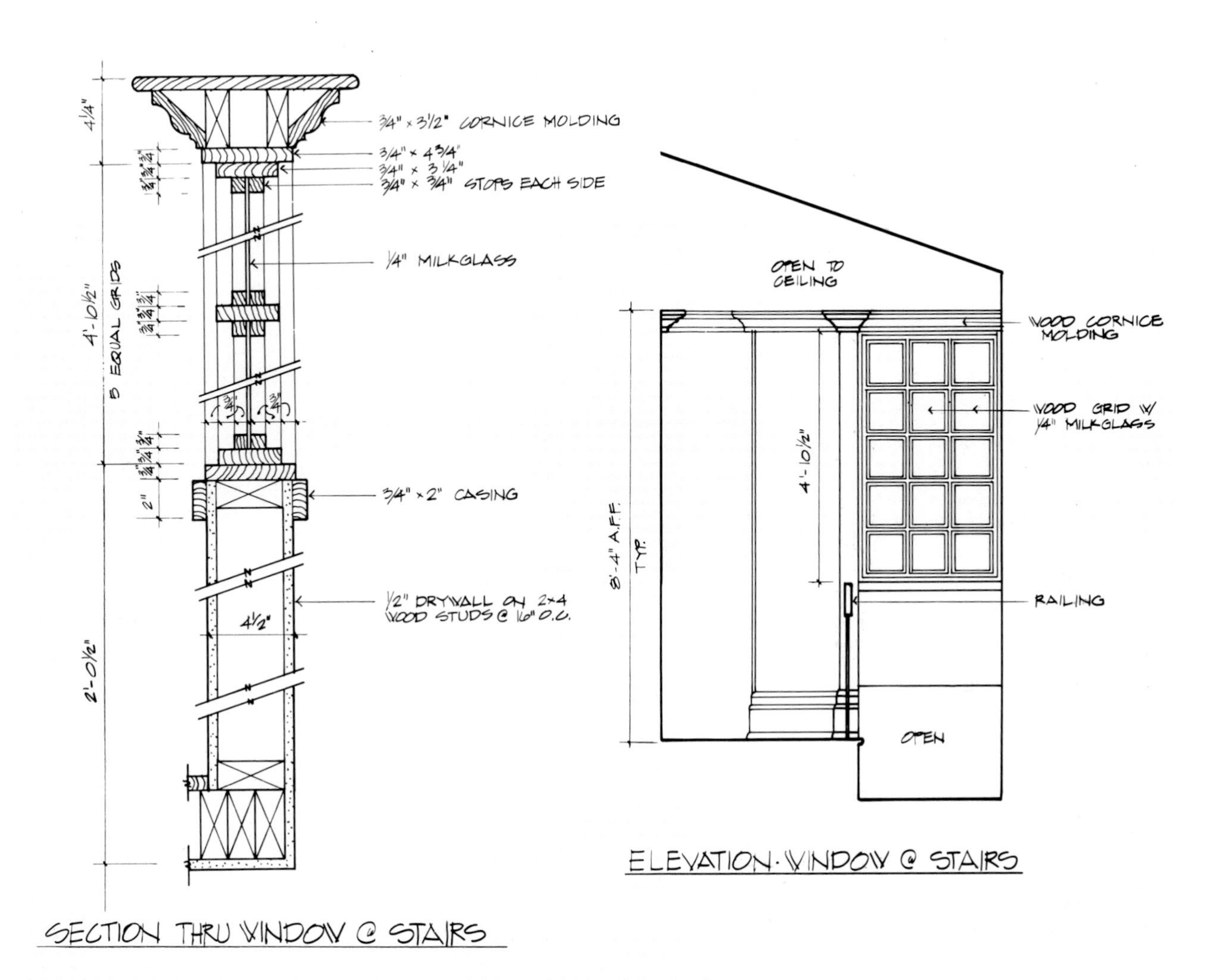
4 1/4"
3/4" x 3 1/2" CORNICE MOLDING
3/4" x 4 3/4"
3/4" x 3 1/4"
3/4" x 3/4" STOPS EACH SIDE
1/4" MILKGLASS
4'-10 1/2"
5 EQUAL GRIDS
3/4" x 2" CASING
1/2" DRYWALL ON 2x4
WOOD STUDS @ 16" O.C.
4 1/2"
2'-0 1/2"
SECTION THRU WINDOW @ STAIRS
OPEN TO
CEILING
WOOD CORNICE
MOLDING
WOOD GRID W/
1/4" MILKGLASS
4'-10 1/2"
8'-4" A.F.F.
TYP.
RAILING
OPEN
ELEVATION · WINDOW @ STAIRS

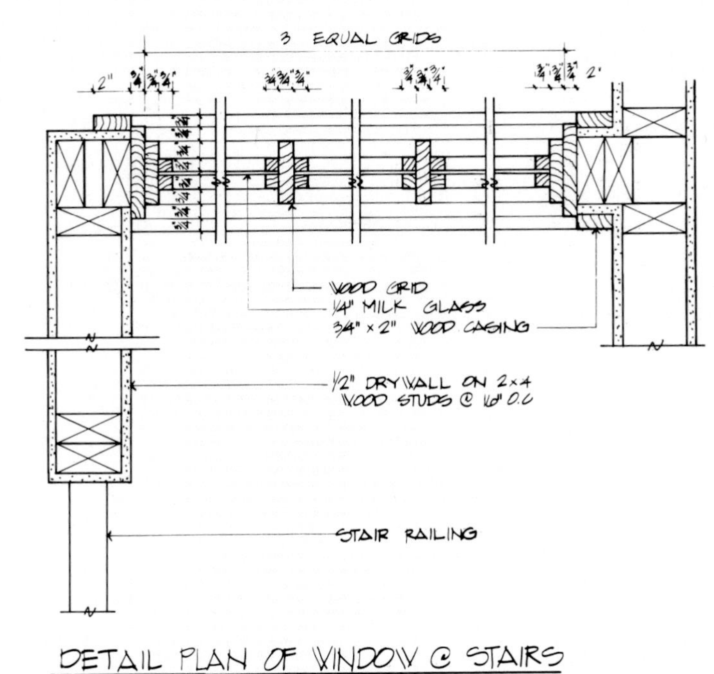
3 EQUAL GRIDS
2"
2"
WOOD GRID
1/4" MILK GLASS
3/4" x 2" WOOD CASING
1/2" DRYWALL ON 2x4
WOOD STUDS @ 16" O.C.
STAIR RAILING
DETAIL PLAN OF WINDOW @ STAIRS

## Plocek Residence

*Warren, New Jersey*

**Architect**
Michael Graves, Architect

**Design Team**
Bruce MacNelly, Job Captain; Terence Smith, Project Manager; Gordon Smith, Seth Warner, Gary Wolf, Natalie Fizer, Pierre Fuhrer, Gary Lapera, Leslie Mason, Peter Hague Neilson, Margaret Perkins, Anita Rosskam, Keat Tan, Juliet Richardson Smith, Donald Strum, Suzanne Strum, Assistants

**General Contractors**
John Bossany, Inc.; Sheldon Cyrlin, C-Shel Construction, Inc.

**Structural Engineer**
Blackburn Engineering Associates

**Photography**
© William Taylor

Tom and Ingrid Plocek had two priorities in mind when, in 1977, they commissioned Michael Graves to design a house for them in the New Jersey Watchung Mountains: to build a house that would take advantage of the site's panoramic views and that would be totally—and idiosyncratically—unique. To those ends, they gave complete artistic license, within the constraints of an average budget, to their architect.

As Graves conceived it, the house is an early example of postmodern classicism, in which overt architectural gestures refer nonspecifically to historical styles to give a subtle and indirect feeling of history—rather than to copy or reinterpret a building, architect, or style.

In the entryway, two enormous piers with flared tops form the first of three exterior entry walls, or layers. This ceremonial entry sets up one axis through the house; another is formed by the more private side entry, which is flanked by angled terrace walls, projecting corner windows, and gateway columns. This entry is surmounted by a vertical window—again with a flared top.

At the point where these two first-floor circulation axes cross, a light-filled space provides vertical circulation to the upstairs and the house proper. Standing in the entrance hall, one looks straight ahead through the space to the termination of the axis: an enormous rojo alicante marble fireplace surmounted by a Graves mural. As one looks up, the top of an oversized column is visible through a light wood trellis. Inside this three-story square room, where a stair winds upward around a 10′–0″ hollow circular column or pavilion capped by a skylight, is the literal and symbolic center of the house.

The walls of the column/pavilion are also hollow; the column is built of two layers of ⅝-inch gypsum wallboard scored at 3-inch intervals to bend around a frame of metal studs. The curved base at the bottom is built of 1 × 12 finish trim nailed to 2-inch wood blocking set on the oak tongue-and-groove floor. Surfaces are of painted gypsum board, except on the top level, where stucco covers the column interior.

Oak stairs with painted aluminum handrails wrap the column, filling the space between column and wall. They begin inside the column and rise up through one of the four door openings, where they meet the exterior wall of the room at a landing, turn, and move up to the top floor. At this middle level, the exterior of the column is square, becoming round again at the top level.

A 1¼-inch slab of polished rojo alicante marble covers the top of the square box at the point where the column's exterior again becomes

circular. Four custom light fixtures, translucent glass lenses set on faux marble and patina bases, sit on the four corners of this square marble shelf. Four windows are placed above the four doorways—along the axes of the house—with angled jambs and sills, allowing more light to pour into the interior of the column while preserving axial views through the space.

At the top of the room, a circular, painted wood grid forms a capital for the column, while also acting as a diffusing screen for the slightly narrower stock aluminum skylight above it. This frame, 15 feet in diameter, was built in four sections, of all straight members, and was then bolted together on-site. It is screwed to two layers of wood blocking in the top of the column wall, which at this level is constructed of two layers of ¼-inch gypsum board over wood studs. The angled frame sits 18.5 degrees from horizontal.

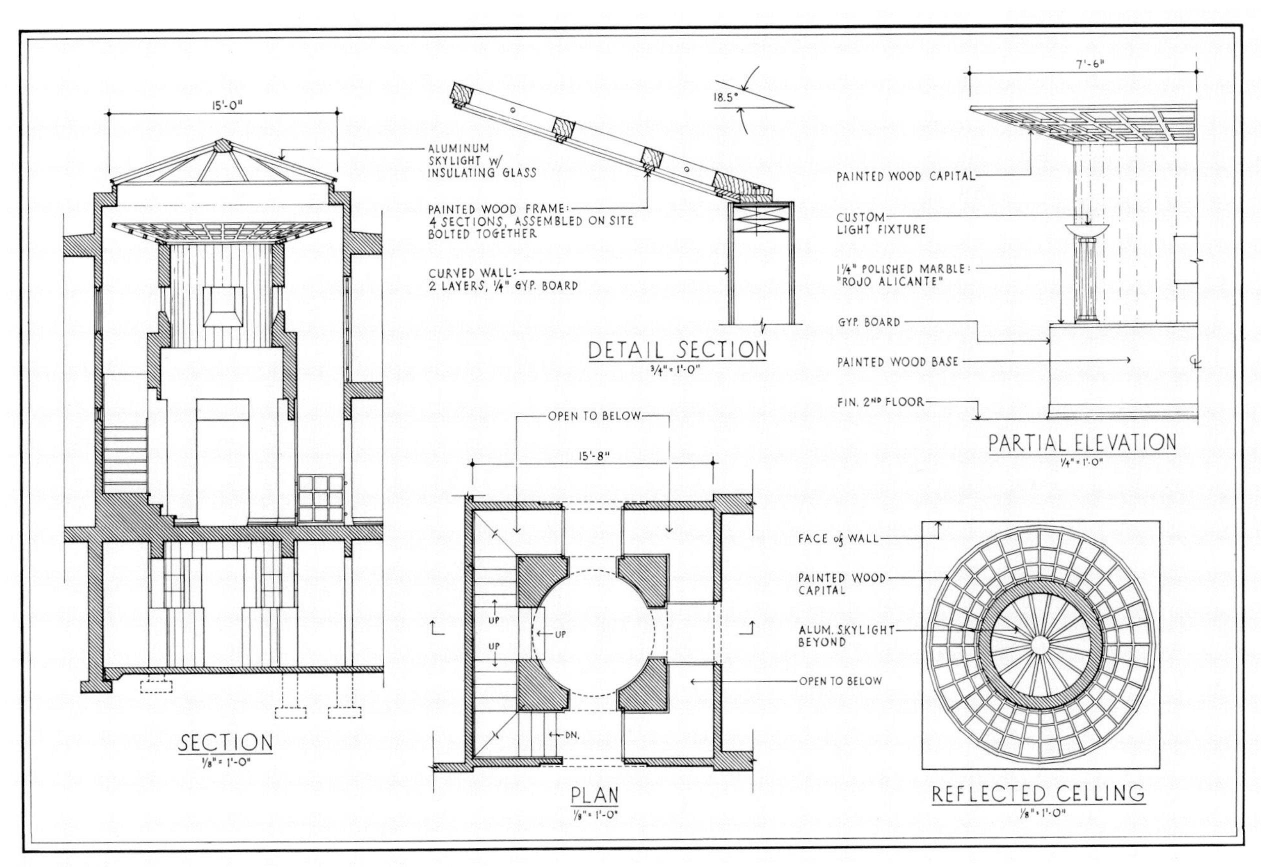
15'-0"
ALUMINUM SKYLIGHT w/ INSULATING GLASS
PAINTED WOOD FRAME: 4 SECTIONS, ASSEMBLED ON SITE BOLTED TOGETHER
CURVED WALL: 2 LAYERS, 1/4" GYP. BOARD
18.5°
DETAIL SECTION
3/4" = 1'-0"
7'-6"
PAINTED WOOD CAPITAL
CUSTOM LIGHT FIXTURE
1 1/4" POLISHED MARBLE: "ROJO ALICANTE"
GYP. BOARD
PAINTED WOOD BASE
FIN. 2ND FLOOR
PARTIAL ELEVATION
1/4" = 1'-0"
SECTION
1/8" = 1'-0"
OPEN TO BELOW
15'-8"
UP
UP
UP
DN.
PLAN
1/8" = 1'-0"
FACE of WALL
PAINTED WOOD CAPITAL
ALUM. SKYLIGHT BEYOND
OPEN TO BELOW
REFLECTED CEILING
1/8" = 1'-0"

# PAVILION

**PRIVATE LOFT**
*New York, New York*

**Architect**
Haigh Space Architects

**Design Team**
Paul Haigh, AIA, Architect;
Barbara H. Haigh, IDSA, Designer;
Jon A. Dick, AIA, Project Architect

**General Contractor**
Clark Construction Corporation

**Fabricators**
Kalwall Glazing (wall glazing);
Zolatone (paint); David Fishbein
Furnituremaker (millwork)

**Photography**


PAUL HAIGH'S APPROACH to his design work varies according to the individual interests, as well as the professional focus, of his respective clients (*see* Kitchen Hood, page 126). For a restorer of sixteenth-century paintings, the architect concentrated on developing a historically referenced, three-dimensional forced perspective.

The forced-perspective concept occurred to Haigh as a viable means by which to resolve the space planning of a railroadlike third-floor loft apartment in a flatiron building in New York's West Village. Despite the generous floor space—2,250 square feet—the 25′–0″ × 90′–0″ dimensions were laterally constraining; previous demolition had also left the loft in poor condition, with plumbing pipes exposed.

Haigh was presented with a client mandate that raised further difficulties. The client wanted to maximize the amount of light available from north/south exposures; conversely, she required a study-cum-guest room that would almost inevitably affect the transmission of light.

Haigh's forced perspective combated the space-planning problem, in part, by enhancing it—by using forced perspective to slightly alter the perception of the apartment's proportions. The stained white-oak floorboards and drywall walls were all slightly tapered or skewed to achieve the illusion.

Beginning at the entryway, every element converges along a central axis that passes through a doorway framed by translucent corner windows and terminates in a blue stained-glass window at the opposite end of the apartment. The window is illuminated like a rear screen projector by the exterior windows of the bedroom beyond its framing partition. The axial progression is intensified by a duct that runs the length of the apartment directly above the passageway, even passing through a circular hole centered above the door.

Haigh responded to the client's request for a study/guest room by creating an autonomous pavilion in the center of the apartment with its own windows and pyramidal skylit roof. The architect rotated the 14′ × 12′–6″ pavilion a slight 3 degrees off-axis to enhance his forced perspective scheme.

Like the rest of the apartment, the pavilion's walls are of drywall, here set on steel studs at 12 inches on-center. In order to provide a visual, thermal, and acoustic barrier for the pavilion, Haigh built the windows and skylight out of Kalwall, a 3⁹⁄₁₆-inch-thick, double-skin fiberglasslike material. Invented as an exterior retrofit finish material, Kalwall provides translucency and corresponding transmission of light into and through the pavilion, while retaining the perception of privacy offered by Japanese rice-paper screens.

The Kalwall panels were set in an integrated aluminum frame. The windows span the length of one wall of the pavilion and wrap around the corners to the two adjacent sides, enhancing the perspective in the "hallway" while also dematerializing and lightening the pavilion's mass.

The skylight's aluminum frame rests on a steel frame that bears on the metal studs in the walls. A gap was left between the pavilion's ceiling and the bottom edge of the skylight frame, which allows ventilation into the pavilion that is induced by a centrally suspended ceiling fan. The perimeter of the skylight is internally lit by discrete uplights, creating a glowing effect at night.

All drywall surfaces are finished with Zolatone white paint, which contains flecks of purple and brown.

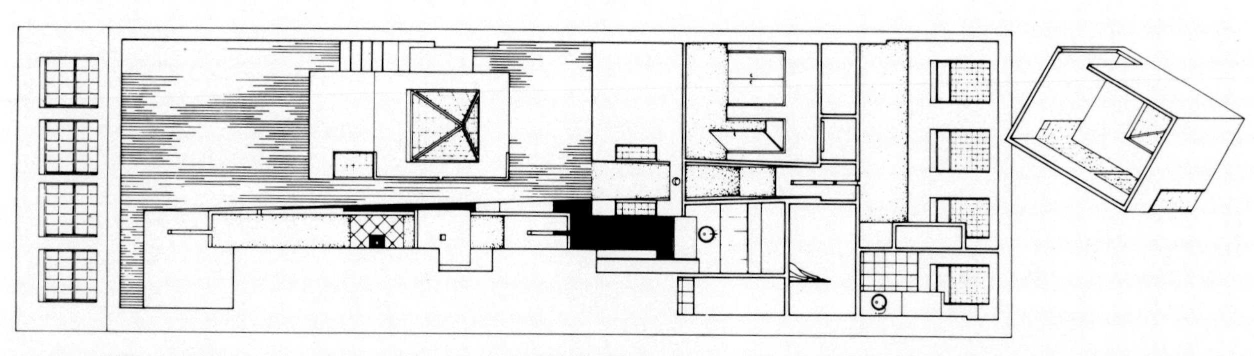

AXONOMETRIC

# Pavilion

**Loft Apartment**
*New York, New York*

**Architect**
Lee H. Skolnick Architecture + Design:
Lee H. Skolnick, AIA, Principal

**Fabricator**
Townhouse Finishings

**Photography**
© Antoine Bootz

An architect's own home is often used as an experimental workshop, or a place in which to try out new ideas and materials at full scale. The interior pavilion Lee Skolnick built in his 2,800-square-foot Chelsea loft in 1985 served just such a purpose. The pavilion was constructed originally to keep bulky storage out of sight; it later metamorphosed, according to plan, into a second bathroom for the child's bedroom behind it.

Skolnick's approach to loft design is "to make the whole space read." Essentially, this sculpted, almost cubical 5′–9″ × 7′–9″ × 7′–6″ box serves as a buffer between the loft's public and private spaces: longitudinally, it divides the living room from the master bedroom; transversely, by means of the 8-inch-high platform (which houses plumbing extensions), it connects to and screens the master bedroom. The platform also defines the main circulation corridor from bedroom access.

The geometric pattern of reveals on each face of the pavilion is formed of two layers. The inner skin of black-painted drywall is nailed to the underlying wooden frame, over which the outer skin of finished plywood panels is glued, with brass grommets screwed as accents into the corners of each panel.

On the living room side, shelves for the display of a pottery collection are cantilevered from grooves in a stuccoed plywood-and-wire lath armature (*axonometric*), which is bolted to the pavilion structure through an intervening sheet of black-painted ¾-inch plywood, creating another black reveal. On this face, the architectural focal point is created by the mirror, which reasserts the actual center of the pavilion, centering on the dining room table.

A second mirror in the inner passage is placed directly opposite the master bathroom. Viewed obliquely, it appears almost as an optical illusion. Its surface is in the same plane as the plywood and features two lines scraped out from the back of the mirror, allowing the black band behind to appear as a continuation of the reveal line. There is another mirror in the master bathroom; upon opening the door, mirrored reflections augment the actual space.

The cube's status as a pavilion is affirmed with a frosted glass window of Japanese inspiration, set in the plane of the black reveal in the main circulation side. Through it, the bathroom borrows light from an overhead corridor fixture.

The intersecting glass clerestory defines the master bedroom.

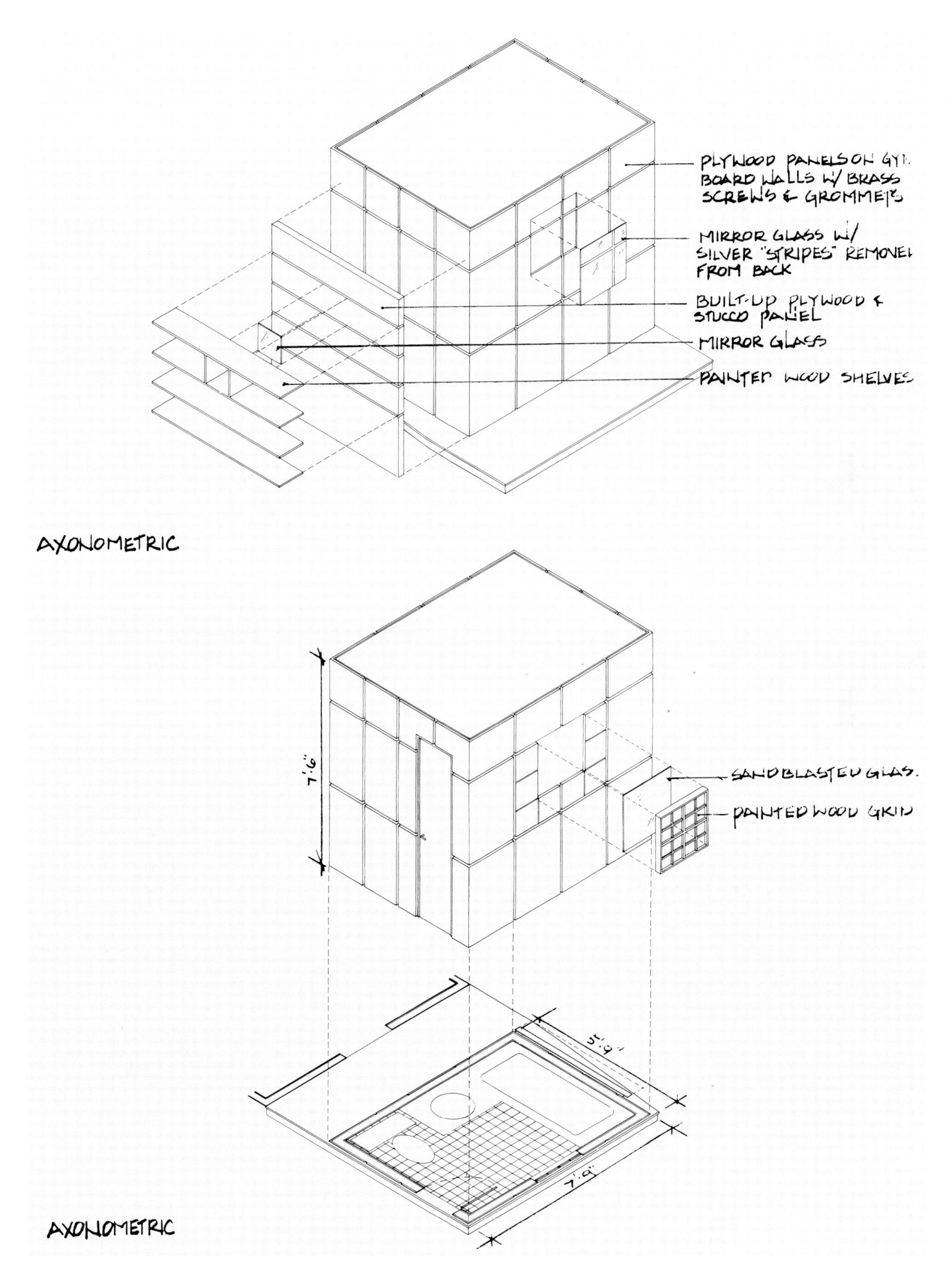
PLYWOOD PANELS ON GYP. BOARD WALLS W/ BRASS SCREWS & GROMMETS
MIRROR GLASS W/ SILVER "STRIPES" REMOVED FROM BACK
BUILT-UP PLYWOOD & STUCCO PANEL
MIRROR GLASS
PAINTED WOOD SHELVES
AXONOMETRIC
7'-6"
SANDBLASTED GLASS
PAINTED WOOD GRID
5'-9"
7'-9"
AXONOMETRIC

## BUCKHEAD RESIDENCE
*Atlanta, Georgia*

**Architect**
Moore Ruble Yudell

**Design Team**
Charles Moore, Principal;
John Ruble, Principal-in-Charge;
Peter Zingg, Project Architect

**Fabricator**
W.P. Stephens Lumber Company

**Photography**
© Bard Wrisley

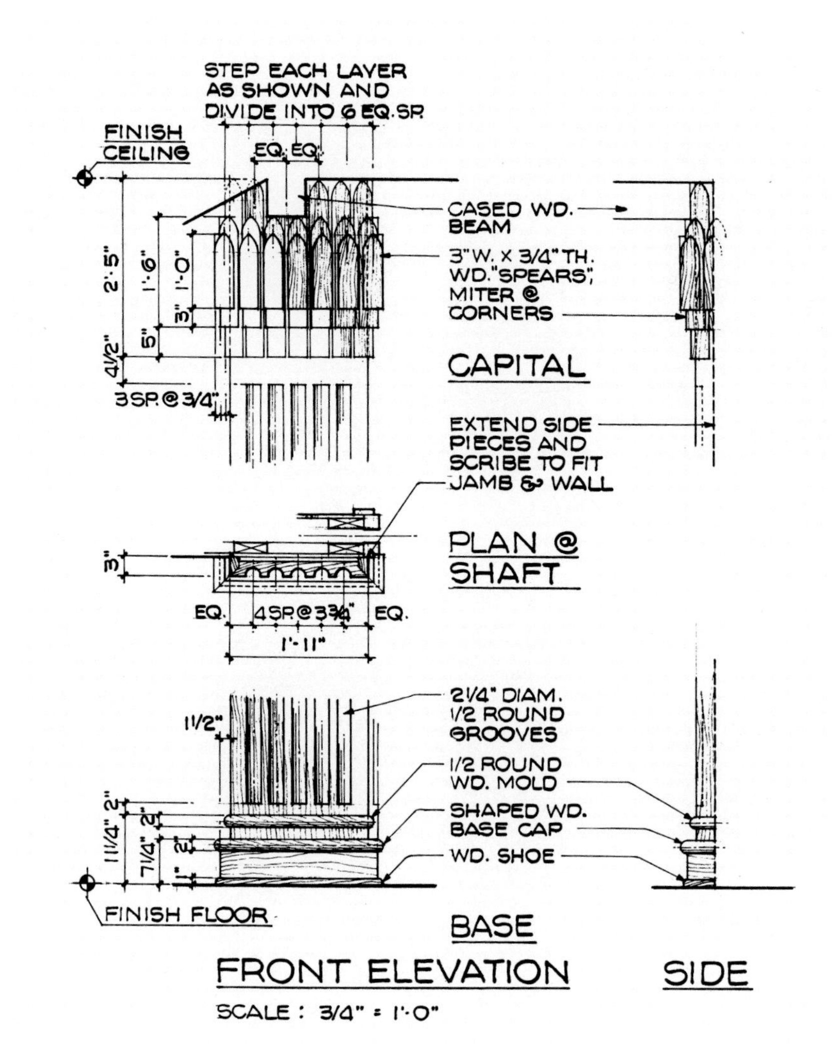


BUCKHEAD IS THE NEIGHBORHOOD in Atlanta in which most of that city's people, given free choice and enough income, would elect to live. But as in other attractive neighborhoods across the country, demand for housing there has long since outstripped supply. Consequently, new houses, some of which strike an unfortunately grandiose pose, are beginning to outnumber Buckhead's quota of gracious antebellum, Victorian, Edwardian and Deco era homes.

In 1983, the scion of an old Buckhead family faced an ironic housing shortage of his own. The landmark mansion his grandparents had built had been turned into a museum, and his own young family was fast outgrowing its current home. Unwilling to leave their neighborhood, and opposed in principle to buying one of the overwrought and overvalued houses being offered by local developers, the client decided to build a "baby grand" house that would, in 3,500 square feet, evoke the graceful proportions of the "concert grand" house in which he had spent his summers. Architects Moore Ruble Yudell were commissioned to design the house that was to be "thoughtfully but sparingly detailed." The architects developed an elegant plan and a number of details that merit attention, particularly the large and small pilasters designed for the living room.

Traditionally, the pilaster is one of the most formal of architectural elements and, like the column, usually represents the stylistic expression of a specific order. Pilasters are set beneath structural elements whose weight, were they columns, they would bear. The smaller pilasters within this room, set beneath cornice moldings and around bays of windows, are in keeping with traditional use. Moore Ruble Yudell's larger, focal-point pilasters, however, represent a radical break with tradition. Two grand pilasters that, at right angles, flank the fireplace, and two others which accentuate the room's entrance archways belong to no clear order, although their capitals resemble the Egyptian lotus variety (*front elevation; capital*). Nor do these grand pilasters play a traditional, self-effacing role of secondary support; rather, they break through the normal limits of cornice moldings and coved ceiling curves as they soar to the 17′–0″ flat ceiling. The cased wood beam that projects from each grand pilaster's capital appears to be less supported by the pilaster than encircled by its capital as it continues to push upward.

The pilasters were crafted by W. P. Stephens, the owner's millwork company. Each element of each pilaster was separately carved; the spears of each capital were individually cut and mitered, then glued and nailed to the shaft by hand (*front elevation; capital*).

## Private Residence
*Pound Ridge, New York*

**Architect**
Haverson/Rockwell Architects, P.C.

**Design Team**
Jay M. Haverson, Principal;
David S. Rockwell, Principal

**Interior Designer**
David Briggs

**General Contractor**
Olav Ranneklev, Ranneklev Brothers Construction

**Structural Engineer**
Rarwood-Weisenfeld

**Drawing**
Ken Hutchinson

**Photography**
© Mark Ross

Barnstorming takes on new meaning when interpreted by architects Haverson/Rockwell in a Pound Ridge, New York, residence. The elegant 6,000-square-foot house is, in fact, a new construction attached to remnants of an old barn that was moved to a new site overlooking a pond. Owned by an architectural millworking contractor and his wife, an antiques dealer, this dream house was developed, according to the architects, to provide plenty of space for "three children, a collection of art and fine furniture, and any future acquisitions that may appeal to the eclectic tastes of the clients."

*Eclectic* may not be quite broad enough a word to describe the house; *polymorphous* might serve in its stead. Not only does the structure incorporate segments from an entirely bucolic barn; the owners also asked that the architects design the new wing in a serendipitous fashion combining Shingle-style, Victorian, and Georgian elements as well. The architects complied with the client request; as the design evolved, it resolved itself into two basic components: a "barn" side, containing the family room, and a "new" side, with everything else.

To connect disparate architectural elements, and to provide a unified backdrop for the clients' diverse possessions, Haverson/Rockwell conceived an ordered, formal arcade or gallery fitted with a long elevation of mirror-image, neoclassical elements. Longitudinally, it unites family room to living room; transversely, outside terrace to dining room and stair hall. It therefore serves as the hub of circulation for the house, and no effort was spared to make it the visual centerpiece as well. The proportions themselves announce this program: the arcade is approximately 35′–0″ × 7′–0″, and its height is 8′–9″ from floor to soffit, with another foot added to the top by a covelit, gabled ceiling.

The fine wooden detailing is extensive enough—and grand enough—to appear in a millworking contractor's dreams. Along each side stand seven pilasterlike Tuscan columns supported by engaged pedestals. The interior facing elevation (into the stair hall and dining room) is open, with only a screen (bearing) wall separating the gallery from the living space. The opposite elevation, however, is fully elaborated into a façade of French windows (except for the two discordant single doors that actually open), surmounted by pairs of single-pane windows, with the columns applied between each set of windows in a manner suggestive of the main Petit Trianon façade (*analytique*).

The 8-inch-diameter columns, which are nonbearing (except for the support of the plywood soffits above them) are of barrel construction, with redwood "staves" assembled, clamped, and glued, then turned on a lathe to produce a cylinder. Each rests on a hollow pedestal of plywood, detailed with stock pine. The lighting soffit running the length of each wall contains both recessed can downlights and incandescent cove lighting to create the impression of a spacious "artificial sky."

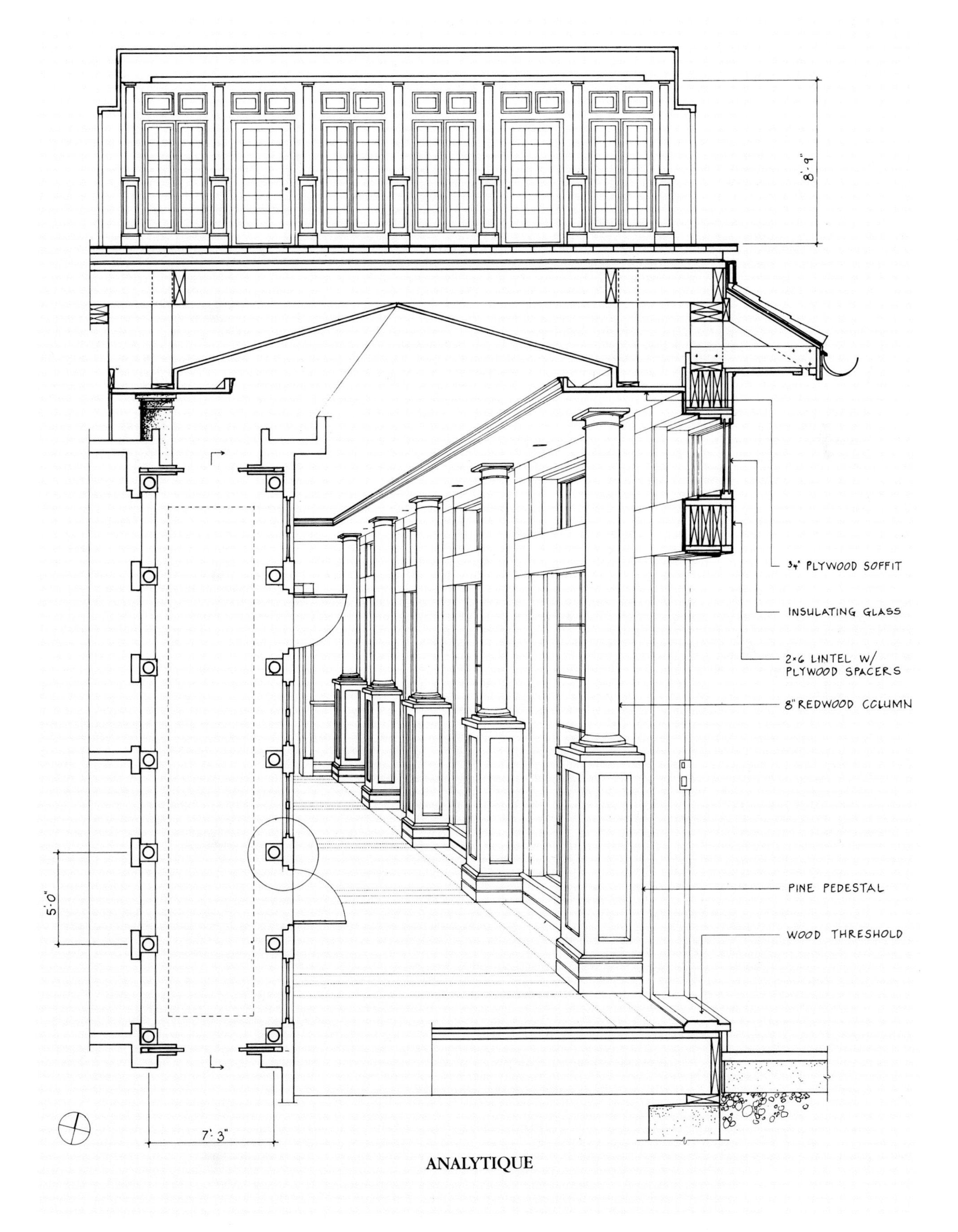
8'-9"
3/4" PLYWOOD SOFFIT
INSULATING GLASS
2×6 LINTEL W/
PLYWOOD SPACERS
8" REDWOOD COLUMN
PINE PEDESTAL
WOOD THRESHOLD
5'-0"
7'-3"

ANALYTIQUE

# Radiator Cover/Closet Cabinetry

**Private Residenc[illegible]**
*Kansas City, Missouri*

**Architect**
Roger Kraft: Architecture • Design

**Design Team**
Roger Kraft, Project Designer;
Mark Peters, Project Architect

**Fabricator**
Bob Falkenberg Company

**Photography**
© E. G. Schempf

Despite 6,000 square feet, the owners of this apartment felt a need for "additional built-in storage" in a number of rooms. But the request made perfect sense to architect Roger Kraft, who conceived the cabinetry as a detailing component "necessary to maintain the continuity of absolutely clean, spare space throughout the apartment" (*see* Ceiling, page 50; Door, page 78).

In the guest bedroom, large existing windows needed to be fitted with new interior trim that, in turn, would work with other wall elements. A corner proved to be particularly problematic: Kraft had to come up with a detailing system that would incorporate a new window frame over existing windows, closet and bathroom doors slightly shorter than the top of the windows, a television cabinet, a radiator cover, and a display area.

Kraft's solution was to unite the window head, frame, sill, and radiator cover in a single sculptural detail, adjoined to an adjacent "panel" consisting of recessed television cabinet, bathroom door, and closet. Together, the segments appear less as disparate parts or stacked elements, and more as a unified "cabinetry wall" (*axonometric*).

A shop was set up in the apartment so that all millwork and cabinetry construction might be performed on-site. The first wall, penetrated by a full-length bank of windows, was covered at the top by a band of ⅝-inch gypsum board, below which was set a wood window frame; both were painted white (*section-elevation*). Below the wooden windowsill, Kraft created a grillwork made of white satin-lacquered wood slats glued to horizontal wooden spacers (*axonometric B*). The entire removable grill, its form inspired by the work of Alvar Aalto, is hung on clips 2 inches out from the face of the radiator.

Three feet from the end of the wall, the sill juts one foot out into the room, with the grillwork turning 90 degrees to follow it, to create a display shelf. The positioning of this shelf creates an immediate view of the piece when one enters the room. The shelf then bends back toward the corner of the room, making a subtle, sculptural reference to the large curve of the opposite wall while also providing transition to the television cabinet (*plan*). On the front of the shelf, parallel to the radiator grill, a white-painted wooden door opens to reveal 11-inch-deep shelves below the display area. The door itself is a full 1¼-inches thick to set it off from the rest of the light wooden grillwork.

The second wall holds three vertical elements: the television cabinet, the bathroom door, and the closet—banded together under one large horizontal panel of painted wood, with each element delimited by a ¼″ × ¼″ reveal. This classical composition is intensified by installing the closet and cabinet doors flush with the wall surface and allowing them to open out, while the central bathroom door is set back and opens in (*plan detail*).

All doors, jambs, and trim are of solid painted wood nailed to blocking. The interior of the television cabinet, which contains a pull-out swivel tray for the set, is finished in painted plywood; all door hardware is white, to match the panel surfaces.

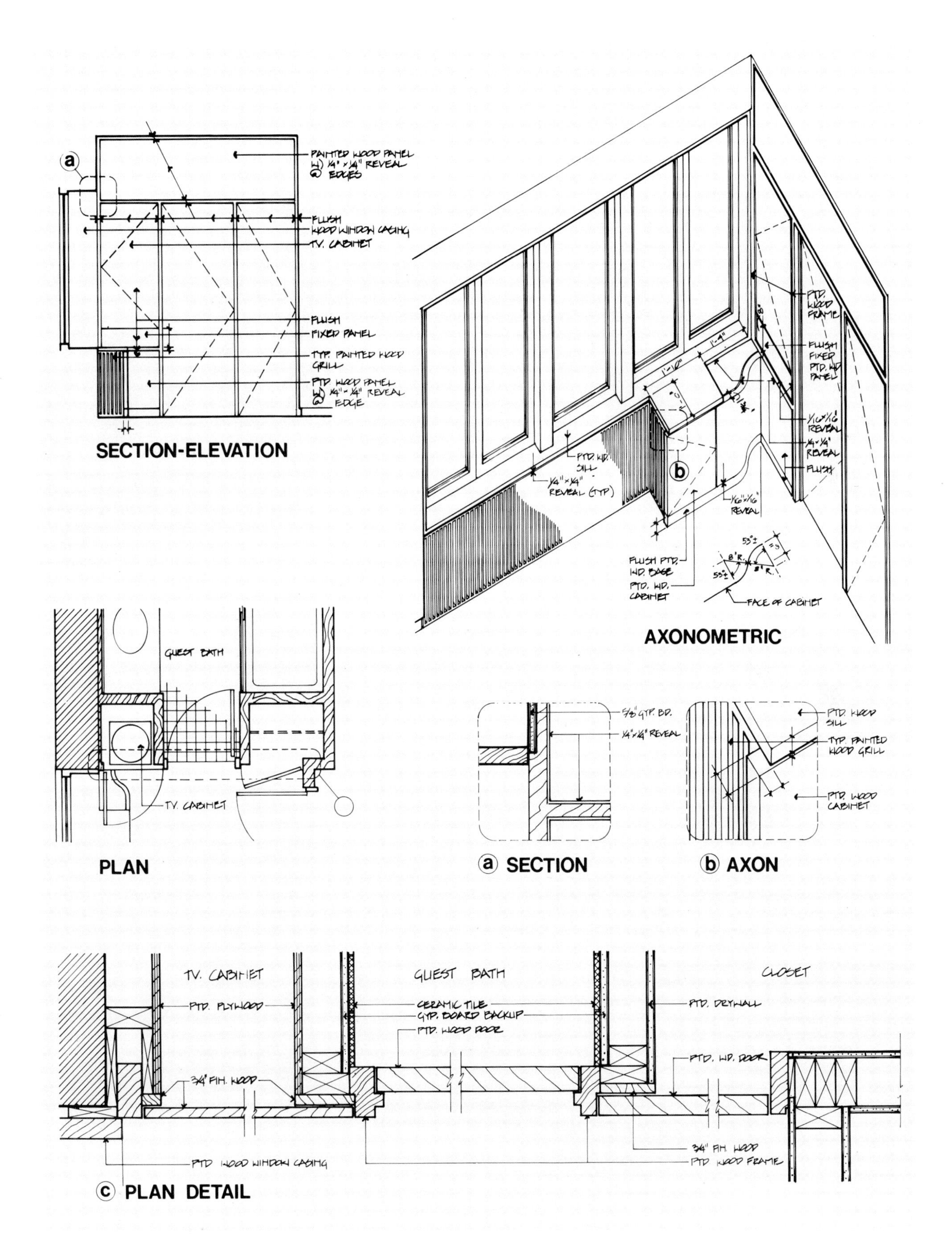

SECTION-ELEVATION
PAINTED WOOD PANEL W/ 1/4" x 1/4" REVEAL @ EDGES
FLUSH
WOOD WINDOW CASING
TV. CABINET
FLUSH
FIXED PANEL
TYP. PAINTED WOOD GRILL
PTD. WOOD PANEL W/ 1/4" x 1/4" REVEAL @ EDGE
AXONOMETRIC
PTD. WOOD FRAME
FLUSH FIXED PTD. WD PANEL
1/16" x 1/16" REVEAL
1/4" x 1/4" REVEAL
FLUSH
PTD. WD SILL
1/4" x 1/4" REVEAL (TYP)
1/16" x 1/16" REVEAL
FLUSH PTD. WD. BASE
PTD. WD. CABINET
FACE OF CABINET
1'-10"
1'-4"
PLAN
GUEST BATH
TV. CABINET
a SECTION
5/8" GYP. BD.
1/4" x 1/4" REVEAL
b AXON
PTD. WOOD SILL
TYP. PAINTED WOOD GRILL
PTD. WOOD CABINET
c PLAN DETAIL
TV. CABINET
GUEST BATH
CLOSET
PTD. PLYWOOD
CERAMIC TILE
GYP. BOARD BACKUP
PTD. WOOD DOOR
PTD. DRYWALL
PTD. WD. DOOR
3/4" FIN. WOOD
PTD WOOD WINDOW CASING
3/4" FIN. WOOD
PTD WOOD FRAME

## PRIVATE RESIDENCE
*Paoli, Pennsylvania*

**Architect**
David C. S. Polk &
Linda O'Gwynn, Architects

**Design Team**
David C. S. Polk, Principal-in-Charge;
Linda O'Gwynn, Project Architect;
Alina Brajtburg, Assistant Architect;
Ellen Concannon, Assistant Architect

**General Contractor**
Hallowell Construction Company

**Structural Engineer**
Nicholas L. Gianopulos and Charles Bloszies, Keast and Hood Company

**Mechanical Engineer**
Basil Greene, Inc.

**Photography**
© Matt Wargo

**FOR A COUPLE** who wished to extend their house into a sylvan landscape, architects David C. S. Polk and Linda O'Gwynn designed a naturalist's house that is, in essence, a series of integrated indoor/outdoor pavilions (*see* Archway/Alcove, page 20).

The pavilions presented the architects with the opportunity to explore the complementary relationships between materials and light. David Polk saw this as "one of the spiritual essences of the house." In one pavilion, "the column, being an antiwall, creates the light, and the light falling on the column creates the pavilion."

To retain a connection among dining room, library, and study—rather than treating each as a conventional room with walls for separation—the library, to which the study communicates through glass doors, was rendered as a balcony over a two-story, 11′–4″-square dining area defined by piers.

The divider between dining room and library becomes horizontal railing rather than vertical wall. Polk describes this detail as "an extension of the lower floor's public realm into the private realm of the upper floor, and as an extension of the first floor architecture into the air."

The piers, which support the corners of the balcony, are constructed of concrete block finished in tinted stucco. Beneath the balcony, pairs of concrete lintels with red-oak infill panels span the 3′–4″ between piers; on the faces of the balcony, support is provided by wood beams. A drywall ceiling is attached to the underside of 2 × 6 wood joists, as the floor of the balcony rests on 2 × 10s.

On the second floor, the finish of the piers shifts from stuccoed concrete to wood, or sets of four 4 × 4 square columns that are finished out to 6″ × 6″ with oak veneer. In plan, they are set at the corners of the 17-inch concrete columns below, leaving a 5-inch gap between them. The columns support the ceiling soffit above, which is also finished in oak trim.

A 3-foot-high rail emerges from the space between the sets of columns. Openwork railing on two sides of the room preserves a sense of connection to the dining area below. On a third side, the railing becomes a glass window wall, and on the fourth, oak panels form the back of a bookshelf, becoming part of the balcony's function as a library. The outer edge of the balcony alternates between built-in oak bookshelves and glass windows and doors. On all sides, the geometry of the oak frames and panels that face the depth of the balcony is extended up into the railing.

Wood pieces are joined by rabbeting and gluing. The wood is finished with a clear satin varnish that gives a slight sheen to the wood surface.

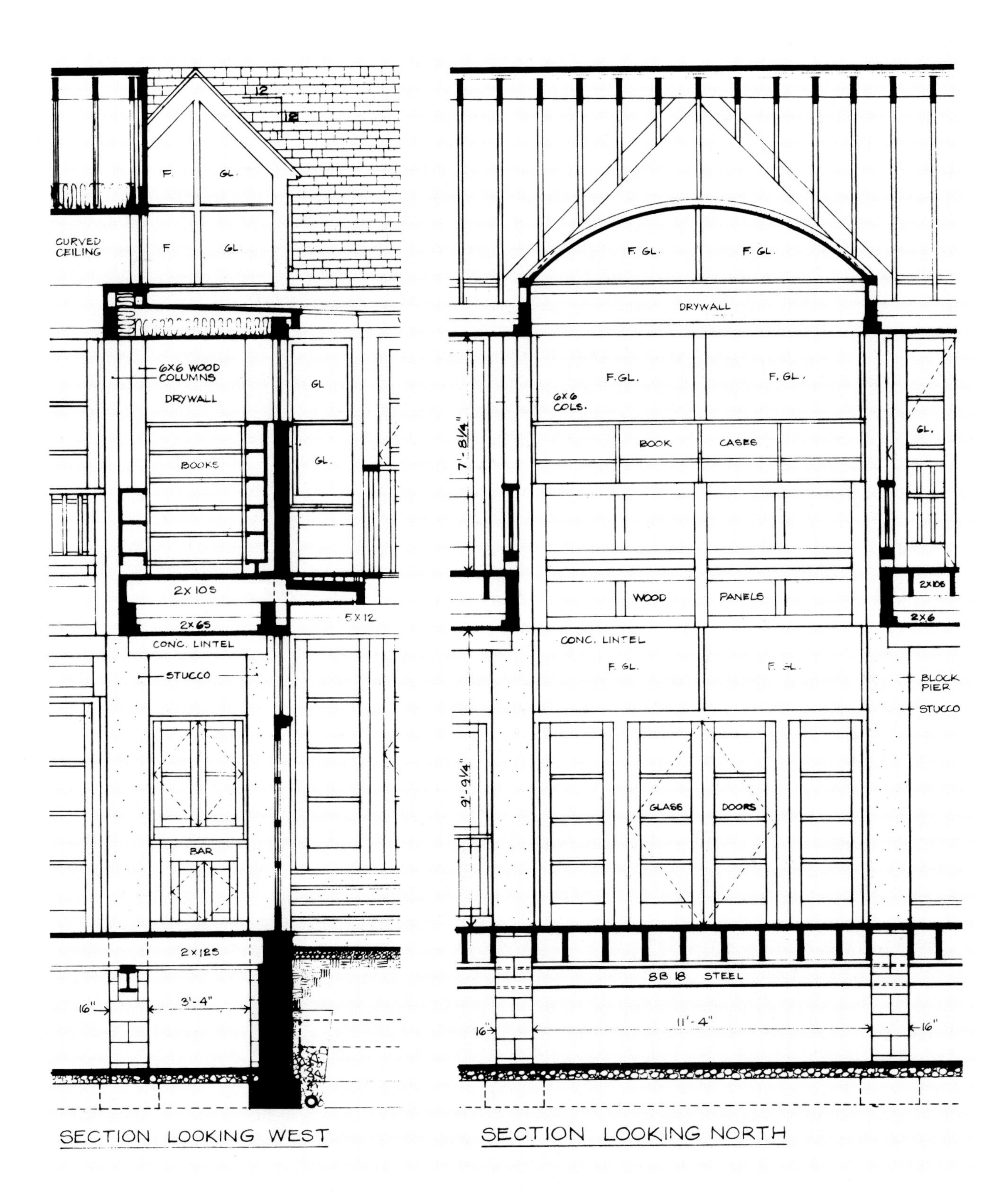
12
12
F
GL
CURVED
CEILING
F
GL
6X6 WOOD
COLUMNS
DRYWALL
GL
BOOKS
GL.
2X10S
2X6S
5X12
CONC. LINTEL
STUCCO
BAR
2X12S
16"
3'-4"
SECTION LOOKING WEST
F. GL.
F. GL.
DRYWALL
F. GL.
F. GL.
6X6
COLS.
7'-8 1/4"
BOOK
CASES
GL.
WOOD
PANELS
2X10S
2X6
CONC. LINTEL
F. GL.
F. GL.
BLOCK
PIER
STUCCO
9'-9 1/4"
GLASS
DOORS
8B 18
STEEL
16"
11'-4"
16"
SECTION LOOKING NORTH

## HORNBUCKLE RESIDENCE
*Santa Rosa Beach, Florida*

**Architect**
James Mount/Architect

**Design Team**
James Mount, AIA, Architect;
Sharon Mount, Interior Designer

**General Contractor**
Steve Landry Construction Company

**Photography**
© Timothy Hursley

THE APPEAL OF A GETAWAY is not limited to the criminal element. On the contrary, police and those who work closely with them value a personal getaway as much, if not more, than the malfeasants they pursue. For Charles Hornbuckle, an active policeman, time to get away with his wife, Margaret, and their daughter is a top priority. Consequently, the Hornbuckle family commissioned architect James Mount to design a vacation home for them in Santa Rosa, Florida, six hours from their home base.

The clients provided Mount with a $71-per-square-foot budget and a simple request for "a cheerful vacation home." Because the design program was unrestricted, the architect enjoyed the rare freedom to develop the house exactly as he wished.

Mount conducted a series of functional studies in order to determine the most versatile dimensions for the space. The result: a 1,500-square-foot plan composed on a grid of 16′–0″ squares. The dining room, living room and kitchen, spaces that occupy three overlapping squares, are also defined by a 3′–0″ change in elevation level.

The architect wanted to keep the 16′–0″ format intact as he formulated a means by which to support the opening for the stairway to the second floor. A multifunctional grid wall "railing" accomplished both goals at once: its openness allows the space to remain basically unaltered, as its full—rather than half—height provides total structural support for the stairwell opening. Parenthetically, the grid's full height also provides an unusual measure of "handrail" safety. Because the stairwell is washed by southern light from an exterior window, geometric shadows that spill across adjacent walls and the tangential floor enhance the grid allusion as they reinforce a sense of scale.

Although the grid railing partition, and the stair treads and floor, are constructed of pine, the treads and floor are bleached, while the grid is painted gray. The grid muntins, therefore, were fabricated of three pieces of painted pine, glued and nailed together. The middle piece sandwiched by the finish surfaces was recessed slightly in an effort to reduce the dimensional feel of the grid. Several coats of polyurethane protect the bleached pine surfaces.

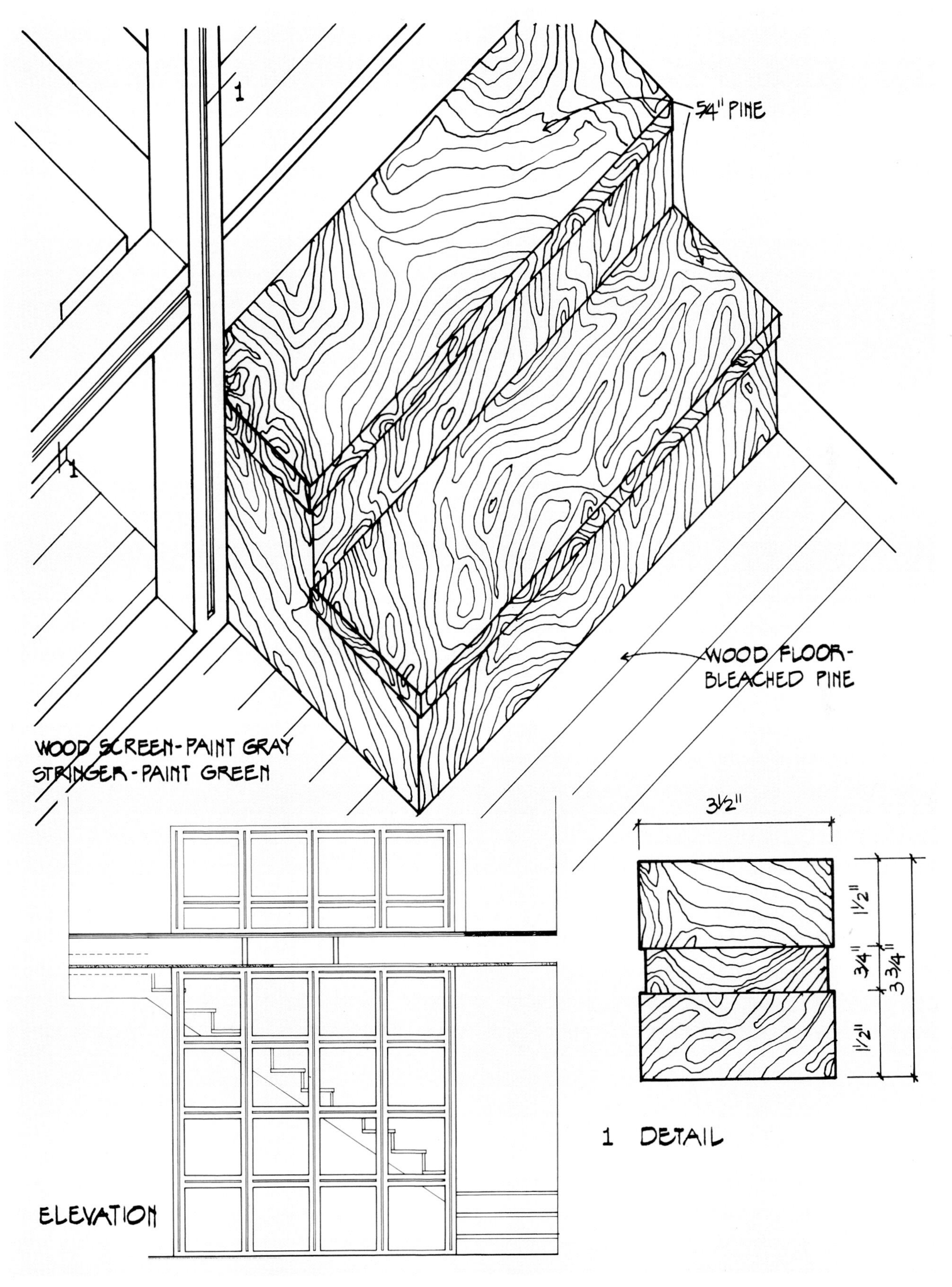
1
5/4" PINE
1
WOOD FLOOR-
BLEACHED PINE
WOOD SCREEN-PAINT GRAY
STRINGER-PAINT GREEN
3½"
1½"
¾"
3 ¾"
1½"
1 DETAIL
ELEVATION

# RAILING

## HARBORSIDE RESIDENCE
*Baltimore, Maryland*

**Interior Designer**
Rita St. Clair Associates, Inc.

**Design Team**
Rita St. Clair, FASID, Principal;
Ted Pearson, ASID, Project Manager

**Fabricators**
The Valley Craftsmen, Ltd. (finishes);
Hough Woodworks (millwork);
Mark Supik (woodwork and staircases);
Crystal Interiors (beveled glass)

**Photography**
© Tim Fields

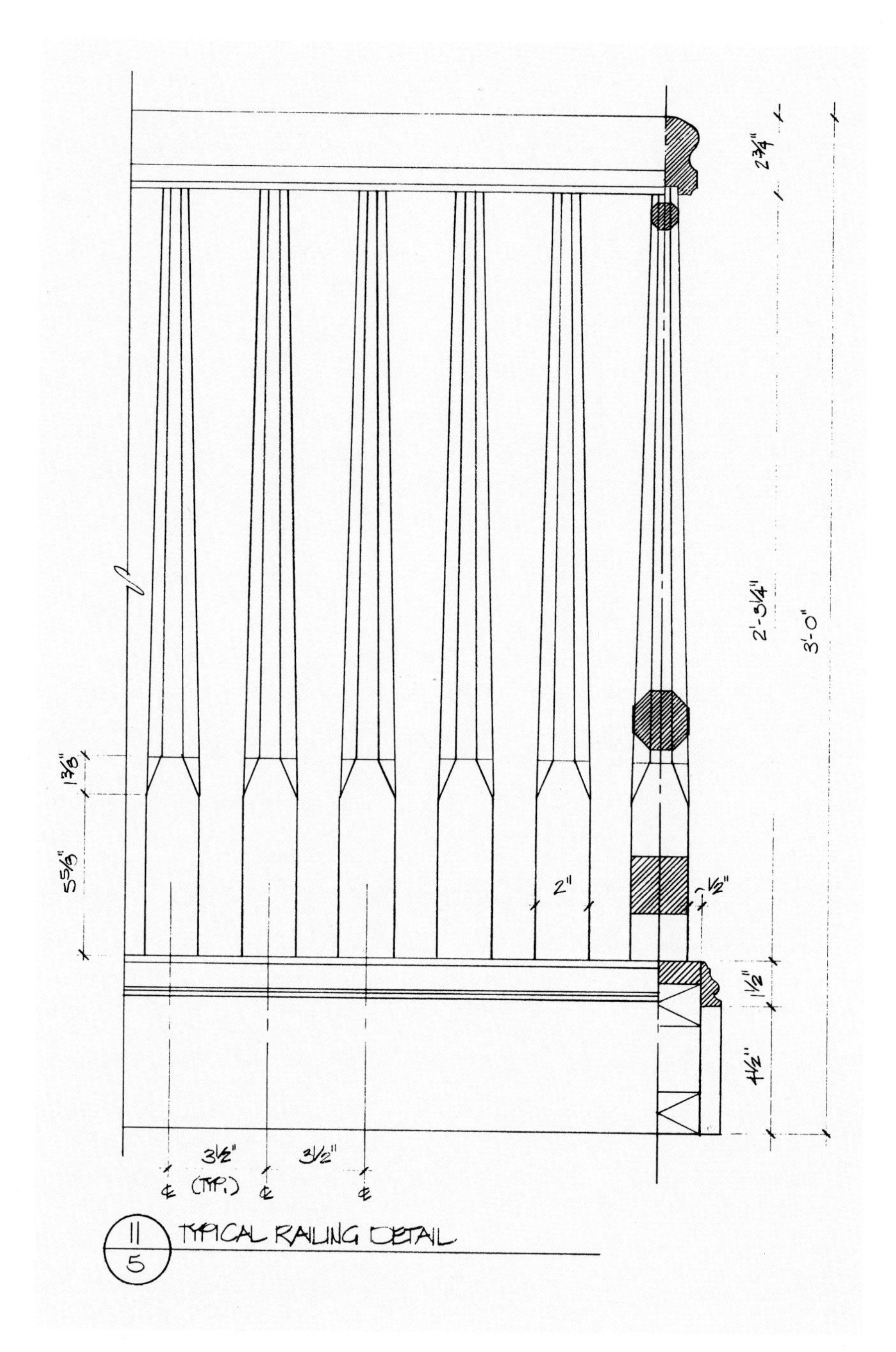


RITA ST. CLAIR, engaged by the owners of a Baltimore harborfront townhouse, utilized rich wood surfaces, natural light, and leaded glass to provide a neo-Edwardian feel to the interior of what is, in fact, all new construction (*see also* Bathroom Cabinets, page 28; Door, page 86; Storage Cabinets, page 208).

It requires more than a cursory examination of the interior to discern the true age of the detailing. The staircase, in particular, is perceived as one that has mellowed with the passage of time and years of hand-polishing.

A closer look tells a different, decidedly contemporary tale. The stair is a slightly splayed ellipse that narrows as it rises upward, combining traditional elements in a nontraditional composition. The plan of the third-floor landing, with its stepped corners and semicircular end, mediates between the curve of the stair and the regular grid of the French doors. The master bedroom, son's bedroom, and bath open onto the landing.

The stair is comprised of cherry and mahogany woods, its hand-carved 2¾"-thick railing set on 2'–3¼" balusters and a 5" wood base. The balusters, which are 2 inches square in plan at the base, taper as they rise, becoming octagonal in plan as the squares' corners are truncated at a height of 5⅝ inches. Their color and placement accentuate the fluted cherry columns on the second floor.

## PRIVATE RESIDENCE
*Greenwich, Connecticut*

**Architect**
Shope Reno Wharton Associates

**Fabricator**
Breakfast Millworks

**Photography**
© H. Durston Saylor

THE PARTNERS of Shope Reno Wharton Associates insist that, despite the million-plus cost, the fondness they have for this particular 6,000-square-foot project is based on the positive relationship they established with their clients. According to Bernard Wharton: "It was a pleasure to work this couple. Their input and participation, on an ongoing basis, enabled us to design and build a house that has become, without question, not just a grand house, but a real family home."

The clients—an investment banker and his wife, an engineer—wanted "a house to grow up in" for their two boys that would emulate "the easy grace and livability of the best houses built during the 1890s." Specific client requests for the interior spaces included "open and private areas; generous circulation; and an overall sense of flow."

The architects developed a Shingle-style derivative house in which all major rooms revolve around a welcoming 10′–0″-wide hallway and stair spine. As viewed from a Dutch entry door, the hallway's generous lateral dimension is accentuated and centered, in elevation, by three integrated and aligned devices: a 7′–0″ newel post; a sphere that sits atop the second-floor landing's railing; and a skylight that is positioned in the center of a coved ceiling directly above the second-floor landing (*stair elevation*).

The architects developed a "Union Jack" detail for their Anglophile clients, which is repeated in millwork detailing throughout the house—in moldings, in the fretwork of upper kitchen cabinet doors, and in two details within details in the central hallway. The newel post is capped by a lantern light fixture that outlines the fretwork grid from within; the stair railing emphasizes the prowlike protrusion of the landing with mirror image, Union Jack railing panels that outline its angles in elevation.

Balusters and grid panels of the railing were painted; the balustrade and sphere were treated with mahogany stain and varnished.

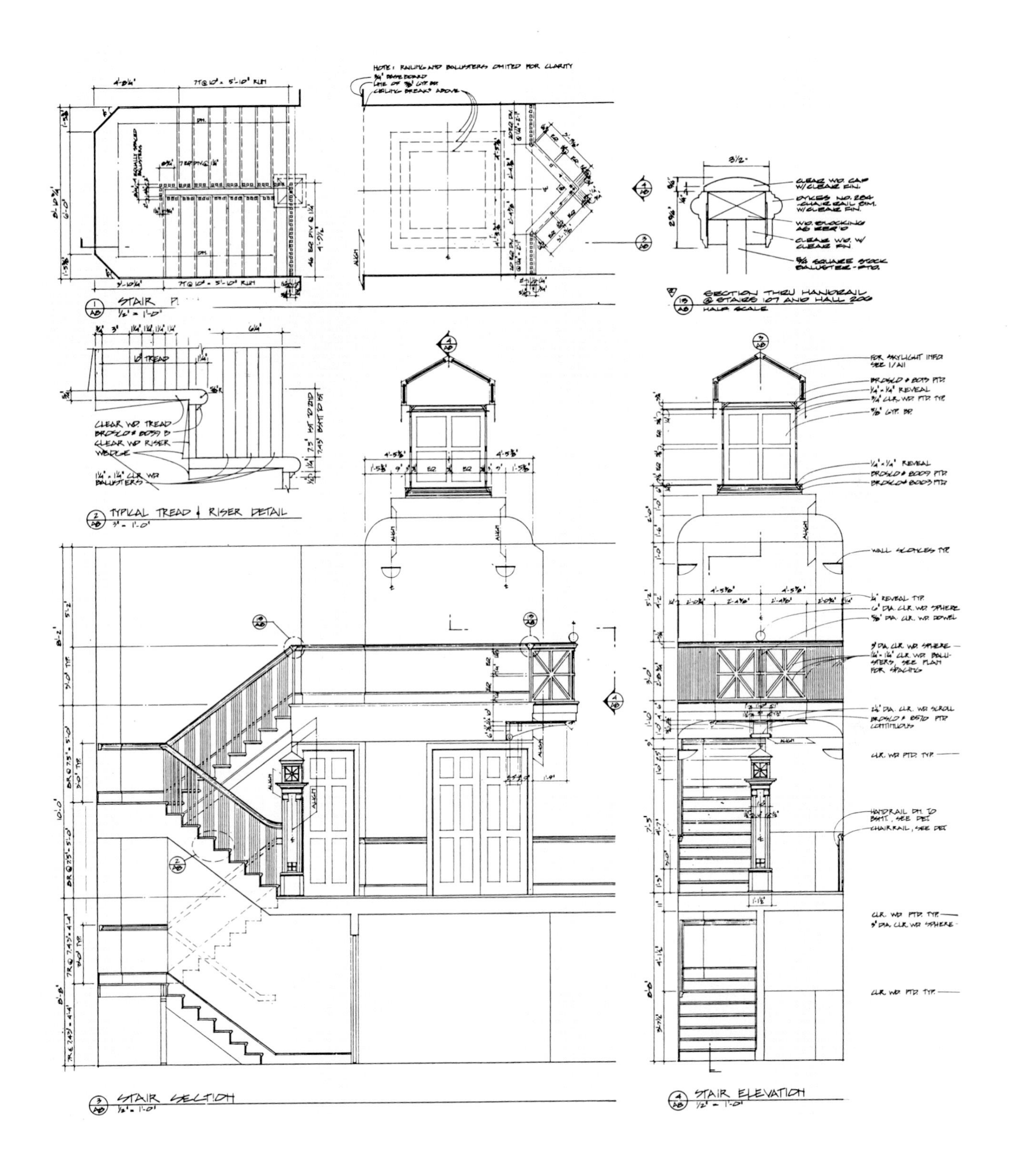

# ROTUNDA

**PETAL HOUSE**
*Los Angeles, California*

**Architect**
Eric Owen Moss • Architect

**Fabricator**
Howard Newhouse

**Photography**

THE PETAL HOUSE—so named for its apparently unfolding roofline (*exterior elevation*)—is owned by West Los Angeleno Brad Culbertson, who with his former wife, Maritza, made the decision to renovate and expand the property in 1984. "New Wave" architect Eric Owen Moss designed the now easily recognizable house, which was, originally, an unassuming, rather dejected post–World War II frame structure (*see* the June 1984 issue of *Progressive Architecture*).

Moss was given a program by the Culbertsons that asked for a new master bedroom suite, an enlarged living room and porch, a new kitchen, and a studio, which was to be added to an existing garage. The architect delivered on all counts in a design tour de force that combines discipline with exuberance, mathematical logic with subjective emotional expression, and sobriety with wit.

Because it was the intent of the project participants—architect and clients alike—to make reference to the increasingly gentrified, yet still industrial, flavor of the surrounding neighborhood, Moss developed a series of both exterior and interior details that allude to, yet depart from and transcend, the architectural forms, finishes, and colors apparent in the immediate area. Although the details are singular and diverse, they are contained within a plan that is clearly organized as an interpretation of the 9-square plan of classical villas.

The entry "rotunda" is one of these details (*see* Joist, page 112; Kitchen Cabinets, page 116). Moss developed the rotunda entry foyer as a circle within a new square porch; it is the only symmetrical element within the new scheme, and is the stem that channels traffic to the public living spaces of the house on the one side, and to the stairs and private bedroom spaces on the other (*floor plan*). The four piers (*rotunda plan*) that define the square are capped, not by a dome as one might expect, but with an inverted dome skylight and light fixture (*rotunda elevation*). The inverted skylight contains fluorescent light fixtures, which are accessed on the second floor. On the first floor, the fixtures are concealed by a 36-inch-wide translucent white dome, fabricated of acrylic plastic, that was nailed to the existing 2 × 6 wood joists. Blocks between the joists accept the plywood furring, to which ½-inch drywall, which forms the ceiling surface, was nailed. The plastic dome protrudes through a circular cut in the drywall, capped by a metal edge that also serves to hide the edge of the skylight (*section*).

The curved front door completes the outline of the circle in the square. The door's wooden frame was constructed of curved horizontal pieces and vertical spacers. Two layers of ⅛-inch tempered Masonite were screwed to either side of the frame to create the door surface. To resolve the integration of a conventional doorknob and lock mechanism into a curved plane, Moss designed a notched recess on the exterior side of the door surface. From the outside, this notch forms a small pocket, which protects the doorknob from weather. The knob assembly was fitted into a solid wood insert that remains perpendicular to the wood jamb (*door plan; exterior knob axonometric*). On the inside, the knob's protrusion is a small, sculptural break in the fluidity of foyer form (*interior knob axonometric; plan and section*).

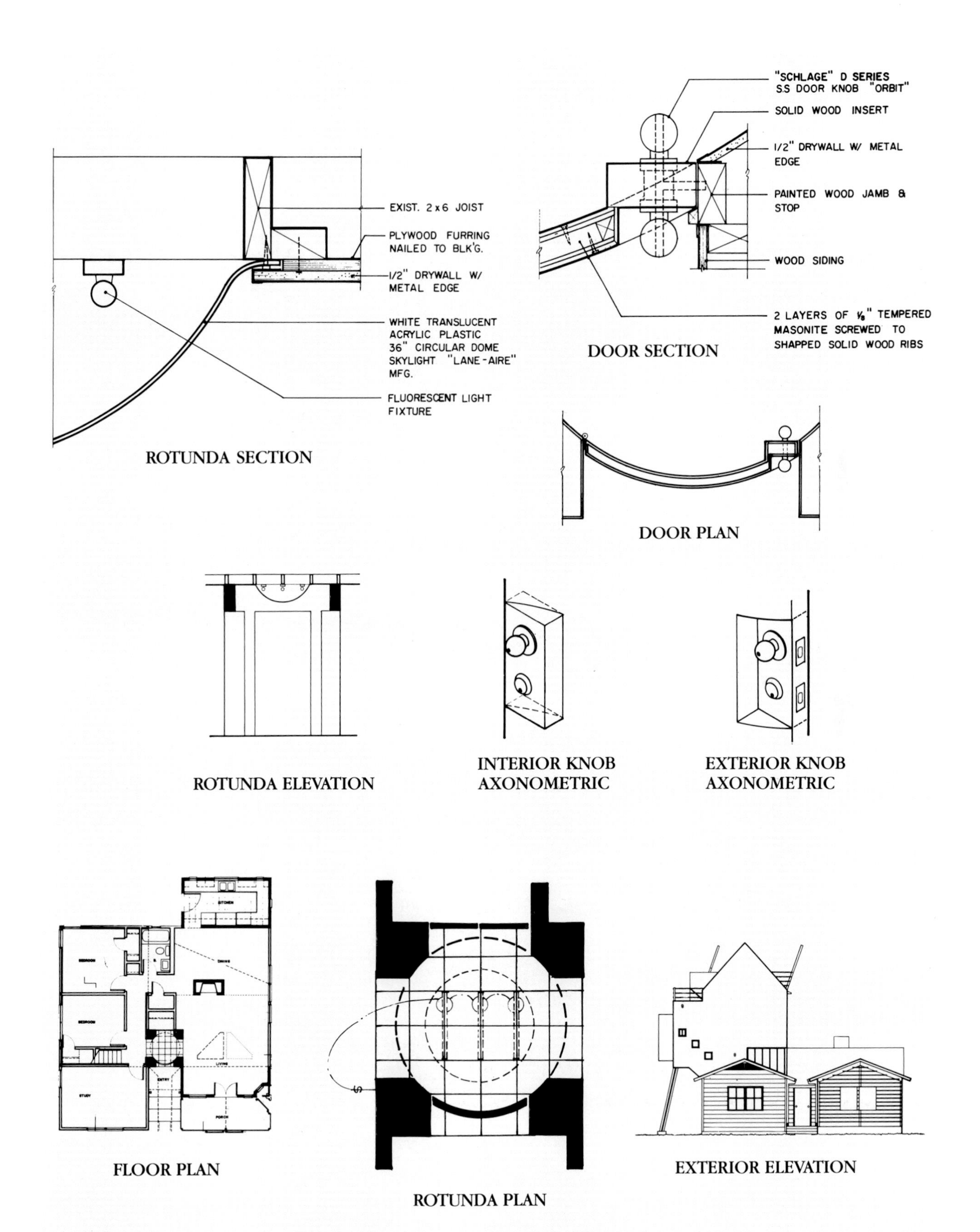


ROTUNDA SECTION

DOOR SECTION

DOOR PLAN

ROTUNDA ELEVATION

INTERIOR KNOB AXONOMETRIC

EXTERIOR KNOB AXONOMETRIC

FLOOR PLAN

ROTUNDA PLAN

EXTERIOR ELEVATION

## Upper East Side Apartment
*New York, New York*

**Architect**
Robert A. M. Stern Architects

**Design Team**
Robert A. M. Stern, Principal;
Paul Whalen, Project Architect;
William Nolan, Grant Marani,
Assistants

**Lighting Consultant**
Cline, Bettridge, Bernstein
Lighting Design, Inc.

**General Contractor**
Scorcia & Diana

**Fabricator**
Phoenix Millwork, Ltd. (cabinets)

**Photography**
© Whitney Cox

In 1984, Robert A. M. Stern faced a common but intriguing design problem: despite the low ceilings and random fenestration of the 1950s "Manhattan modern" apartment building in which his clients lived, the project program called for a 2,700-square-foot penthouse renovation that would, when finished, achieve the feel of traditional, figured space. "Finding the appropriate balance between the real and ideal, the existing space and the desired effect," according to the architect, "became the project's primary challenge."

A challenge that this world-renowned architect considered somewhat less troublesome was to develop a totally new floor plan—a footprint that would clarify circulation and increase the perceived height of the apartment's existing 9′–0″ ceilings. Working with a "fairly generous New York City budget," the Stern design team began its transformation of the apartment by gutting the existing space.

The centerpiece as well as the pièce de résistance of the new apartment plan is an elegant entry rotunda, which acts as a foyer to principal entertaining spaces. The perfectly round, 11′–0″-diameter room is exquisitely finished in "streamlined classical" paneling of African avodire veneer and limba hardwoods that, by their coloration and simple forms, find the comfortable stylistic meeting point between the eighteenth century and the Eisenhower era. Paneled walls are surmounted by a saucer domed ceiling, which in turn is crowned by a lanterned oculus. The "dematerialized" ceiling of dome and lantern visually extends the ceiling horizon, although the room's actual ceiling height was lowered to accommodate the dome/lantern detail.

The form of the domed ceiling was achieved by applying several smooth coats of plaster to lath framing. The dome seems to be supported by the paneled walls, but its lath framework is, in fact, suspended on hangers from the concrete slab of the roof above to accommodate the additional height of the 1′–3″-diameter lantern (*section facing south*).

The meticulously detailed, finely crafted lantern is, technically, nothing more than an aggrandized light box. But its form, as well as its finishes—which include a burnished gold leaf apex and a miniature painted hardwood colonnette positioned in front of sandblasted glass panes—is subtly and impressively rendered (*partial reflected ceiling plan; section through oculus*).

Not a single planar surface in this controlled rotunda was neglected; the room's collective finishes were further enriched by the imposition of an inlaid hardwood floor. Paneled walls accommodate both much needed general storage below and numerous display shelves above.

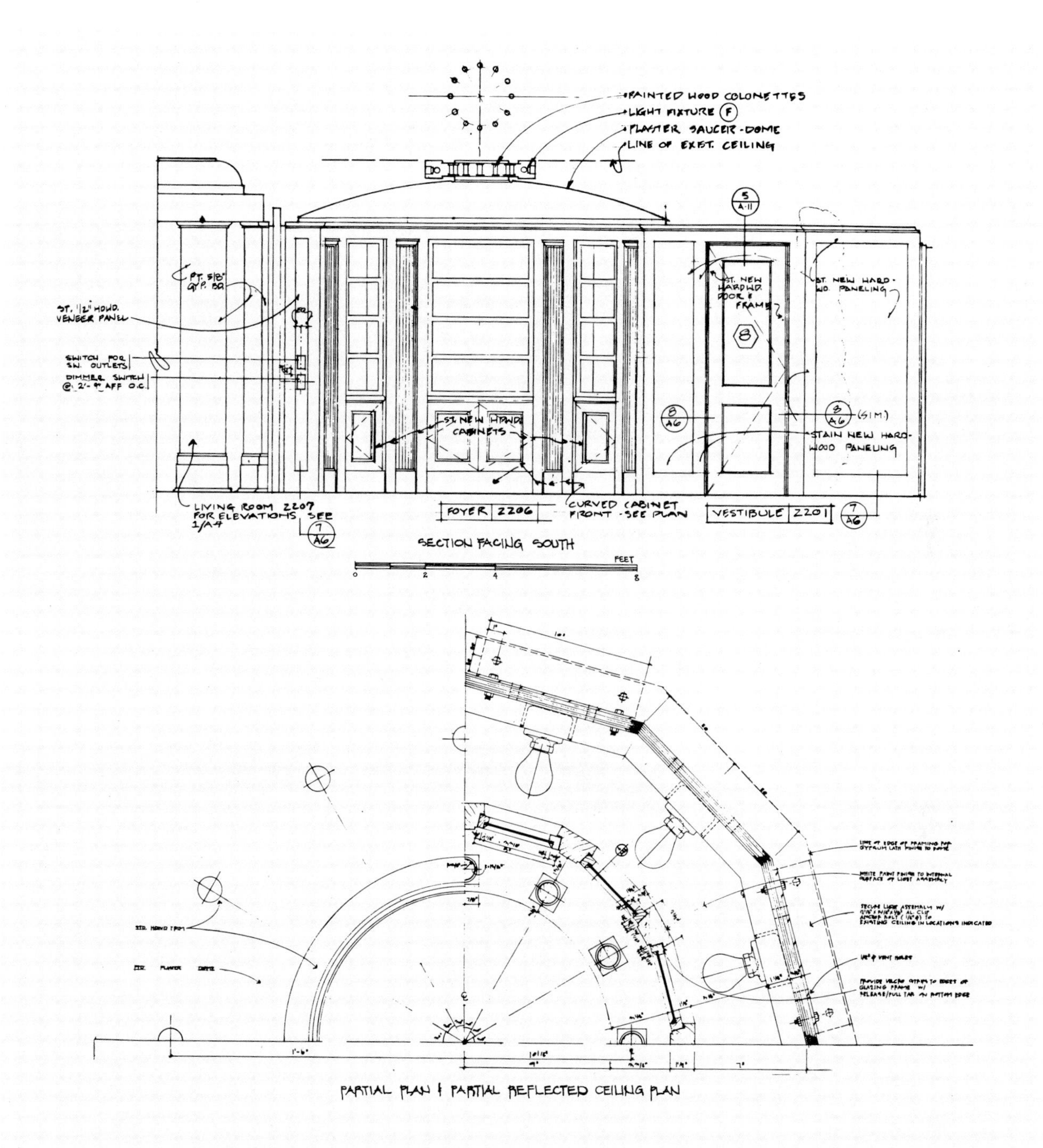


SECTION FACING SOUTH

PARTIAL PLAN & PARTIAL REFLECTED CEILING PLAN

SECTION THROUGH OCULUS

INCHES
0 3 6 12

# ROTUNDA

**YADAVA RESIDENCE**
*Chicago, Illinois*

**Architect**
Pappageorge Haymes Ltd.

**Fabricator**
Wangler Construction

**Photography**
© Paul D'Amato

THE COSMOPOLITAN Yadava family wanted an "urbane American" house that would be conducive to the traditional style of entertaining they had known in India. The couple—both doctors—asked architects Pappageorge Haymes to design their new home with appropriate formality; the result is a symmetrical 7,500-square-foot house constructed as a perfect 50′–0″ × 50′–0″ square on three levels. At its center there is a breathtaking two-and-a-half story, 15′–0″-diameter rotunda that has become, because of its circular configuration as well as its central location within the plan, the focal point of virtually all household activities.

To fully appreciate the well-orchestrated circulation pattern established by the rotunda, it is necessary to view the plan "as if one were moving counterclockwise around the face of a clock." Entry to the house is achieved at the 6:00 position. An archway, at the 3:00 position, provides ceremonial entrance to the living and dining rooms. At 12:00, French doors lead to the kitchen, as well as to a stair that spirals to a recreation room for the Yadavas' two children. The main staircase to the second floor, as well as a hallway to maids' rooms, is located at 9:00. At 7:30, side-by-side doors access a standard kitchen-size wet bar. Display niches occur, respectively, at 5:30, 2:30, and 10:30—two of which back diagonally set fireplaces in adjoining rooms (*rotunda plan*). A circulation hallway on the second floor, punctuated by windows, overlooks the first floor of the rotunda and follows its curve.

Extravagant in scale and elegant in appearance, the rotunda was, nonetheless, constructed quite reasonably on a 1983 budget of $100 per square foot. The rotunda's radius was framed in on studs placed 12 inches on center. Two layers of ¼-inch drywall were moistened and then screwed into the stud framing, after which a skim coat of plaster was applied.

A skylight that penetrates the parapet roof is headed on all four sides and supported by roof rafters that transmit the load down the curved walls (*parapit* [sic] *roof detail*).

Pappageorge Haymes designed a number of smaller details within the rotunda to maximize its visual impact, both indoors and out. The extra half-story, containing the skylight and a carefully scaled row of clerestory windows, projects up from the roofline so that it may be seen from an exterior as well as interior perspective. A continuous cove light fixture was mounted at the second-floor ceiling line, which spotlights the detailing of the extra half-story, as it enhances the dome illusion of the floating dish ceiling (*elevation*).

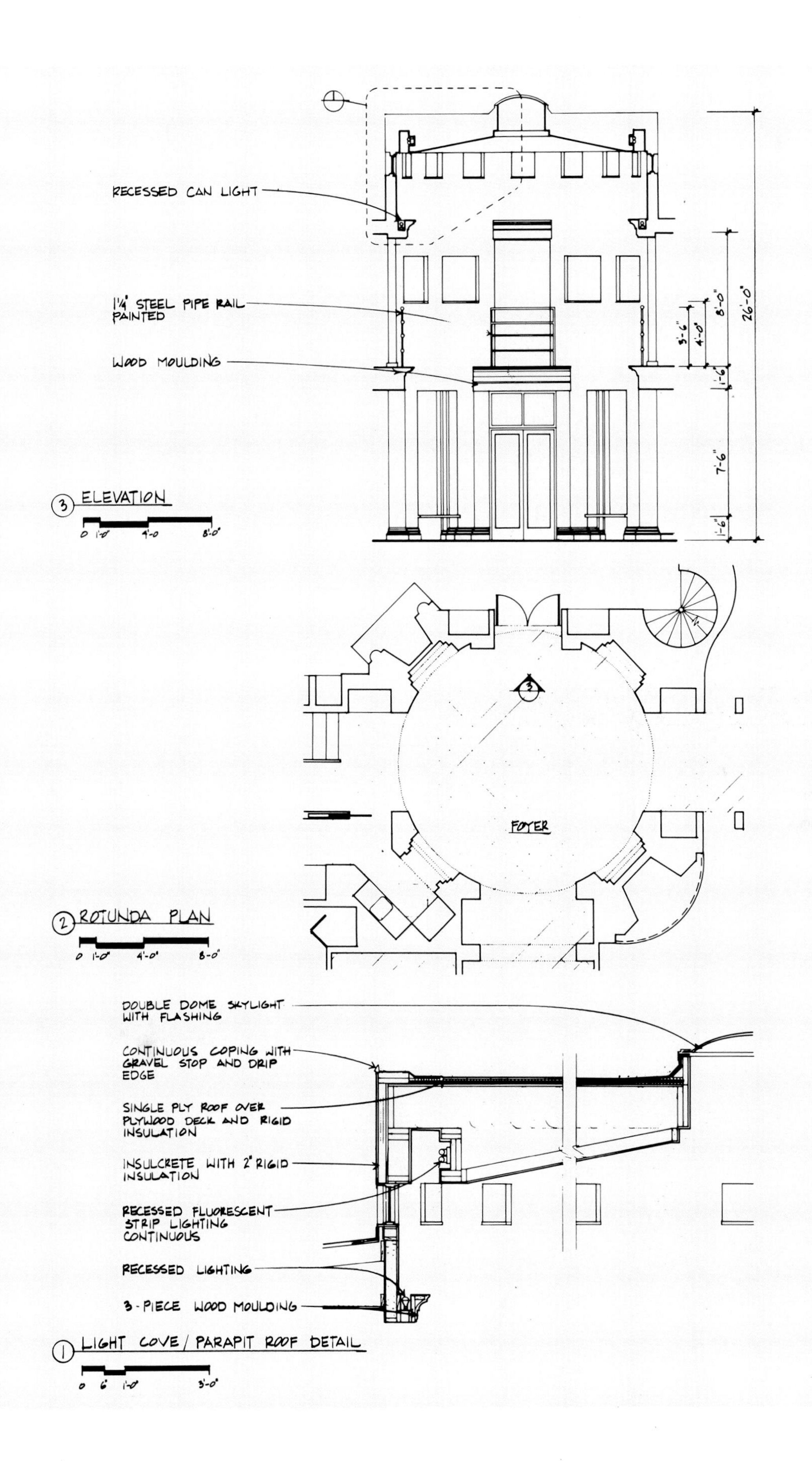
RECESSED CAN LIGHT
1¼" STEEL PIPE RAIL PAINTED
WOOD MOULDING
26'-0"
8'-0"
3'-6"
4'-0"
1'-6"
7'-6"
1'-6"
3 ELEVATION
0 1'-0" 4'-0 8'-0"
FOYER
2 ROTUNDA PLAN
0 1'-0" 4'-0" 8'-0"
DOUBLE DOME SKYLIGHT WITH FLASHING
CONTINUOUS COPING WITH GRAVEL STOP AND DRIP EDGE
SINGLE PLY ROOF OVER PLYWOOD DECK AND RIGID INSULATION
INSULCRETE WITH 2" RIGID INSULATION
RECESSED FLUORESCENT STRIP LIGHTING CONTINUOUS
RECESSED LIGHTING
3-PIECE WOOD MOULDING
1 LIGHT COVE / PARAPIT ROOF DETAIL
0 6" 1'-0" 3'-0"

# Shower Enclosure

**Greenwich Village Loft**
*New York, New York*

**Architect**
Anderson/Schwartz Architects

**Design Team**
Frederic Schwartz, Partner-in-Charge; Janice Kitchen, Assistant

**General Contractor**
Peter Austerin

**Fabricators**
Steve Stretnjak (tile and glass block); Marble Modes (granite); Peter Jevremov, Metal Forms Studio (metal bracket)

**Photography**
© Elliott Kaufman

**Bathrooms in general,** and bathtubs and shower enclosures in particular, are important to urbanites. People subjected to constant stress want more from their bathrooms than a few windowless cubic feet in which to wash away accumulated city grime; they long for a meditative retreat in which to soothe jangled nerves and collect private thoughts.

In 1988, Dr. Mark Phillips and Sylvia Stela, frazzled but joyful at the arrival of Sarah, their first child, commissioned architects Anderson/Schwartz to renovate their Greenwich Village loft apartment. At the top of their list of priorities: a separate bedroom for the baby and, for the parents, a rejuvenating master bathroom.

Frederic Schwartz restored equanimity to the household first by reconfiguring the space plan, and second, and perhaps more important, by transforming the master bath into a luxurious environment that soothes, not only by the spaciousness of its shower enclosure, but also by its monochromatic tones.

Schwartz, who has a special interest in pattern and decoration in architecture, specified glass block in varying sizes and textures for the fabrication of the shower enclosure "curtain" wall—in particular, ripply, water-inspired block, in combination with glass blocks that are channeled, gridded, sandblasted, and clear (*elevation*). Three graduated shades of granite that cover adjacent surfaces, as well as small, color-corresponding ceramic tiles, give the room additional, subtle textural variety. The overall impact of pattern interplay is heightened by the multiple imagery reflected in a curvilinear wall-mounted mirror.

A detail's fabrication is usually more complex than its straightforward finished form may imply. The mortar joints between each glass block in this bathroom were meticulously grouted (*shelf and curb details*); each bracket was crafted of burnished stainless steel and attached by exposed stainless steel screws (*bracket detail*).

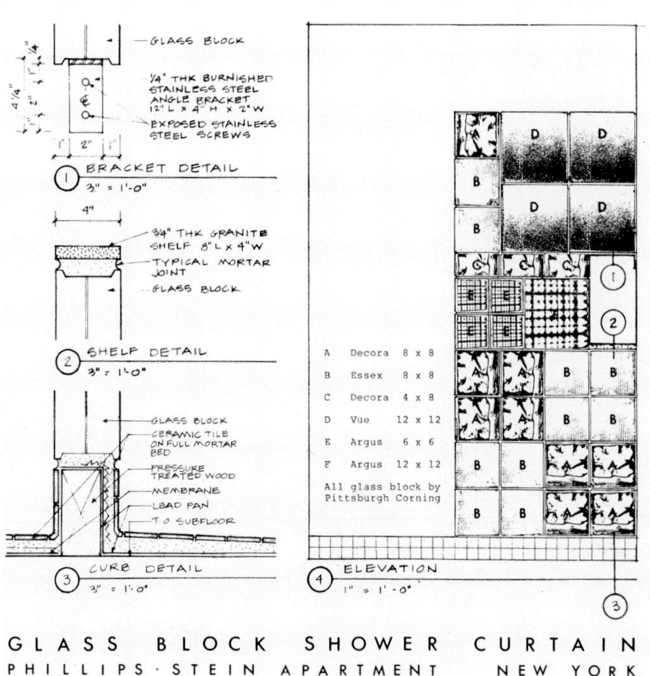

# Shower Enclosure

**Harbor Country Residence**
*Sawyer, Michigan*

**Architect**
Tigerman/McCurry, Architects

**Design Team**
Margaret McCurry, AIA, Partner-in-Charge; John Holbert

**General Contractor**
David Z & Co.

**Fabricator**
Twin Cities Glass

**Photography**
© Judy Neisser

Two fast-paced city dwellers yearned for a weekend country house that would encourage them to enjoy "a slower, antebellum pace." Architect Margaret McCurry, of Tigerman/McCurry, responded by designing a 1,800-square-foot residence that is, although thoroughly up-to-date in its mechanical systems and construction technique, replete with nostalgic detailing allusion (*see* Bookcases/ Door Surrounds, page 42).

The master bathroom, located at one end of the second story beneath a soaring gable, provided a perfect spot for such power of retro-suggestion. McCurry imposed a modern porcelain tub directly beneath the ceiling gable (*elevation @ bath*); she then partly enclosed it, against spillage, with clear panes of channel-mounted glass and, for shower usage, a welded stainless steel curtain rod that conforms, concentrically, to the interior shape of the tub basin (*plan @ bath*).

The shower rod, which was cut from a template, is braced in position both vertically and horizontally. It is suspended from the ceiling (*elevation detail-hanger*) and is bolted to the wall (*plan detail-bracket*).

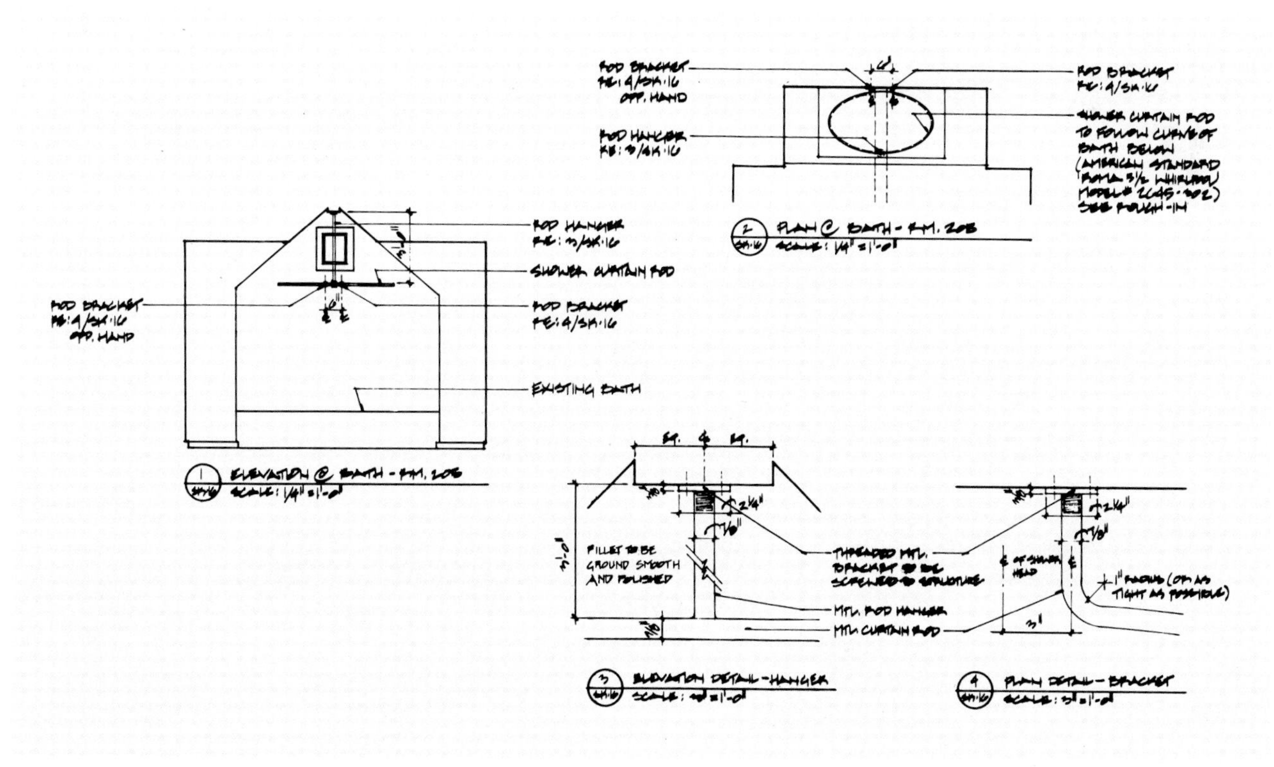

# Shower Enclosure

## Muniak Residence
*New York, New York*

**Architects**
William McDonough Architects

**Design Team**
William A. McDonough, AIA, Principal; Joseph Vance, Project Manager; Janet Roseff; Mark Rylander; Carl Finer; Steve Pynes; Judy O'Buck Gordon; Shelley Brock

**General Contractor**
Dennis Leftwick, Romac Construction

**Fabricators**
Eric Bauer, Fayston Iron and Steel Works (steel and wood); Bob Solari, Vermont Marble (marble); Fordham Marble (marble)

**Drawings**
Judy Choi

**Photography**
© H. Durston Saylor

A CLIENT COUPLE of architect William McDonough, owners of a 5,000-square-foot Victorian brownstone in Manhattan, were determined to have separate bathroom space, not because they suffer any irreconcilable differences, but because their respective preferences in bathroom design are nearly polar opposites. One way to reconcile the couple's diverging tastes was to divide the healthy bathroom budget so that "a frescoed plaster grotto" could be developed for the wife, and a "Loos-inspired bathroom sculpture" for the husband.

McDonough designed a streamlined, structurally focused bathroom for the husband in which requisite functional fixtures appear in radically chic form. Despite its linear austerity, the bathroom is sybaritic, finished in lustrous stainless steel and marble. The bathroom is, in essence, a refined rendition of the conceptual theme that is manifested in detailing throughout the house—"simple elements simply enjoined" (*see* Staircase, page 198).

The allotted space for the bathroom, although relatively small—5′-0″ × 7′-6″—offered geometric interest in the form of a slight angle cutting through one wall. McDonough capitalized on that triangular suggestion by creating a composition of three independent elements: two cylinders—one implied and one real—for the sink and shower, and an apparently freestanding wall that supports the toilet. According to the architect: "The bathroom is a simple composition with very strong materials—large-scale elements becoming more refined as their detail grows smaller and more refined."

The brushed-side, polished-rim stainless steel toilet (a standard prison fixture) was attached with concealed pins to a 3-inch freestanding vertical slab of Vermont verde antique marble. This slab's rear elevation also supports stacked towel shelves.

The two cylinders—sink and shower—were conceived as a suite of elements. The sink's cylinder is created by the opposition of two Elkay RLR-12 stainless steel basins: one forming the sink itself, the other inverted directly overhead to become the reflector of a light fixture. The light basin is attached to the ceiling by a custom-built, welded stainless steel ring frame. The frame is attached to wood cross-blocking between existing joists and is slotted to receive studs welded to the back of the sink rim. A housing, without trim and with a MR16 quartz lamp, sits above the basin's "drain."

At the sink level, another verde antique marble triangular slab intersects the floor-to-ceiling cylinder to form the sinktop. A ⅛-inch stainless steel plate was screwed to the wall as its bottom edge was bent out 90 degrees to support the stone slab and act as a backsplash. A kerf at the back edge of the stone receives the steel plate, but stops short of the edge of the stone to conceal the plate's edge. Another custom stainless steel ring frame, slotted to

receive the marble slab, supports the basin. The whole assembly sits on a stainless steel cylinder of square-section steel tubes formed into hoops and wrapped by a stainless steel skin (*plan-shower*). A removable panel at the back allows access to the plumbing stack.

The shower is similarly constructed, with steel sheets bent around a frame of square-tubed steel "hoops" and studs. Vertical welds between the skin panels are concealed by ¼-inch stainless steel rods; the gap that allows entry to the shower is bridged at the top by another steel rod. This element supports a thin stainless steel mesh "chain mail" shower curtain. The circular steel pan that forms a floor drain is set through a hole in the floor on its own leveling screws on the ¾-inch tongue-and-groove subfloor. The floor hole was cut off-site to Mylar templates (which will not shrink or stretch) before the stone was installed. The bottom hoop of the shower frame was set into a bed of silicone on the flanged edges of the steel pan and then bolted into pretapped holes. The inner skin of the shower was then welded into place. The pan's assembly includes a continuous perimeter support for the stainless steel grating.

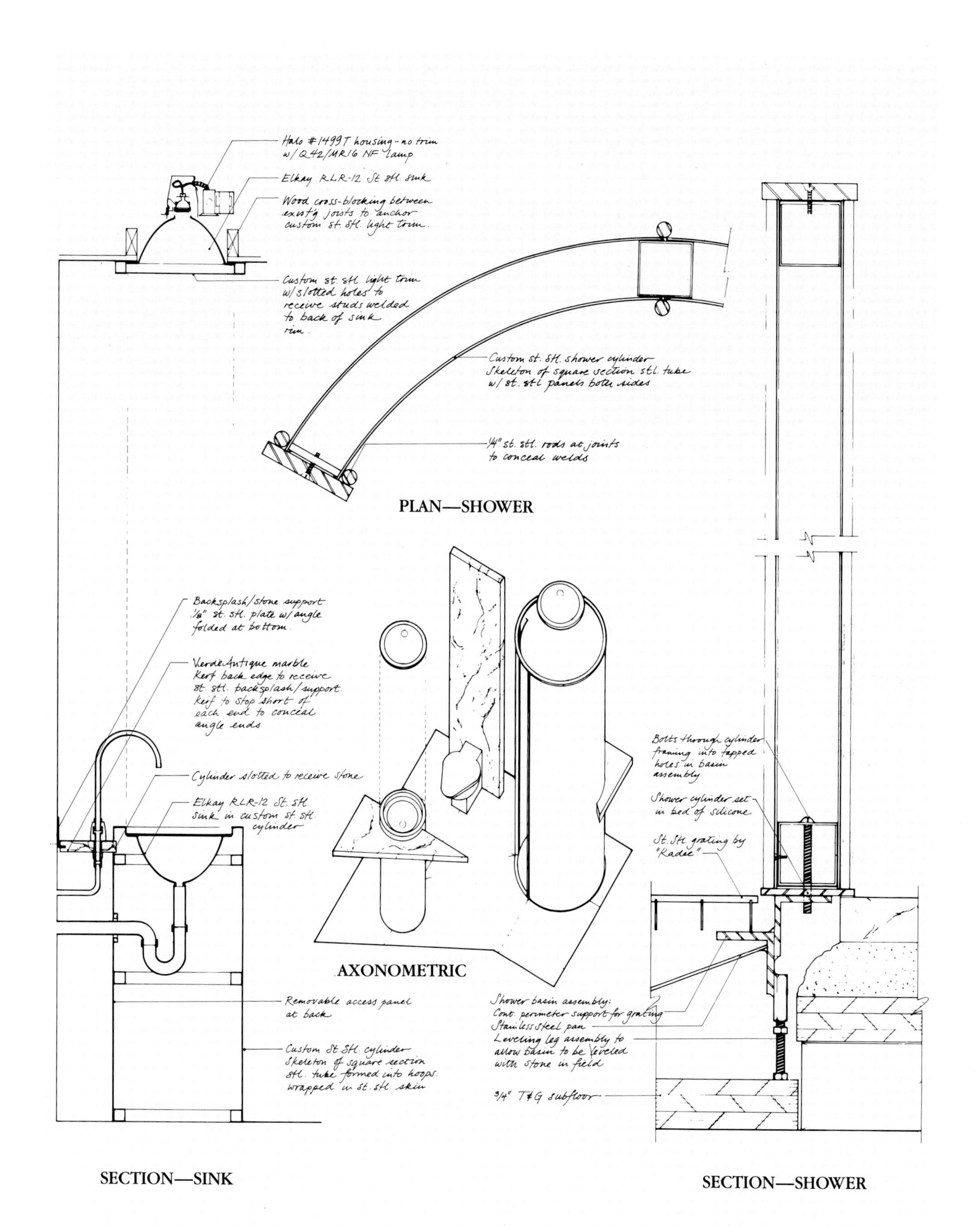
Halo #1499T housing - no trim w/Q42/MR16 NF lamp
Elkay RLR-12 St stl sink
Wood cross-blocking between exist'g joists to anchor custom st. stl. light trim.
Custom st. stl. light trim w/slotted holes to receive studs welded to back of sink rim.
Custom st. stl. shower cylinder Skeleton of square section stl. tube w/ st. stl panels both sides
1/4" st. stl. rods at joints to conceal welds
Backsplash/stone support 1/8" st. stl. plate w/ angle folded at bottom.
Verde Antique marble Kerf back edge to receive st. stl. backsplash/support. Kerf to stop short of each end to conceal angle ends
Cylinder slotted to receive stone
Elkay RLR-12 St. stl. sink in custom st. stl. cylinder
Removable access panel at back
Custom St. Stl. cylinder Skeleton of square section stl. tube formed into hoops. wrapped in st. stl. skin
Bolts through cylinder framing into tapped holes in basin assembly
Shower cylinder set in bed of silicone
St. Stl. grating by "Kadee"
Shower basin assembly: Cont. perimeter support for grating Stainless Steel pan Leveling leg assembly to allow basin to be leveled with stone in field
3/4" T&G subfloor

PLAN—SHOWER

AXONOMETRIC

SECTION—SINK

SECTION—SHOWER

# Shower Enclosure

**Private Residence**
*Chicago, Illinois*

**Architect**
Pappageorge Haymes Ltd.

**General Contractor/Fabricator**
Capital Construction Group

**Photography**
© Wayne Cable

In 1987, a successful Chicago trader in his mid-twenties decided it was high time to make a long-term investment of his own—in urban high-rise, lakefront real estate. He promptly purchased a 2,400-square-foot, two-story penthouse, and then turned to architects Pappageorge Haymes to transform his new acquisition into a "personal design statement." That statement was to reflect "something loftlike, but chic and first-rate in quality."

The client's primary wish, for an upscale loftlike ambience, presented the design team with little challenge; an essentially open plan, offset by a select number of enclosed private spaces, filled the footprint bill. A far greater challenge, according to the architects, was to "correctly, and three-dimensionally, interpret 'chic' and 'first-rate' for a client who gave us both a free hand and a generous build-out budget of $500,000." Their eventual answer: exquisite details throughout the apartment that were crafted by hand in sumptuous finish materials (*see* Partition, page 148).

The design team appropriated 320 square feet from the overall plan for the development and construction of a spectacular second-level, master bathroom/spa—a sensualist's paradise that incorporates into one space a double vanity, a combination shower/steam room, and a large whirlpool tub.

So that the tub could be inset flush with the floor, the floor was raised 2′–6″ to a platform height. Access to the platform is gained via jigsaw, ziggurat stairs, a subtlety that not only adds to the composition a dramatic diagonal design element, but also avoids a potentially awkward conflict in elevation at the intersection point with the windows (*master bath platform plan*).

A superiority of form within the spa is as obvious as its functional quality. An unusually sophisticated combination of three contrasting, but complementary, finish materials proclaims the room's pizzazz. Floors, stairs, and counters are tiled in three incrementally sized squares of flamed and polished granite; shower and steam room wall panels are rendered in laminated layers of cracked tempered glass; fixtures, faucets, and mirror mounts are fabricated of polished brass (*elevation; section*).

Meticulous planning is evident in even the smallest detail. An ergonomically scaled depression has been created in the steam room floor to facilitate the option of a supine posture while bathing (*elevation*); recessed channels hold cracked glass panels invisibly in place (*steam/shower room ceiling and base details*); and a shaving mirror and supply shelf have been mounted onto cracked glass walls without visible support (*glass shower shelf detail*).

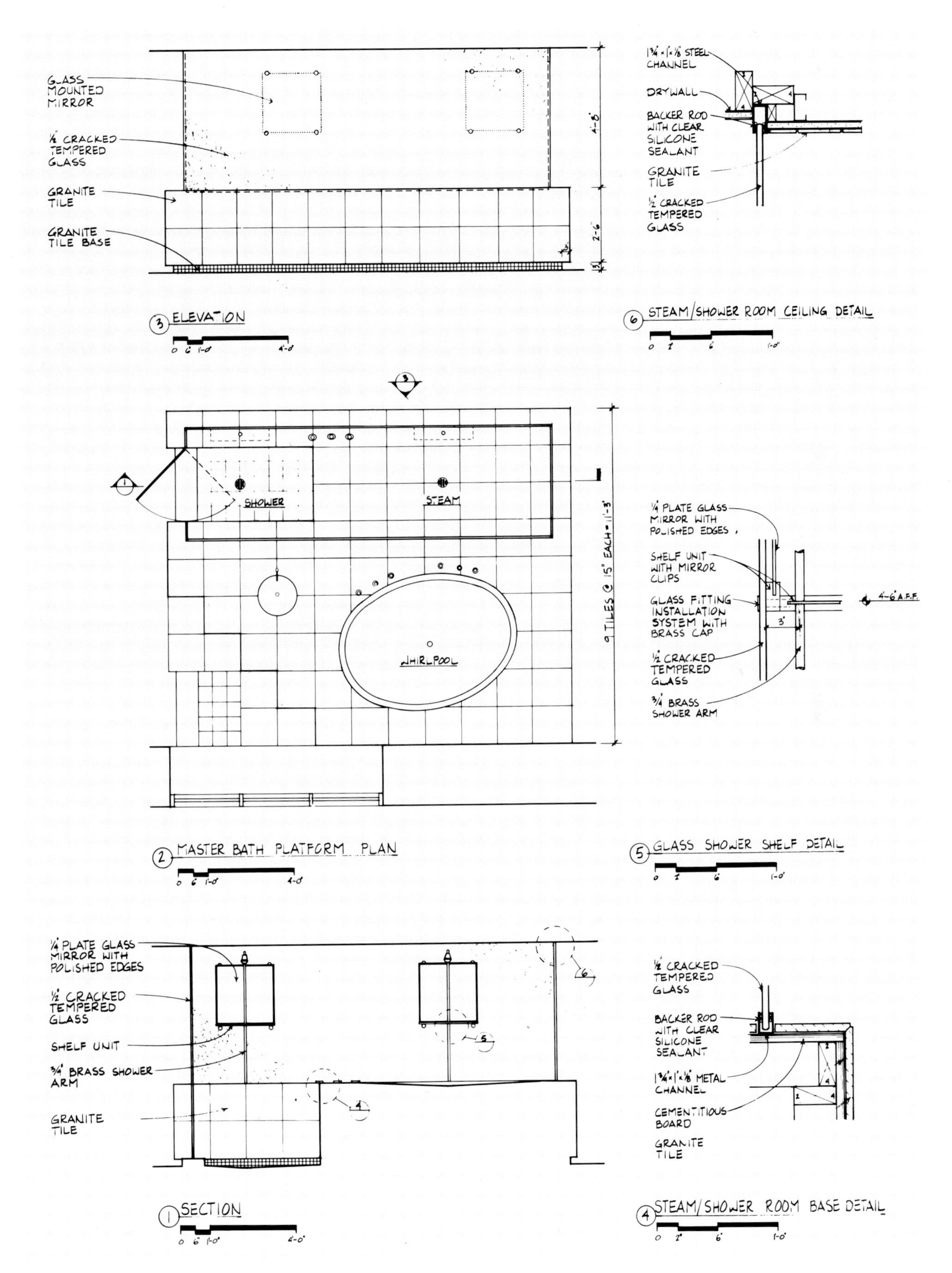
GLASS MOUNTED MIRROR
½ CRACKED TEMPERED GLASS
GRANITE TILE
GRANITE TILE BASE
4'-8"
2'-6"
3 ELEVATION
0 6 1'-0" 4'-0"
1¾×1"×⅛ STEEL CHANNEL
DRYWALL
BACKER ROD WITH CLEAR SILICONE SEALANT
GRANITE TILE
½ CRACKED TEMPERED GLASS
6 STEAM/SHOWER ROOM CEILING DETAIL
0 2 6 1'-0"
SHOWER
STEAM
WHIRLPOOL
9 TILES @ 15" EACH = 11'-3"
2 MASTER BATH PLATFORM PLAN
0 6 1'-0" 4'-0"
¼ PLATE GLASS MIRROR WITH POLISHED EDGES
SHELF UNIT WITH MIRROR CLIPS
GLASS FITTING INSTALLATION SYSTEM WITH BRASS CAP
½ CRACKED TEMPERED GLASS
¾ BRASS SHOWER ARM
4'-6" A.F.F.
3"
5 GLASS SHOWER SHELF DETAIL
0 2 6 1'-0"
¼ PLATE GLASS MIRROR WITH POLISHED EDGES
½ CRACKED TEMPERED GLASS
SHELF UNIT
¾ BRASS SHOWER ARM
GRANITE TILE
1 SECTION
0 6 1'-0" 4'-0"
½ CRACKED TEMPERED GLASS
BACKER ROD WITH CLEAR SILICONE SEALANT
1¾×1"×⅛ METAL CHANNEL
CEMENTITIOUS BOARD
GRANITE TILE
4 STEAM/SHOWER ROOM BASE DETAIL
0 2 6 1'-0"

# Shower Enclosure

**Private Residence**
*Aspen, Colorado*

**Architect**
Harry Teague Architects

**Design Team**
Harry Teague, Principal;
Dennis Cyrus, Project Manager;
Glenn Rappaport, Suzannah Reid,
Ron Robertson, Associates

**General Contractor**
Michael McNamara, Hanson
Construction, Inc.

**Fabricator**
Steve Parzybok, Paradox Structures
(metal work)

**Photography**
© John Vaughan, Russell MacMasters
& Associates, Inc.

In 1974, architect Harry Teague designed a house in Aspen for an independent filmmaker and his wife. Although Teague chose a "log cabin" style that was both relatively economical and suggestive of the Colorado mountain environment, he split the primary mass of the structure with an axial skylit gallery in order to achieve the light, airy effect he sought. His clients loved the end result so much that, as their business and family grew, they recommissioned Teague to add to their home no fewer than six times (*see* Window, page 224).

Teague's sixth effort, a two-story master bedroom and bath/spa, brings the master living quarters up to the standard set by earlier additions. Its centerpiece is a shower/steam room big enough for two, designed as a relaxing environment that contains a whirlpool spa, exercise equipment, a wet bar, and comfortable wicker furniture.

A prerequisite of a steam room, where the temperature can reach 110 degrees, is resistance to the corrosive effects of steam. Glass is an ideal resistant material; used here to form the ceiling of the shower, it allows the infusion of light from above, as it also allowed Teague to allude to the shimmering light cast through the house's original gallery skylight. Glass block was specified to coordinate with the ceramic tile used for the seats and wall surfaces inside the shower, as well as the floor and lower wall tile of the outer spa (*axonometric*).

Teague set 7′–8″-high walls of grouted 4′–8″ glass blocks into a welded, sandblasted, stainless steel frame. In the vaulted ceiling, which was built on a wooden form, metal strips were inserted into the grouting for extra strength (*axonometric*).

The entire assembly rests on typical frame construction covered with Wonder-Board, to which the ceramic tile was grouted. The back wall includes two 18-inch square windows—at eye level for those sitting on the benches—that bring outdoor light directly in. The windows were fabricated of triple-layer heat-mirrored glass, in which two glass panes sandwich a plastic layer coated with a very fine metallic material. This process allows ultraviolet light in, but keeps infrared out (*axonometric*).

The shower door was fabricated as a sandblasted stainless steel frame enclosing frosted glass panes, which were silicone-mounted flush with the door surface. A rubber gasket seals the door opening.

In the large spa room, the shower is flanked by bearing steel columns; the romantic fluted capitals are constructed of sandblasted stainless steel. The columns were faux painted to resemble the verde antique marble chips set in the spa room's tile walls.

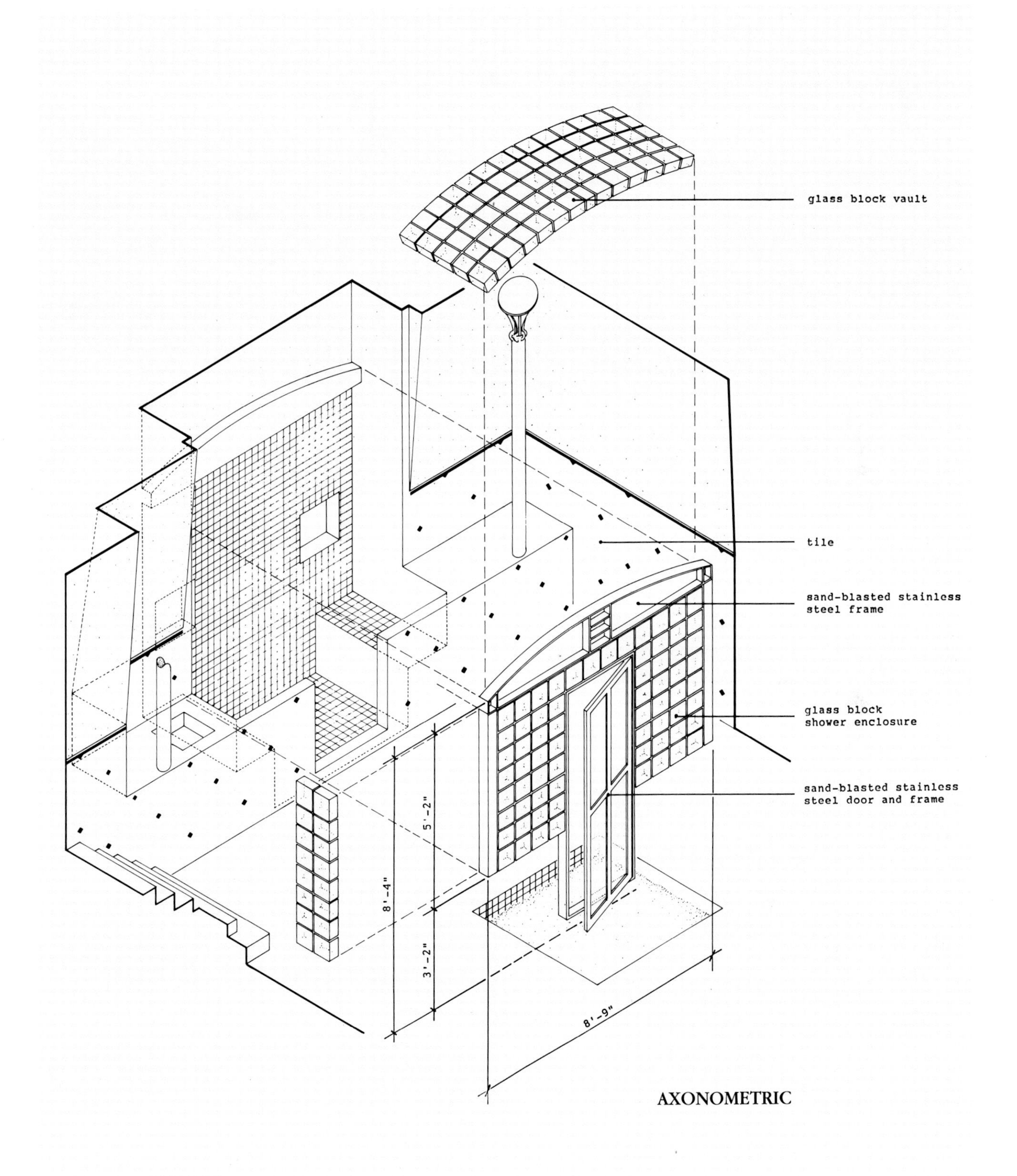
glass block vault
tile
sand-blasted stainless
steel frame
glass block
shower enclosure
sand-blasted stainless
steel door and frame
5'-2"
8'-4"
3'-2"
8'-9"

AXONOMETRIC

## BERGREN RESIDENCE
*Venice, California*

**Architect**
Morphosis

**Design Team**
Thom Mayne, Principal; Michael Rotondi, Principal; Gianluigi Irsonti; Mahmood Michale Saee; Rachel Vert; Tom Adolph; Jay Vanos; Eric Khan; Alex Rudeamen; Kathy Rea

**Electrical Consultant**
Saul Goldin

**Mechanical Consultant**
The Sullivan Partnership, Inc.

**Structural Consultant**
Gordon Polon

**Photography**
© Tim Street-Porter/ESTO

MORPHOSIS DESIGNED this award-winning 850-square-foot, back-lot addition to a house in Venice, California—a closely knit and tightly sited beach community dominated by bungalows. The owner occupies the main house; her son—a professor of architecture at UCLA and the Southern California Institute for Architecture—occupies the addition, which contains a library, lounge space, study space for writing, a bedroom and bath, as well as a roof deck.

Thom Mayne and Michael Rotondi, principal architects of Morphosis, saw the project as an opportunity to design a house in miniature and, therefore, to develop a prototype for a small family dwelling on a restricted urban site. The owner and her son saw the new addition as an opportunity to expand the existing house, and as a space that would in the future serve as either a guest house or a separate rental dwelling.

The miniaturized house—constructed of concrete slab, wood frame, asphalt shingle walls, and metal wall panels—consists of three formal masses. The main element is a large rectilinear volume, rotated off the axis of the main house, that contains working and sleeping areas. The second element, on the axis of the existing house, is a small linear mass that contains the library. Finally, an element consisting of three components combines skylights and detached volumes to house a roof deck, a bath, and a future kitchen—all set on the new axis.

The 6′–5″ × 8′–4″ bathroom, which is positioned at the end of the main workspace, is accessed through double doors at the stair landing. The bathroom completes the central axis of the main volume, which passes through the bathroom's centrally placed doors, sink, tub, and window. A toilet sits in its own alcove off-axis, rotated back to the orientation of the library and existing house.

The tub and sink were fabricated of steel as one piece incorporating the tub's outer shell, the vertical fins, and the horizontal shelf that sup-

ports the sink and medicine cabinets. The fins were bolted to vertical wooden supports that continue into the ceiling, and were further stabilized by stainless steel diagonal rods with adjustable couplings (standard yacht hardware) that counterbalance the weight of the cabinets.

The double medicine cabinets, which were mounted parallel to the bath's axial double doors, were fabricated of paint-grade wood with mirrors on both sides. Each cabinet is half the width of the gap between the steel fins and can swing 180 degrees. When closed, the cabinets form a continuous mirror for sink and tub; when open, they allow a continuous view through a square window in the back wall of the bathroom.

Cost control was an important consideration in the fabrication of the bathroom, as it was for the entire addition. Consequently, the tub shell was lined with standard ceramic white tile, applied on Thin-Set over mortarboard. The 18″ × 24″ Brazilian blue marble countertop was salvaged by the architects as a remnant from an earlier restaurant project. The 10-inch diameter spherical steel basin was purchased for $29 from a store that, according to the architects, "couldn't wait to get rid of it." Plumbing and fixtures are stock inventory. The floor was covered with industrial carpeting.

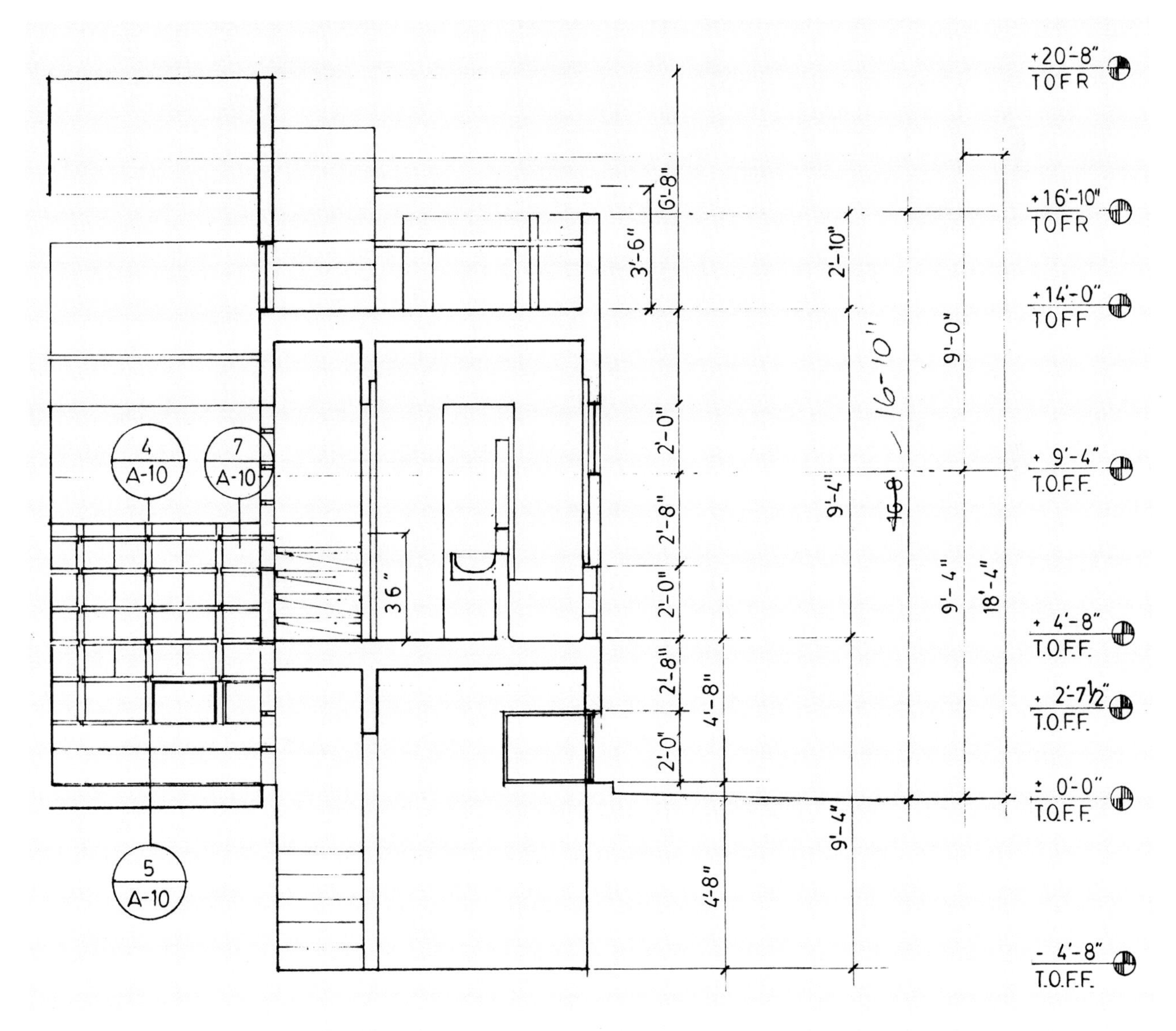


SECTION C-C
1/4"= 1'-0"

# Sink/Cabinet/Wall

**Private Residence**
*Sag Harbor, New York*

**Architect**
Lee H. Skolnick Architecture + Design

**Design Team**
Lee H. Skolnick, AIA, Principal;
Kurt Ofer, Assistant

**Fabricator**
Bert Numme

**Photography**
© Lee H. Skolnick

Two well-known artists who are stimulated by everyday life in Manhattan nonetheless make a point of escaping the city in summer and early fall by retreating to their property on Long Island. In 1986, they commissioned architect Lee Skolnick to make a compound of the property by remodeling the existing house and designing two additional studio buildings, one of which was to be attached to the house and the other, detached.

The artists are often in France, where inclusion of "bathroom" facilities in the dressing area is common. They thus feel little need for privacy and tend to think of the living process as a totality without preconceived notions. Because these clients were clearly receptive to new ideas about the forms a bedroom/ bathroom could take, Skolnick demolished existing walls and partitions on the second floor of the house to create a new master suite that not only occupies the entire floor, but is almost entirely open.

Having made the decision to allow the sink to face into the bedroom, Skolnick's challenge was to design a functional sink cabinet that would also be a nice piece of furniture. The architect resolved the problem by rendering the cabinet in finely grained hardwood against a freestanding wall that screens spray from the shower (*axonometric*).

The cabinet, which contains all the plumbing for sink and shower, is faced with mahogany (for resistance to the effects of water and humidity, as well as for richness of tone). Bolted to it are two solid brass brackets; these in turn are welded to the two solid brass rails of the armature, which bears the sink proper and its flanking frosted glass counter surfaces (*axonometric*).

The sink basin itself is china, which is glazed on the inside but not on the outside. Skolnick reports that he searched "far and wide" for a perfectly hemispherical sink with the patina of unglazed china on the outside. He finally located one through a dealer in French hardware; the look that results is, intentionally, very French.

The French look is strengthened by the faucets, which are, paradoxically, from the Chicago Faucet Company. They are mounted directly through the mahogany wall without touching the sink.

The mirror is set with adhesive directly into the paneling, underlying the mahogany.

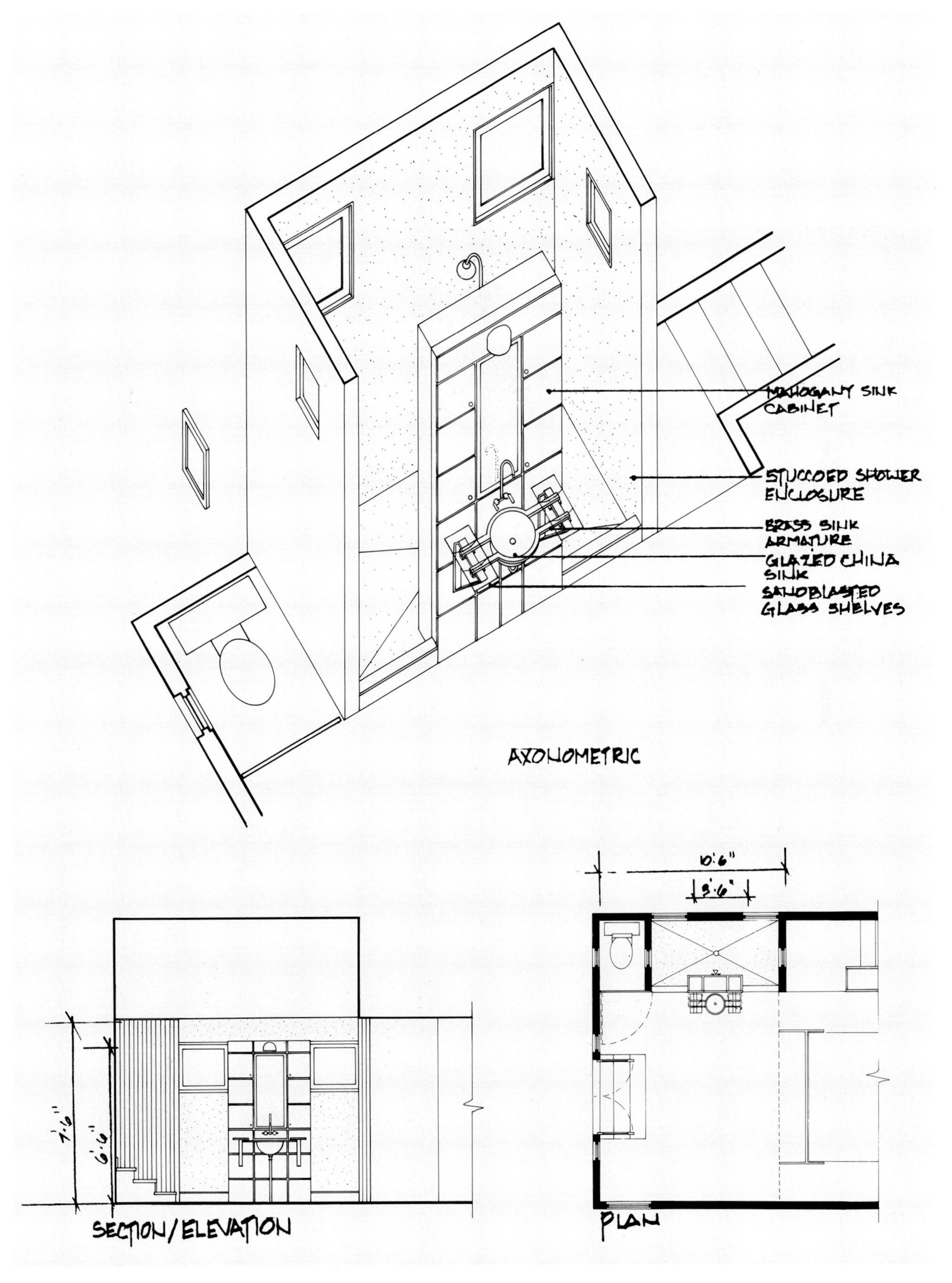
MAHOGANY SINK CABINET
STUCCOED SHOWER ENCLOSURE
BRASS SINK ARMATURE
GLAZED CHINA SINK
SANDBLASTED GLASS SHELVES
AXONOMETRIC
10'6"
3'6"
7'6"
6'6"
SECTION/ELEVATION
PLAN

### LEHRMAN RESIDENCE
*Washington, D.C.*

**Architect**
David M. Schwarz/Architectural Services, P.C.

**Design Team**
David Schwarz, Margaret Flinner

**Fabricators**
Clevenger Corporation (finish carpentry); A. F. Schwerd Manufacturing Company (column); Focal Point, Inc. (moldings)

**Photography**
© Jim Hedrich, Hedrich-Blessing

CREATING ENOUGH SPACE to house "a great many personal possessions" was the primary challenge for architect David Schwarz in designing the apartment of a Washington, D.C., art collector. Fortuitously, the Schwarz firm had designed the building in which the apartment was located; because construction was under way but not complete, the architect was able to include a number of timely changes, some of which were structural, to meet the client's needs.

Because the client owned a large number of oversize canvases, ceiling height became an issue of immediate concern. Schwarz had specified dropped ceilings containing recessed light fixtures in the construction documents, but for this particular apartment, he was able to redesign the actual slabs with lighting recesses already in place, eliminating the need for a suspended ceiling.

To further accommodate the display of large canvases, Schwarz designed a series of independent walls: flat, freestanding planes that support the artwork and create a progression of spaces throughout the apartment. The planes were set on the diagonal to allow a free circulation flow among them. More structural changes—including the relocation of several columns—were implemented to accommodate a freer plan.

The client asked Schwarz to provide an area within the apartment for the presentation of video art—a request that required Schwarz to design custom enclosures for an extensive inventory of electronic equipment, including a system of stereo speakers and a screen for a projection television. Because there was no ceiling in which to hide the equipment, Schwarz designed an enclosure that is both in keeping with and in counterpoint to the aesthetic of the rest of the apartment.

A 20-inch concrete column that marked one corner of the space designated as the video "room" inspired Schwarz to create a modern "entablature" that defines the space, as it contains the high-tech equipment. The entablature concept, according to the architect, "is appropriate to video art, as it plays on classical ideas of theater, proscenium, and stage."

A stock 5′–9″-high Roman Corinthian fluted wood column was set in line with the existing concrete column, together creating the ends of the proscenium. Schwarz de-

signed a 1′–8″-square × 1′–3″-high wood base with classical molding to support the column and one of the stereo speakers. The base was constructed of ¾-inch paint-grade finish wood over 2x supports, with a flush speaker grill as one of four fascia panels.

The column supports the 11-foot-long entablature above it, which breaks at the edge of the concrete column and continues again on the other side, set off on both sides by 2-inch reveals. The entablature was fabricated of 2 × 3 framing that was covered, front and back, with wood trim and stock plaster dental molding. The entablature also supports stereo speakers, as well as a 5″ × 6″ × 6′–0″ enclosure for the video screen. From below, the opening for the screen appears only as a 1-inch reveal running between the two columns on the underside of the entablature.

The 15-inch-high entablature stops 5½ inches short of the ceiling and contains cove lighting fixtures on the interior of the upper cornice. Light shines up through the open 2′–7⅛″-wide top of the cornice to reflect from the ceiling. Power for the lighting, as well as connections for the speakers and screen, is carried through electrical conduit in the hollow wood column. The projection unit and all controls are contained in a hollow coffee table in the video area; a panel in the side of the table opens up when the projector is in use. The table's classical molding edge and the wood base built around the concrete column are subtle extensions of the entablature's classical language.

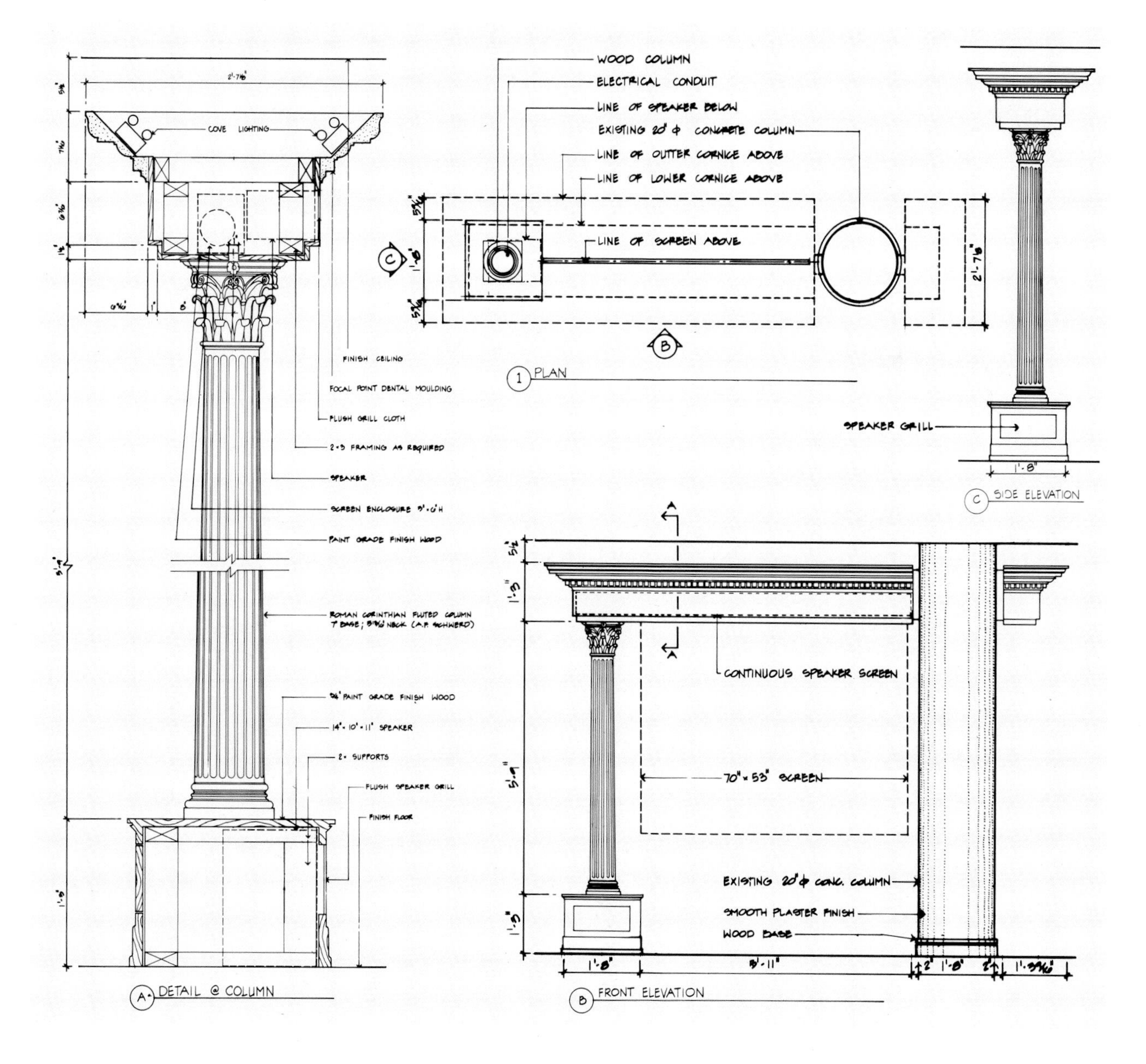

# SOFFIT

**LIBROS HOUSE**
*Chester Springs, Pennsylvania*

**Architect**
David C. S. Polk, Architect

**Design Team**
David C. S. Polk, Principal-in-Charge; John David Rulon, Project Architect; Gautam Bhatia, Assistant Architect; Faith Baum, Assistant Architect

**General Contractor**
George K. Page

**Photography**
© John Chew, courtesy of Sotheby's International Realty

A COUPLE with grown children wanted a small house on a large piece of property. But the perfect site already had a house on it; consequently, the decision was made, with architect David C. S. Polk, to reduce, reconfigure, and remodel the existing structure.

The clients asked for generous living spaces to be augmented by only one bedroom for themselves and another for guests. To achieve this, the house was gutted and the roof was removed, after which the entrance courtyard was recomposed with a new wall.

The existing exterior living room wall had only a small window and, therefore, no significant connection to the terrace. Polk redesigned this room to be the grand space of the house, building up from its stone base with a combination of existing stone walls and new oak and glass walls to a double-height, barrel-vaulted wood ceiling.

The terrace wall forms the support for one side of the vault. Polk designed a 4′–0″-thick wall to support the monumental roof, but rather than creating a solid wall out of wood or stone, he designed a wide zone of space of lighter wood members and large areas of glass.

This juncture of glass to barrel vault is defined by a roughly 4-foot double soffit. The soffit is actually an "L" in section: on the interior side, a composite beam—four Douglas fir 4 × 12s nailed together with a 2 × 6 and a 2 × 8 nailed to the top (to resist bending compression)—is clad on the other three sides in plywood that supports the vertical loads. Perpendicular to the composite beam, a hollow, insulated, plywood box beam resists the lateral thrusts of the vault. One of the 2 × 10s is nailed to the top of the two 3 × 8s, projecting roughly 6 inches out to the exterior of the house. This beam creates a flat surface to support the upper plywood layer of the box beam. At the outer edge of this surface, a 2 × 4 supports the plywood roof. Two pieces of wood trim wrap the face and underside of this upper plywood box, stopping 2 inches short of the soffit face to create a drip molding. At the uppermost corner, a final square section of trim forms a stop for the two layers of flashing.

The soffit is, in fact, a double soffit; the lower one forms a head for the doorway and lower windows, as well as a sill for the upper band of glass. This secondary soffit provides shade from the summer sun while preserving the wall's lightness and transparency. It is constructed of white oak trim and panels over edge beams of two 2 × 6s and one 2 × 8. An angled wood sill on the top edge of this soffit receives the glass and projects out over the face to keep water from draining down the wood surface. On the underside, the window heads are formed of oak trim nailed to the 2x beams.

All visible soffit panel surfaces are of white oak, nailed to the beams with the nails sunken and hidden. Polk chose this wood because it is "darker and calmer" than red oak. The jambs at the stone end walls are of oak trim over wood blocking; wood-to-stone joints are caulked inside and out.

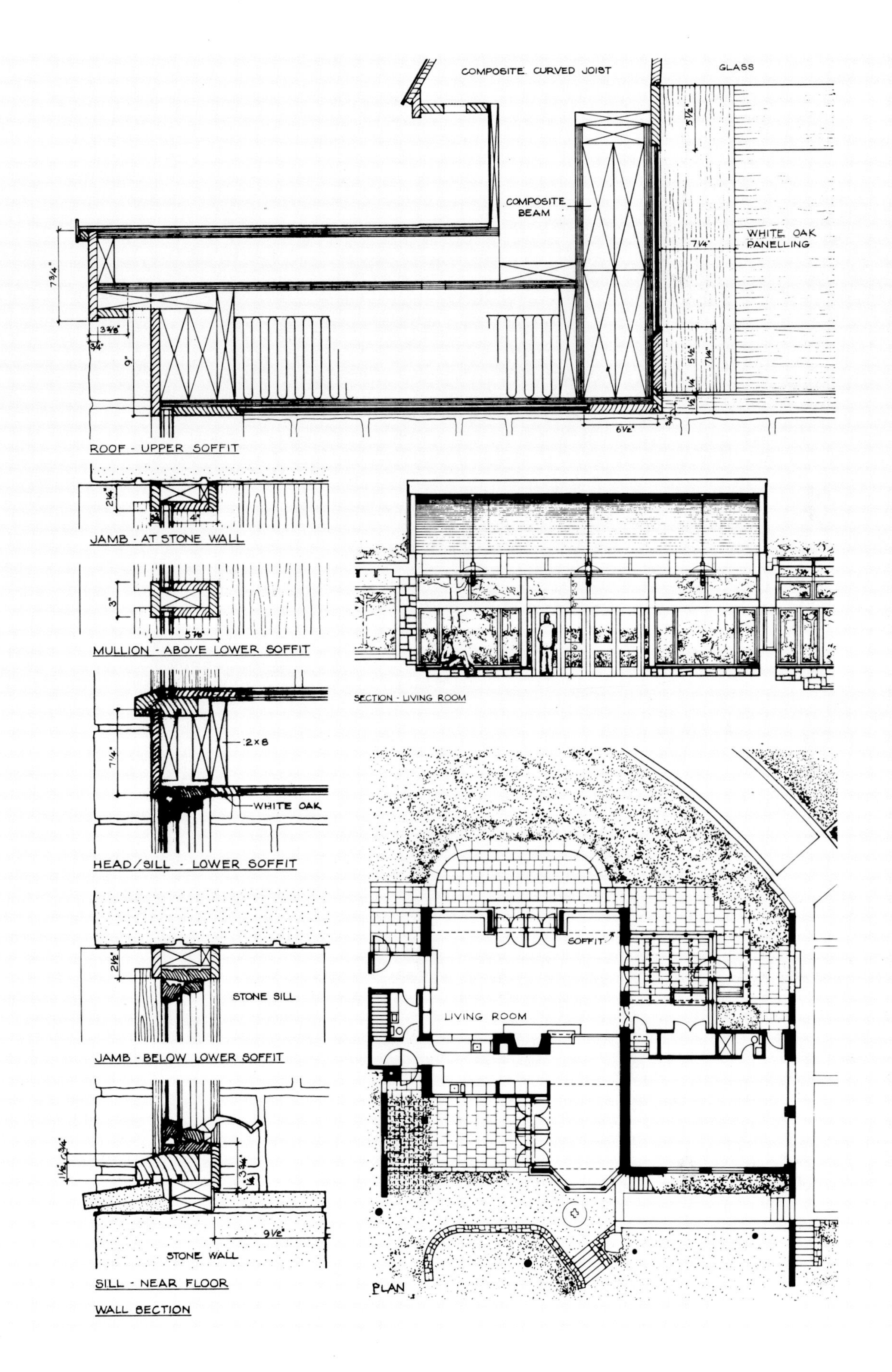
COMPOSITE CURVED JOIST
GLASS
COMPOSITE BEAM
WHITE OAK PANELLING
ROOF - UPPER SOFFIT
JAMB - AT STONE WALL
MULLION - ABOVE LOWER SOFFIT
2x8
WHITE OAK
HEAD/SILL - LOWER SOFFIT
STONE SILL
JAMB - BELOW LOWER SOFFIT
STONE WALL
SILL - NEAR FLOOR
WALL SECTION
SECTION - LIVING ROOM
SOFFIT
LIVING ROOM
PLAN

## Private Residence
*Charleston, South Carolina*

**Architect**
Charleston Architectural Group (since disbanded), c/o Eubank + Thompson, Architects

**Design Team**
Steven Ross Thompson, Project Architect and Detail Design; William F. Riesberg; Charles Menefee, III; Huston Eubank

**General Contractor**
Trudeau-Wolf Construction

**Fabricator**
Jowers and Ramberg Wood Works

**Photography**
© Terry Richardson

In 1983, Victor Barrette commissioned Charleston Architectural Group to design a modern house empathetic with Charleston, South Carolina's historic architectural vocabulary and current building restrictions.

Given a modest budget with which to design the 2,250-square-foot contemporary house, the architects reconciled the client's program requirements by incorporating into their taut design a traditional low-country piano nobile scheme. By positioning the public areas of the house on the second story, views of the Ashley River and fresh air from the prevailing southerly winds are provided, while privacy from the boulevard outside is maintained.

The staircase hall—the point of transitional connection between the street-level entry and the upstairs living quarters—was given careful detailing attention. The architects emphasized the piano nobile parte by designing the stair as an element that extends down from the second floor to the entrance hall. The floor of the ground story stair hall was finished in a checkerboard pattern of black and white tile—a formal, generic field on which the stair lands (*partial plan*).

The staircase was constructed as a fine piece of furniture, its joints and connections concealed. Two 2¼″ × 12″ stringers, each laminated together from three ¾-inch pieces of red oak, extend from the base to the balcony. The round-edged treads, laminated of two ¾-inch oak pieces, were lag-bolted to the stringers (*section*). The balusters, set on 3-inch centers, are 1½″ × ¾″ pieces of mahogany and extend from the cut in the stringer to a similar cut in the rail. The alternate mahogany/oak banding pattern is completed by a 1½-inch bullnose mahogany cap that sits on top of the oak rail, set off by a ¼-inch reveal.

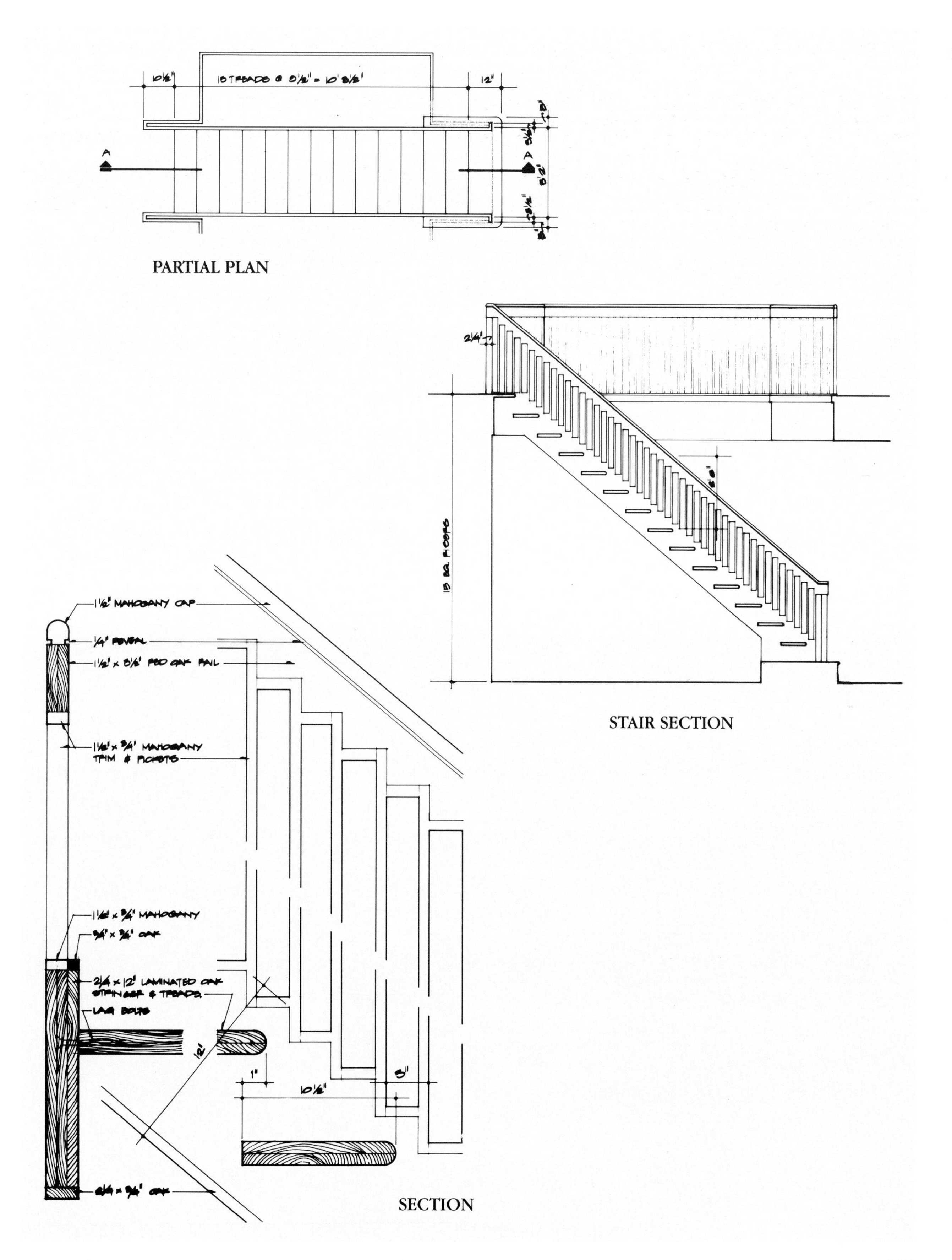


PARTIAL PLAN

STAIR SECTION

SECTION

# STAIRCASE

**PRIVATE RESIDENCE**
*Washington, D.C.*

**Architecture/Interior Design**
Hartman-Cox Architects

**Design Team**
George Hartman, Partner-in-Charge; William Grater; John F. Dale

**Fabricators**
E. A. Baker Company, Inc. (general contractor); Taney Stair Corporation (stairs)

**Photography**
© Robert C. Lautman

SOME PEOPLE PREFER to buy a house before buying art; others purchase art, piece by piece, and then search for a house that will accommodate their collection. A Washington, D.C., couple with grown children had assembled a significant collection when they purchased a 22,000-square-foot, 1920s mansion. The maintenance and display of the collection were of paramount concern.

The owners turned to architects Hartman-Cox to renovate the entire structure. Hartman-Cox gutted and rebuilt the interior, concentrating on the refurbishment and new development of fine detail.

The original house boasted a striking, two-story, semicircular staircase that Hartman-Cox would have liked to preserve. Instead, they pragmatically demolished the rotted original and had it rebuilt in similar form, extending the stair down one story to the ground floor.

The staircase was shop-fabricated, flight by flight. Each flight is self-supporting; the structural support and integrity of each flight is provided by formed, laminated pine stringers to which treads and risers are glued and screwed (*section detail*). Internal blocking is employed for extra rigidity and tread support.

Imbouee wood was specified for the treads because of its consistent, close grain, as well as its ability to maintain a high polish. Balusters of turned poplar, doweled into the treads, bear the weight of the solid mahogany banister (*section detail*).

Once fabricated, each flight was lifted into place and affixed with steel angles bolted to floor joists and stringers. The walls of the stairwell were then finished in plaster over metal lath (*section detail*).

In order to avoid marring the stairwell walls with vents, Hartman-Cox developed a ¾-inch slot for required HVAC return air that is masked behind the lip of the outside stringer. Air is drawn through the stair itself into a plenum concealed in the wall.

Hartman-Cox topped the stairwell with a semicircular laylight that echoes the configuration of the stair itself. Three recessed light fixtures highlight the stair's sculptural quality. The construction is similar to that of the laylight in the ballroom (*see* Ceiling, page 48).

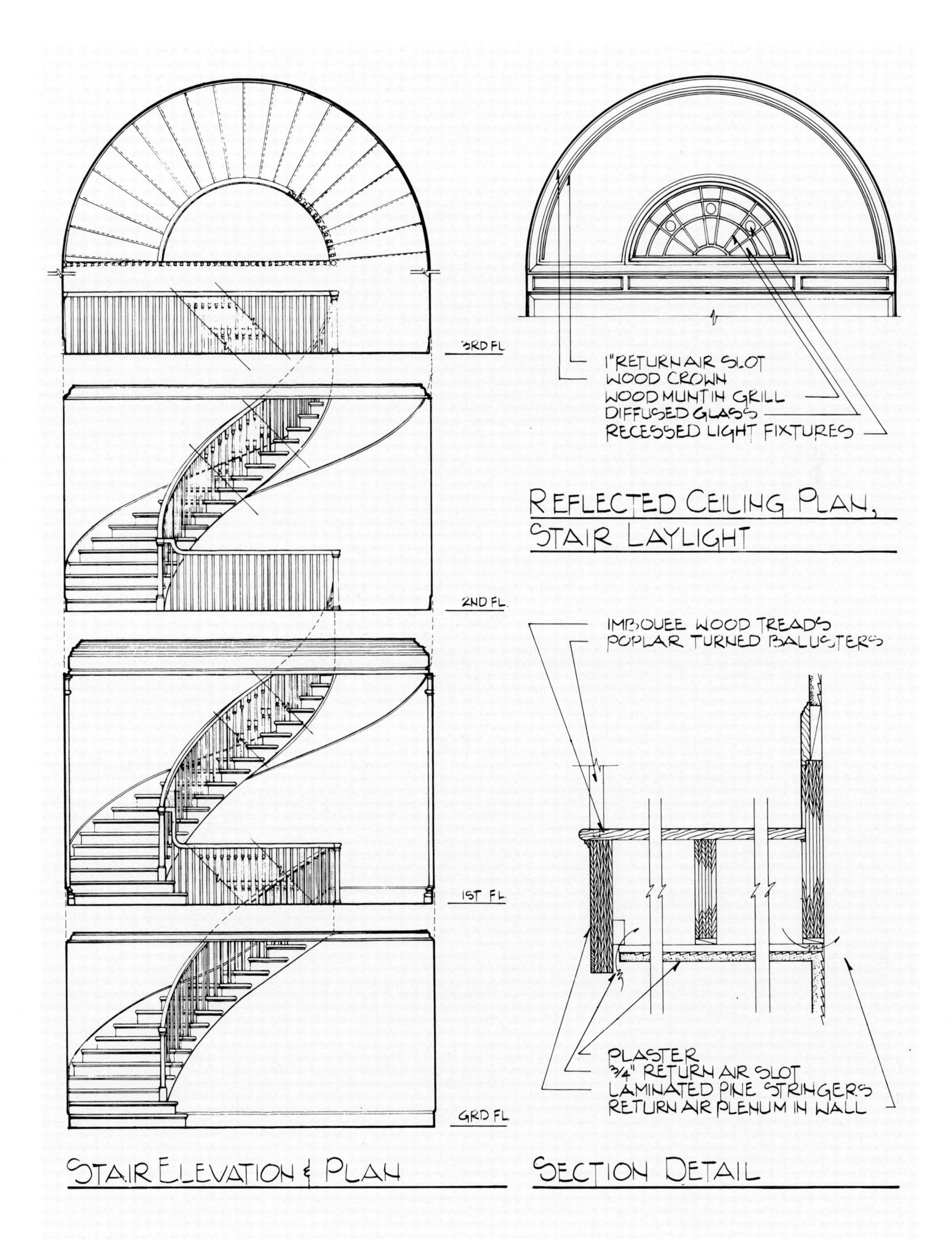
3RD FL
2ND FL
1ST FL
GRD FL
STAIR ELEVATION & PLAN
1" RETURN AIR SLOT
WOOD CROWN
WOOD MUNTIN GRILL
DIFFUSED GLASS
RECESSED LIGHT FIXTURES
REFLECTED CEILING PLAN,
STAIR LAYLIGHT
IMBOUEE WOOD TREADS
POPLAR TURNED BALUSTERS
PLASTER
3/4" RETURN AIR SLOT
LAMINATED PINE STRINGERS
RETURN AIR PLENUM IN WALL
SECTION DETAIL

## MUNIAK RESIDENCE
*New York, New York*

**Architect**
William McDonough Architects

**Design Team**
William A. McDonough, AIA, Principal; Joseph Vance, Project Manager; Janet Roseff; Mark Rylander; Carl Finer; Steve Pynes; Judy O'Buck Gordon; Shelley Brock

**General Contractor**
Dennis Leftwick, Romac Construction

**Fabricators**
Eric Bauer, Fayston Iron and Steel Works (steel and wood); Christopher A. Clark, Clark Construction Corporation (fresco plaster)

**Photography**
© H. Durston Saylor

THE MUNIAK FAMILY was impressed with architect William McDonough's taut and elegantly controlled architectural style; consequently, they persuaded him to renovate their 5,000-square-foot Victorian brownstone on Manhattan's Upper West Side with "his cerebral sensibility." Sasha Muniak—an aficionado of the work of architect Adolf Loos—and Joanna Muniak—an admirer of Etruscan architecture (as well as of interior decoration and color in general)—asked only that McDonough design the house as "an extensive exploration of detailing possibilities" (*see* Shower Enclosure, page 180).

McDonough sought a serene, tectonic character in his design that would make consistently integrated transitions from conceptual ideas to literal realization. The architect wanted to create details that would engender an understanding of the making of things; to produce "simple elements simply enjoined."

Bolstered by client enthusiasm and an adequate budget, McDonough began the transition from conceptualization to realization by tearing down an earlier, hodgepodge addition and gutting most of the brownstone's interior. Only some of the original building's details—the Victorian entranceway, carved mahogany staircase, oak paneling, oak doors, and exterior window casings—were saved for restoration. The demolished structure was then replaced with a larger, two-story addition.

McDonough is a thoughtful architect who not only weighs options carefully before making decisions, but also considers the perception of weight and mass in addition to scale. Therefore, it is the basement that was fitted with heavy Norwegian stone finishing slabs, which not only appeal to Joanna Muniak's Etruscan tastes, but also lend an appropriate air of solidity and permanence to the foundation level.

On the first floor—replanned as family room, kitchen, and dining room—McDonough used somewhat lighter materials in both form and finish to emphasize the vertically oriented transitional quality of Brescia marble and Minnesota limestone, elements that were further lightened in the kitchen with ash, cherry, and stainless steel.

The focal point of the new plan—a finely wrought stainless steel and cherry wood staircase—was positioned within the new two-story, glass-walled dining room addition next to the kitchen. The staircase serves as both a ceremonial and choreographic connection between the dining room and the music room on the parlor floor above. McDonough designed the staircase to represent the transition from one era to another, as well as to reinforce the evolution, from floor to floor, of massively scaled finish materials to those of exquisite delicacy—or, in his own words, "to create a layered enfilade between the existing and the new."

The stairway, with its balcony, is the fourth of four major elements in the composition of the dining room. McDonough saw each element as autonomous, but becoming increasingly refined and delicate. The first element, the stone floor, is the most solid and simple. The second, the massive wall panels of tinted plaster, act as both surface and object, the gaps between them allowing views through to the kitchen and music room. These panels become piers in both a literal and figurative sense. The third element is the gridded window wall, composed of 6-inch-deep, oxidized, oiled and waxed steel fins fitted with standard storefront aluminum glazing. The fourth—and most refined—element is the stairway itself.

Conceptually, the staircase is a very thin plate of stainless steel with a cherry "runner" that acts almost as a carpet of wood, flowing over the steel as a liquid would. McDonough's ideas about the dining room composition are exhibited within each support of the staircase: each is composed of assemblies of horizontal and vertical steel plates that grow increasingly refined and delicate from the bottom to the top. The plates decrease in number from three at the level of the baluster support, to two at the baluster itself, to a single plate that supports the wood handrail.

The stair is supported by a landing assembly set on a length of wide flange steel I-beam, to which two ⅜-inch steel plates—set back ½ inch from the edges—were welded (*landing support assembly; section-handrail/balcony*). The W-section penetrates the floor to rest on a footing in the cellar below. The stringer assemblies, each composed of two ½″ × 5″ steel plates, bear on this steel "box section," as does a double cross-piece of tread/baluster supports. The plates are of cold-rolled milled steel, which was sandblasted and lacquered.

For each tread/baluster support, a ½-inch steel plate was welded between the two members of each stringer assembly and notched to receive the support. The baluster

support itself was fabricated of three horizontal steel plates; at each end two vertical steel plates were welded between the three supports to form the balusters. Thus, the balusters and supports hold each other together by their welded joint (*detail-railing and balcony assembly*).

The stairs were formed of stainless steel decking that bears on the stringers and baluster/tread supports. The tread/riser units were formed of L-shaped sections of decking that were welded together. Similarly, the cherry runner was fabricated in L-shaped tread/riser units with beveled edges, attached with screws through slotted holes in the back of the steel decking. A ⅛-inch gap was left between the riser of each unit and the tread of the next to allow for differential movement.

The handrail is supported by single 1½-inch steel plates welded between the two plates of each baluster. The rail, a 2-inch round section of oiled cherry, was attached to a stainless steel post, welded to the top of the support plate by means of a 3/16-inch brass pin that passes through the rail and the steel post. The steel support plate was cut to match the curve of the handrail.

Below the wood rail, ¼-inch stainless steel rods connect the balusters, passing through holes drilled in the paired steel plates. The holes were connected by short lengths of ½-inch-diameter stainless steel sleeves; rods were threaded at both ends and capped by brass acorn nuts bearing against the face of the final baluster (*detail-horizontal rod connection*).

The balcony is supported by two beams, each composed of two ½″ × 9″ stainless steel plates with a third 11¼″ plate welded between them. Each beam bears at both ends on steel plates in the masonry party walls. The center plate in each beam was notched to receive the baluster/deck supports, and was welded to the steel balcony deck by plug welds underneath the cherry runner. The runner was beveled 2 inches from each edge.

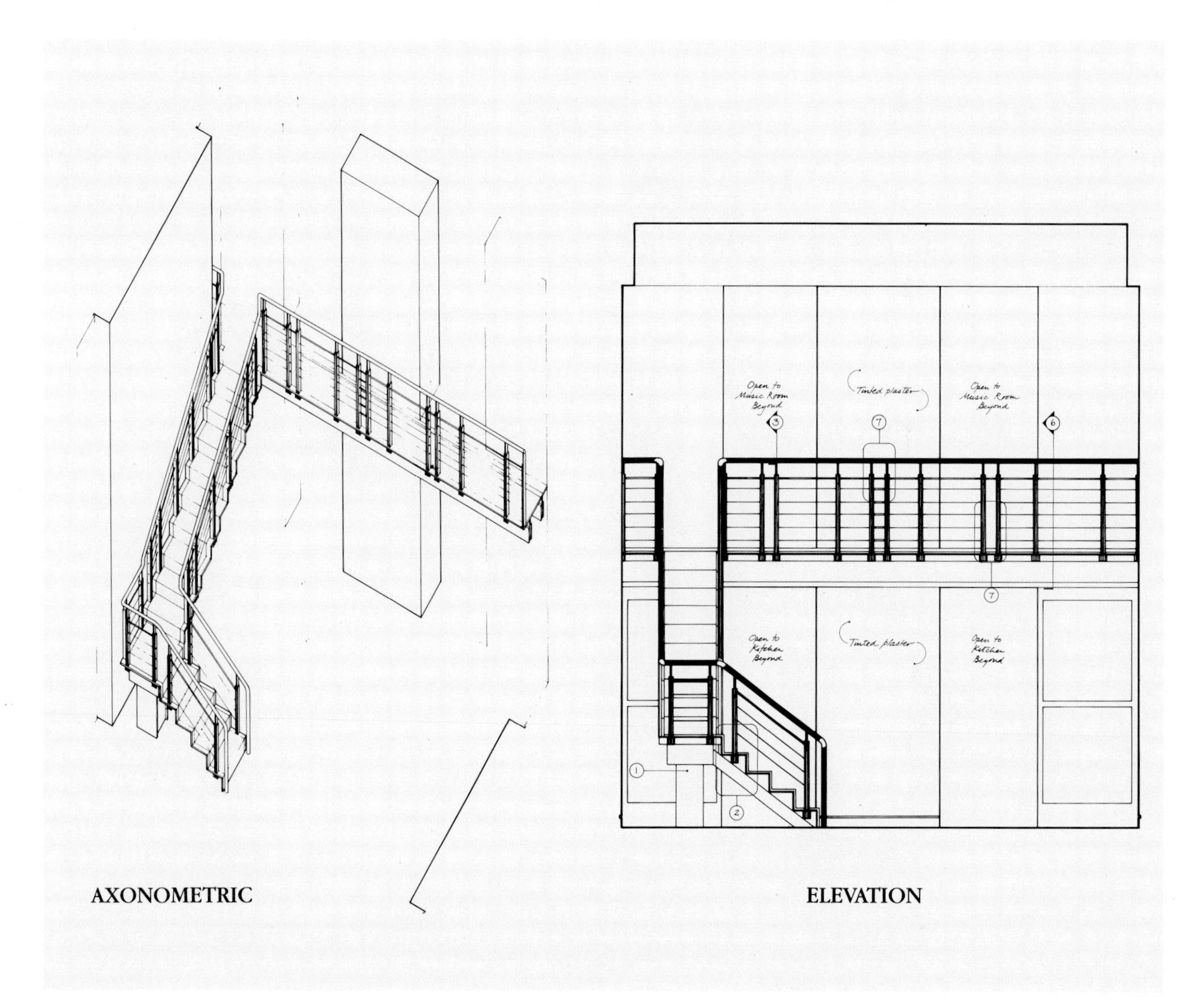


AXONOMETRIC

ELEVATION

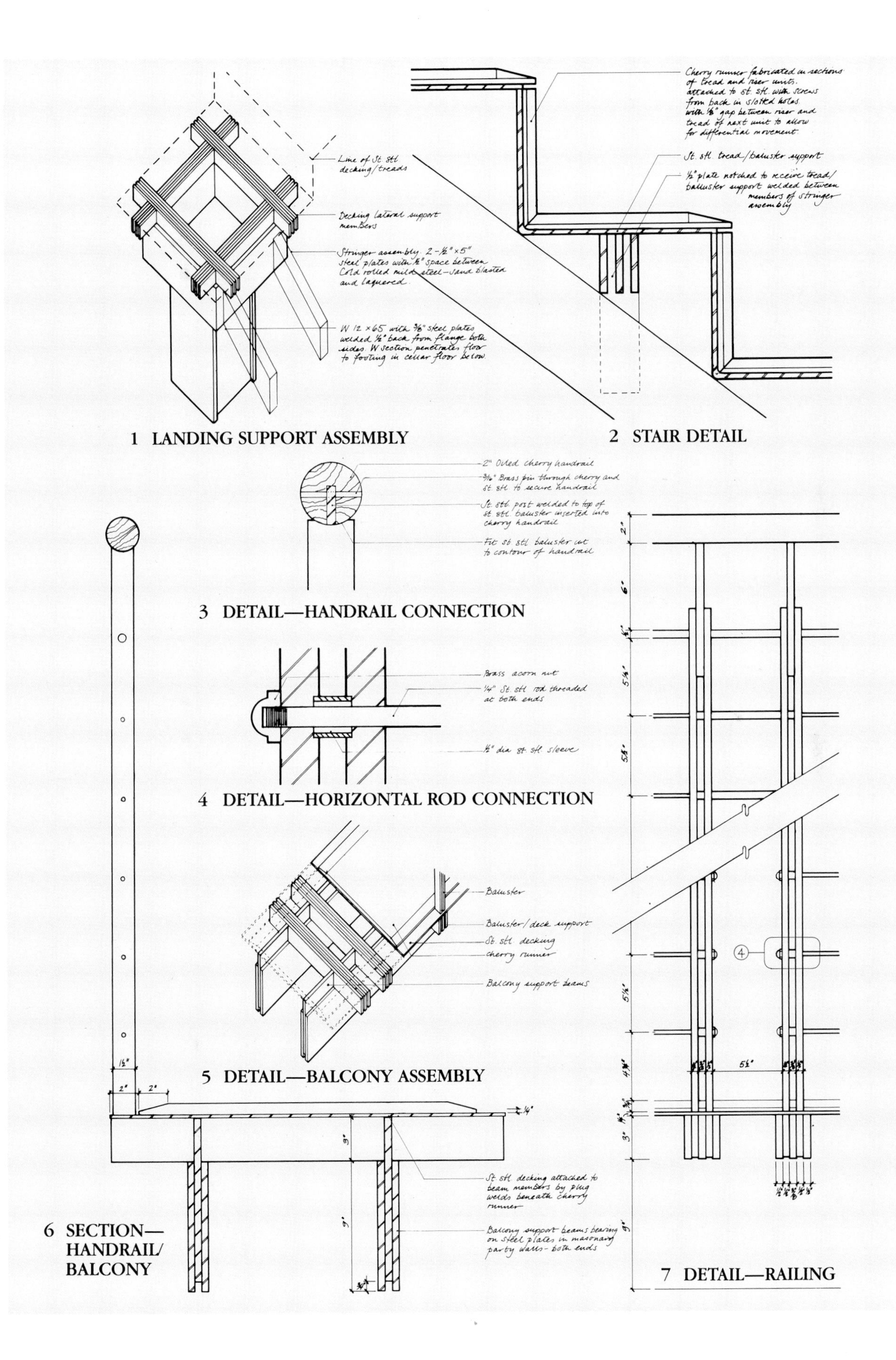


1 LANDING SUPPORT ASSEMBLY

2 STAIR DETAIL

3 DETAIL—HANDRAIL CONNECTION

4 DETAIL—HORIZONTAL ROD CONNECTION

5 DETAIL—BALCONY ASSEMBLY

6 SECTION—HANDRAIL/BALCONY

7 DETAIL—RAILING

# Staircase

**Private Residence**
*East Hampton, New York*

**Architect**
Robert A. M. Stern Architects

**Design Team**
Terry Brown, Project Architect;
Roger Seifter, Project Architect;
Bonnie Fisher, Interiors Assistant

**General Contractor**
Pat Trunzo

**Photography**
© Roberto Schezen

In 1983, Robert A. M. Stern built a summer house for a discerning empty nest couple who loved the style and quality of nineteenth-century Shingle-style houses, but wished to avoid their typical plan. The clients asked Stern to develop such a house with "fewer, but bigger rooms," including a bathroom for every bedroom; a master suite; a professional kitchen; large, interconnected entertaining spaces; and accommodations for a small, seasonal staff.

The design team developed a 3,600-square-foot floor plan that is centered by an airy and grandly scaled entry hall. The layout and oversized scale of the hall is further enhanced by a double-story "vertical circulation element"—a staircase that encourages informal, seated sociability on its broad bank of amphitheaterlike lower treads.

The stair is a sculptural element, the generous scale of which invites one to equate the space with the concept of gracious hospitality. According to Stern: "The staircase was rendered as a simple, abstract version of the traditional Stickley furniture that was placed throughout the house. Its handrail grid was specifically designed to recall the English Arts and Crafts movement that, following John Ruskin's lead, developed a modern aesthetic from traditional craftsmanship" (*lattice details*).

The staircase was constructed of oak treads, pine risers, and poplar trim. Its typical underside and stringer construction is hidden by paneling (*elevations, east and west*). The staircase composition was completed by the imposition of a similarly scaled, oversized window at the landing level (*elevation, north*).

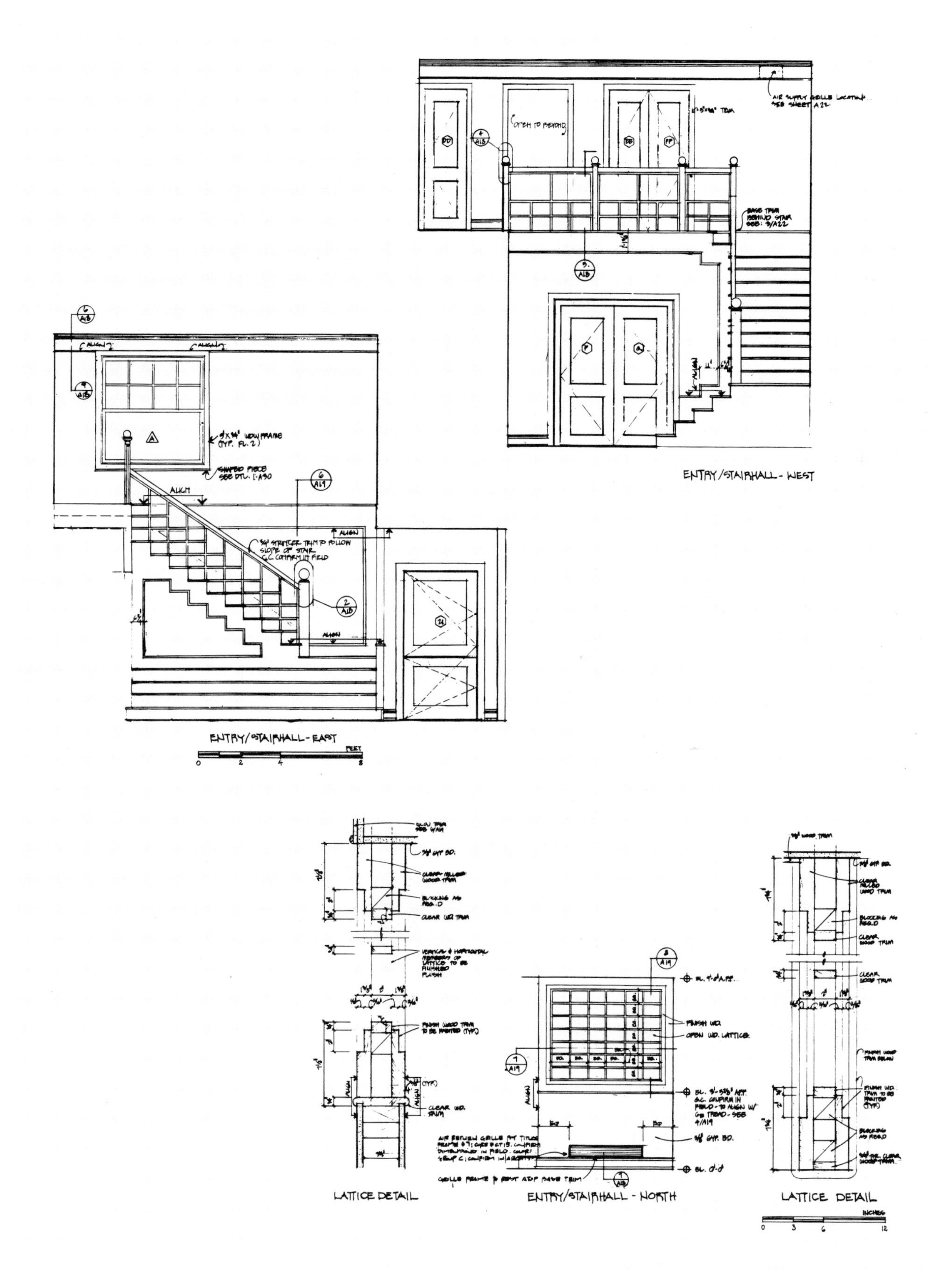
ENTRY/STAIRHALL - WEST
ENTRY/STAIRHALL - EAST
LATTICE DETAIL
ENTRY/STAIRHALL - NORTH
LATTICE DETAIL
ALIGN
FINISH WD.
OPEN WD. LATTICE

### TIGERMAN/MCCURRY RESIDENCE
*Southwest harbor country, Michigan*

**Architect**
Tigerman/McCurry, Architects

**Design Team**
Margaret McCurry, AIA;
Stanley Tigerman, AIA

**Fabricator**
Richard Brychta, Brychta Woodshed

**Photography**
© Margaret McCurry, Tigerman/McCurry, Architects

WEEKEND HOUSES are frequently small and are usually constructed on very tight budgets. Ingenious design solutions are therefore sought from the architect, who can rescue a "basic box" with good detailing.

Margaret McCurry and Stanley Tigerman became their own conflicting-demand clients when they decided to build a 1,000-square-foot weekend house that "would be comfortable for two" but which—when family and friends were in tow—"could comfortably sleep ten."

Their intriguing solution was to develop a double-height "plaza or gathering space," which is overlooked, at either end, by private loft bedrooms. The bedrooms are accessed not by square-foot-consuming staircases, but by steeply pitched ladders.

The ladders were modeled on ship's stairs that allow just enough tread depth for a toehold. The actual degree of pitch for the ladders was established by setting the most prominent tread 2′–1″ from the wall; the resulting angle is "steep but avoids personal injury" (*side elevation*). Bullnosed treads serve as safety-conscious handgrips, as do metal tubular railings bolted to the wall at the loft level (*side and front elevations*).

The 20′–0″ span of the loft would normally have required a truss for structural support. Tigerman/McCurry substituted a structural, and ceremonial, archway at the top of the ladder that, in fact, carries an equivalent load.

The ladders were constructed, as was the entire house, with unusual craftsmanship by Richard Brychta of Brychta Woodshed in New Buffalo, Michigan.

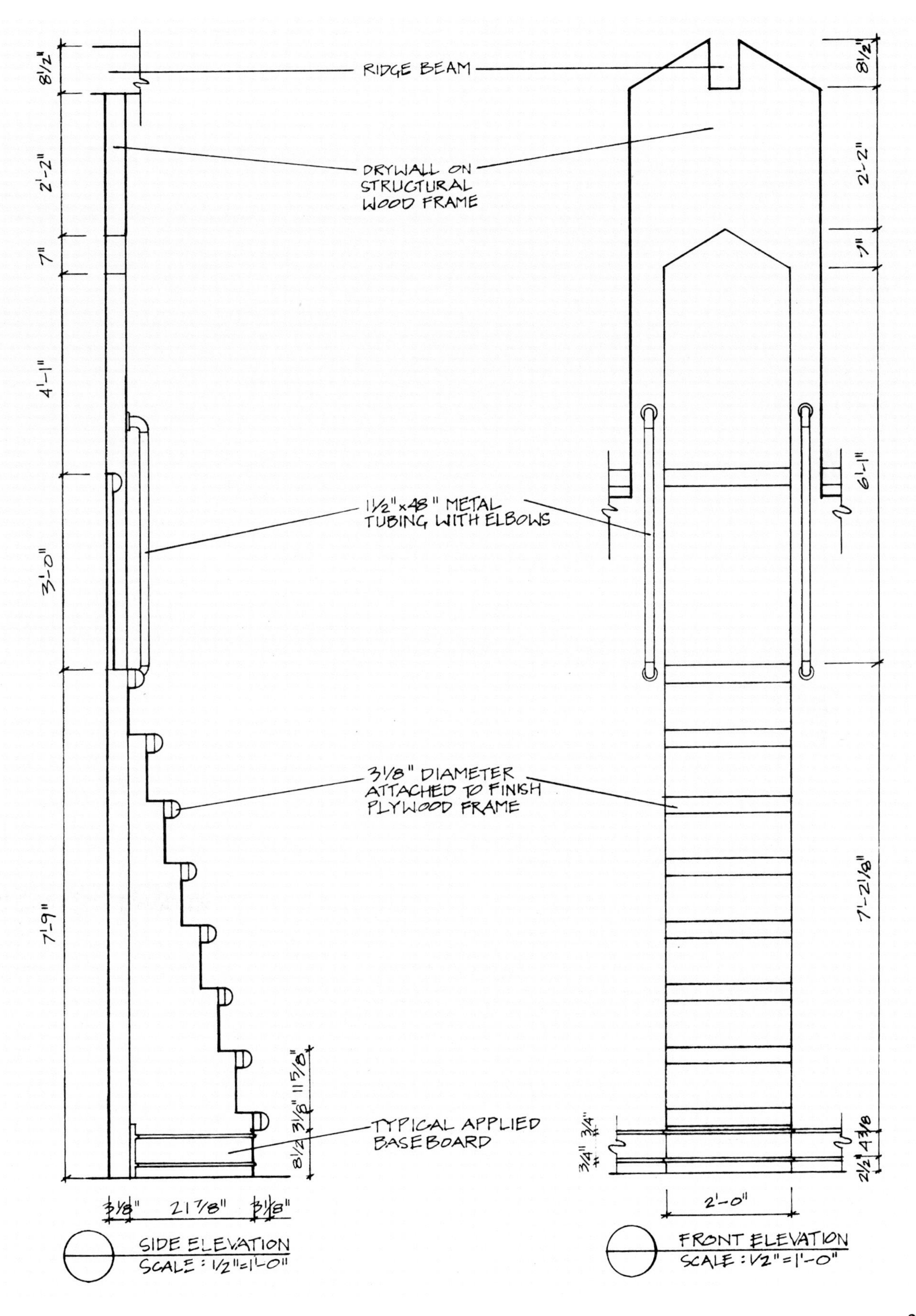

RIDGE BEAM
DRYWALL ON STRUCTURAL WOOD FRAME
1 1/2" x 48" METAL TUBING WITH ELBOWS
3 1/8" DIAMETER ATTACHED TO FINISH PLYWOOD FRAME
TYPICAL APPLIED BASEBOARD
8 1/2"
2'-2"
7"
4'-1"
3'-0"
7'-9"
11 5/8"
3 1/8"
8 1/2
3 1/8"
21 7/8"
3 1/8"
6'-1"
7'-2 1/8"
4 3/8
2 1/2
3/4"
2'-0"
SIDE ELEVATION
SCALE: 1/2"=1'-0"
FRONT ELEVATION
SCALE: 1/2"=1'-0"

# Storage Cabinet

**Fifth Avenue Residence**
*New York, New York*

**Architect**
Steven Holl Architects

**Design Team**
Steven Holl, Principal-in-Charge; Mark Janson, Project Architect; Joe Fenton, Project Architect

**Fabricator**
Terry DeAngelis

**Photography**
© Paul Warchol

As a bachelor and student of architecture, Andrew Cohen's priorities for renovating his three-bedroom Fifth Avenue co-op apartment were decidedly atypical. In discussions with his architect and instructor, Steven Holl, Cohen placed little emphasis on issues of square footage allocation, privacy, or other domestic amenities; instead, he asked only that Holl use the renovation as an exploration in architectural theory and craftsmanship. To that end, he committed a generous budget.

Holl's design solution utilizes two overriding architectural themes that unify the complex space of the L-shaped apartment. First, as a counterpoint to the vertical emphasis of Manhattan's urban fabric, Holl introduced a horizontal band throughout the entire space: a ⅝-inch acid-treated brass channel set 4′–9″ above the floor. The channel divides the lower wall, of finished white plaster, from an upper band of gray, integral-color plaster. For practical purposes, the channel functions as a screed between the upper and lower layers of plaster.

Holl's second unifying theme, set out in three sandblasted glass drawings in the foyer, was to treat the three major areas of the apartment as distinct elements relating to three modes of architectural composition: linear, volumetric, and planar. The dining room's chandelier, table, chairs, and carpet are all composed of linear elements, while in the living room, a cylindrical sofa, a solid coffee table, and a carpet patterned with geometric solids follow a volumetric system.

The final area, the bedroom/study, is composed in a "planar mode." Whereas in the living room walls are treated as thick solids, in the bedroom/study they become thin sheets. A drafting table/desk formed of black and white wooden planes is attached to a low, thin wing wall projecting out into the room.

The wall screening the bedroom drops down from a ceiling soffit; however, the face of the wall is set back from the face of the soffit to allow the wall to read as a separate plane. The wall's thin planar nature is intensified: on the right, it drops back to allow access to a closet; on the left, a portion of the upper panel swings into the bedroom to create a window; and in the center, an entire section, wider at the top than at the bottom, pivots to create a door into the bedroom. Through this door the final element is visible: a large blue-stained "planar cabinet" that occupies most of the back wall.

Built in three panels, the floor-to-ceiling unit was constructed in three vertical sections by cabinetmaker Terry DeAngelis. It is fabricated entirely of solid ash pieces, splined together with a recessed countertop of honed marble. Storage is provided by drawers and pivot-door cabinets with brass flush ring, white plastic, and open-hole pulls.

According to Holl: "The composition of the cabinet openings is based on musical and mathematical proportions."

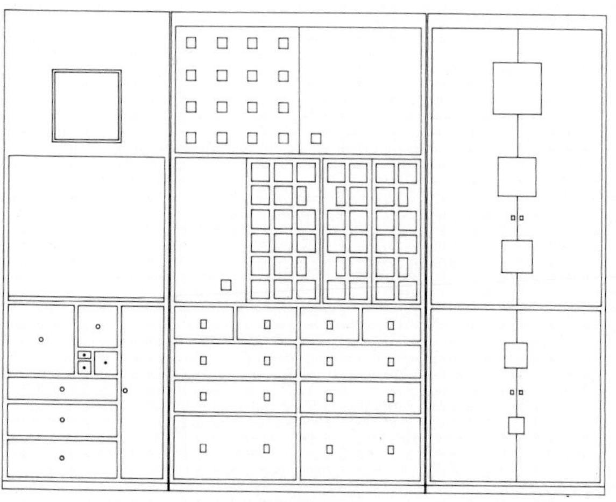

ELEVATION

## LAWRENCE RESIDENCE
*Hermosa Beach, California*

**Architect**
Morphosis

**Design Team**
Thom Mayne, Principal;
Michael Rotondi, Principal;
Benjamin Caffey, Project Manager;
Frank Lupo, Project Manager;
Marlou Vengelers, Project Manager;
Kazu Arai, Project Manager

**Mechanical Consultant**
The Sullivan Partnership, Inc.

**Structural Consultant**
Erdelyi Moon Mezey

**Photography**
© Peter Aaron/ESTO

DESIGNING WITHIN the constraints of an unusually narrow site in Hermosa Beach, California, challenged Morphosis to develop a number of innovative solutions, in both spatial organization and detailing form (*see* Kitchen Hood, page 128).

The clients made clear to Morphosis their wishes that both the house's "public space" (the semicircular air shaft bordered by the double staircases) and private area (the master bedroom) be as expansive as possible. Specifically, the master bedroom was to extend the entire width of the second floor, in effect occupying, together with its own balcony, an entire "wing." The balance of the master suite, the bathroom and dressing areas, had to be squeezed into a long, narrow space behind the second-floor landing. Morphosis elected to remove the bathroom from the bedroom; as a result, the dressing area also serves as a conduit between the two.

This corridorlike solution (the width of the passage proper is about 3′–6″) had the virtue of running along the exterior wall, providing the opportunity for lots of windows. The architects' choice was to use glass blocks to build up translucent, sparkling surfaces that preserve privacy (*elevation: south wall at wardrobe*).

Morphosis specified material finishes in the wardrobe corridor to make the confined area feel luxurious. In addition to the glass blocks, they provided custom-built cabinetry of naturally finished, solid white oak, with neoprene pulls for the drawers.

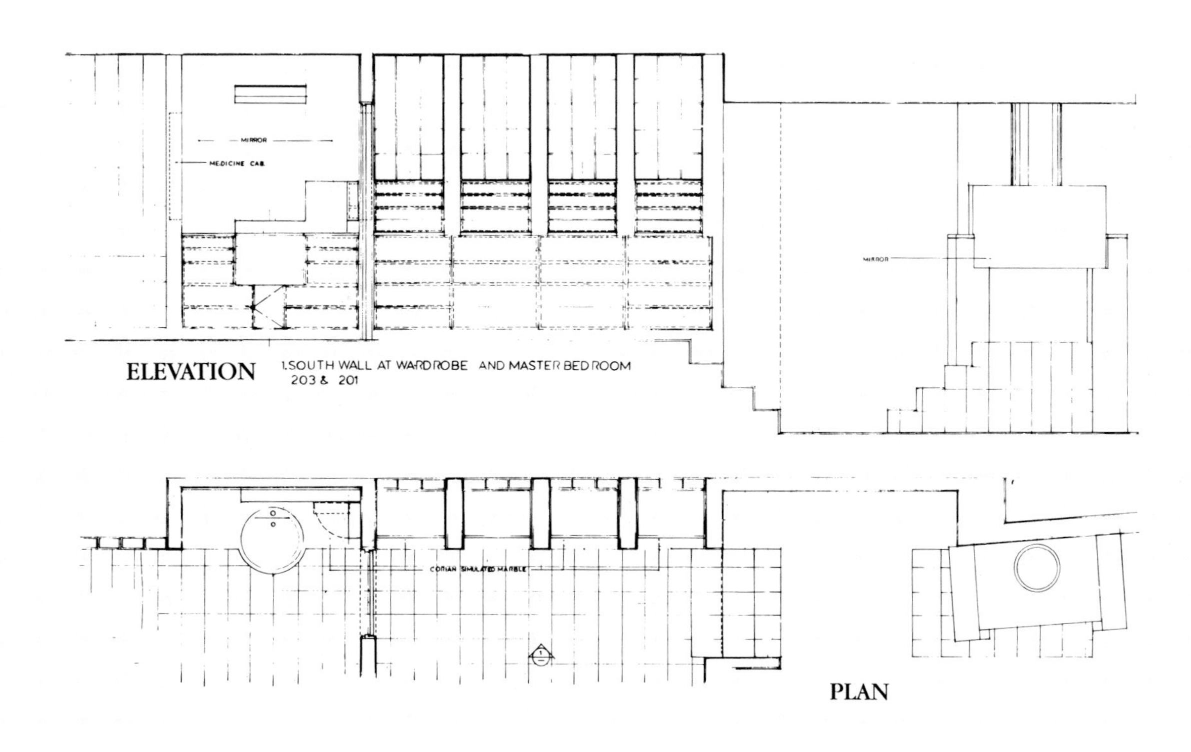

## Harborside Residence
*Baltimore, Maryland*

**Interior Designer**
Rita St. Clair Associates, Inc.

**Design Team**
Rita St. Clair, FASID, Principal;
Ted Pearson, ASID, Project Manager

**Fabricators**
The Valley Craftsmen, Ltd. (finishes);
Hough Woodworks (millwork and cabinetry); Kardell Studios (leaded and stained glass)

**Photography**
© Tim Fields

When the owners of this brand-new Baltimore harborfront townhouse asked for a "classical, neo-Edwardian" interior, Rita St. Clair drew on her vast experience in renovating both public and private older buildings in developing the detailing package, combining intricate design with craftsmanship in a series of details that define and refine the 4,500-square-foot space (*see also* Bathroom Cabinets, page 28; Door, page 86; Railing, page 168).

The living room was to receive particular and lavish detail. Therefore, in addition to a mantel and overmantel, paneling, baseboards, and cornices, the designer developed two mirror-image storage cabinets.

The storage cabinets were built as one part of an integrated wall system of display elements. The wall system includes a set of sliding leaded-glass doors in mahogany frames, which slide into pockets behind flanking bookshelves to reveal a pass-through into the kitchen.

The display cabinet is set off from this desk area by a nonstructural black lacquered column and a mahogany beam. The cabinet consists of two 1′–0″-wide by 1′–1¾″-deep niches framing a 2′–5″-wide by 1′–10½″-deep central cabinet with glass double doors. The top of the entire cabinet is integrated into the 1′–0″-high mahogany ceiling molding, the cabinet's narrow vertical proportions giving the room a sense of height.

The two side niches each hold four fixed shelves for memorabilia lit by vertical strips of low-voltage lighting placed in the outer corners. The fixtures are obscured by the reeded mahogany stiles that frame both niches and cabinet, allowing light from an unseen source to wash in toward the center of the cabinet. The edge of each shelf is faced with reeded trim similar to the stile pieces, and the ash burl spandrel panels above the niches are similarly outlined.

The semielliptical head of the central glass cabinet rises above the tops of the side niches. The leaded glass door, set in a wood frame, has an elaborate scroll design at the base, made of opaque glass to obscure modern audio and video equipment. The translucent glass is also used for a border strip around the edge of the cabinet doors, providing a transition between the wooden frame and the glass infill. The interior of the glass case is lit with low-voltage light strips.

The cabinet and niches are visually supported from below by a 2′–6″-high wooden cabinet with central double doors and a recessed shelf, and by two sets of three stacked drawers on the sides.

The drawers and cabinet sit on a 6-inch-high mahogany base. The entire piece is constructed of mahogany with ash burl panels and brass hardware.

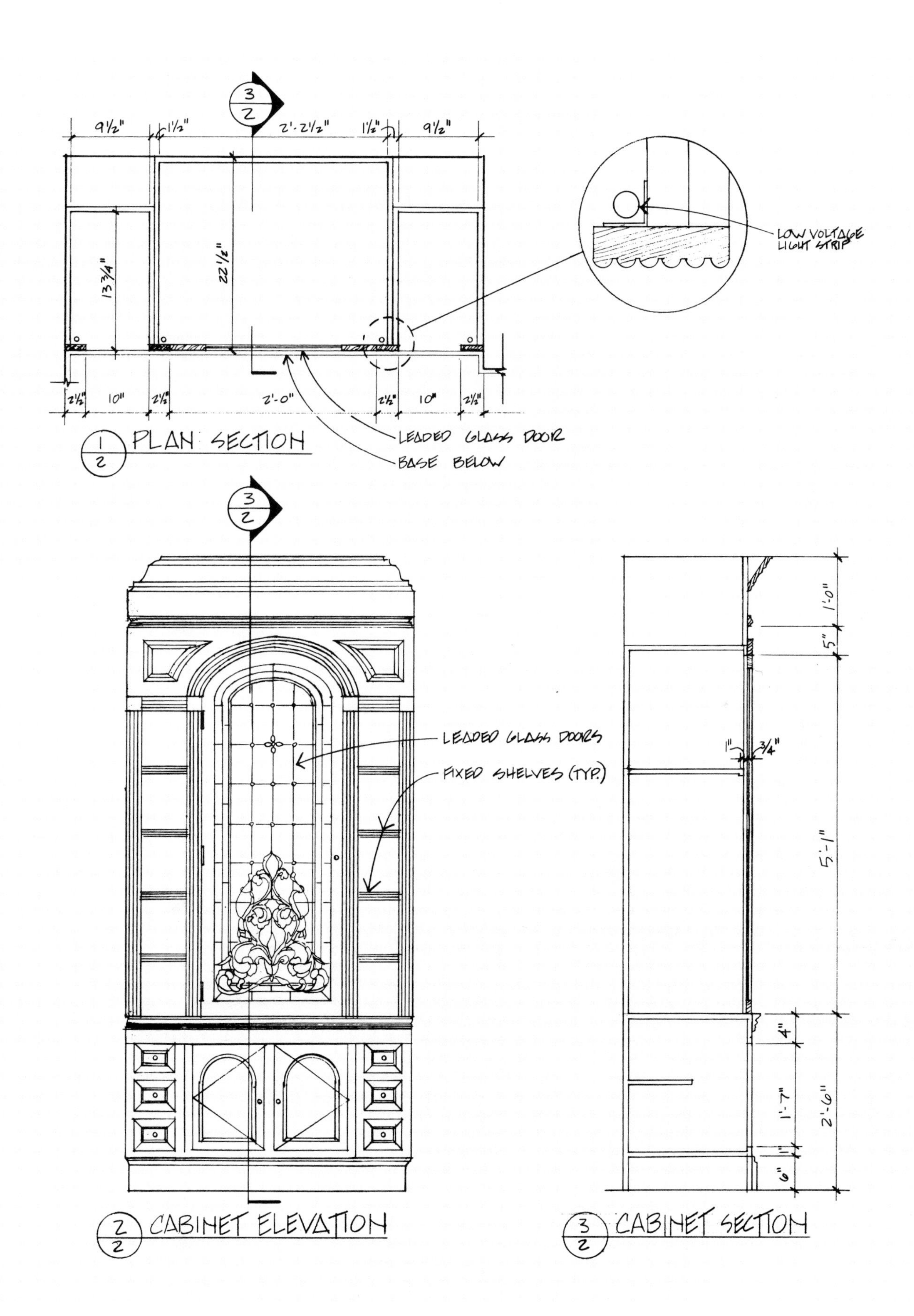
9½"
1½"
2'-2½"
1½"
9½"
13¾"
22½"
2½"
10"
2½"
2'-0"
2½"
10"
2½"
LOW VOLTAGE LIGHT STRIP
LEADED GLASS DOOR
BASE BELOW
PLAN SECTION
LEADED GLASS DOORS
FIXED SHELVES (TYP.)
1'-0"
5"
1"
3/4"
5'-1"
4"
1'-7"
2'-6"
1"
6"
CABINET ELEVATION
CABINET SECTION

# Storage Wall

## O'Keefe Residence
*New York, New York*

**Architect**
Alan J. Buchsbaum

**Design Team**
Alan Buchsbaum, Partner-in-Charge; Marc L'Italien, Project Architect; Corey Delany, Project Coordinator

**Consulting Architect**
Frederic Schwartz, Anderson/Schwartz Architects

**General Contractor**
Dandt Contracting

**Fabricators**
Gino Cassara, Marvel Aire Mechanical (HVAC/electrical); Peter Jevremov, Metal Forms Studio (door finish); Taro Suzuki (paint and special effects); Marble Modes (marble)

**Photography**
© Peter Aaron/ESTO

In the worlds of fantasy created by film and television set designers, all things are possible. Models simulate cities; façades represent buildings; and shadowbox sets serve as "stand-ins" for actual rooms. Adherence to accurate dimensioning, therefore, is essentially irrelevant to a milieu in which the camera, or the eye of the eventual beholder, is the only perception that counts.

In the real world, an antithetical truth prevails. Architects and interior designers, working with actual spaces that are—or will be—inhabited by real people, must calculate both vertical and horizontal dimensions down to the correct fraction of an inch. The architect's or interior designer's job is, therefore, particularly problematic when there are not many inches with which to work.

In 1985, actor Michael O'Keefe, who starred in *The Great Santini* and *Ironweed*, bought a townhouse duplex in Manhattan's Chelsea district that measured only 19′–0″ across. Because a general circulation staircase and hallway occupied 6 of those limited feet, only a lateral dimension of 13′–0″ was available to designers Alan Buchsbaum and Marc L'Italien on each of the two floors.

The design team demonstrated a facile combination of space-planning agility and detailing skill by developing a floor-to-ceiling storage wall that incorporates both East and West Coast characteristics: the storage wall—from a New York perspective—clears the room of impedimenta as it separates living from service spaces; its freespirited form and a few special effect finishes strongly evoke the witty sophistication of Los Angeles.

Buchsbaum and L'Italien designed the wall as a "storage wall ruin" that hints at classicism as it avoids post-modernist cliché. The wall's multiple spaces, planes, and contoured surfaces were intentionally planned to contrast with the original plaster wall it faces.

The storage wall was fabricated as stud wall construction covered by drywall, from which ¾-inch painted plywood bookshelves and storage compartments emerge (*sections A and B; elevation*). The intricately cut finish surfaces of the most prominent plane—those that are superimposed and cut away from the cabinets—are also constructed of ¾-inch painted plywood (*section C*). Jagged edges of these surfaces were fabricated by attaching metal lath to the frame, which was plastered to meet the edges of the plywood (*axonometric*).

There are details within details in this storage wall—among them, an internal light fixture concealed in the bulkhead above the stripped and burnished metal entry door; a stereo component shelf that reiterates the jagged edge pattern of the outer plane; and clean kick spaces that alternate in a positive/negative rhythm with the intentionally broken baseboards. A sophisticated palette of flat, semigloss and high-gloss paints completes this three-dimensional tour de force.

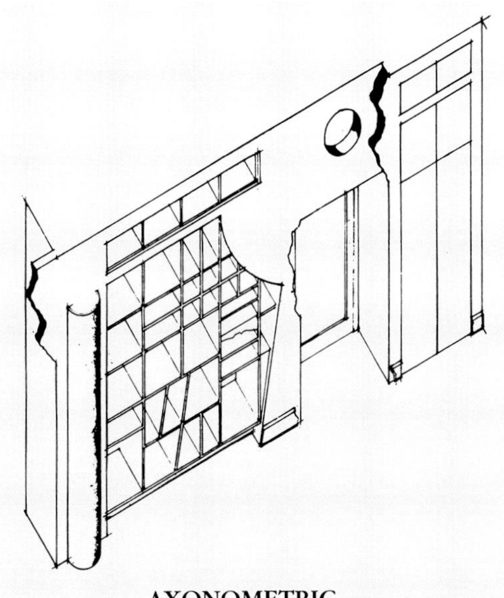

AXONOMETRIC

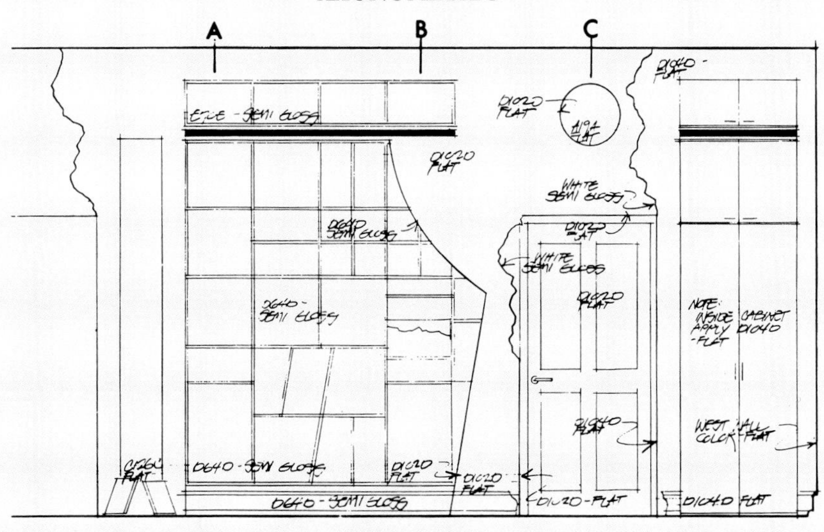


ELEVATION

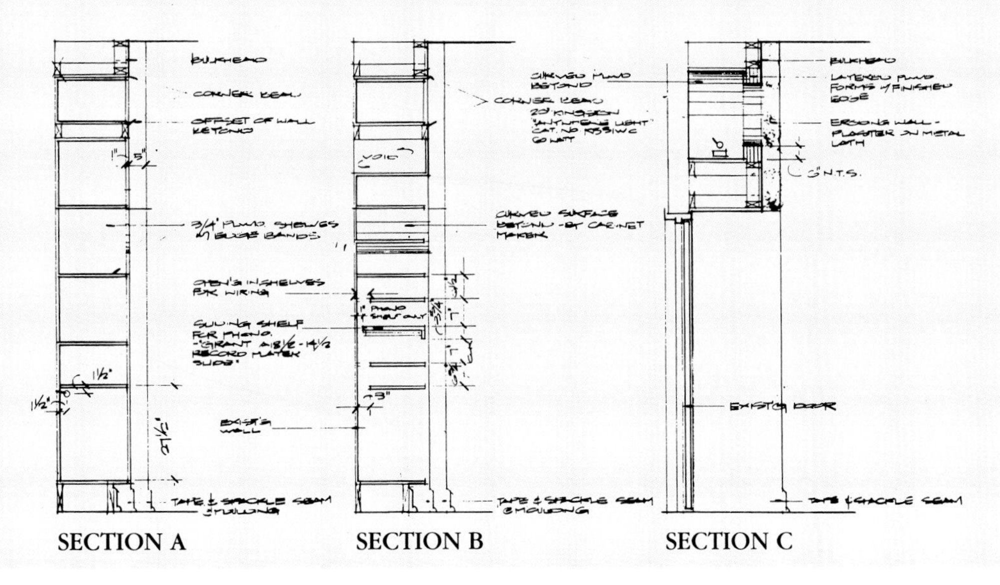

SECTION A SECTION B SECTION C

## DAVIES RESIDENCE
*Tucson, Arizona*

**Architect**
Paul T. Edwards, Architect;
Bonnie Bridges, Production Assistant

**Structural Engineer**
John Grenier, P.E., Grenier Structural, Inc.

**General Contractor**
Tortolita Construction

**Fabricators**
Terry Darr, Blue Construction (truss fabrication); Woody's Wrought Iron (steel plate fabrication)

**Photography**
© James Brett

THE DAVIES, both longtime residents of the Arizona desert, turned to architect Paul Edwards, of Tucson, to actualize their dream of "a house nestled in the local northwest desert foothills" because his professional reputation is one of interpreting "archaeological layers of regional history" into viable—and award-winning—contemporary structures.

The Davies asked for a house that would not only "feel rooted, aesthetically, in the continuum of desert life," but would also incorporate "as many passive solar features as possible." Edwards responded by developing a 2,432-square-foot plan that used the shape and finish materials of the structure itself to achieve a historical time-line reference as well as impressive climate control.

Bedrooms at either end of the plan are constructed as white stucco masses that recall eighteenth-century Sonoran rowhouses found in the barrios of Tucson, and an interior communal living space is defined by "ruined" adobe walls that recall Mexican plazas as well as Anasazi Indian dwellings from prehistory to the middle ages. These areas, in turn, are ordered and organized by a raised, overhanging roof that shelters the house in "an abstracted, Anglo influence" form, which developed in the nineteenth century with the coming of the railroad to Tucson (*building section*).

Historical reference continues inside the house. The roof is supported by heavy timber trusses and peeled pine poles that recall the stately resort hotels built in the area during the 1930s. The scale and unrefined quality of the timbers, trusses, and connector plates allude to early local mining communities, now ghost towns.

The trusses were designed by Edwards and sized by a structural engineer (*web, ridge, and beam connections*). Trusses were field-fabricated on-site and raised into position with a crane; "rusting" of the steel connector plates was accomplished by spraying them with water (*center plate detail*).

Despite area temperature fluctuations, ranging from freezing to 110 degrees, the Davies house maintains its warmth and cool temperatures through natural ventilation and passive solar techniques. In summer, warm air rises to the 22′–0″ ridge line, where it is vented through two thermostatically controlled vents in the Dutch gables. Awning windows at floor level allow cooler air to be drawn into the house. Plastered concrete block walls with sand-filled cells have 2 inches of stuccoed rigid insulation applied to the exterior to create a captive mass for thermal energy storage. A roof-mounted thermostatically controlled evaporative "swamp" cooler supplements natural ventilation at times of peak heat load.

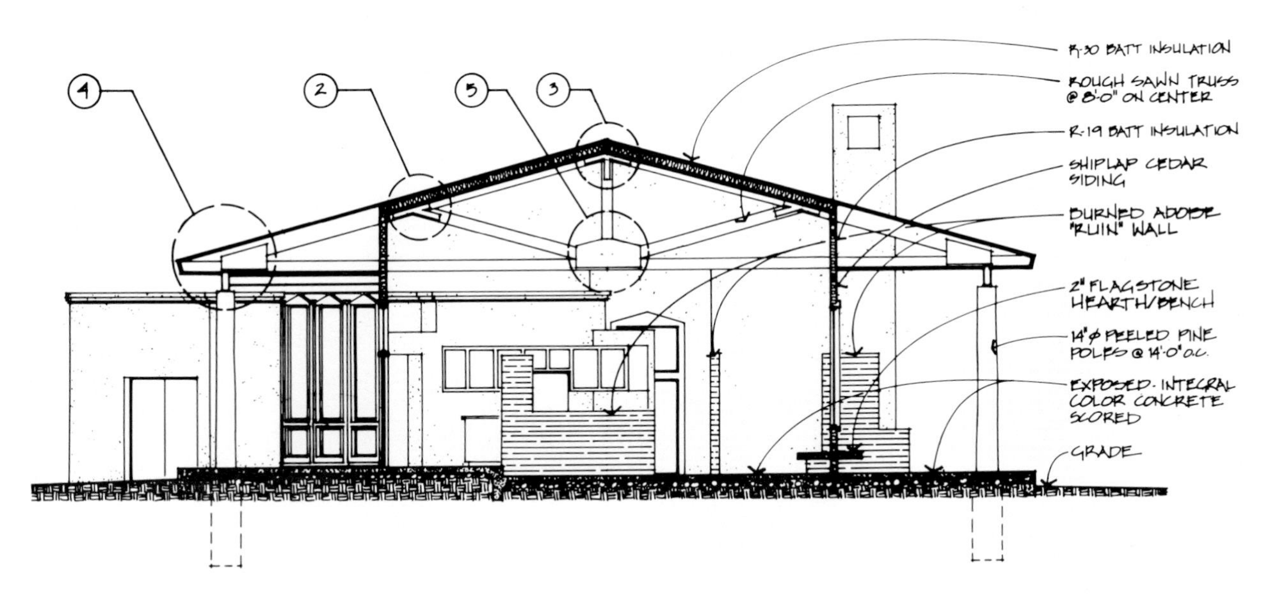
4
2
5
3
R-30 BATT INSULATION
ROUGH SAWN TRUSS @ 8'-0" ON CENTER
R-19 BATT INSULATION
SHIPLAP CEDAR SIDING
BURNED ADOBE "RUIN" WALL
2" FLAGSTONE HEARTH/BENCH
14"ø PEELED PINE POLES @ 14'-0" O.C.
EXPOSED INTEGRAL COLOR CONCRETE SCORED
GRADE

1 BUILDING SECTION
SCALE: 1/4" = 1'-0"

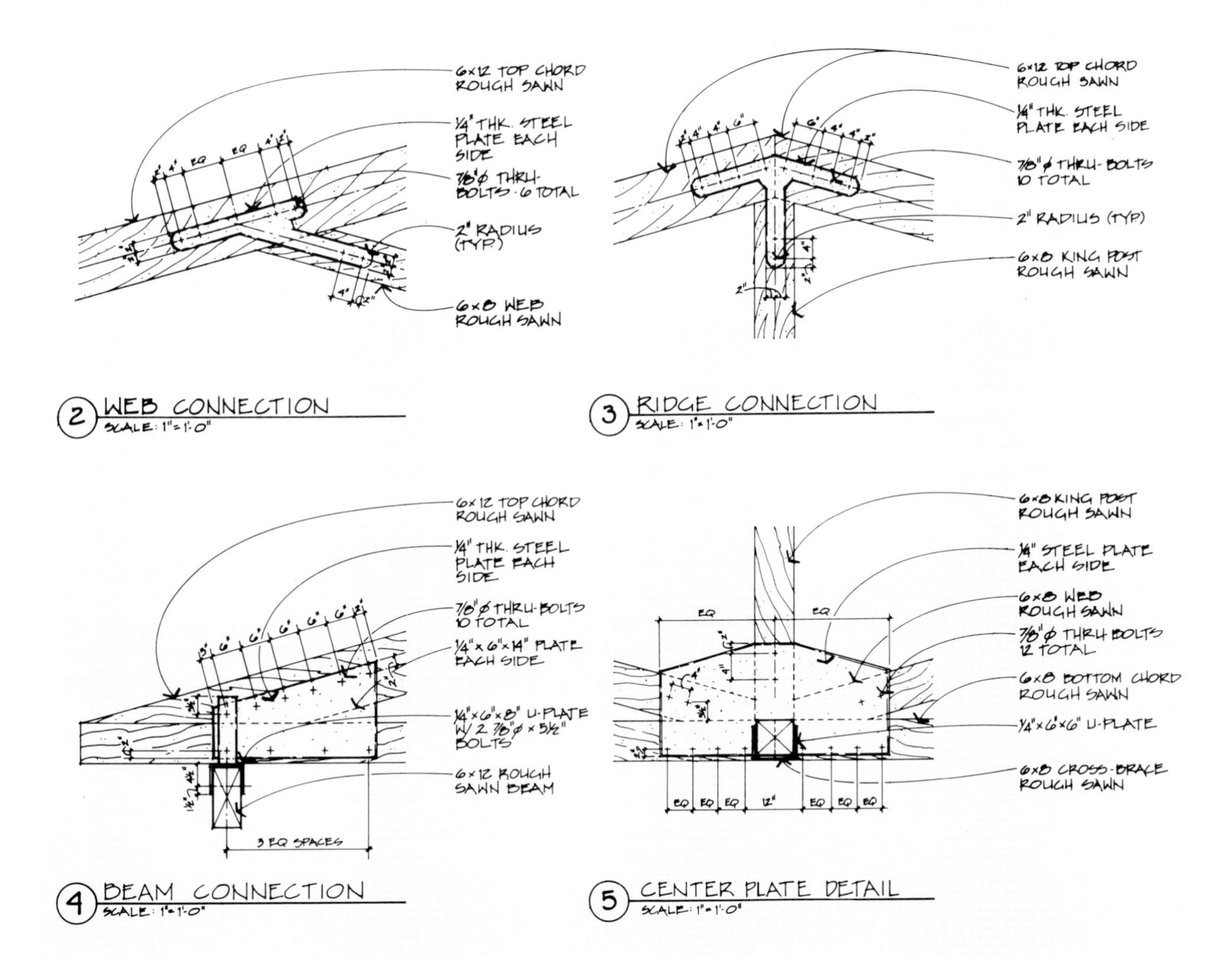
6×12 TOP CHORD ROUGH SAWN
1/4" THK. STEEL PLATE EACH SIDE
7/8"ø THRU-BOLTS - 6 TOTAL
2" RADIUS (TYP.)
6×8 WEB ROUGH SAWN
2 WEB CONNECTION
SCALE: 1" = 1'-0"
6×12 TOP CHORD ROUGH SAWN
1/4" THK. STEEL PLATE EACH SIDE
7/8"ø THRU-BOLTS 10 TOTAL
2" RADIUS (TYP)
6×8 KING POST ROUGH SAWN
3 RIDGE CONNECTION
SCALE: 1" = 1'-0"
6×12 TOP CHORD ROUGH SAWN
1/4" THK. STEEL PLATE EACH SIDE
7/8"ø THRU-BOLTS 10 TOTAL
1/4" × 6" × 14" PLATE EACH SIDE
1/4" × 6" × 8" U-PLATE W/ 2 7/8"ø × 5 1/2" BOLTS
6×12 ROUGH SAWN BEAM
3 EQ SPACES
4 BEAM CONNECTION
SCALE: 1" = 1'-0"
6×8 KING POST ROUGH SAWN
1/4" STEEL PLATE EACH SIDE
6×8 WEB ROUGH SAWN
7/8"ø THRU BOLTS 12 TOTAL
6×8 BOTTOM CHORD ROUGH SAWN
1/4" × 6" × 6" U-PLATE
6×8 CROSS-BRACE ROUGH SAWN
5 CENTER PLATE DETAIL
SCALE: 1" = 1'-0"

## GUCCIONE RESIDENCE
*New York, New York*

**Architect**
SPGA Group, Inc.

**Design Team**
Sidney Philip Gilbert, Principal-in-Charge; Daniel Goldschmidt, Project Manager

**General Contractor**
Cauldwell-Wingate Co., Inc.

**Fabricators**
Port Morris Tile & Terrazzo Corp. (tile and terrazzo); Nordic Interior Inc. (millwork); Roth Painting Co., Inc. (paint); Pace Plumbing Corp. (plumbing); Burgess Steel Products Corp. (structural steel)

**Photography**
© Wolfgang Hoyt

BOB GUCCIONE is a man who knows what he likes and has earned the means to buy it. The editor and publisher of *Penthouse* and *Omni* magazines, Guccione and his wife purchased a townhouse and a carriage house close to Manhattan's Central Park. After interviewing twenty-five firms, they commissioned Sidney Philip Gilbert & Associates to renovate the two structures as one to create a 50-foot-wide, 23,000-square-foot residence reminiscent of San Simeon.

Guccione, an admirer of the grand Renaissance patrons of the arts, sought a "palazzo in neo-Tuscan" style. Gilbert was dispatched on research trips to Italy and other countries over a five-year period to collect design ideas. One result is the railing overlooking the pool, styled after the railing in Gore Vidal's Italian home; another is the course of columns by the pool, inspired by those on the set of Guccione's movie *Caligula*. Guccione had his own ideas as well, which he drew convincingly for Gilbert, granting the architect the latitude to design with only minimal budget restraints.

The pool room is one of the focal points of the palazzo. The pool itself was installed at the basement level; it is overlooked by the main entrance to the house. Removal of the first floor allowed a 20-foot-high space to be gracefully framed by a groin-vaulted ceiling.

The vault spans 22 feet over the pool. Longitudinally, three spans are used; on the west wall, the transverse vaults result in three segmental arches spanning 13′–4″ on either side and 15′–10″ in the center (*west elevation-swimming pool*).

The rhythm of the vault arches is echoed below, more forcefully, by a series of five semicircular arches of the same Roman brick as the vaults, applied decoratively to the wall and springing from four fantastic Italian terra-cotta fountainheads. The wave-like arch rhythm is further reinforced by two symmetrically placed pairs of arched windows cut out of the plaster surface, which, according to Gilbert, "include a touch of both Le Corbusier and Mexican Colonial in their lineage."

In contrast to the movement expressed by the walls, the pool proper represents smooth repose. Surrounded by pavement of Mexican tile and coping of rose levanto marble, the pool is lined with glass mosaic tile touched with silver markings. The odor of chlorine was avoided in and around the pool room by the use of a special filtering system, as humidity was controlled by maintaining a slight negative air pressure in the space.

Lighting is chiefly artificial, with ambient light provided by chandeliers and underwater pool lights. Recessed cans wash the walls with parabolas of illumination that further augment the rhythm of the three spans of arches.

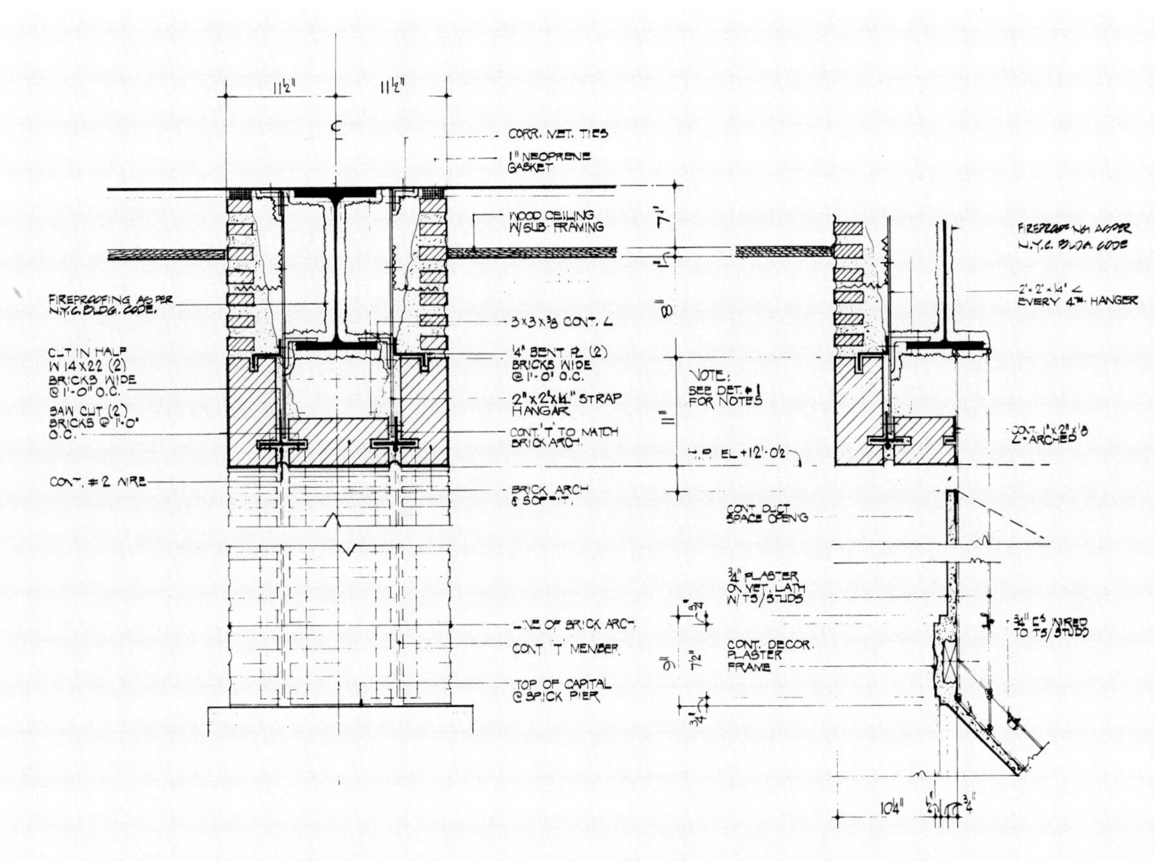


1 DET. @ BRICK ARCH

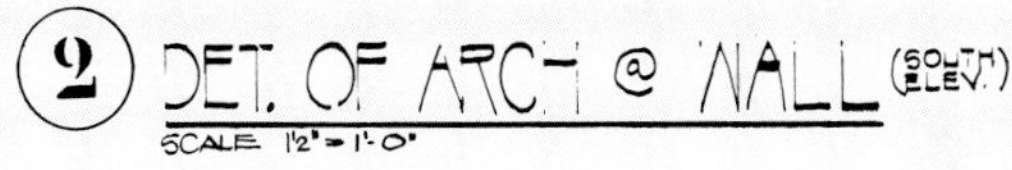


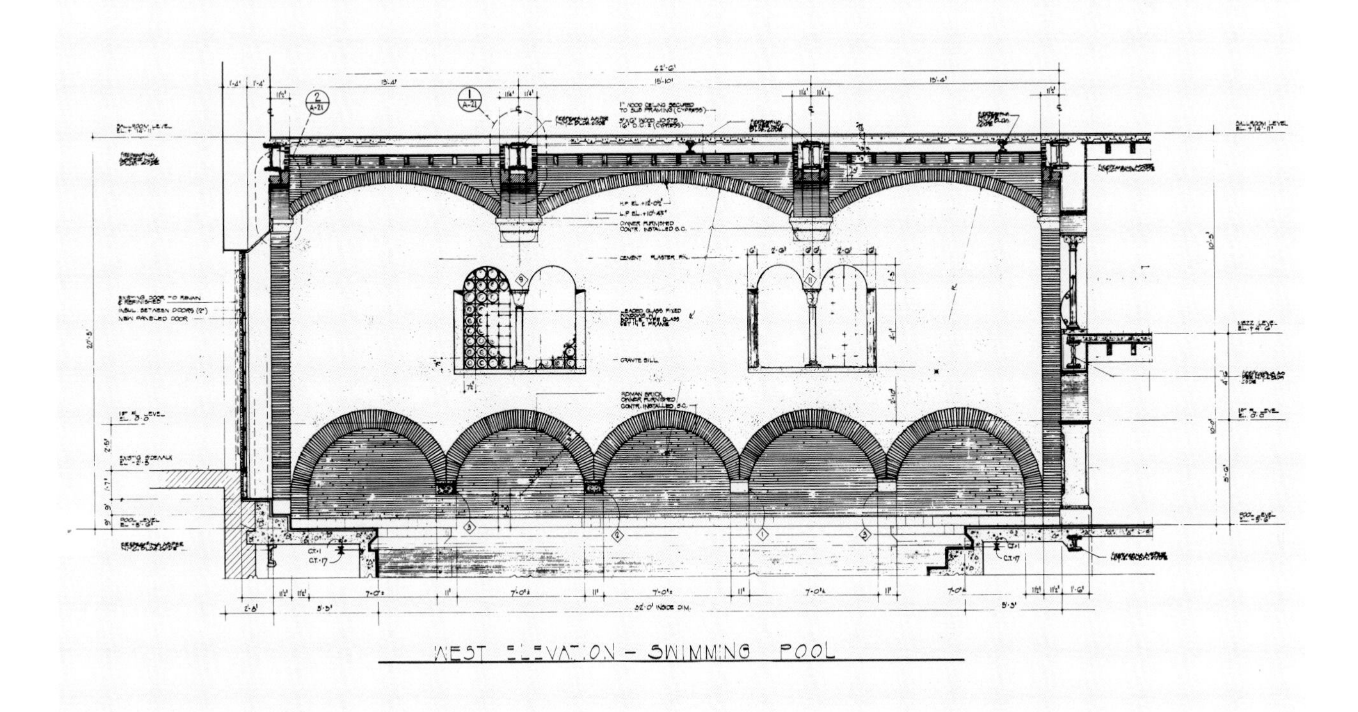

WEST ELEVATION – SWIMMING POOL

## PRIVATE RESIDENCE
*East Hampton, New York*

**Architect**
Norman Jaffe, AIA, P.C., Architects

**Design Team**
Norman Jaffe, AIA, Architect;
Keith Boyce, Project Associate

**Fabricators**
David Webb; Robert E. Otto, Inc. (glasswork); Southampton Welding and Iron (metal work)

**Photography**
© Norman McGrath

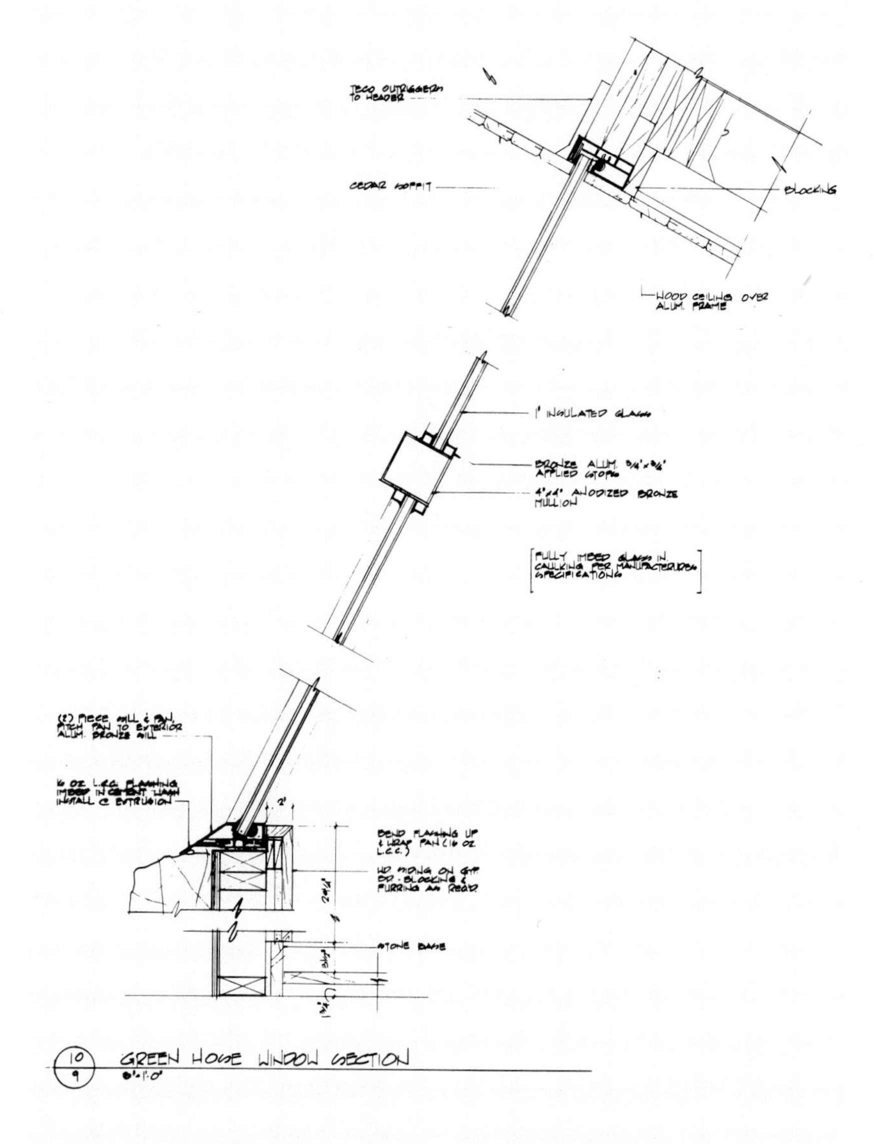


IN DESIGNING this 5,000-square-foot house in East Hampton, New York, architect Norman Jaffe sought to produce a composition of "interconnecting structure and landform." As a metaphor for this juxtaposition of the natural and the man-made, Jaffe used the formal device of intersecting rectangles and radial forms throughout the plan. Trees and other plant materials were brought right up to the house to heighten the contrast. The construction materials—oxidized copper, weathered cedar, and Westchester granite—were chosen to a similar end, natural elements that have been manipulated by man and then left to change slowly under the force of nature.

Defining the point of connection in such a scheme—the barrier between the man-made house and the natural environment—created an important detailing challenge. Jaffe designed the large living room window wall as a mediating element between structure and nature; its construction is of factory-extruded bronze and aluminum, while the form is a gently sloping and curved surface.

The window frame itself is similar to conventional storefronts. On the inside, the aluminum-framed cedar ceiling carries right out to the edge of the glass. A prefabricated aluminum head is attached to wooden blocking and header beams behind the ceiling surface. On the outside, an outrigger joins the header beams, the aluminum head assembly, and an exterior cedar soffit.

The window itself is of 1-inch insulated glass. At the level of the second-floor balcony, a 4″ × 4″ aluminum mullion receives the upper and lower panes of glass, holding them in place with four ¾″ × ¾″ anodized bronzed stops.

At the base, a two-piece aluminum bronze sill and pan sit on wood blocking. The pan is pitched to the sill and, with 16-ounce flashing, is bent up and wrapped around it. The flashing is then embedded in a cement wash.

On the interior, a 2-inch piece of wood siding that forms a small sill is mitered to a 30-inch-high panel of wood siding set not at the angle of the window, but perpendicular to the floor. Both are attached to gypsum board over wood blocking and furring. At the bottom, a 3½-inch-high stone base, set back an inch from the panel surface, forms a reveal and a joint with the floor.

## PRIVATE APARTMENT
*New York, New York*

**Architect**
Charles Patten Architects

**Design Team**
Charles Patten, AIA, Principal; Robert Rossi, Rich Oechsler, Maureen Cornwell, Paul Knapton, Project Team

**General Contractor**
Glenn Muller, Metro Design, Inc.

**Fabricator**
Jules Edlin, Inc.

**Photography**
© H. Durston Saylor

THE 4,000-SQUARE-FOOT, 1920s Park Avenue apartment that Charles Patten remodeled (*see* Partition, page 146) for an investment broker and his family offered a number of challenges, all of which derived from the design standards of architects who practiced during the first part of the twentieth century. Architects from that era saw their task as one of dividing the gross square footage assigned to any one apartment into a group of appropriately sized subspaces with smooth walls, doors, windows, plumbing, and if necessary, electrical outlets and finished floors—and nothing more. In other words, those architects generally did not see their job as one that would include any integration of the inhabitants' life-style into the design. Tenants or owners would come and go; they were, as far as the structure was concerned, interchangeable. In this era, the inverse is true, and roles once routinely assigned to freestanding furniture have been integrated into structure as personalized "built-in" details.

In this apartment's master bedroom, Patten fashioned a stylish and comfortable built-in solution to a frequent problem suffered by those who try to read in contemporary beds: the lack of a headboard. Many victims of this state of affairs make do by propping their pillows against the wall for support, often wishing that the wall could somehow be softened. Here, Patten created a soft wall surface that acts as a headboard, as part of a complete niche for the bed that includes built-in spotlighting and side surfaces (*axonometric*).

The padded headboard itself consists of five long plywood panels, wrapped in polyester-and-dacron padding and a finish surface of silk. The panels are hung on removable "Z" clips nailed to the stud wall.

Each side cabinet contains a sizable storage drawer. In order to render a "softer" textural surface analogous to the padded wall, the cabinet tops were fabricated of a single sheet of travertine, with a matte finish rather than a polished one.

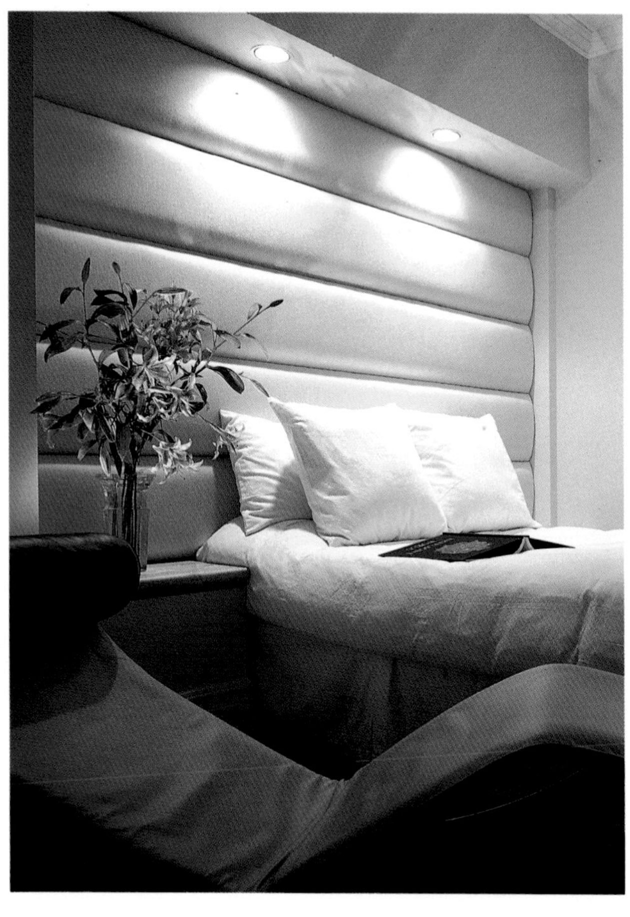

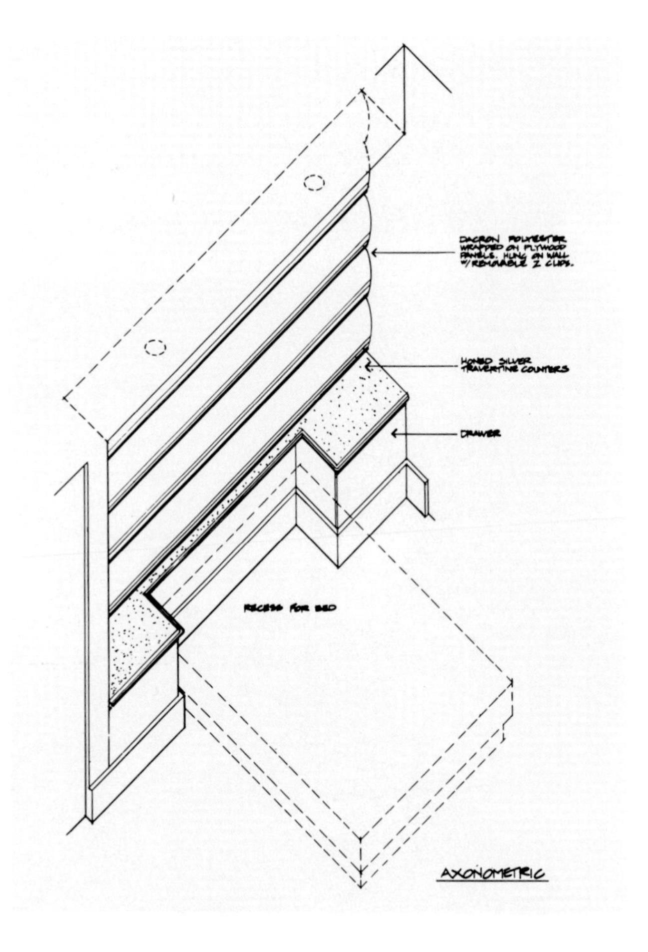

## LOG HOUSE

*Steamboat Springs, Colorado*

**Architect**
Tigerman/McCurry, Architects

**Design Team**
Margaret McCurry, AIA, Partner-in-Charge; John Holbert; Karen Hollander; J. T. Dallman; June Nelson-Steinke

**Fabricators**
Alpine Log Home Company (logs); Weather Shield Manufacturing, Inc. (windows)

**Photography**
© Margaret McCurry, Tigerman/McCurry, Architects

PRIVATE LIFE-STYLES are rarely as stereotypical as an individual's choice of professional career might suggest. An example of this anomaly: the rustic, log-construction "dream house" that Margaret McCurry, of Tigerman/McCurry, designed on a 35-acre parcel of Colorado mountainside for an upscale Chicago art gallery owner.

The client—father of three children and recently remarried—envisioned the house as, first and foremost, "an informal family gathering place," one that would be "intentionally antithetical to the ritualized, formal atmosphere of gallery life." Secondary, but specific, client priorities included log construction, a "cook's kitchen," and a bedroom for each child.

McCurry approached the design, detailing, and specification of finishes for the 5,000-square-foot house with suitable caution. "Log design and construction," according to McCurry, "is a tricky business. Logs, unlike lengths of sawn lumber, are neither straight nor square." After researching a number of suppliers, the architect selected the Alpine Log Home Company because "Alpine provides, in addition to raw materials, a service package that includes engineering, costing, shipping, and an on-site construction consultant."

Working collaboratively with Alpine and the project carpenter, McCurry developed a number of custom details that both compensate for the lack of log dimensioning regularity and provide a standardized trim scale that is in keeping with the large scale of the logs (*interior elevation*).

One of the most striking of these details is a "shadowbox" window frame that was constructed as follows: rough window openings were cut from the logs with a chain saw; openings were then framed out on all four sides with 1½″ × 9¼″ wood blocks. Wood finish trim was set into each framed opening to form heads, jambs, and sills (*typical jamb*). Each stock casement window was then installed asymmetrically, in a setback position over a wood block, which is itself centered over a flat-cut log (*typical sill*); finally, vertical wood trim splines were chiseled into grooves in the logs and scribed to them to form the side of each shadowbox (*section*).

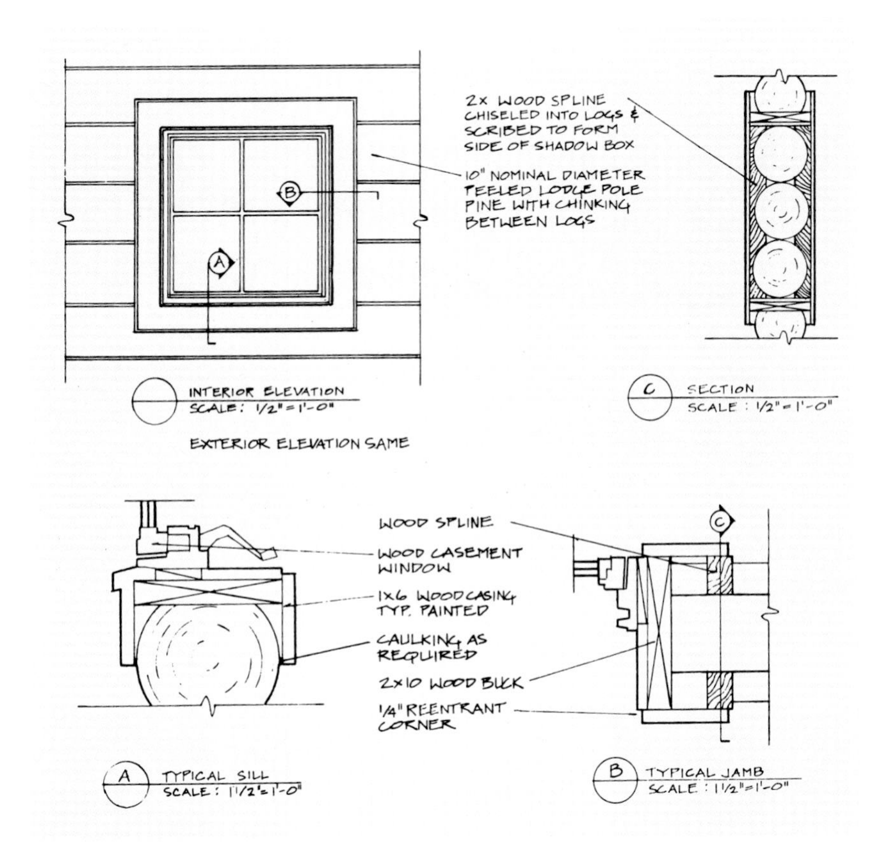

## REID RESIDENCE
*Northern Ohio*

**Architect**
Centerbrook Architects

**Design Team**
Jefferson B. Riley, AIA,
Partner-in-Charge;
Walker J. Burns, AIA, Project Manager

**General Contractor**
Roman Yoder and Son

**Photography**
© Peter Mauss/ESTO

A "DRAMATIC VISTA OF TREETOPS" and "a floor plan conducive to entertaining" were high on the list of client priorities when Centerbrook Architects, of Essex, Connecticut, began to develop plans for the Reid family's large, 5,500-square-foot house.

Because such a substantial house was to be built on a small, one-acre lot in a densely built Ohio suburb in which lateral privacy from neighbors is a perennial problem, Centerbrook designed—on "an average to generous budget"—a U-shaped house around a central, walled courtyard. Entrance into the courtyard, and the house beyond, is achieved by passing through a ceremonial archway cut into the courtyard wall.

Entry into the house itself, completed in 1987, evokes not so much a sense of ceremony, but rather a subliminal anticipation of "event"—a subliminal reaction caused by the impact of the tree-shaped window that overlooks and dominates the entry hall from its position above the staircase. The window was positioned within the hall to serve as a landmark by which to orient oneself within the sprawling plan from adjacent rooms; it was writ large and shaped specifically to mimic the canopy of graceful trees that are visible through it.

The 13′ × 10′ window (*elevation*) was assembled from Marvin components, customized to accommodate Centerbrook's design. All window segments are constructed of double-insulated glass panes separated by real muntins (*details A, sill; B, muntin; and C, jamb/head*). Although the bottom edge of the window manifests an obvious relationship to the staircase it surmounts, the dimensional ratio of window frame to stair tread width is different—"a design disparity," according to Centerbrook's Jeff Riley, "intended to relieve what might have been, otherwise, a plodding mathematical progression."

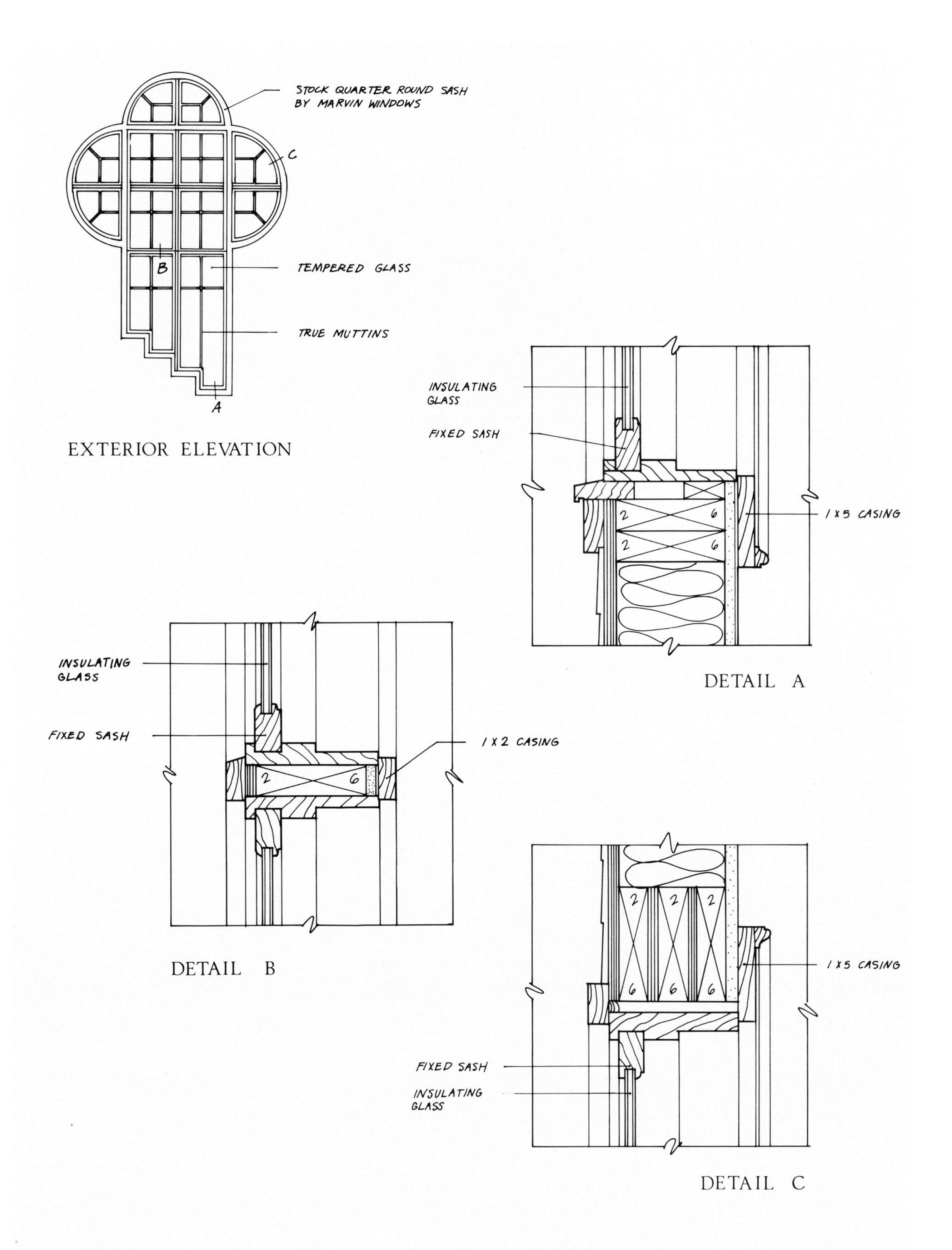
STOCK QUARTER ROUND SASH
BY MARVIN WINDOWS
C
B
TEMPERED GLASS
TRUE MUTTINS
A
EXTERIOR ELEVATION
INSULATING
GLASS
FIXED SASH
2
6
2
6
1 X 5 CASING
DETAIL A
INSULATING
GLASS
FIXED SASH
1 X 2 CASING
2
6
DETAIL B
2
2
2
6
6
6
1 X 5 CASING
FIXED SASH
INSULATING
GLASS
DETAIL C

## PRICE RESIDENCE
*Southern California*

**Architect**
Bart Prince, Architect

**Fabricators**
Eric Johnson; David Bartholomew, Glass Arts Center (stained and leaded glass)

**Photography**
© Joe Price

THERE ARE TWO schools of thought in regard to properties with enviable views: one maintains that the house and its interior should present a noncompetitive, neutral character; the other insists that creating a domestic environment as rich in color and form as the outdoors is only fair in the balance of power with nature. Joe and Etsuko Price, sympathetic to the latter philosophy, commissioned Albuquerque architect Bart Prince to design an intricately configured, complexly detailed pleasure dome that would also take advantage of a beautiful Pacific Ocean view.

Prince designed the 4,700-square-foot, southern California house as a series of three independent but interconnected "pods" that cantilever around a central bundle of wood columns. As the pods rotate around the central "spine," they also step down the steep coastal site toward the ocean. The clients' first priority—"a private room"—is located within the upper, most secluded level. Because the room would occasionally be used to entertain guests, the Prices also wanted it to include a bar and liquor storage space.

The joint between the two sections of the room is created by the obtuse angle formed by the intersection of the room's two main walls; one of wood, the other of stained glass. At the corner, two glue-laminated columns create a center point, around which the stairs and a curved teak counter with circular teak sink rotate.

The stained glass window wall, one of four in this private section of the house, becomes a focal point for the room. The window is integrated with a 3-foot-high cylindrical teak cabinet below. The outer edge of the window is formed by a set of radiating copper mullions holding stained glass panels with copper stops.

A pair of copper-clad wood columns divide this fixed glass "arch," and another set of copper-clad wood frames separates it from a pair of interior panels of a more free-form design. The inner and lower edges of these secondary panels are formed by L-shaped stainless steel frames with a radiating pattern.

The window wall can also break down: the inner panels pivot out around the central wood spine into a semicylindrical "shell" of ¼-inch Plexiglas, allowing a view of the ocean outside framed by the outer band of stained glass. The edges and "roof" of this shell are tied back to the copper and wood frame, while the main copper and wood roof projects over the whole assembly, providing shade and protection from hot or inclement weather.

Beneath this operable glass wall, the cylindrical teak cabinet with two rotating shelves provides liquor storage that is accessible through a curved teak door. The cabinet projects through the plane of the wall and receives the bottom edge of the Plexiglas cylinder, at which point a triangular section of copper flashing connects the whole assembly to the exterior wall.

The top of the cabinet is teak, supported by 2 × 4 framing, but two quarter-circular tabletops of lavender Plexiglas—each attached to a pivoting window so it too can rotate outward—add an extra layer above the teak.

All cabinetwork and mullions were built in place. Art glass was shop-fabricated from templates made on the site.

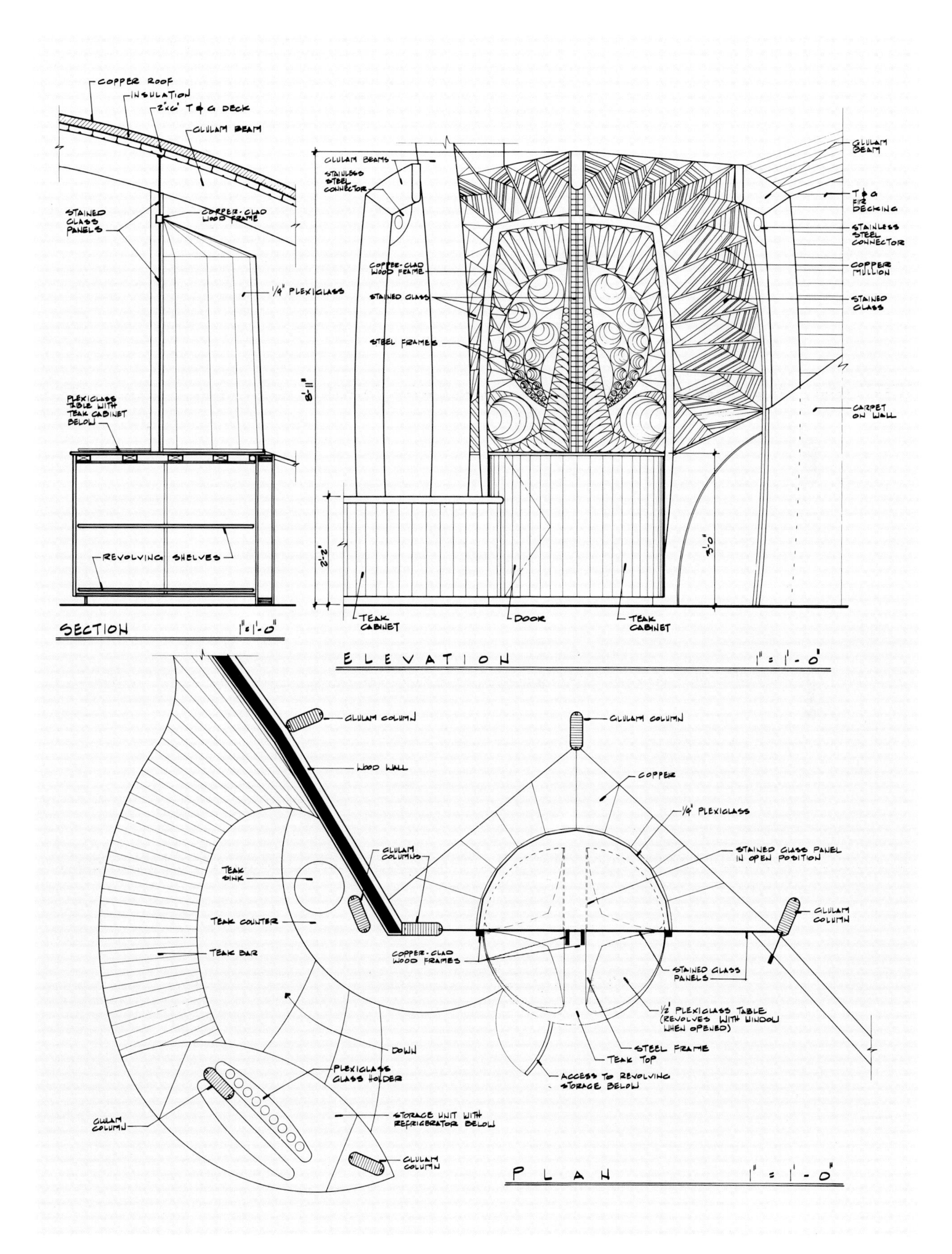
COPPER ROOF
INSULATION
2"x6" T & G DECK
GLULAM BEAM
STAINED GLASS PANELS
COPPER-CLAD WOOD FRAME
1/4" PLEXIGLASS
PLEXIGLASS TABLE WITH TEAK CABINET BELOW
REVOLVING SHELVES
SECTION 1"=1'-0"
GLULAM BEAMS
STAINLESS STEEL CONNECTOR
COPPER-CLAD WOOD FRAME
STAINED GLASS
STEEL FRAMES
8'-11"
2'-2"
TEAK CABINET
DOOR
TEAK CABINET
3'-0"
GLULAM BEAM
T & G FIR DECKING
STAINLESS STEEL CONNECTOR
COPPER MULLION
STAINED GLASS
CARPET ON WALL
ELEVATION 1"=1'-0"
GLULAM COLUMN
WOOD WALL
GLULAM COLUMNS
TEAK SINK
TEAK COUNTER
TEAK BAR
COPPER-CLAD WOOD FRAMES
DOWN
PLEXIGLASS GLASS HOLDER
STORAGE UNIT WITH REFRIGERATOR BELOW
GLULAM COLUMN
GLULAM COLUMN
GLULAM COLUMN
COPPER
1/4" PLEXIGLASS
STAINED GLASS PANEL IN OPEN POSITION
GLULAM COLUMN
STAINED GLASS PANELS
1/2" PLEXIGLASS TABLE (REVOLVES WITH WINDOW WHEN OPENED)
STEEL FRAME
TEAK TOP
ACCESS TO REVOLVING STORAGE BELOW
PLAN 1"=1'-0"

## PRIVATE RESIDENCE
*Aspen, Colorado*

**Architect**
Harry Teague Architects:
Harry Teague, Principal

**General Contractor**
S.L.O.W. Construction

**Photography**
© John Vaughan, Russell MacMasters & Associates, Inc.

AS AN INDEPENDENT FILMMAKER'S business grew, the home office within his family's Aspen house became too small to contain it. In 1978, he asked Aspen architect Harry Teague to create an office/studio addition for the house, which the architect had designed three years earlier (*see* Shower Enclosure, page 184).

The client wanted the addition to house a film library and screening room, as well as an office and a studio. It was his particular wish to keep the addition—which would inevitably generate noise—physically apart from the family quarters of the house so that acoustical privacy might be provided for each. Teague placed the addition on the north side of the house, at a distance that avoided shadowing the naturally lighted living room. Teague positioned the windows of the addition so that the main house would not be visible from them, thereby providing another layer of separation.

One of Teague's design motifs in both the house and the addition is an eclectic mix of technical solutions, geometric shapes, and varied materials. His influences in this regard include his Yale professors, Charles Moore and Robert Venturi, as well as noted industrial designers Walter Dorwin Teague, Jr. and Sr.—his father and grandfather.

Teague combined a number of finish materials—both natural and manufactured, rustic and industrial in the construction of the addition. One prime example of this juxtapositioning of diverse materials may be seen in the design of the bridge, which was necessitated by the separation of the house and the studio.

Since the bridge is essentially the commute between the client's home

and his place of work, Teague wanted to make the everyday transition something special. He designed the bridge with simple 2 × 6 wood framing. The bottom of the structure was cut in the shape of an arch, a form the architect felt to be appropriate for a bridge, although it was not constructed as a structural arch because of cost considerations. The exterior façade of the bridge was covered with wood siding over plywood, nailed to the 2 × 6 frame.

Aspen's strong natural light suggested to the architect a way of diffusing light while allowing it to penetrate into the bridge space. To match the arched curve of the underside of the bridge, Teague designed an arched "window" of fiberglass that runs across the span of the bridge; Lascolite panels of corrugated translucent fiberglass were then nailed to either side of the 2 × 6 framing, which passes through the "windows"—a device that allows the framing to be vaguely visible through the translucent panels.

Translucency became transparency when Teague placed three square spruce framed windows within the larger fiberglass window. The clear windows were placed in what the architect asserts is a musical composition that ties into the rest of the house—a theme of repetition with variation. The clear windows allow a view out, as the fiberglass window fosters the infusion of light in. The spruce trim for the deep-frame windows rests on 2 × 6 head and sill beams nailed between the studs. Glass panes are held in place with square spruce stops.

Above and below the large arched window, the interior surface of the stud walls was covered in flakeboard. Fiberglass insulation filled the gap between the flakeboard and the exterior wood panels. Wood floorboards that are perpendicular to the span of the bridge continue the motif of rough finishes, a startling and intentional contrast to the white drywall peaked ceiling, and the elegantly finished wood and glass door (with brass lever) at the end of the bridge.

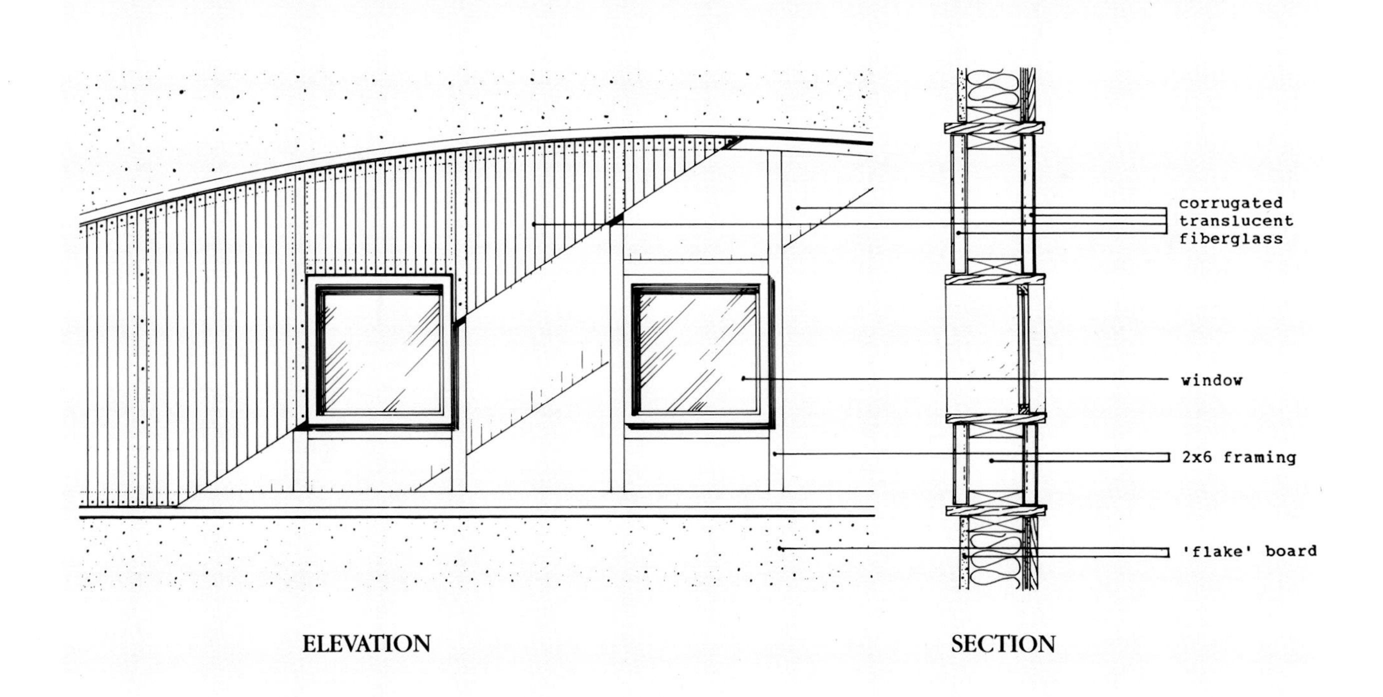


ELEVATION

SECTION

## SHOPE RESIDENCE
*Greenwich, Connecticut*

**Architect**
Shope Reno Wharton Associates

**Fabricator**
Finsterwald Art Glass (glass)

**Photography**
© H. Durston Saylor

THERE ARE NOT MANY architects who have as much hands-on experience in actual building construction as does Allan Shope, a principal of Shope Reno Wharton Associates; before taking up architecture as a career, Shope was, for several years, a highly skilled woodworker. That experience proved invaluable when, in 1987, he and his wife, Julie, a television producer, decided to build a home of their own in New England, on a 4-acre wooded site next to a lake. Their long-term plan was to build, in phases, "a non-invasive, naturalists' house" that would "integrate with the site without the flora and fauna disruption caused by bulldozers."

Phase one—the completed 500-square-foot "heart of the house"—was constructed of materials gathered from the site: stone that blends in with the craggy knoll on which the house is erected and—because Shope owns milling equipment and kilns—white oak judiciously logged from the overall acreage. The quarter-sawn white oak, according to the architect, "was time-consuming to work with, but worth the investment of labor to achieve the beautiful wood grain pattern visible on many of the exterior details."

The interior of the diminutive Shope residence revels in craftsmanlike detail as well. All windows were not only leaded, but also were handcrafted—by Shope and glass expert Thomas Finsterwald. The windows, which incorporate nineteen different types of glass—prism, silk, frosted, and bubble glass, among them—intentionally create rainbow reflections and lacelike patterns on interior wall and floor surfaces as shafts of natural day- and moonlight pass through them.

The square windows were designed as gridded panels that recall the Vienna Secessionist movement in a totally contemporary context. All panels are encased in mitered and painted crown moldings; the moldings are encased and framed by generously proportioned plain painted trim (*elevations; wall section*). The resulting recessed depth of the windows enhances a perception of the house as one built with a sense of solidity and permanence.

There is a pleasing rhythm to the windows: some are single squares; others are stacked vertically in pairs; still others appear in horizontal ranks.

Shope completed phase one of construction in "a year's worth of weekends." According to this particularly patient and philosophical architect: "The entire house will probably be finished by 1991."

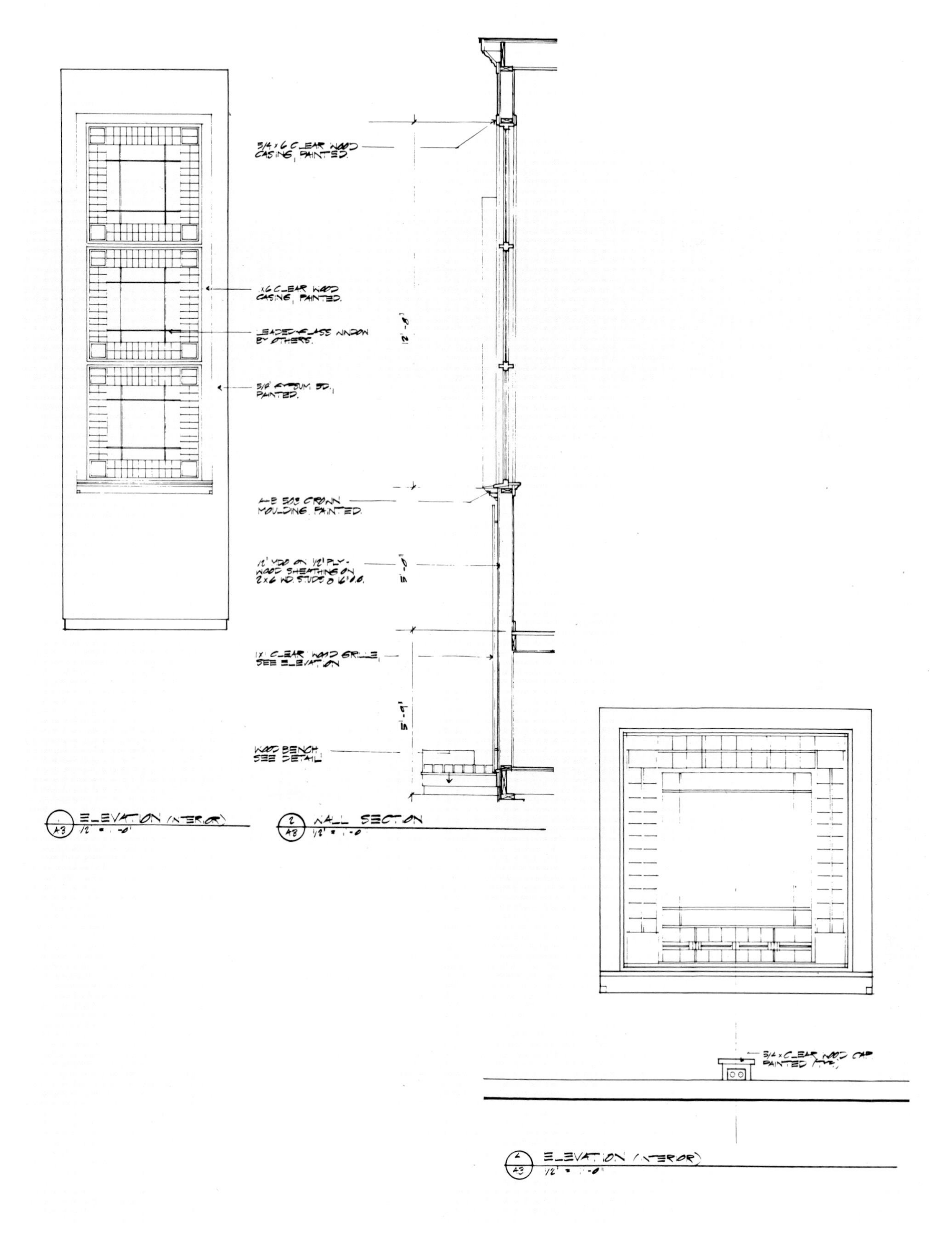
3/4 x 6 CLEAR WOOD
CASING, PAINTED.
CASING, PAINTED.
BY OTHERS.
PAINTED.
12'-0"
MOULDING, PAINTED.
5'-0"
1x CLEAR WOOD GRILLE,
SEE ELEVATION
5'-9"
WOOD BENCH
SEE DETAIL
ELEVATION
WALL SECTION
2
A3
ELEVATION
A3

**PRIVATE RESIDENCE**
*Darien, Connecticut*

**Architect**
Shope Reno Wharton Associates

**General Contractor**
Olson Byxbee Corporation

**Photography**
© H. Durston Saylor

A CHARMING 1890s VICTORIAN HOUSE is home to a young, energetic family in Darien, Connecticut. The image conjured is idyllic, but as anyone who has ever lived in such a rambling gingerbread palace can verify, even 5,000 square feet of living space does not necessarily mean that individual rooms are spacious, or that they are laid out in a footprint conducive to modern living.

The clients—parents of two preschool boys—wanted a new family room located not in a distant recess of the house, but connected to the kitchen. In 1985, the couple commissioned Shope Reno Wharton Associates to design a family room addition that would "contain plenty of bookshelves; encompass a view of the anchorage in Five Mile River; and be childproof in construction while presenting a light and airy, whimsical feeling."

Provided with a budget of $80,000, the design team gave the clients not only an enviable family room, but also a new two-car garage. Occupying the second floor of the new peaked roof addition, the family room is connected to the kitchen by a stairway that feeds into a fenestrated bridge, which provides additional elegance.

The sparsely furnished, 400-square-foot family room accommodates plenty of floor-oriented play space, as recessed bookshelves along two walls store many books. A bay window set in under the gable of the ceiling provides an extra, nostalgic amenity: not only does the bay afford expansive views of the river as it floods the space with light, it also forms the perfect nook for a built-in windowseat with integral side tables.

Like many Shope Reno Wharton details, the windowseat is constructed of clear hardwood over plywood framing that has been shop-sprayed with enamel in a dust-free environment (*elevation/section*). To avoid potential injury to the children during boisterous game playing, the windowseat cushion platform was finished with a bull-nosed edge set over a reveal (*finish trim + casing details*). The maple "Ode to Boulee" spheres placed at the front of the two triangular side tables similarly prevent the children from making direct contact with sharp corners, as they invite the children to see, touch, and understand a geometric form in three dimensions (*plan*).

Other details were planned with the children in mind, to foster their exposure to ideas: naturally finished maple plugs that punctuate the windowseat fascia at evenly spaced intervals serve as a rudimentary counting system; the staircase railing partition is surmounted by a clear and painted hardwood colonnade, constructed from small pieces of maple, that is intended to "subliminally predispose the children to appreciate architecture."

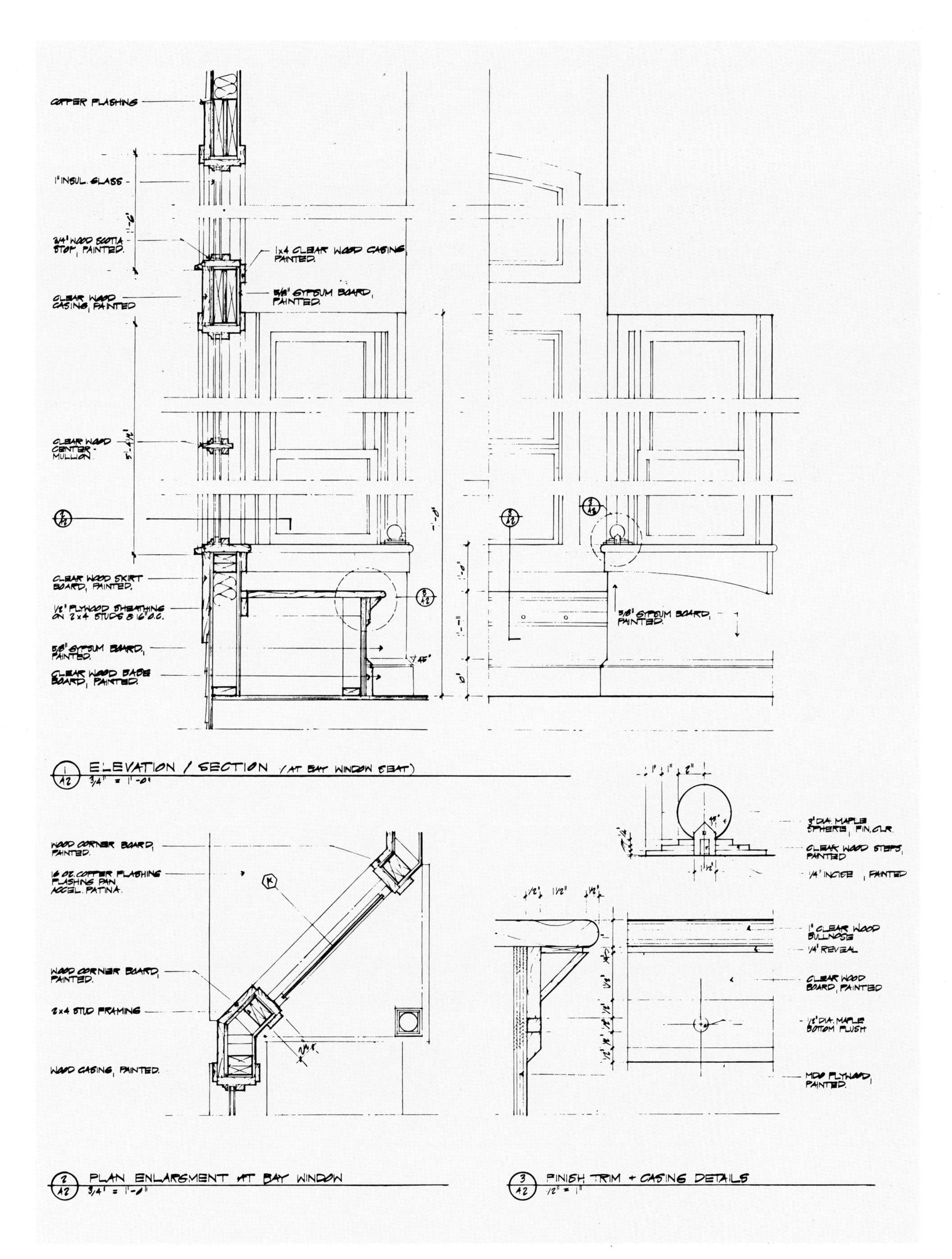
COPPER FLASHING
1" INSUL. GLASS
3/4" WOOD SCOTIA STOP, PAINTED.
1x4 CLEAR WOOD CASING, PAINTED.
5/8" GYPSUM BOARD, PAINTED.
CLEAR WOOD CASING, PAINTED
CLEAR WOOD CENTER MULLION.
CLEAR WOOD SKIRT BOARD, PAINTED.
1/2" PLYWOOD SHEATHING ON 2x4 STUDS @ 16" O.C.
5/8" GYPSUM BOARD, PAINTED.
CLEAR WOOD BASE BOARD, PAINTED.
5/8" GYPSUM BOARD, PAINTED.
ELEVATION / SECTION (AT BAY WINDOW SEAT)
3/4" = 1'-0"
WOOD CORNER BOARD, PAINTED.
16 OZ. COPPER FLASHING FLASHING PAN ACCEL. PATINA.
WOOD CORNER BOARD, PAINTED.
2x4 STUD FRAMING
WOOD CASING, PAINTED.
PLAN ENLARGEMENT AT BAY WINDOW
3/4" = 1'-0"
3" DIA. MAPLE SPHERE, FIN. CLR.
CLEAR WOOD STEPS, PAINTED
1/4" INCISE, PAINTED
1" CLEAR WOOD BULLNOSE
1/4" REVEAL
CLEAR WOOD BOARD, PAINTED
1/2" DIA. MAPLE BOTTOM FLUSH
MDO PLYWOOD, PAINTED.
FINISH TRIM + CASING DETAILS
1/2" = 1"

# Window Wall

**Richardson Residence**
*Wynnewood, Pennsylvania*

**Architect**
David C. S. Polk, Architect

**Design Team**
David C. S. Polk, Principal-in-Charge;
Richard T. Rice, Project Architect;
Anna Ku Lau, Assistant Architect

**General Contractor**
Oscar Temple

**Photography**
© David C. S. Polk

The parable of the tortoise and the hare began to have real meaning for the Richardson family of Wynnewood, Pennsylvania. Attorney James Richardson—an admirer of the work of Frank Lloyd Wright—his wife, and three young children started the renovation of their house in 1968 and continued working on it themselves until 1972. The family performed some of the carpentry and masonry and most of the electrical and plumbing work; the parents subcontracting the rest.

The 3,700-square-foot addition was to be nearly twice the size of the original house. The Richardsons wanted a large master suite and a room large enough (56′ × 35′) for a sizable indoor pool. Architect David C. S. Polk, called to the rescue, found the combination of Richardson's interest in architecture, the heroic effort of the family, and the site—an old white-washed stone house—intriguing.

Despite the small size of the existing house relative to the addition, Polk's design took a number of cues from the original architecture. The dimensions of the existing house affected, but did not determine, the dimensions of the addition. Polk expanded upon the idea of the old house's thick stone walls with deep-set windows, creating even thicker walls in the addition. But where the windows in the old walls became small spaces filled with light, the new walls were themselves made of space and light rather than material. They became habitable, providing places for a desk, a stair, a seat, a bathtub.

The second-floor master suite—containing bedroom, study, baths, and dressing alcove—is "a house within a house." A double row of square wood columns define a thick exterior "wall" of space that contains various functions: a seating alcove in the bedroom, a tub in the bathroom, a desk in the study, planters at the corners, and—in the center—a spiral stairway.

The master-suite wall was designed to dissolve the barrier between inside and outside. As a counterpoint to the thickness of this zone, the actual barrier between interior and exterior is a single-pane glass wall—something more feasible in the days of low-cost heating fuel. Just as at Wright's "Fallingwater" house in Bear Run, Pennsylvania, the wall's glass corners and intersections are butt-jointed and glued, and the top of the glass sits flush in the ceiling to intensify the transparency of the wall. The bottom of an external wood gutter sits flush with the ceiling plane, furthering its sense of infinite extension into the landscape.

The corners at the ends of the addition are also dissolved, where they invert and step into the house to form spaces for exterior planters. The central stairway sits within a square projecting bay, twice the width of the double row of columns, with its window posts centered on its walls rather than at the corners. The corners are butted and glued glass, dematerializing the boundary between interior and exterior at a typically solid juncture.

The wall's columns are of two types. The interior line is constructed of 4½-inch-diameter steel pipe columns surrounded by fir blocking, while the exterior columns are Douglas fir 6 × 6s. Both are finished with 1x Philippine mahogany trim to a final dimension of 7½ inches. Trim joints are typically rabbetted and glued.

Like the columns, the posts and mullions are square cornered, without reveals. One-quarter-inch plate glass is set into rabbetted corners of the mahogany trim and secured with square mahogany stops. The window wall is set flush into a 7½-inch-wide mahogany trim in the ceiling plane (to match the width of the wood columns), supported by two 2 × 6s above. A mahogany sill and drip molding sit on a wood stud wall, finished with two layers of stucco on the exterior and one layer of plaster on the interior.

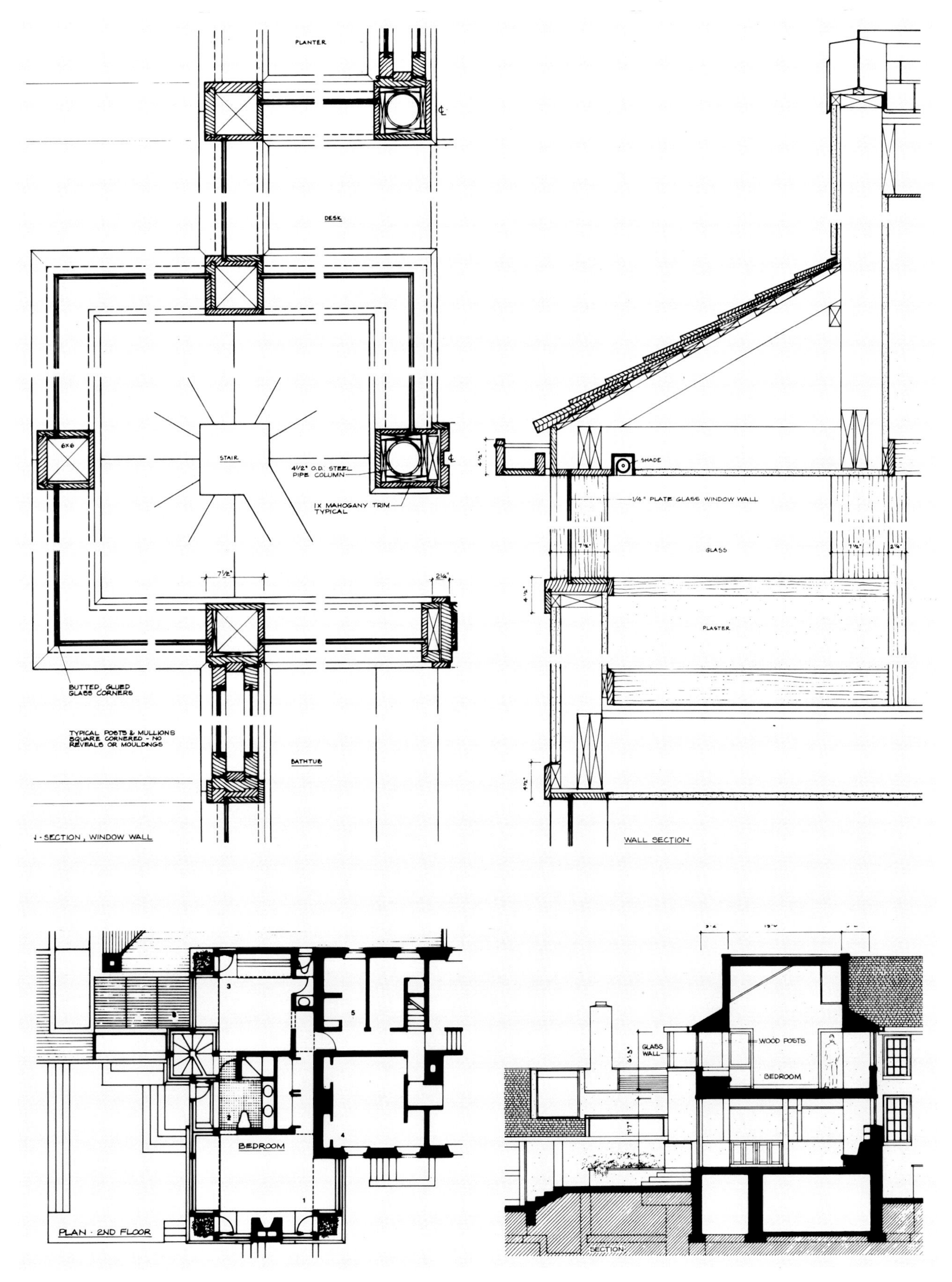
PLANTER
DESK
6x6
STAIR
4 1/2" O.D. STEEL PIPE COLUMN
1X MAHOGANY TRIM TYPICAL
7 1/2"
2 1/4"
BUTTED GLUED GLASS CORNERS
TYPICAL POSTS & MULLIONS SQUARE CORNERED - NO REVEALS OR MOULDINGS
BATHTUB
SECTION, WINDOW WALL
SHADE
1/4" PLATE GLASS WINDOW WALL
GLASS
PLASTER
WALL SECTION
BEDROOM
PLAN · 2ND FLOOR
GLASS WALL
WOOD POSTS
BEDROOM
SECTION

# WINDOW WALL

**POOL HOUSE**
*Chicago, Illinois*

**Architect**
Tigerman/McCurry Architects

**Design Team**
Stanley Tigerman, AIA, Architect; Frederick Wilson; Chuck Renner

**General Contractor**
John Teschky, Inc.

**Fabricators**
Illinois Brick (brick); Hispanic Design (floor tile); Thomas Melvin Painting Company (trompe l'oeil painting)

**Photography**
© Barbara Karant, Karant and Associates

NECESSITY IS OFTEN the mother of invention, as clients of Chicago architect Stanley Tigerman can attest. An investment consultant, his wife—a finance attorney—and their three children entertained frequently. The family unilaterally yearned for an indoor pool. However, the density of their suburban site restricted the width of a pool pavilion to 20 feet. The clients, therefore, assumed that a pool was impossible.

The architect disagreed, acquainting the family with the attractions of lap pool swimming. The result: a 2,400-square-foot pool enclosure that is 20 feet wide and 90 feet long. Taking cues from the formal ground floor of the existing house, Tigerman sought to design an equally elegant, if more powerful, environment for the pool below.

In plan, the pavilion surrounds the 4-foot-deep linear lap pool, which has a central dogleg for a Jacuzzi and play pool. A classically inspired archway helps to separate the main pool from the "water inglenook" while preserving the room's linearity.

On the opposite side of the pool, a colonnade creates a 90-foot window wall. Tigerman's choice of the Tuscan order for the columns together with the room's height/span ratio determined a set of eighteen bays on a 5-foot module. The piers of the exterior wall are of brick masonry, and the interior is constructed of "greenboard"—treated drywall that retards moisture—over wood studs. The Tuscan pilasters' postmodern classical details are created from various pieces of standard wood moldings and painted poplar flat, half-round, and quarter-round trim. Where projections are necessary, the trim is built out over wood blocking. Between the pilasters, operable wood casement windows with fixed, small-paned toplights were imposed to incorporate modern convenience to a classical window wall.

A sconce is mounted on each pilaster, and a piece of wood molding spans the sky-mural ceiling between each pair of "capitals." Faux marble finishes and a wainscoting of blue and white checkerboard tiles, matching those that line the edge of the pool, enhance a grotto effect. The tile wainscoting also serves the practical purpose of keeping moisture from seeping into the drywall.

After all pieces had been set in place, a waiting period of one year allowed shrinkage or settling to reveal cracks, which were then filled and refinished.

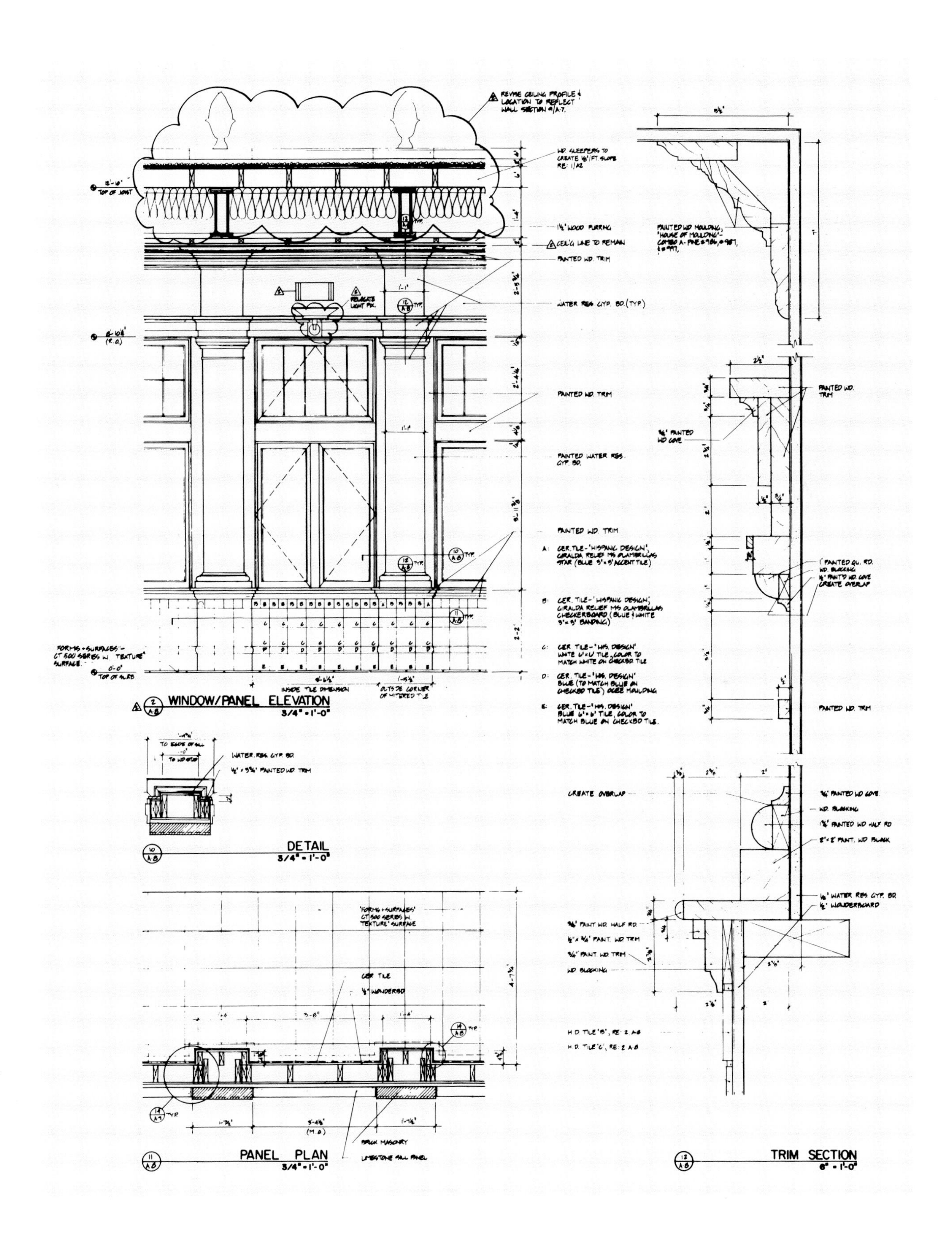
WINDOW/PANEL ELEVATION
3/4" = 1'-0"
DETAIL
3/4" = 1'-0"
PANEL PLAN
3/4" = 1'-0"
TRIM SECTION
6" = 1'-0"
PAINTED WD. TRIM
WATER RES. GYP. BD. (TYP)
CEIL'G LINE TO REMAIN
1½" WOOD FURRING
PAINTED WATER RES. GYP. BD.
CREATE OVERLAP
BRICK MASONRY
LIMESTONE SILL PANEL

### The Cupola House
*Fripp Island, South Carolina*

**Architect**
Dowling Architects—Atlanta

**Design Team**
G. Geddes Dowling III, AIA, Principal-in-Charge of Design; Elizabeth Dowling, Ph.D., AIA, Architect; Chris Bishop, Intern Architect

**General Contractor**
Ray Ward and Company

**Exterior Photography**
© G. Geddes Dowling III

Certain well-designed beach houses evoke a sense of emotional connection to happy seaside experiences one enjoyed in the past; others foster a sense of physical connection to admired, and perhaps faraway, regional styles of architecture; still others invite one—within both communal and carefully planned private spaces—to relax, unwind, and recharge the emotional and physical energies that have been debilitated by the stresses and strains of everyday life.

The best beach houses offer their owners and guests all of these qualities. And the Cupola House, designed in 1984 by Dowling Architects—Atlanta, clearly ranks among the "best of the best."

The Cupola House received both state and regional American Institute of Architects (AIA) Awards of Excellence in 1984 and 1985 for practical as well as aesthetic reasons: effective use of minimal space (four bedrooms/three baths plus generous public spaces in an enclosed area of 2,500 square feet) and effective climate control, accomplished by raised piling foundations, casement windows, roof overhangs, thick insulation, separate heat pumps on each floor, sloped ceilings to thermal chimneys, as well as both soffit and ridge beam heat vents (*section @ cupola*). But the real joy of the house is in the unusual number of amenities it provides—among them, a gracious floor plan, ceiling heights up to 16 feet, and three ocean-oriented spaces including a sun deck, a generously scaled screened porch, and an owner's cupola.

It is the last of these amenities—the cupola—that is deserving of special praise. The cupola room is accessible only by climbing a ship's ladder from the second floor (*axonometric*). Consequently, it sits apart from the rest of the house, crowning the roof line like a jaunty burgee at the top of a flagpole. The cupola room, first and foremost, serves its owners and guests as a magical aerie from which to view a 360-degree panorama of ocean, sky, marsh, and woodland. But it is also well loved by local fishermen, who refer to it, quite literally, as a landmark, and by other island inhabitants who proudly refer to it as an example of local architectural distinction.

The cupola was specifically designed for the owner, a former Navy captain who wanted a "ship's bridge" room in which to keep his telescope, nautical charts, and celestial navigation equipment. The cupola, and its cantilevered deck, were also to serve the captain as a quiet retreat in which he might at once survey and escape from the tumult and happy exuberance of visiting grandchildren.

The cupola design answered all of his priorities in 100 square feet of "carpenter classical construction." No special budget pertained to the cupola and its deck; rather, the detail was developed within the financial framework of the $60-per-square-foot overall project budget. Finish materials were minimal, consisting of stock casement windows and rough, rotary-sawn cypress plywood paneling, sealed with clear varnish, which covers both walls and ceiling.

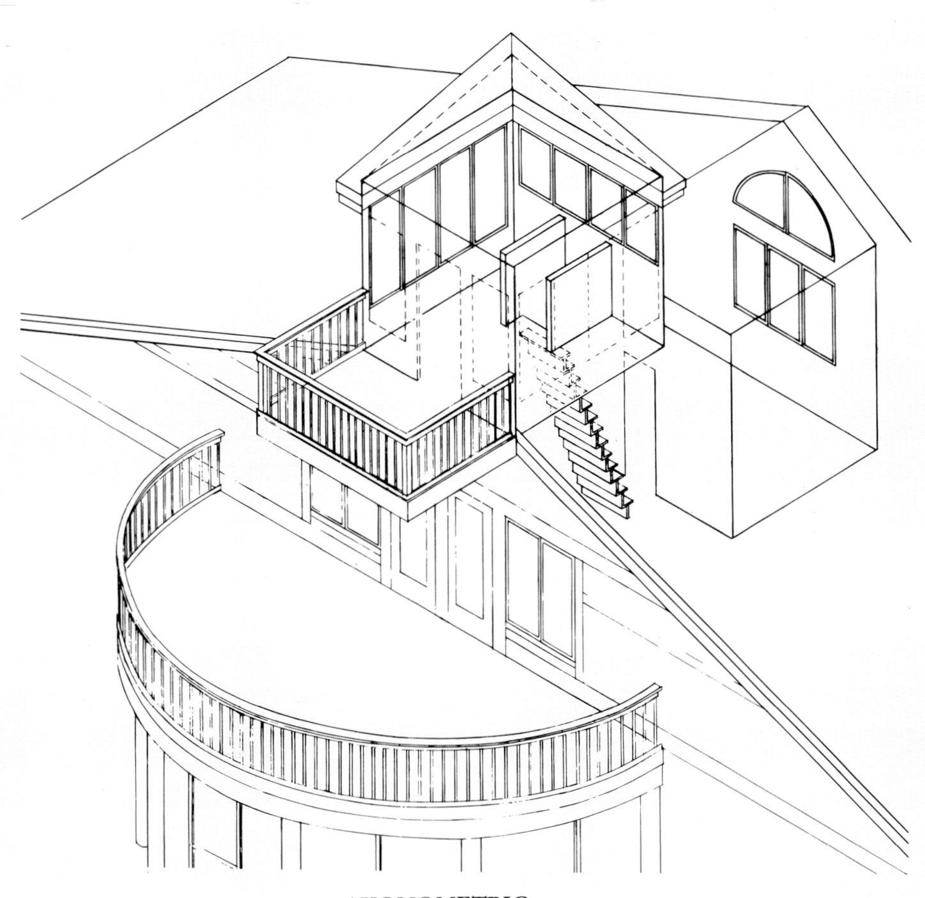

AXONOMETRIC

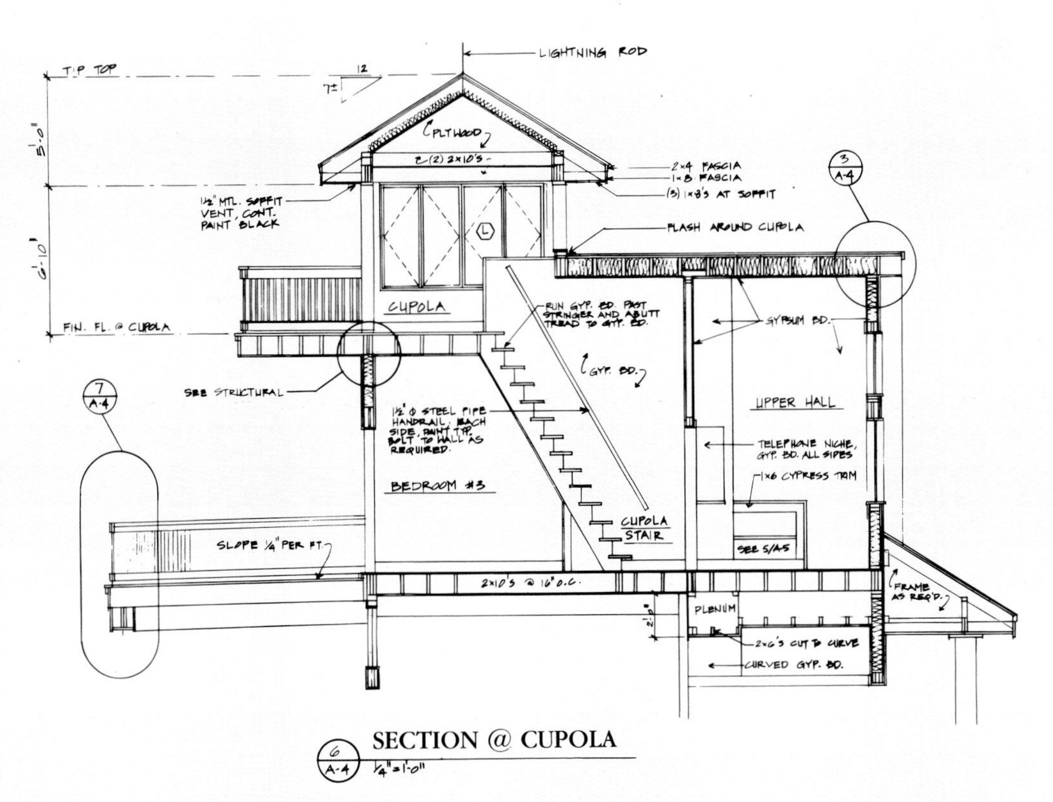
LIGHTNING ROD
TIP TOP
12
7±
5'-0"
6'-10"
PLYWOOD
2 (2) 2x10's
2x4 FASCIA
1x8 FASCIA
(3) 1x8's AT SOFFIT
3
A-4
1½" MTL. SOFFIT VENT, CONT. PAINT BLACK
L
FLASH AROUND CUPOLA
CUPOLA
RUN GYP. BD. PAST STRINGER AND ABUTT TREAD TO GYP. BD.
GYPSUM BD.
FIN. FL. @ CUPOLA
GYP. BD.
SEE STRUCTURAL
7
A-4
1½" ϕ STEEL PIPE HANDRAIL, EACH SIDE, PAINT TYP. BOLT TO WALL AS REQUIRED.
UPPER HALL
TELEPHONE NICHE, GYP. BD. ALL SIDES
1x6 CYPRESS TRIM
BEDROOM #3
CUPOLA STAIR
SLOPE ¼" PER FT.
SEE 5/A5
2x10's @ 16" O.C.
FRAME AS REQ'D.
PLENUM
2'-0"
2x6's CUT TO CURVE
CURVED GYP. BD.
6
A-4

SECTION @ CUPOLA
1/4" = 1'-0"

## CLOSE PEGASE WINERY

*Napa Valley, California*

**Architect**
Michael Graves, Architect

**Design Team**
Michael Graves, Project Architect;
Terence Smith, Associate-in-Charge;
Juliet Richardson Smith, Job Captain;
Ronald Berlin; Peter Hague Neilson;
Alexey Grigorieff; Leslie Mason

**Associate Architect**
Heidi Richardson,
Richardson • Butler Associates

**General Contractor**
Friederich Company, Inc.

**Drawings**
Ronald Berlin

**Photography**
© William Taylor

THE FOUNDER and owner of the Close Pegase Winery in Napa Valley, California selected Michael Graves to design the winery after sponsoring an intense architectural competition. The client, an entrepreneur and art collector, devoted a generous budget to the design and development of the 70-acre estate, which in addition to the winery, terraces, and gardens was to include a spacious 6,700-square-foot villa for his family.

Graves took design cues from the Eastern tradition of drawing nature into the house through intermediate spaces: formal gardens, porches, and verandas. An outdoor atrium forms the center of the plan, around which gather the passages and rooms of the house. The exterior of the house is finished in stucco with a clay tile roof, while windows and doors are constructed of unstained mahogany.

One of the villa's "intermediate spaces" is a wintergarden that connects the living and dining rooms. It is designed to be an actual garden, presenting an arrangement of plants and trees. Because the living and dining rooms are set at right angles to each other, the wintergarden acts as a termination for the two axes of the winery.

The octagonal structure is framed in wood 2x columns and beams, and finished in dark, green-stained cedar, an extremely weather resistant material ideally suited to the wintergarden's exposure to frequent storms from the south. The radiating floor pattern of the garden is composed of hand-glazed French tiles specifically requested by the owner.

Each of the wintergarden's eight sides is composed of three vertical panels of square-paned glass lights; the central panel is two panes wide, the outer panels, one pane wide. A narrow wood band at 7′–0″ demarcates exterior doorways and passages to the dining and living rooms; a wider band at 13′–0″ creates a 2′–0″ clerestory. Sheet-metal sconces, in the shape of quarter cylinders, are set in this band, in the center of every panel. These are mirrored by eight ceiling light fixtures set in 3′–6″ from each wall.

In the center of the ceiling, a 6′–0″-wide octagonal cupola extends 11′–6″ above the roof, each side a vertical band of single glass panes identical to those used in the walls below. The cupola is supported on beams, each formed of seven pieces of 2 × 6 wood laminated together with glue. Stained western red cedar trim covers wood blocking that is attached to this glue-laminate frame. The trim steps down from the interior of the cupola, covers the ceiling, and finishes out the ceiling molding of the wintergarden walls.

The wood frame wall is capped by a 2 × 8 and an 8 × 8 beam that also support the exterior cornice. Wood blocking is nailed to two layers of ¾-inch plywood on top of the 8 × 8; this blocking supports a plywood roof with metal flashing and a cedar cornice. Three strips of fascia trim form the cornice's drip moldings, with the uppermost molding notched to receive the edge of the roof's metal flashing.

The window frame, sash, trim, and stops are all of mahogany; mahogany trim also covers an 8 × 8 beam at the clerestory level. This beam receives the head of the window wall below, as well as the two beveled and lapped pieces of mahogany that form the clerestory sill. The sheet-metal sconce is set into a well created by wood blocking built off the 8 × 8 and framed by mahogany trim.

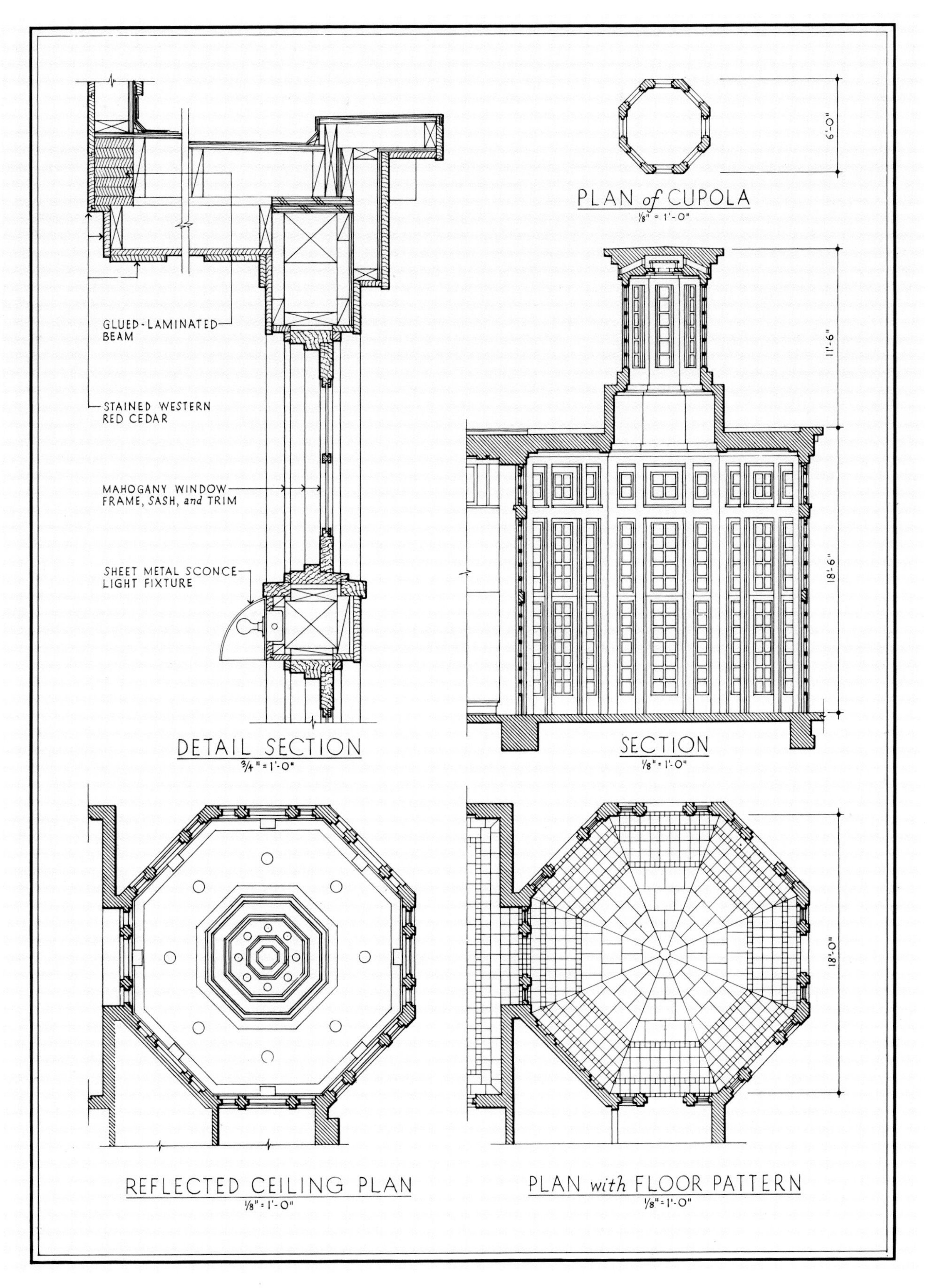
6'-0"
PLAN of CUPOLA
1/8" = 1'-0"
GLUED-LAMINATED BEAM
STAINED WESTERN RED CEDAR
MAHOGANY WINDOW FRAME, SASH, and TRIM
SHEET METAL SCONCE LIGHT FIXTURE
11'-6"
18'-6"
DETAIL SECTION
3/4" = 1'-0"
SECTION
1/8" = 1'-0"
18'-0"
REFLECTED CEILING PLAN
1/8" = 1'-0"
PLAN with FLOOR PATTERN
1/8" = 1'-0"

# Credits and Sources

## Architects/Designers

Anderson/Schwartz Architects, New York, New York: *pp. 114–15, 136–37, 178, 210–11*

Armstrong Cumming Architects, New York, New York: *pp. 36–37*

Alan J. Buchsbaum, c/o Anderson/Schwartz: *pp. 210–11*

Centerbrook Architects, Essex, Connecticut: *pp. 14–15, 38–39, 94–95, 220–21*

Charleston Architectural Group, c/o Eubank + Thompson, Architects, Charleston, South Carolina: *pp. 194–95*

Dick Clark Architecture, Austin, Texas: *pp. 32–33*

William M. Cohen, Architect, New York, New York: *pp. 130–31*

David Coleman Architecture, Burlington, Vermont: *pp. 76–77*

James Cutler Architects, Winslow, Washington: *pp. 96–99*

Dowling Architects—Atlanta, Atlanta, Georgia: *pp. 234–35*

Paul T. Edwards, Architect, Tucson, Arizona: *pp. 212–13*

J. Frank Fitzgibbons, Architect, Los Angeles, California: *pp. 16–17*

Peter L. Gluck and Partners, Architects, New York, New York: *pp. 60–61, 143*

Michael Graves, Architect, Princeton, New Jersey: *pp. 152–53, 236–37*

Graham Gund Architects, Cambridge, Massachusetts: *pp. 110–11, 142*

Gwathmey Siegel & Associates, Architects, New York, New York: *pp. 10–11*

Haigh Space Architects, Greenwich, Connecticut: *pp. 126–27, 154–55*

Hartman-Cox Architects, Washington, D.C.: *pp. 48–49, 196–97*

Haverson/Rockwell Architects, P.C., New York, New York: *pp. 160–61*

Don A. Hawkins & Associates, Washington, D.C.: *pp. 56–57*

Steven Holl Architects, New York, New York: *pp. 40–41, 80–81, 206*

Norman Jaffe, P.C., Architects, Bridgehampton, New York: *pp. 88–89, 216–17*

Kelly and Lehn, Kansas City, Missouri: *pp. 100–101, 144–45*

Roger Kraft: Architecture • Design, Kansas City, Missouri: *pp. 50–51, 78–79, 134–35, 162–63*

Ira Kurlander, San Francisco, California: *p. 12*

Claudia Librett Design Studio, New York, New York: *pp. 31, 72–73*

Machado and Silvetti Associates, Inc., Boston, Massachusetts: *pp. 74–75, 102–3*

MacNelly • Cohen Architects, Vineyard Haven, Massachusetts: *pp. 24–25*

William McDonough Architects, New York, New York: *pp. 82–83, 90–91, 180–81, 198–201*

Moore Ruble Yudell, Santa Monica, California: *pp. 52–53, 62–63, 158–59*

Morphosis, Santa Monica, California: *pp. 128–29, 186–87, 207*

Eric Owen Moss • Architect, Culver City, California: *pp. 112–13, 116–17, 172–73*

James Mount/Architect, Atlanta, Georgia: *pp. 122–23, 166–67*

Pappageorge Haymes Ltd., Chicago, Illinois: *pp. 34–35, 124–25, 148–49, 176–77, 182–83*

Charles Patten Architects, New York, New York: *pp. 146–47, 218*

David C. S. Polk & Linda O'Gwynn, Architects, Philadelphia, Pennsylvania: *pp. 20–21, 164–65, 192–93, 230–31*

Bart Prince, Architect, Albuquerque, New Mexico: *pp. 222–23*

Quinn and Searl, Architects, Chicago, Illinois: *pp. 46–47, 64–65, 104–5*

Rudolph & Associates, P.C., Chicago, Illinois: *pp. 26–27, 84–85, 108–9, 138–39*

Michael Schuster Associates, Cincinnati, Ohio: *pp. 18–19, 150–51*

David M. Schwarz/Architectural Services, P.C., Washington, D.C.: *pp. 190–91*

Shope Reno Wharton Associates, Greenwich, Connecticut: *pp. 9, 44–45, 58–59, 118–19, 120–21, 132–33, 140–41, 170–71, 226–27, 228–29*

Sally Sirkin Interior Designs, Los Angeles, California: *pp. 22–23, 30, 92–93*

SITE Projects, Inc., New York, New York: *p. 13*

Lee H. Skolnick Architecture + Design, New York, New York: *pp. 68–69, 156–57, 188–89*

Architects Snyder • Snyder, Philadelphia, Pennsylvania: *pp. 54–55*

SPGA Group, Inc., New York, New York: *pp. 214–15*

Rita St. Clair Associates, Inc., Baltimore, Maryland: *pp. 28–29, 86–87, 168–69, 208–9*

Robert A. M. Stern Architects, New York, New York: *pp. 66–67, 174–75, 202–3*

John M. Strite, Haverford, Pennsylvania: *pp. 70–71*

Harry Teague Architects, Aspen, Colorado: *pp. 184–85, 224–25*

Tigerman/McCurry, Architects, Chicago, Illinois: *pp. 42–43, 179, 204–5, 219, 232–33*

William Turnbull Associates, San Francisco, California: *pp. 106–7*

## Lighting Consultants

Cline, Bettridge, Bernstein Lighting Design, Inc., New York, New York: *pp. 174–75*

Claude Engle, Washington, D.C.: *pp. 48–49*

Clark Johnson, Johnson Schwinghammer Lighting Consultants, New York, New York: *pp. 114–15, 136–37*

## General Contractors

Alan Custon Building, New York, New York: *pp. 114–15, 135–37*

Peter Austerin (*address not available*): *p. 178*

E. A. Baker Company, Inc., Takoma Park, Maryland: *pp. 48–49*

Banner Construction Company, Kaneohe, Oahu, Hawaii: *pp. 92–93*

John Bossany, Inc., Warren, New Jersey: *pp. 152–53*

BT Equipment, Smithfield, Rhode Island: *pp. 102–3*

Capital Construction Company, Chicago, Illinois: *pp. 182–83*

Cauldwell-Wingate Co., Inc. New York, New York: *pp. 214–15*

Charter Construction, Seattle, Washington: *pp. 96–99*

Clark Construction Corporation, New York, New York: *pp. 154–55*

Robert Coe Builders, Inc., Austin, Texas: *pp. 32–33*

C. S. Construction., Burlington, Vermont: *pp. 76–77*

C-Shel Construction, Inc., Somerville, New Jersey: *pp. 152–53*

Dandt Contracting (*address not available*): *pp. 210–11*

Deak Construction, Inc., New Milford, Connecticut: *pp. 31, 72–73*

C. I. Duncan Company, Inc., Malvern Pennsylvania: *pp. 54–55*

Friederich Company, Inc., Saint Helena, California: *pp. 236–37*

Hallowell Construction Company, Wayne, Pennsylvania: *pp. 20–21, 164–65*

Hanson Construction, Inc., Aspen, Colorado: *pp. 184–85*

Harder Construction, New York, New York: *pp. 82–83*

J & B Construction, Cincinnati, Ohio: *pp. 18–19, 150–51*

William A. Kelly & Co., Katonah, New York: *pp. 60–61*

Kissner Company, Chicago, Illinois: *pp. 46–47, 64–65*

Richard Knight, Edgartown, Massachusetts: *pp. 24–25*

Landon and Hall, Guilford, Connecticut: *pp. 14–15*

Steve Landry Construction Company, Shalimar, Florida: *pp. 166–67*

Len Van Builders, Wayne, New Jersey: *pp. 66–67*

Martin Construction, Inc., New York, New York: *pp. 126–27*

Metro Design, Inc., Bronx, New York: *pp. 146–47, 218*

Nicely and Nicely, Ligonier, Pennsylvania: *pp. 94–95*

Octagon House Construction, New York, New York: *pp. 36–37*

Olson Byxbee Corporation, Darien, Connecticut: *pp. 228–29*

George K. Page, Spring City, Pennsylvania: *pp. 192–93*

P. D. Associates, Point Reyes Station, California: *pp. 106–7*

S. N. Peck, Builder, Inc., Chicago, Illinois: *pp. 26–27*

Ranneklev Brothers Construction, Bedford, New York: *pp. 160–61*

Romac Construction, New York, New York: *pp. 90–91, 138–39, 180–81, 198–201*

Robert P. Schultz, Inc., Schaumburg, Illinois: *pp. 138–39*

Scorcia & Diana, Elmont, New York: *pp. 174–75*

E & L Shilo Company, Fox Lake, Illinois: *pp. 104–5*

C. M. Stretmater Construction Company, Clarksville, Maryland: *pp. 56–57*

Oscar Temple, Philadelphia, Pennsylvania: *pp. 230–31*

John Teschky, Inc., Glenview, Illinois: *pp. 232–33*

TORTOLITA CONSTRUCTION, Tucson, Arizona: *pp. 212–13*

TRUDEAU-WOLF CONSTRUCTION, Mount Pleasant, South Carolina: *pp. 194–95*

PAT TRUNZO, East Hampton, New York: *pp. 202–3*

WRANGLER CONSTRUCTION, Elmhurst, Illinois: *pp. 176–77*

RAY WARD AND COMPANY, Seabrook, South Carolina: *pp. 234–35*

EDWARD WORTHINGTON CONSTRUCTION COMPANY, Carmel, New York: *pp. 130–31*

ROMAN YODER AND SON, Middlefield, Ohio: *pp. 220–21*

DAVID Z & CO., Bridgemen, Michigan: *p. 179*

ZZI CONSTRUCTION COMPANY, INC., Brookline, Massachusetts: *pp. 110–11, 142*

## FABRICATORS

ALEXANDER & WRIGHT MILLWORKS, INC., Vineyard Haven, Massachusetts: *pp. 24–25*

ALPINE LOG HOME COMPANY, Victor, Montana: *p. 219*

AMERICAN LAMINATES, Kansas City, Kansas: *pp. 100–101*

AMSCO, Honolulu, Hawaii: *pp. 92–93*

ARCHITECTURAL PRESERVATION GROUP, Warwick, Rhode Island: *pp. 120–21*

AUDIO COMMAND SYSTEMS, Los Angeles, California: *pp. 22–23, 92–93*

E. A. BAKER COMPANY, INC., Takoma Park, Maryland: *pp. 48–49, 196–97*

BANNER CONSTRUCTION COMPANY, Kabeohe, Oahu, Hawaii: *pp. 92–93*

BEST WAY MARBLE COMPANY, Los Angeles, California: *p. 30*

BLUE CONSTRUCTION (*address not available*): *pp. 212–13*

JIM BOHN, INC., PAINT AND WALLCOVERINGS, North Hollywood, California: *pp. 22–23*

BREAKFAST MILLWORKS, Branford, Connecticut: *pp. 44–45, 118–19, 170–71*

WILLIAM BROWER, FLOOR INSTALLER, Franklyn, Massachusetts: *pp. 110–11, 142*

BRYCHTA WOODSHED, New Buffalo, Michigan: *pp. 204–5*

BURGESS STEEL PRODUCTS CORPORATION, Englewood, New Jersey: *pp. 214–15*

CAPITAL CONSTRUCTION GROUP, Chicago, Illinois: *pp. 182–83*

CASTELLUCCI STONE, INC., Providence, Rhode Island: *pp. 102–3*

LANIE AND MAREK CECULA, New York, New York: *pp. 72–73*

CHARLES CHAMOT, New York, New York: *pp. 72–73*

CHARTER CONSTRUCTION, Seattle, Washington: *pp. 96–99*

CLARK CONSTRUCTION CORPORATION, New York, New York: *pp. 198–201*

CLEVENGER CORPORATION, Beltsville, Maryland: *pp. 190–91*

COLONIAL WOODWORKING, INC., South Norwalk, Connecticut: *pp. 132–33*

HENRY COOK, Brooklyn, New York: *pp. 136–37*

HOWARD CROUCH, Redhook, New York: *pp. 144–45*

CRYSTAL INTERIORS, MIRROR AND GLASS CUTTERS, Baltimore, Maryland: *pp. 28–29, 168–69*

TERRY DEANGELIS, CABINETMAKER, New York, New York: *pp. 80–81, 206*

TIM DONOVAN TILE, Austin, Texas: *pp. 32–33*

DUTCHMAN PLUMBING, Austin, Texas: *pp. 32–33*

EBNER WOODWORK CORPORATION, Bronx, New York: *pp. 88–89*

JULES EDLIN, INC., New York, New York: *p. 218*

STEVEN ETHRIDGE, ELECTRICIAN, Chicago, Illinois: *pp. 104–5*

BOB FALKENBERG COMPANY, Kansas City, Missouri: *pp. 50–51, 78–79, 134–35, 162–63*

FAYSTON IRON AND STEEL WORKS, Fayston, Vermont: *pp. 180–81, 198–201*

FINSTERWALD ART CLASS, Brooklyn, New York: *pp. 226–27*

DAVID FISHBEIN, FURNITUREMAKER, Newbury Port, Massachusetts: *pp. 154–55*

FOCAL POINT, INC., Atlanta, Georgia: *pp. 190–91*

FORDHAM MARBLE, Bronx, New York: *pp. 180–81*

H. P. FRISCH, MASONRY, Lynwood, Washington: *pp. 96–99*

JOHN FURNESS (*address not available*): *pp. 38–39*

MARISA GEISY, CUSTOM FINISHER, Long Beach, California: *pp. 16–17*

GIANNINI & HILGART, GLASSWORK, Chicago, Illinois: *pp. 84–85*

GLASS ARTS CENTER, Newport Beach, California: *pp. 222–23*

TARO SUZUKI (*address not available*): *pp. 210–11*

TORBEN JENSEN WOODCRAFT CO., Chicago, Illinois: *pp. 84–85, 138–39*

TOWNHOUSE FINISHINGS, Hoboken, New Jersey: *pp. 68–69, 156–57*

TREITEL-GRATZ, Long Island City, New York: *pp. 60–61*

TWIN CITIES GLASS, Stevenville, Missouri: *p. 179*

THE VALLEY CRAFTSMEN, LTD., Baltimore, Maryland: *pp. 28–29, 168–69, 208–9*

VERMONT MARBLE, Proctor, Vermont: *pp. 180–81*

WEATHER SHIELD MANUFACTURING, INC., Medford, Wisconsin: *p. 219*

DAVID WEBB, Montauk, New York: *pp. 216–17*

WOODY'S WROUGHT IRON, Tucson, Arizona: *pp. 212–213*

WRANGLER CONSTRUCTION, Elmhurst, Illinois: *pp. 176–77*

ZAHMER SHEET METAL, Kansas City, Missouri: *pp. 100–101*

DAVID Z & CO., Bridgemen, Michigan: *p. 179*

ZOLATONE, Los Angeles, California: *pp. 154–55*

FRANK ZORC, Atlanta, Georgia: *pp. 122–23*

## ENGINEERS

BASIL GREENE, INC., Erdenheim, Pennsylvania: *pp. 20–21, 164–65*

BESIER GIBBLE NORDEN, Old Saybrook, Connecticut: *pp. 14–15*

BLACKBURN ENGINEERING ASSOCIATES, Princeton, New Jersey: *pp. 152–53*

GRENIER STRUCTURAL, INC., Tucson, Arizona: *pp. 212–13*

JOONG LEE, Scarsdale, New York: *pp. 130–31*

KEAST AND HOOD COMPANY, Philadelphia, Pennsylvania: *pp. 20–21, 164–65*

RARWOOD-WEISENFELD, New York, New York: *pp. 160–61*

## OTHER CONSULTANTS

APTEKAR ARTS MANAGEMENT, Cambridge, Massachusetts: *pp. 110–11*

SAUL GOLDIN, ELECTRICAL CONSULTANT, Los Angeles, California: *pp. 186–87*

CHIP HUNTER, FEASIBILITY CONSULTANT, HUNTER/HAAS REAL ESTATE, Cincinnati, Ohio: *pp. 18–19*

RAY LINDAHL, STRUCTURAL CONSULTANT, San Francisco, California: *pp. 106–7*

ERDELYI MOON MEZEY, STRUCTURAL CONSULTANT, San Francisco, California: *pp. 128–29, 207*

GORDON POLON, STRUCTURAL CONSULTANT, Santa Monica, California: *pp. 186–87*

HEIDI RICHARDSON, ASSOCIATE ARCHITECT, RICHARDSON • ASSOCIATES, San Francisco, California: *pp. 236–37*

MICHAEL SAPINSKY, AIA, ARCHITECT, New York, New York: *pp. 31, 72–73*

THE SULLIVAN PARTNERSHIP, INC., MECHANICAL CONSULTANT, LOS ANGELES, CALIFORNIA: *PP. 128–29, 186–87, 207*

## PHOTOGRAPHERS

PETER AARON/ESTO, Mamaroneck, New York: *pp. 12, 66, 97, 129, 207, 210*

JOHN ALDERSON, Chicago, Illinois: *p. 34*

JAIME ARDILES-ARCE, New York, New York: *pp. 22, 30*

ANTOINE BOOTZ, Brooklyn, New York: *pp. 68, 156*

JAMES BRETT, Tucson, Arizona: *p. 212*

RICHARD BRYANT, New York, New York: *p. 10*

WAYNE CABLE, CABLE STUDIOS, Chicago, Illinois: *pp. 148, 182*

JOHN CHEW, Wayne, Pennsylvania: *p. 192*

WHITNEY COX, New York, New York: *p. 174*

PAUL D'AMATO, Chicago, Illinois: *p. 176*

MARK DARLEY/ESTO, Mamaroneck, New York: *pp. 40, 50, 78, 80*

TIM FIELDS, Baltimore, Maryland: *pp. 28, 87, 169, 208*

RON FORTH, Cincinnati, Ohio: *pp. 18, 150*

JEFF GOLDBERG/ESTO, Mamaroneck, New York: *p. 60*

JEFF HEATLEY, East Quoque, New York: *p. 88*

JIM HEDRICH, HEDRICH-BLESSING, Chicago, Illinois: *p. 190*

JOHN HOLLIS ENTERPRISES, INC., Evanston, Illinois: *pp. 84, 108, 138*

WOLFGANG HOYT, New York, New York: *p. 214*

GREG HURSLEY, Austin, Texas: *pp. 32, 33, 77*

TIMOTHY HURSLEY, Little Rock, Arkansas: *p. 166*

WARREN JAGGER PHOTOGRAPHY, Providence, Rhode Island: *pp. 110, 111, 142*

BARBARA KARANT, KARANT AND ASSOCIATES, Chicago, Illinois: *p. 232*

ELLIOTT KAUFMAN, New York, New York: *pp. 126, 155, 178*

CHRIS KILMER, Kansas City, Missouri: *p. 134*

GEORGE LAMBROS, Chicago, Illinois: *pp. 46, 65, 104*

ROBERT C. LAUTMAN, Washington, D.C.: *pp. 48, 196*

CHRISTOPHER LITTLE, New York, New York: *p. 83*

HUGH LOOMIS, Philadelphia, Pennsylvania: *p. 122*

MAXWELL MACKENZIE, Washington, D.C.: *p. 57*

PETER MAUSS/ESTO, Mamaroneck, New York: *p. 220*

NORMAN MCGRATH, New York, New York: *pp. 11, 14, 36, 39, 74, 94, 106, 130, 143, 217*

JUDY NEISSER, Chicago, Illinois: *p. 179*

JOE PRICE, Newport Beach, California: *p. 222*

TERRY RICHARDSON, Charleston, South Carolina: *pp. 194*

MARK ROSS, New York, New York: *p. 160*

ABBY SADIN/SADIN PHOTOGRAPHY GROUP, Chicago, Illinois: *p. 124*

H. DURSTON SAYLOR, New York, New York: *pp. 9, 31, 44, 54, 58, 72, 90, 118, 120, 132, 140, 146, 170, 180, 199, 218, 226, 228*

E. G. SCHEMPF, Kansas City, Missouri: *pp. 78, 100, 162, 218*

ROBERTO SCHEZEN, New York, New York: *p. 202*

TIM STREET-PORTER/ESTO, Mamaroneck, New York: *pp. 62, 112, 116, 172, 186*

WILLIAM TAYLOR, Princeton, New Jersey: *pp. 152, 153, 236*

BRUCE VAN INWEGEN, VAN INWEGEN PHOTOGRAPHY, Chicago, Illinois: *pp. 26, 42*

JOHN VAUGHAN, RUSSELL MACMASTERS & ASSOCIATES, INC., San Francisco, California: *pp. 184, 224*

ALEX VERTIKOFF, Venice, California: *p. 52*

PETER VITALE, New York, New York: *p. 92*

PAUL WARCHOL, New York, New York: *pp. 13, 102, 206*

MATT WARGO, Philadelphia, Pennsylvania: *pp. 20, 164*

BARD WRISLEY, Atlanta, Georgia: *p. 159*

TOSHI YOSHIMI, Los Angeles, California: *p. 16*

# GLOSSARY

**ANGLE BLOCK** a small block, usually shaped like a right-angled triangle, glued and tacked into the corner of a frame to stiffen it.

**APRON** (1) a panel or board below a window board projecting slightly into a room.
(2) vertical asphalt on a fascia or overhang of a roof.

**ARRIS** an external angular intersection between two planes; the sharp edge of a brick.

**ASTRAGAL** a rabbeted wood or T-shaped metal bar that holds the panes of glass in a window.

**BEVEL** a surface meeting another surface at an angle that is not a right angle.

**BOOKMATCHED** paneling that has been split in two and unfolded to give a symmetrical grain pattern.

**BOOT** a projection from a concrete beam or floor slab to carry the facing brickwork.

**BULLNOSE** the rounding of an arris; in general, any rounded edge or end of a brick, a step, a joiner's plane, etc.

**CASING** (1) the exposed frame or trim around a door or window.
(2) a timber or similar enclosure on the face of a wall, floor, or ceiling, made to accommodate pipes or cables in a chase or other duct.

**CLEAR TIMBER** wood that is free from defects and knots; usually obtained from the bottom section of trees.

**COFFER** a panel in a ceiling, deeply recessed to make a decorative pattern.

**COMBED JOINT** a joint made up of interlocking projections called tenons that fit into corresponding mortises.

**CONDUIT** a metal, plastic, or fiber tube fitted to a wall, ceiling, or other part of a building and used as an encasement to cables.

**CORNICE** (1) a molding at the top of an outside wall that overhangs the wall and throws drips away from it.
(2) a molding at a junction between an inside wall and the ceiling.

**DOVETAIL** a joint often used in the corners of boxes or fine joinery. It differs from the combed joint in that the interlocking tenons are fan-shaped, like a pigeon's tail. They are thicker at the end than at the root and therefore cannot be easily pulled out from the corresponding mortise.

**ESCUTCHEON** a metal plate around a keyhole.

**FASCIA BOARD** (1) a wide board set vertically on edge, fixed to the rafter ends, wall plate, or wall. It carries the gutter around the eaves.
(2) the wide board over a shop front.

**FURRING** wood or metal strips used to create a cavity within an outer wall to keep out dampness or to provide air space; this process itself is also known as furring.

**GLUE-LAMINATED COLUMNS** columns that are constructed of layers of wood laminated together with glue to provide more strength and stiffness than in a single wood member.

**GROIN** the ridge or curved line where the soffits of two vaults intersect.

**GROMMET** a hemp washer soaked in joining compound and fitted between the back nut and the socket of a connector to make a tight joint. Many other grommets exist.

**GYPSUM BOARD** square-edged plasterboard available in standardized sizes replacing plaster and lath in modern wall construction; Sheetrock; wall board; drywall.

**HEADER** a brick laid across a wall to bond together the different parts of a wall, and, by extension, the exposed end of a brick.

**HVAC** heating, ventilating, and air conditioning.

**JIG** a clamp or other device for holding work or guiding a tool so that repetitive jobs can be done accurately without repeating the marking.

**JOIST** a rectangular lumber from 5 cm. up to 127 cm. thick and 10 cm. or more wide, graded for its bending strength loaded on edge and used vertically for supporting the floor above.

**KERF** a cut or notch made with a cutting tool.

**LATH** a sawn or split strip of wood formerly used in new work as a base for plaster. More generally it is any material, such as fiberboard or plasterboard, used as a base for plaster.

**LEWIS** a metal device used in the hoisting of masonry units; uses a dovetail tenon to fasten to a mortise cut into the masonry.

**LINTEL** a small beam over a door or window head, usually carrying the wall load alone.

**MASTIC** a quick-setting waterproof pointing or plastering material containing litharge and linseed oil, now replaced by portland cement.

**MILLWORK** prefabricated doors, windows, panels, stairs, etc., made at the mill and partly fabricated there.

**Miter** an angle joint between two members of a similar cross section. Each is cut at the same bevel—45 degrees for a right-angle corner—so that the straight line of the joint is seen to bisect the angle.

**Mortise** (1) a rectangular slot cut in one member, in which usually a tenon from another member is glued or pinned, or a lock is fixed.
(2) a rectangular sinking cut in a stone to receive a cramp or other locking device or a lewis.

**Molding** a continuous projection or groove used as a decoration, to throw shadow, or sometimes to throw water, away from a wall.

**Mullion** a vertical dividing member of a frame between the lights of a door or window, which may be further subdivided into panes by glazing bars.

**Muntin** (1) a subsidiary vertical framing member in a door, framed into the rails and separating the panels; usually of the same width as the stiles.
(2) a glazing bar or a mullion.

**Nose** (1) any blunt overhang.
(2) the lower end of the shuttling stile of a door or casement.

**Particle Board** boards made from sawdust, wood chips, flax stalks, etc., under pressure with or without added adhesive.

**Pier** (1) the load-bearing masonry in a building between two openings.
(2) short buttresses on one or both sides of a wall, bonded to it to increase its stability.

**Pilaster** a rectangular pier, sometimes fluted, projecting from the face of a wall and having a capital, shaft, and base. It buttresses the wall.

**Plenum** a method of air-conditioning a factory or large building by keeping the pressure in it above atmospheric pressure. Clean air is blown into the rooms near the ceiling level and foul air is withdrawn near floor level at the same side of the room, or allowed to escape through cracks in doors and windows.

**Pointing** term for the finishing of joints in masonry; also, the material used for this purpose.

**Purlin** a horizontal member supporting the common rafters in a roof.

**Rabbet** a long, step-shaped rectangular recess cut in the edge of a timber, such as the part cut from each side of a rail to form a tenon on the end of it.

**Reveal** the outer part of a jamb visible in a door or window opening and not covered by the frame. It is the visible part to a window or other opening.

**Riser** the vertical part of a step, or its height.

**Rout** to cut and smooth wood in a groove using a tool called a router.

**Runner** a horizontal member that carries the joists of the formwork under a concrete slab or the folding wedges of an arch.

**Scribe** mark and shape a member to fit an irregular surface.

**Scrim** coarse canvas, or cotton or metal mesh, used for bridging the joints between board, sheet, or slab coverings before they are plastered, and as reinforcement for fibrous plaster.

**Sill** the lowest horizontal member of a framed partition, of frame construction, or of a frame for a window or a door.

**Skid** a short length of wood used for packing walling stones to the correct height when laying them.

**Skim Coat** a very thin finishing coat usually of plaster usually applied to drywall.

**Soffit** (1) the under-surface of a cornice, stair, beam, arch, vault, or rib or the uppermost part of the inside of a drain, culvert, or sewer. Generally, it is any under-surface except a ceiling.
(2) the lining at the head of an opening.

**Stretcher** a brick or stone laid with its length parallel to the length of the wall.

**String** a sloping board at each end of the treads, housed or cut to carry the treads and risers of a stair.

**Tenon** an end of a rail or similar member, reduced in area at its end to enter a mortise in another member.

**Transom** a horizontal beam, particularly the stone or timber bar separating the lights of a window or a door from the fanlights over it.

**Tread** the horizontal part of a step, or its length.

**Truss** a frame, today generally made of steel, used to carry a roof or other load and built up wholly from members in tension and compression. Trusses are usually spaced about 3 m. apart, but their spacing is fixed by the design of the purlin.

**Wainscot** wood paneling on boards up to chair height in a room.

# Index

Senior Editor: Cornelia Guest
Assistant Editor: Mindy Nass
Designer: Areta Buk
Production Manager: Hector Campbell
Manufactured in Japan by Toppan Printing Co.
Set in 10-point ITC Garamond Light